The Supernatural
Source Book

The Supernatural
Source Book

A Handbook of Precepts and Practices to Dominate the World

Wade Baskin

CASTLE BOOKS

This edition published in 2006 by
CASTLE BOOKS ®
A division of Book Sales, Inc.
114 Northfield Avenue
Edison, NJ 08837

Originally published as *The Sorcerer's Handbook*

This edition published by arrangement with and permission of
Regeen Runes Najar
New York, NY

ISBN-13: 978-0-7858-2187-8
ISBN-10: 0-7858-2187-2

Printed in the United States of America

Foreword

Signs, symbols, archetypes, correspondences—between the visible and the invisible, the microcosm and the macrocosm —testify to the persistence in the deepest oceans of the mind of an age-old longing to achieve through magic a goal still beyond the reach of science. That goal is a coherent view of man and his universe. Drawn together from many different sources and presented in this book in simple, down-to-earth terms are thousands of fascinating items relating to the art of manipulating the forces that control the universe.

All the entries are arranged alphabetically and cross-indexed to provide ready access to the wide variety of materials associated with sorcery. Frequently further references are supplied at the end of an entry. In most instances the reader can find additional information on a subject by referring to the names or expressions mentioned in a particular entry.

Sorcery, as used in this book, embraces the world of the supernatural and the precepts or practices through which men through the ages have sought to dominate their universe. Universal and timeless, sorcery appealed to primitive minds, to the earliest literate thinkers, and to occult philosophers from Hellenistic times through the Middle Ages and into the modern era. Only during the period between 1450 and 1750 did it degenerate into witchcraft in the Christian nations. Its enduring appeal is attested by the tremendous current of interest in occult phenomena that now embraces all levels of society and sophistication.

The handbook incorporates materials from some of my earlier publications and those of Harry E. Wedeck, with whom I have collaborated. I have also profited by consulting the works of many scholars of occultism, including Lewis Spence, A. E. White, William Howitt, Éliphas Lévi, Rossell Hope Robbins, Julien Tondriau, Roland Villeneuve, Richard Cavendish, Jeffrey Burton Russell, and Robert Charroux.

Finally, a word of gratitude to those who have helped to prepare the handbook: to my wife Vlasta, who typed and corrected much of the material; to Betty Keeton, whose efficiency as a secretary enabled me to find the time needed for research; and to my colleagues Ralph Cherry, Jorge Morales, and Lewis Warren, who in their several ways contributed to the completion of the undertaking.

The Supernatural Source Book

A

A.'. A.'.

Symbol of a secret society founded by Aleister Crowley. Expelled from the Order of the Golden Dawn, which he had joined in 1898, Crowley founded the Argentinum Astrum (Silver Star) and began to publish the secrets of his rivals in *The Equinox*. The new society failed to attract many illustrious members. By 1914 its membership had dwindled to 38.

Aamon

In medieval European demonology, one of three wicked spirits in the service of Satanachia, who commanded the first legion of the infernal regions.

Aanro

In theosophy, the second division of Amenti, the abode of the supreme being. The celestial field of Aanro is surrounded by an iron wall. The field is covered with wheat, which to the Egyptians symbolized the law of retribution or karma. The dead who glean the celestial field and pass beyond the first of three bounds enter the state of bliss. Gleaners who fail to clear the first bound proceed to the lower regions.

Aaron

Hebrew miracle worker. Jehovah used him to perform many miracles, including the transformation of a rod into a flower. He was the first high priest mentioned in the Old Testament (particularly Exodus, Deuteronomy, and Numbers), the brother of Moses, and the spokesman of Moses in Egypt. It was Aaron who fashioned the Golden Calf and encouraged others to worship it.

In theosophy he is the Illuminated, the chief of the hierarchy of the initiated seers.

Aaron

Famous Byzantine sorcerer. He is reputed to have possessed Solomon's magic key and to have been an adept in the black arts. In demonology he is credited with commanding legions of infernal spirits.

Aaron's Rod

A magic wand embellished by a serpent. When cast before the Egyptian Pharaoh, it turned into a serpent.

Ab

In Semitic magical tradition, Ab is a month characterized by special features. A man who crosses a river on the 20th day of the month is likely to become ill, and one who eats pork on the 30th will be plagued with boils.

Abaddon

In demonology, the chief of the demons of the seventh century. St. John in the Apocalypse applies the word, which means The Destroyer, to the king of the grasshoppers.

Abadie, Jeanette

A French sorceress who lived in the Gascon village of Sibourre. A demon carried her while she was asleep to the Sabbat, where she awoke to find herself surrounded by a large company. She noticed that the chief demon, like Janus, had two faces. She saved herself from the stake by confessing all that had happened and renouncing sorcery.

Abaris

Scythian sorcerer and high priest of Apollo. He was given a golden arrow by Apollo. On it he could ride through the air like a bird. The Greeks called him the Aerobate. Pythagoras is supposed to have been his pupil and stolen the arrow from him. Abaris controlled the weather, banished sickness, foretold the future, and lived without eating or drinking. He sold to the Trojans his famous talisman, the Palladium (a state of Minerva), which protected the town where it was placed. Modern occultists make Abaris one of the Initiators of mankind.

Abathakathi

An African enchanter. See Zulus.

Abatur

In mysticism, the father of the demiurge of the universe, the third life.

Abben-Ragel

An Arabian astrologer, generally known by the Latin name of Alchabitius. His tenth-century treatise on astrology was translated into Latin and printed in 1473, under the title *De Judiciis seu fatis stellarum.* Many of his predictions were fulfilled.

Abdelazys

Tenth-century Arabian astrology. His much-prized treatise on astrology was translated into Latin and published in 1473. The best edition is that published in Venice in 1503, under the title *Alchabitius cum commento.*

3

Abednego
Biblical figure frequently referred to by fire walkers. He survived after Nebuchadnezzar, king of Babylonia, had cast him and his fellow prisoners, Meshach and Shadrach, into a blazing furnace. The miraculous survival of the three men is mentioned in the Book of Daniel (3:12).

Abgurvadel
The magic blade of Icelandic wizardry was used in occult operations.

Abhamsi
In mysticism, a designation of the four orders of beings: gods, demons, pitris, men. Pitris are the ancestors of mankind.

Abigor
Demon who commands sixty infernal legions. He appears as a handsome cavalier on a winged horse. He knows the future and all the secrets of war.

Ab-i-Hayat
In mysticism this term denotes the water of immortality that confers eternal life and eternal youth.

Ablanathanalba
In Gnosticism, a term similar to "Abracadabra." It reads the same from either end and was used as a charm in Egypt. It may mean "Thou art a father to us."

Abou-Ryhan (Mohammed-ben-Ahmed)
An Arabian astrologer credited with judicial astrology. He is supposed to have possessed to a remarkable degree the power to predict future events.

Abracadabra
A magic word of unknown origin. It is widely supposed to ward off evil, sickness, and death. Quintus Serenus Sam-

4

monicus, who accompanied the Emperor Severus to Britain in the year 208, mentions it in a poem as a cure against tertian fever. DeFoe mentions it in his *Journal of the Plague Year*. Eliphas Levi discusses the "magic triangle" at length and connects it with other occult concepts, including the symbolism of the Taro. For best results, the word should be arranged in the shape of a triangle and worn around the neck. The word is commonly written:

```
A B R A C A D A B R A
A B R A C A D A B R
A B R A C A D A B
A B R A C A D A
A B R A C A D
A B R A C A
A B R A C
A B R A
A B R
A B
A
```

Some scholars say that the word is a corruption of the sacred Gnostic term "Abraxas," a magic formula meaning "Hurt me not."

Others insist that it derives from the Aramaic *abhadda kedabrah,* "Disappear, O sickness, from this world." The magical formula was used extensively by early Gnostics seeking the help of benevolent spirits in combatting affliction.

Abraham the Jew
Alchemist, magician, and philosopher (born about 1362). He began his occult studies under the guidance of his father, continued under a man named Moses, and embarked on extensive travels. He finally reached Egypt, where he learned a number of invaluable secrets from Abramelin. Armed with this secret wisdom and a number of documents

5

which Abramelin had given him, he returned to Europe, settled in Wurzburg in Germany, and delved into alchemy. He instructed his two sons in magic, settled immense dowries on his three daughters, and performed acts of magic before many famous people, including the Emperor Sigismund of Germany and Henry VI of England.

Most of the facts concerning him and his activities are contained in a curious manuscript stored in the Arsenal Library in Paris. The French manuscript, written in a style indicating that the scribe was a semi-literate 18th-century Frenchman, purports to be a translation from Hebrew. Its Anglicized title is The Book of the Sacred Magic of Abramelin, as Delivered by Abraham the Jew unto His Son Lamech. It consists of an account of Abraham's travels in search of wisdom. The second part is based on the documents which Abraham brought with him from Egypt and deals with the rudiments of magic: What is magic? What things should be considered before undertaking a magical operation? How are spirits summoned? The last part gets to the heart of the matter, telling how to induce visions, retain familiar spirits, raise storms, change into different forms or shapes, fly through the air, destroy buildings, heal diseases, discover thefts, and walk under water. Most of these feats are accomplished by employing cabalistic squares or letters.

Samuel Mathers translated Abraham's work under the title *The Book of the Sacred Magic of Abramelin the Mage* (1932).

Abramelin
A sorcerer known through Samuel Mathers' translation of a manuscript written in French in the eighteenth century but purporting to be a French translation of a Hebrew document, completed in 1458. The central doctrine of *The Book*

of the Sacred Magic of Abramelin the Mage is that the cosmos is populated by hosts of angels and demons. The demons work under the direction of the angels. Man stands between the angelic and the demonic forces. To him are attached a guardian angel and a wicked demon. Initiates can control the demons. See Abraham the Jew.

Abraxas

A mystic term in vogue among the Gnostics. It can be traced to Basilides of Alexandria, who used it in the second century as a title for the divinity. In Greek numeration, the seven letters of the word denote the number 365, the days of the solar year, representing a cycle of divine action. Moreover, 365 was supposed to be the sum total of the spirits who emanated from God.

When engraved on stones or gems and worn as a charm, the word protects a person against harm. There are several classes of amulets based on the sacred name of the Gnostic spirit: those with the head of a cock, lion, human being, Seraphis, or Anubis (or those in the shape of a dung-beetle, serpent, sphinx, or monkey); those consisting of Hebraic letters; and those of diverse and even more whimsical design.

Abred

In Celtic religion, the inner circle where all things have their source. See Druids.

Abstinence

Ritual magic requires careful preparation. To summon a demon, the magician first prepares himself by abstinence or by some other means which will heighten his powers. Eliphas Levi recommends thorough cleansing before undertaking a magical operation, a minimum of sleep, and abstinence from sex, intoxicating drink, and meat.

Achmetn
An Arab soothsayer who flourished in the ninth century A.D. He was the author of *The Interpretation of Dreams*.

Aconite
A cardiac and respiratory sedative. It is a common ingredient of flying ointment used by medieval witches.

Adam, Book of the Penitence of
Title of a manuscript in the Arsenal Library in Paris. It shows that Seth was an initiate of occult science. He saw the Tree of Life after he was allowed to advance beyond the gate of the earthly paradise. The guardian angel gave him three seeds from the tree that resulted from the grafting together of the Tree of Life and the Tree of Knowledge and told him to place them in his father's mouth when Adam died. From Adam's mouth sprang the burning bush through which God revealed his holy name to Moses and which Moses used to make a magic wand. This was placed in the ark of the covenant, then planted on Mount Zion by David, then cut by Solomon to form the pillars that were placed at the entrance to Solomon's temple. A third portion was ultimately made into the cross on which Jesus was crucified.

Adam Kadmon
A Hebraic expression associated with the Aramaic expression Adam Kadmaah. Of mystical significance, it denotes the prototype of mankind.

Adamantius
A Jewish physician of Constantinople. During the reign of the Roman Emperor Constantine he produced a treatise on physiognomy, a branch of the occult arts.

Adams, Evangeline

American astrologer (1874-1932). She is credited with having elevated the science of astrology through a series of amazingly accurate predictions which were broadcast nationally. The excitement generated by her broadcasts brought about cancellation of her radio program.

She cast horoscopes for the most prominent people of her time, such as J. P. Morgan and Mary Pickford. Among the accomplishments that brought her into the limelight was her prediction of the outbreak of World War II. By accurately casting the horoscopes of the members of the jury assembled for her trial, she won the legal right to practice her profession.

Adepts

Men who through self-denial and self-improvement master the occult sciences and prepare themselves to assist in the ruling of the world. They are supposed to possess superior knowledge and powers. According to Lewis Spence:

They can control forces both in the spiritual and physical realm, and are said to be able to prolong their lives for centuries. They are also known as the Great White Brotherhood, Rishis, Rahats, or Mahatmas. Those who earnestly desire to work for the betterment of the world may become apprentices or *chelas* to *Adepts,* in which case the latter are known as "masters," but the apprentice must first have practiced self-denial and self-development in order to become sufficiently worthy. The master imparts teaching and wisdom otherwise unattainable, and helps the apprentice by communion and inspiration. Madame Blavatsky alleged that she was the apprentice of these masters, and claimed that they dwelt in the Tibetan Mountains.

Adeptus Exemptus

One of the ten grades in Aleister Crowley's cabalistic system. It corresponds to sephira 4, or Jupiter, and completes the student's training in practical magic.

Adeptus Major
One of the ten grades established by Aleister Crowley in his cabalistic system. It corresponds to sephira 5, or Mars. Here the adept obtains a general mastery of magic.

Adeptus Minor
One of the grades or ranks established in Aleister Crowley's cabalistic system. It corresponds to sephira 6, the sun, and involves the attainment of "the Knowledge and Conversation of the Holy Guardian Angel," a rite of sex-magic.

Adramelech
Mathers lists Adramelech as one of the ten evil sephiroth, commanded by Sammael, the angel of poison. Children were sacrificed to Adramelech in ancient times. His cult probably originated in Syria and later was introduced into Samaria.

In demonology, he is regarded as the grand chancellor of Hell, superintendent of the Devil's wardrobe, and president of the high council. He reveals himself in the shape of a mule or a peacock.

Ady, Thomas
Author of one of the most rational protests against witch-hunters, entitled *A Candle in the Dark, or a Treatise concerning the nature of witches and witchcraft: being advise to the judges, sheriffs, justices of the peace and grandjurymen what to do before they pass sentence on such as are arraigned for their lives as witches* (1656).

Aerial Demons
One of the six classes of demons identified by medieval theologians. They roam through the air but remain close to human beings. They can fashion bodies for themselves

from thin air. Moved by passion like men, they can cause natural disturbances. They can be invoked by sorcerers and often change their shape.

Aerolite

A stone or meteorite presumed to be of divine origin and worthy of veneration. Aerolites were worshiped in Phoenicia, Syria and elsewhere in the ancient world.

Aeromancy

Divination based on wind directions. Variations include the practice of casting sand or dirt into the wind and studying the shape of the resulting dust cloud to determine the answer to a question as well as that of using a specified number of seeds which, when thrown into the wind, scatter and settle into a pattern which can then be interpreted in much the same manner as tea leaves.

Aethrobacy

In mysticism, this term is equivalent to levitation, that is, moving in the air without external support.

African Builders' Architects

A mystical association founded by C. F. Koffen (1734-1797) for the purpose of supplying Egyptian, Christian, and Templar mysteries to the initiate. It had branches at Worms, Paris, and Cologne. Its several grades were designated as inferior (Apprentice of Egyptian Secrets, Initiate into Egyptian Secrets, Cosmopolitan, Christian Philosopher, Alethophilos) and superior (Esquire, Soldier, Knight).

Agaberte

Daughter of the Scandinavian giant Vagnoste, she was a powerful enchantress. A nature hag, she rarely appeared in her own shape. She was believed to be capable of overturning mountains and causing streams to dry up. A legion of demons helped her to accomplish her magical feats.

Agaliarept

Grand general of the infernal spirits. He commands Buer, Gusoyn, and Botis. He has the power to discover all secrets and unveil the greatest mysteries. He commands the second legion of spirits.

Agathodemon

A Greek term designating a beneficent demon that accompanies a person throughout his life. Socrates had such a demon.

Ages, Astrological

Anciently, a period of some 2,000 years during which the point of the Spring Equinox recedes through one sign of the Zodiac Constellations. Since the constellations have no precise boundaries, the points of beginning and ending are mere approximations. However, it is absurd to date the beginning of the precessional cycle, of presumably 25,800 years, from the particular time in history when it was decided no longer to treat the Equinox as a moving point, but instead to freeze it at no degrees Aries. It is probable that midway between the Equinoctial points are the Earth's Nodes, where the plane of its orbit intersects that of the Sun, at an inclination of approximately 50 degrees; but since the Equinoctial point is now considered as a fixed point and the motion takes place only within its frame of reference, it appears that a study of the circle which the celestial pole describes around the pole of the Ecliptic will be required in order to determine when it passes an East point, to mark the time of beginning of the first twelve astrological ages of 2150 years each, into which the precessional cycle is subdivided. On this manner of reckoning, the Earth might now be in the Capricorn Age, as well as any other. Historical records show the Equinox as having once begun in Taurus, at which time Taurus was regarded as the first sign of the Zodiac.

Ages of Civilization

In mysticism, after the Great Flood submerged the continent of Atlantis, seven cycles of civilization followed. They are know as the epochs of the Ancient Indian, the Persian, Egyptian, Greco-Roman, Anglo-Saxon or Sardis, Philadelphia, Laodicea.

Each epoch constitutes a progression of the human soul, wherein operate the soul-body, the life-body, the physical-body.

Each civilization lasts one twelfth of the Platonic year, that is, 2160 years.

In the first post-Atlantean age, the physical world was an illusion and of a transitory character. People then were concerned primarily with the spiritual world.

The Persian period dated from 5,000 B. C. to 3,000 B. C. It was marked by the two principles of good and evil, Ahura Mazda and Ahriman respectively. There was a continuous conflict between the light and the darkness, light representing the good and virtuous and darkness symbolizing the forces of evil.

The span of 3000 B. C. to 747 B. C. belonged to the Egypto-Chaldean or Assyrian-Babylonian-Egyptian-Hebraic culture. This age was marked by the triad of Osiris, his consort Iris, and their son Horus. In this age too the mystery cults flourished in the Near East, in the Mesopotomian area, in the Mediterranean littoral, and in Egypt. The next civilizations —the Greco-Roman and the Anglo-Saxon era—extend from 747 B. C. to 1413 A. D. Man has now become aware of himself and his physical environment.

The sixth civilization will be the ancient Persian era "resurrected." It will be called Philadelphia, and will be characterized by human love and spiritual interests.

The seventh civilization, termed Laodicea in the Apocalypse, will involve the concept of hope and the future life.

Agla

A cabalistic term used to invoke demons. An acronym composed of the Hebrew expression *Athah gabor leolom, Adonai* (Thou are powerful and eternal, O Lord)—or possibly *Aieth gadol leolam Adonai* (God will be great forever)—the term appears on many scrolls and amulets.

Aglaophotis

An herb growing in the deserts of Arabia and used to invoke demons.

Agnes

First person accused of witchcraft in England. She was exonerated in 1209, after she had passed the test by red-hot iron.

Agnishmattas

In occultism, one who has been "sweetened by fire." The term refers to a class of Pitris, or solar ancestors. They are the counterparts of our lunar ancestors, the Barhishads.

Agnus Dei

A disc of wax stamped with the figure of a lamb. Worn about the neck, it offers protection against spells. Judges at witchcraft trials were advised to wear the Agnus Dei, and to have it contain "some salt consecrated on Palm Sunday and some Blessed Herbs." The authors of the *Malleus Maleficarum* observed that these items "have a wonderful protective virtue known not only from the testimony of witches, but from the use and practice of the Church."

Agonaces

An ancient sorcerer reputed to have lived 7,000 B.C. and taught witchcraft to Zoroaster.

Agrippa

A grimoire shaped like a man and written in black on purple pages. It should be hidden in a special room. Initially it was the property of priests alone, but its owners were easily identified since they reeked of sulphur and smoke.

Agrippa von Nettesheim

German occultist (1486-1535). He was a German diplomat, physician, philosopher, and author. He made religion an amalgam of cabalistic mysticism, neo-Platonism, and Christianity. He traveled widely, lectured in Italy on Hermes Trismegistus, and wrote *De occulta philosophia* (1510), a defense of magic and a synthesis of occultism and science. In his book he explains how to summon spirits:

If you would call any evil spirit to the circle, it first behooveth us to consider and to know his nature, to which one of the planets he agreeth, and what offices are distributed to him from the planet.

This being known, let there be sought out a place fit and proper for his invocation, according to the nature of the planet, and the quality of the offices of the same spirit, as near as the same may be done.

For example, if his power be over the sea, rivers or floods, then let a place be chosen on the shore, and so of the rest. . . .

These things being considered, let there be a circle framed at the place elected, as well for the defense of the invocant as for the confirmation of the spirit.

In the circle itself there are to be written the general divine names, and those things which do yield defense unto us; the divine names which do rule the said planet, with the offices of the spirit himself; and the names, finally of the spirits which bear rule and are able to bind and constrain the spirit which we intend to call.

Agrippa's work on occult philosophy is divided into three books. The first book deals with the study of the elements and culminates with the study of the three worlds and analogical correspondents, the theoretical basis of all occult science. He develops the theory of sympathies and antipathies at length, then takes up the first principles of astrology. He devotes several chapters to astral influences, theurgy, magical substances, divination, and preparation for magical operations.

The second book is devoted to the numerical and astrological study of the Cabala. The third book deals with magical training and practice. The esoteric teachings of the Cabala are the subject matter of several chapters.

Agrusadapariksay
Ancient Hindu treatise on occultism.

Aguerre, Pierre D'
Sixteenth-century French sorcerer. During the time of Henry IV he was accused of using witchcraft to kill several persons. Witnesses testified that he had used a golden baton to conduct the Sabbat.

Ahola
A Hopi kachina. He represents the spirit who controls the growth and reproduction of all living things. During the ceremonial dances performed at the yearly summer solstice, he enters the body of a male dancer wearing a white shirt and green moccasins and carrying a ceremonial wand and a gourd full of sacred water. He then dictates the dancer's movements. Like other kachinas, he appears on earth frequently as the intermediary of the gods to help deserving people.

Aiguillette
The French word for ligature.

Ain Soph
In cabalistic mysticism, this expression denotes the limitless, nameless deity.

Aio
Among the Hopi Indians, a spiritual guide. He lends a helping hand to mortals who wish to communicate with the gods.

Aiwass
The spirit who dictated Aleister Crowley's first important work on magic, the *Book of the Law* (1904).

Aix-en-Provence
French city, scene of a famous outbreak of diabolical possession during the first part of the seventeenth century. Madeleine de Demandolx de la Palud stated that her ex-confessor, Father Louis Gaufridi, had been her lover at the Ursuline convent at Marseille. Transferred to Aix in 1609, she suffered convulsions and diabolical attacks. Father J. B. Momillon tried in vain to exorcise the "green demon" Gaufridi had imposed upon her. She contaminated five other nuns.

After Sébastien Michaélis, the Grand Inquisitor, failed in his attempts at exorcism, François Domptius took charge.

One of the nuns, Louise Capeau, acknowledged that she was under the control of three demons: Verrine, Grésil, and Sonnillon. Madeleine was possessed by 6,666 demons led by Belzebuth. Gaufridi finally confessed under torture that he had signed a pact with the Devil. Though he later recanted, he was burned alive on April 30, 1611.

Akasa

In Pythagorean thought, the fifth element. It is a celestial ether or astral light that occupies all space. In certain Buddhist teachings, it is the cosmic spirit-substance, the vast reservoir of being. Akasa (or Akasha) is one of the five elementary principles of nature studied in Hindu Yoga.

Akashic Records

Detailed cosmic accounts of the activities of everyone who has ever lived or will ever live. Predicated on the doctrine that "all that ever was *is*" and "all that will ever be *is*," the records are supposed to have enabled some seers to discover the details of their past lives, determine how best to conduct themselves in working off karmic debts, and make accurate predictions concerning the future. An individual who succeeds in gaining access to the records may not use what he learns for personal advancement other than along spiritual lines. The concept of fatalistic records is important in philosophies and religions stressing reincarnation.

Akkadian Magic Tablets

The Akkadians were among the earliest peoples to leave records of their magic formulas. One incantation against disease was recorded on a tablet:

> The wicked god, the wicked demon, the demon of the desert, the demon of the mountain, the demon of the sea, the demon of the marsh,
>
> Spirit of the heavens, conjure it! Spirit of the earth, conjure it!

Another tablet records a conjuration against seven demons known as Maskim:

> They are seven! They are seven!
> In the depths of the ocean, they are seven!
> In the brilliancy of the heavens, they are seven!

They proceed from the ocean depths, from the hidden retreat.

They are neither male nor female, those which stretch themselves out like chains, they have no spouse, they do not produce children; they are strangers to benevolence.

The enemies! The enemies!
They are seven! They are seven! They are twice seven!
Spirit of the heavens, may they be conjured!
Spirit of the earth, may they be conjured!

Still another Akkadian magic tablet reveals the triple repetition characteristic of magic formulations:

Wicked demon, malignant plague, the Spirit of the earth had made you leave his body.

May the favorable genius, the good giant, the favorable demon, come with the Spirit of the earth.

Incantation of the powerful, powerful, powerful god. Amen.

To cure ulcers the Akkadians resorted to the use of this incantation:

That which does not go away, that which is not propitious,
That which grows up, ulcers of a bad kind,
Poignant ulcers, enlarged ulcers, excoriated ulcers, ulcers,

Ulcers which spread, malignant ulcers,
Spirit of the heavens, conjure it!
Spirit of the earth, conjure it!

Aksakof, Alexander

Russian spiritualist (b. 1832). Influenced by Swedenborg, he was instrumental in bringing many well-known mediums to Russia.

Albert the Great

Dominican scholar (1193-1280) whose interests extended to the realm of the occult. Tradition credits him with summoning up the dead and writing occult treatises. Also known as Albertus Magnus, he is supposed to have devised a brass android with a speaking head. The artificial man, assembled over a period of 30 years, in accordance with the teachings of astrology, was able to answer all kinds of questions. Albert's pupil, Thomas Aquinas, finally became upset and smashed the android.

The learned occultist recorded the following incantation for banishing sickness:

> Ofano, Oblamo, Ospergo.
> Hola Noa Massa.
> Light, Beff, Cletemati, Adonai,
> Cleona, Florit.
> Pax Sax Sarax.
> Afa Afca Nostra.
> Cerum, Heaium, Lada Frium.

Albetti, Gabrina

Victim of one of the first witch trials in Italy. In 1375 she was tried at Reggio on the charge of teaching other women how to sacrifice to the Devil. One of them testified that Gabrina, a woman of some means, had told her to kneel nude at night, look up at the brightest star, and say "I adore thee, o great Devil." The secular tribunal condemned her to be branded and to have her tongue removed.

Albigenses

A sect that arose in Italy and southern France in the eleventh century. Also called New Manicheans and Cathari, they taught the transmigration of the souls of the unperfected. They were almost exterminated by the Inquisition. Catholic writers charged them with believing that men's souls were demons lodged in mortal bodies in punishment of their crimes. Their enemies said that they believed Lucifer to be a rebellious son of God, that other rebellious angels were driven from Heaven along with him, and that the rebellious son had created the world and its inhabitants.

Albigerius
An ancient Carthaginian seer. In a trance state he could make his soul leave his body and wander at will. His feats are mentioned by St. Augustine.

Albumazar
An Asiatic astrologer who flourished in the ninth century A. D. He was the author of many astrological treatises that exerted a great influence in the Middle Ages.

Alchabitius
See Abben-Ragel.

Alchemical Symbolism
Depth psychologists view alchemical symbolism as confirmation of the existence of a collective unconscious. The alchemist in his mystical search for the Aristotelian *materia prima,* or ground of all things, discovers hidden elements of his own soul and thereby brings about a reconciliation of his ego-bound consciousness and the form-seeking power of the collective unconscious. The sense of completion or fulfilment which he experiences takes the place of the desired physical transmutation of metals. Titus Burckhardt, in a work recently (1967) translated into English under the title *Alchemy, Science of the Cosmos, Science of the Soul,* discredits depth psychologists and develops the idea that "man himself is the dull lead that by a refining process can become Gold of the Sun." See Hitchcock.

Alchemy
The forerunner of chemistry seems to have originated in

Alexandria during the first century A. D. when the practical art of metallurgy developed by the Egyptians was fused with the philosophical speculations of Greek philosophy and the mysticism of the Middle Eastern religions. Hermes Trismegistus was credited with originating the art of alchemy.

Although in the beginning alchemy was a practical series of chemical operations based on the accepted theory of nature and matter, the mystically minded soon developed alchemical ideas and stressed divine revelation, the search for the divine elixir, and the secret of immortality. The pseudo-science reached its zenith in the Middle Ages, when learned men like Roger Bacon believed in the transmutation of the base metals into gold. History records that more than one impostor was put to death for failing to produce the philosopher's stone.

According to Titus Burckhardt, alchemy has probably existed since prehistoric times and with certainty since the middle of the first millennium before Christ. Gold and silver, earthly reflections of sun and moon, were sacred symbols, and the procurement of these noble metals was a priestly activity. The oldest surviving alchemical representations are on Egyptian papyri and may recall the derivation of the word from the ancient Egyptian *kême,* an expression meaning black earth and referring to the land of Egypt. "Black earth" may have been a symbol of *materia prima*—Aristotle's ground of all things. Though much of the oral tradition has been lost, the texts ascribed to Hermes-Thoth and named the *Corpus Hermeticum* point to a genuine tradition incorporating elements such as those found in the *Emerald Tablet,* which alchemists writing in Arabic and Latin regard as the summation of their art.

22

Alchemy probably received the form in which we now know it in Alexandria, where it borrowed motifs from Greek and Asian mythologies. It was readily assimilated into Christian beliefs as the philosopher's stone became a symbol of Christ, and into the world of Islam, where Hermes Trismegistos was identified with Enoch (Idrîs) and the esoteric interpretation of the Islamic credo reestablished its emphasis on the "oneness of existence." Hundreds of alchemical texts flowed from the school which Jâbir ibn Hayyân founded in the eighth century. Alchemy in Europe was revitalized by Byzantine influences during the Renaissance, reached new peaks in the seventeenth century, and had declined to the status of a pseudo-science in the eighteenth century, even though Newton and Goethe gave it more than passing attention.

One system of designating the multiple stages of the alchemical work relies on colors and may reflect ancient metallurgical processes. Blackening of the philosopher's stone is followed by bleaching which in turn is followed by reddening. It is worth noting that the three principal colors, which may be separated by a whole series of intermediate colors, correspond to the three fundamental tendencies (gunas) of the "ground of all things" (Prakriti) in Hindu cosmology: black symbolizes downward movement, away from the Origin; white is the upward aspiration toward the Origin and Light; and red is the tendency toward expansion along the plane of manifestation (rajas). Putrefaction, fermentation, and trituration, performed in darkness, divest the original matter of its initial form. Then it is bleached to a silvery white, using Quicksilver. Reddening is accomplished by the use of sulphur.

Traditionally, the grand objects of alchemy were (1) the discovery of the process for transmuting baser metals into gold or silver; (2) the discovery of an elixir for prolonging life indefinitely; and (3) the manufacture of artificial beings endowed with life (*homunculi*). The transmutation was to be accomplished by a powder, stone, or elixir called the Philosopher's Stone. Basing their conclusions on the study of nature's secrets, the alchemists arrived at the axiom that "whatever is below is like that which is above and vice versa." They divided nature into four main regions, the dry, the moist, the warm, the cold. Nature is the divine breath, the invisible yet ever active central fire. The alchemist must be artful, truthful, patient, and prudent. The Philosopher's Stone is the combination of the male and female seeds that engender gold. A. E. Waite summarizes the alchemical process once the secret of the stone is unveiled:

> There is the calcination or purgation of the stone, in which kind is worked with kind for the space of a philosophical year. There is dissolution which prepares the way for congelation, and which is performed during the black state of the mysterious matter. It is accomplished by water which does not wet the hand. There is the separation of the subtle and the gross, which is to be performed by means of heat. In the conjunction which follows, the elements are duly and scrupulously combined. Putrefaction afterwards takes place. . . . Then, in the subsequent congelation the white colour appears, which is one of the signs of success. It becomes more pronounced in cibation. In sublimation the body is spiritualised, the spirit made corporeal, and again a more glittering whiteness is apparent. Fermentation afterwards fixes together the alchemical earth and water, and causes the mystic medicine to flow like wax. The matter is then augmented with the alchemical spirit of life, and the exaltation of the philosophic earth is accomplished by the natural rectification of the elements.

24

Serious students of the alchemistic writings have inferred that the grand object of the Hermetic adepts was the spiritual regeneration of man.

At the highest level alchemy teaches that all is contained in all. Its magesterium (power to transmute) is the realization of this principle on the plane of the soul by means of the creation of an elixir. The elusive elixir unites in itself the soul's powers and thus can change both the psychic world and the material world. In its pristine purity the soul can receive and reflect supraconceptual, pristine truth. Thus the alchemists who made *materia prima* the ground of the soul set for themselves a goal consonant with the teachings of any of the world's great religious systems. An alphabetical listing of older works on alchemy is given in A. E. Waite's *Lives of the Alchemystical Philosophers* (1888).

In concluding his book A. E. Waite states:

I have little personal doubt, after a careful and unbiased appreciation of all the evidence, that the Magnum Opus has been performed, at least occasionally, in the past, and that, therefore, the alchemists, while laying the foundation of modern chemistry, had already transcended its highest results in the metallic kingdom. Now, the Hermetic doctrine of correspondences which is, at any rate, entitled to the sincere respect of all esoteric thinkers, will teach us that the fact of their success in the physical subject is analogically a substantial guarantee of the successful issue of parallel methods when applied in the psychic world with the subject man. But the revelations of mesmerism, and the phenomena called spiritualism, have discovered thaumaturgic possibilities for humanity, which in a wholly independent manner contribute to the verification of the alchemical hypothesis of development in its extension to the plane of intelligence. These possibilities I believe to be realizable exclusively along the lines indicated in Hermetic parables.

See Elixir of Life, Emerald Table, Hermes Trismegistus.

Alchindus
An Arabian sage who wrote a work entitled *The Theory of the Magic Arts*. He lived in the eleventh century.

Aleph
Éliphas Lévi had this to say about the first letter in the Hebrew alphabet:

> The first letter in the alphabet of the sacred language, Aleph, **א** , represents a man extending one hand towards heaven and the other to earth. It is an expression of the active principle in everything; it is creation in heaven corresponding to the omnipotence of the word below. This letter is a pantacle in itself—that is, a character expressing the universal science. It is supplementary to the sacred signs of the Macrocosm and Microcosm; it explains the Masonic double-triangle and five-pointed blazing star; for the word is one and revelation is one.

Aleuromancy
This is a phase of divination by means of flour. Messages, enclosed in balls of dough, are regarded as prophetic of future events. The practice is still in vogue among the Chinese.

Alexander the Paphlagonian
Magician (2nd century A. D.). A native of Abonotica, he established (2nd century A.D.) an oracle under his own direction. His success continued for twenty years. He was consulted by Emperor Marcus Aurelius.

Alfarabi
Alchemist (born at the end of the ninth century A. D.).

26

Born at Farab, now known as Othrar, in Asia Minor, he passed for the greatest philosopher of his time. He wandered incessantly, collecting the opinions of many thinkers on the secrets of nature. Many Hermetic works are attributed to him.

Alfridarya

A science that conceives all planets as influencing man. It is also assumed that each planet controls a certain number of years in a person's life. This science is somewhat akin to astrology.

Alkabetz, Solomon

A cabalist who belongs in the sixteenth century. He lived in the cabalistic center of Safed, in Palestine.

Allegiance to Satan

A witches' Sabbat opened with a ritual of allegiance to Satan. Guazzo's *Compendium Maleficarum* (1626) describes the ritual:

> When these members of the devil have met together, they light a foul and horrid fire. . . .They approach him to adore him, but not always in the same manner. Sometimes they bend their knees as suppliants, and sometimes they stand with their backs turned. . . . Going backwards like crabs, they put out their hands behind them to touch him in supplication.

All Hallow's Eve (Halloween)

A festival of Druidic origin, celebrated on October 31, on the evening before All Saints' Day. The Druids believed that Saman, the lord of death, on this occasion summoned the souls of evil men condemned to inhabit animal bodies. Witches, demons, and the spirits of the dead assemble on this night.

Allier, Elisabeth

Demoniac successfully exorcised in 1639 by François Faconnet. The two demons who had possessed her for twenty years admitted that they had entered her body by means of a crust of bread which they had put into her mouth when she was seven. They fled from her body in the presence of the Holy Sacrament. The demons were named Orgeuil and Bonifarce.

Allmuseri

Secret African society whose rites resemble those of the Cabiric and Orphic Mysteries. The neophytes are taken into the forest, where they undergo a symbolic death. Then the initiates take the neophytes to a temple, anoint them with palm oil, and place them on probation. After 40 days the initiates greet the neophytes with hymns of joy and escort them to their homes.

Ally

A Yaqui spirit who confers knowledge and power on the person who is strong and courageous enough to find and dominate him. See Castaneda, Carlos.

Almagest

The title of a treatise on astronomy by Ptolemy. The *Almagest* was also used in astrological studies.

Almuten

In astrology, the planet of chief influence in a Nativity by virtue of essential and accidental dignities. This term, of Arabian origin, is infrequently used in modern astrology.

Alocer

Grand duke of Hell, depicted as a horned horseman with the head of a lion. He commands 36 legions. His dragon-footed horse is enormous. He teaches the secrets of Heaven and the liberal arts.

28

Aloe

A plant used by the ancient Semites to ward off evil spirits. Its flowers were hung from the door-lintel.

Alomancy

A method of divination by means of salt.

Alphitomancy

This is a branch of divination by means of wheaten or barley cakes. These were used in a kind of trial by ordeal. A person accused of a crime was presumed, if guilty, to be incapable of swallowing such cakes and was consequently condemned.

Alphonsus de Spina

Author of the first book ever printed on witchcraft: *Fortalicium Fidei* (Fortress of the Faith), printed in 1467.

Alroy, David

A Bagdadi magician and false prophet who belongs in the twelfth century. He was reputed to have performed many miracles. He was put to death by his father-in-law. His adherents, however, remained faithful to his memory.

Alrunes

Female sorceresses capable of assuming many different shapes. They are supposed to be able to predict the future, and they are still consulted by some Norwegians.

Aluqa

A female demon who is at once a succubus and a vampire. She depletes men and causes them to commit suicide.

Alveydre, Saint Yves D'

A modern occultist, Saint Yves d'Alveydre tried to establish interrelationships between letters, colors, and the planets.

Aman

One of the demons who possessed Sister Jeanne des Anges. Aman was among the first of the demons whom she managed to expel.

Amandinus

A stone which confers on the wearer the power to solve any question concerning dreams or enigmas.

Amanita Muscararia

Hallucinogenic fungus, also called fly agaric. When several fungi are arranged in a circle, they constitute a fairy ring. Closely related to the deadly destroying angel, the red-capped fungus contains a strong alkaloid and is used to provoke long-lasting hallucinations. It has been used for centuries in Siberia and is well known in Mexico, where it has a place in mushroom cults.

Amaranth

A flower symbolizing immortality. A crown made from amaranths is supposed to bring fame and favor to the wearer.

Amazarak

One of the fallen angels. He taught the secrets of sorcery to men. See Book of Enoch.

American Society for Psychical Research

This society, with headquarters in New York and a branch in California, was founded in 1885 and reorganized in 1904. The purpose and the scope of the society is to investigate claims of telepathic clairvoyance, precognition, retrocognition, veridical hallucinations and dreams, psychometry, dowsing, and other forms of paranormal cognition; also claims of paranormal physical phenomena such as telekinesis, materialization, levitation, and poltergeists. The society also studies writing, trance speech, hypnotism, alterations of personality, and other subconscious processes in so far as they may be related to paranormal processes; in short, all types of phenomena called parapsychological, psychic, or paranormal.

Amphiaraus

Famous soothsayer. Knowing that he would die at Thebes, he tried to hide and avoid going to war. He died there but was restored to life. He healed the sick by showing them in a dream the remedies they should use. He founded many oracles.

Amulets

Objects worn by a person to ward off evil influences. Examples include rings, scarabs, stones, the teeth of animals, ivory phalli, and plants. The Jews used sacred letters, sacred verses, and secret words known to cabalists.

Anachitis

A stone used in divination for the purpose of conjuring water spirits.

Anancithidus

A stone used for invoking demons.

Ananisapta

A cabalistic term. It was written on parchment as an apotropaic talisman against disease.

Anataskarana

In occultism, this is the bridge between the higher manas and the lower manas, or between the spiritual ego and the personal soul.

Anatomical Signs

In astrology, the signs are associated with different parts of the human anatomy, as follows:

Aries: head
Taurus: neck
Gemini: arms
Cancer: chest
Leo: back and heart
Virgo: abdomen
Libra: loins, kidney
Scorpio: organs of generation
Sagittarius: thighs
Capricorn: knees
Aquarius: legs
Pisces: feet

Androgyne

Term designating a person who has both male and female characteristics; hermaphrodite. In Egyptian tradition androgynism is a recurrent theme. The Talmud and other Hebraic works depict Adam, the first man, as an androgynous being. Maimonides interpreted the sentence "He created them male and female" to mean: "Adam and Eve were created together, joined back to back. . . . Somehow they were two and yet they were united." Plato stated a similar theme: "Love . . . reduces two beings to one and in some way restores human nature to its former state of perfection. Each of us is but half a man, a half separated from its whole. . . . These halves are always seeking their mates. The desire and search for unity is called love." Alchemists, cabalists, and sorcerers or magicians, like the Templars whose Baphometic statues suggest the androgynous nature of man, have helped to preserve the Platonic theme. Cabalistic teachings stress the principle that man is truly complete only when he is both male and female. The androgyne or hermaphrodite who watched over the beginning and end of every process involving initiation and magic symbolized the alchemists' famous "union of opposites." In recent times magicians seeking to dominate the world with the help of supernatural forces have often considered one of the first steps in their undertaking to be the full development of their own androgynous natures.

Android

A human-shaped automaton. Among the most famous androids, some of which were said to be animated by the Devil, were Descartes' Francine and Hoffmann's Coppelia.

Angekok

In Greenland, according to William Howitt (*The History of The Supernatural*, 1863):

> The inhabitants pay little regard to the good Pirksama; meaning, in their language He above there; because they know that he will do them no harm, but they zealously worship the evil power, Angekok, from whom their priests, medicine-men, and conjurors are also named; and all the operations of the magicians are supposed to become effectual from the cooperation of Angekok and his inferior spirits.

Angel of Augsberg

Agnes Bernauer, a beautiful woman, was born in Biberach about 1410. She was drowned as a witch in 1435. She worked as a servant in Augsburg before Albrecht, Duke of Bavaria, fell in love with her and, against the wishes of his father, recognized her as his wife. At the father's insistence, and in the absence of her husband, she was pronounced guilty of having bewitched Albrecht. German poets have immortalized her name.

Angels of the Four Cardinal Points

On Tuesday the angels ruling the east are Friagne, Guael, Damael, Calzas, and Aragon. Those ruling the west are Lama, Astagna, Lobquin, Soncas, Jaxel, Isael, and Irel. The north is ruled by Rahumel, Hyniel, Rayel, Seraphiel, Ma-thiel, and Franciel; the south by Sacriel, Janiel, Galdel, Osael, Vianuel, and Zaliel. On Sunday the angels of the east are Samael, Bachiel, Atel, Gabriel, and Vionatraba. The west is ruled by Anael, Pabel, Ustael; the north by Aiel, Aniel, Vel, Aquiel, Masgabriel, Sapiel, and Matuyel; and the south by Hadudiel, Mascasiel, Charsiel, Vriel, and Natomiel. For Friday the cabalistic lists are: east—Serchiel, Chedusitaniel, Corat, Tamael, and Tenaciel; west—Turiel, Coniel, Babiel, Kadiel, Maltiel, and Husatiel; north—Peniel, Penael, Penat, Raphael, Raniel, Dormiel; and south—Porna, Sachiel, Chermiel, Samael, Santanael, and Famiel. For Wednesday the angels or spirits are: east—Mathlai, Tarmiel, Baraborat; west—Ierescue, Mitraton; north—Thiel, Rael, Iarahel, Venahel, Velel, Abuiori, and Ucirnuel; south—Milliel, Nelapa, Babel, Caluel, Vel, and Laquel. For Monday the list is: east—Gabriel, Madiel, Deamiel, Janael; west—Sachiel, Zaniel, Habaiel, Bachanael, Corabiel; north—Mael, Virael, Valnum, Baliel, Balay, Husmastran; south—Curaniel, Dabriel, Darquiel, Hanum, Anayl, and Vetuel.

Angurvadel
In Icelandic legend, this was a sword that possessed magic properties.

Animal Magnetism
A term given by Anton Mesmer to hypnotism. It implies a responsive influence existing between the heavenly bodies, the earth, and animated beings. Mesmer himself wrote:

> The human body has a property which renders it susceptible of the influence of the heavenly bodies, and of the reciprocal action of those which environ it. It manifests its analogy with the magnet, and this has decided me to adopt the term of animal magnetism.

Anolist
Anciently, a diviner who conjured demons at an altar.

Anpsi
A term used in parapsychology to denote "animal psi," or the ability of an animal to communicate with the environment.

Ansuperomin
Sixteenth-century French sorcerer. He became notorious during the reign of Henry IV for his participation in witches' Sabbats.

Anthropomancy
Divination by inspection of human entrails. Gilles de Rays (Rais) is supposed to have engaged in the practice of anthropomancy.

Anthropophagy
The practice of eating human flesh. Witches were supposed to engage in anthropophagy at the Sabbat. Marie de Sains testified at the trial of Gaufridi that she had slaughtered several children and eaten their hearts. De Lancre states that the bones of victims were preserved for as long as a year and cooked with herbs that softened them.

Anthroposophy
An esoteric spiritual science, conceived by Rudolf Steiner (1861-1925). It postulates the need for a spiritual science to bring man into harmony with his environment and with the universe itself. It has followers and exponents in many countries, and has set up Rudolf Steiner Schools.

Antipathies
In astrology, the unaccountable aversions and antagonisms people feel toward each other when positions in their Nativities are in conflict.

Apion

An Alexandrian who flourished in the first century A. D. He was reported to have conjured Homer's spirit, to ascertain the epic poet's parentage and birthplace.

Apis

In Egyptian religion, a sacred bull, symbol of fertility. He was credited with oracular powers.

Apocryphon Iohannis

The *Secret Book of John*. This is a treatise, recently discovered, that belongs in the corpus of the Gnostic writings in Egypt.

Apollonius of Tyana

A Pythagorean philosopher who flourished in the first century A. D. He traveled widely, lecturing on occultism, and gained a reputation throughout Asia Minor, where temples were dedicated to him. During the Middle Ages his reputation became legendary. His ghost is supposed to have been evoked by Eliphas Levi, in London, in 1854.

Many tales are told of his clairvoyant and magical powers.

At Ephesus, for instance, he warned the people of the approach of a terrible plague. . . . (He) pointed out to the people a poor, maimed beggar, whom he denounced as the cause of the pestilence. . . . The wretch was soon covered with a mound of stones. When the stones were removed no man was visible, but a huge black dog, the cause of the plague. . . . At Rome he raised from death . . . a young lady. . . . (He) saved a friend of his, Menippus of Corinth, from marrying a vampire. . . .

His disciples did not hesitate to say that he had not died at all, but had been caught up to heaven, and his biographer (Philostratus) casts a doubt upon the matter. At all events, when he had vanished from the terrestrial sphere, the inhabitants of his native Tyana built a temple in his honour, and statues were raised to him in various other temples. . . . He himself practised a very severe asceticism, and supplemented his own knowledge by revelations from the gods. . . . It is possible that (he) borrowed considerably from Oriental sources, and that his doctrines were more Brahminical than magical. (Lewis Spence.)

Apotropaic Ceremonies

In pagan religions, these ceremonies, involving incantations, spells, and sacrifices, were intended to divert or drive away malefic gods or spirits that might prove harmful to human life and activities.

Apotropaion

A charm that protects one against evil spirits or the Evil Eye.

Apotropaism

A defensive or protective form of magic. By means of incantations, spells, rituals, and amulets apotropaic magic aims to ward off malefic forces.

Apparition

A term designating any visible object of supernatural origin. Famous in literature is the ghost of Hamlet's father, visible only to Hamlet. Apparitions are most commonly considered to be dead souls or entities returning to familiar surroundings to accomplish a particular goal. Primitive societies treat both dreams and drug-induced states of consciousness as apparitions.

Appellation of Bacchus

When an initiate in the Orphic mystery cult performed all the rites and ate the living raw flesh of an animal, thus absorbing Dionysus himself, the god of life, he became a Bacchus. After that, the Orphic votary abstained from meat.

Applied Numerology

Apart from the mystic significance of numbers in esoteric works such as the cabalistic writings, numerology, in a popular sense, is used in practical application. It claims to disclose hidden talents in a person, to predict coming events, to attain a well-balanced attitude to living. In this pragmatic sense, applied astrology combines with numerology to form a synthesis of calculations on life cycles and their impact on the ordinary man.

Apports

Objects materialized by a medium or serving to indicate the presence of invisible spirits. Because of the possibility of fraud, apports are viewed with extreme suspicion by many skeptics who participate in seances. Perfumed scents, tooting horns, flowers, small animals, etc. are reported examples of apports.

Apsaras

In Vedic writings, an undine or water nymph. Gautama Buddha was tempted by legions of these big-breasted nymphs. In occultism, an apsara is a sleep-producing plant or an inferior force of nature.

Apuleius

Roman philosopher (2nd century A. D.). In *De Magia* he credits Zoroaster and Oromazus with the invention of magic:

Have you heard that magic is an art acceptable to the immortal gods: a noble art since the age of Zoroaster and Oromazus, the inventors, and handmaiden to the heavenly beings?

Apuleius was accused of securing a wife by magic practice. In his defense he delivered a speech, still extant, in which he discussed the range and characteristics of magic. The speech includes a great amount of material on occult and supernatural techniques.

Apuleius himself had been initiated in the mystery cult of Isis.

His book, *The Golden Ass,* relates the adventures of a man changed into a donkey and reveals much concerning the mysteries of Isis. Medieval demonographers turned him into a great enchanter.

Aquarius

The approaching Age of Aquarius, beginning about the year 2,000 is supposed to be marked by international harmony. The modern astrologer's Great Year lasts approximately 26,000 years. Its twelve sections correspond to the signs of the zodiac. It is generally agreed that the Age of Leo, when sun worship predominated, ended about the year 8,000 B. C.; the Age of Cancer, marked by moon cults, around 6,000 B. C., the Age of Gemini, marked by the influence of Mercury and the invention of writing, in 4,000 B. C.; the Age of Taurus, which brought in the worship of the bull or the Golden Calf, in 2,000 B. C.; the Age of Aries, conspicuous for ram worship, about the time of Christ's birth; and that the Age of Pisces, marked by the growth of Christianity, is now drawing to a close. Aquarius, the celestial Water Carrier, symbolizes service to others.

Aquatics

One of six classes of demons identified by the medieval theologians, following the suggestions of John Wierus. They wreak havoc at sea. When they take on bodies, they often appear as females, and as nereids, nymphs, or naiads.

Aquinas, Thomas

Italian scholastic teacher (1225-1274). Called The Angelic

Doctor, he stated in his *Sententiae:* "Magicians perform miracles through personal contracts made with demons."

Aradia

Title of a book published in a rare edition by Charles Leland in 1899 (*Aradia, or The Gospel of the Witches*). Having heard that a pagan gospel existed, he commissioned an Italian witch, Maddalena, to obtain a copy for him. The text and his translation of it suggest that the verse parts had been handed down orally with few changes since their composition at a time (probably the 14th century) when the witch cult was practiced by underlings who were instructed to murder their masters and to use magic to destroy the crops of Christian farmers.

Tana, the Etruscan name for Diana, was the supreme goddess, "Queen of Witches All." She (the Moon) fell in love with her brother Lucifer (the Sun), had intercourse with him, and gave birth to Aradia, the female Messiah of the cult. Tana instructed her daughter to descend to the earth and teach the secret of magic power to mortals, the downtrodden, who were to use witchcraft to gain against their oppressors to gain their freedom.

Aradia instructed her pupils and told them that she must return to heaven. Her pupils were to meet once each month, when the moon was full, in a forest or in some deserted place, and worship Tana. They were to be naked at the meeting, for nakedness was a sign of their freedom. After extinguishing the lights, they were to play the game called Benevento, which meant having sexual intercourse with each other, then take part in a ritual feast.

The sacred supper consisted of meal, salt, honey, and water. Each of these elements was the object of a special conjuration. A special conjuration for Cain resulted in a revelation of the suppliant's fate. A conjuration for Tana, including the baking of special cakes, may have been part of the ritual. It contains features found in other ancient religions:

> You shall make cakes of meal, wine, salt and honey in the shape of the crescent moon, and say: "I do not bake the bread, nor with it salt, nor do I cook the honey with the wine: I bake the body and the blood and the soul, the soul of Diana, that she know neither rest nor peace, and ever be in cruel suffering till she will grant what I request, what I do most desire, I beg it of her from my very heart! and if the grace be granted, O Diana! in honour of thee will I hold this feast and drain the goblet deep, we will dance and wildly leap, and if thou grantest the grace which I require, then when the dance is wildest, all the lamps shall be extinguished and we will freely love!" And thus it shall be done: all shall sit down to supper all naked, men and women, and the feast over, they shall dance and sing and make music, and then love in the darkness. (Leland.)

Aradia had the power to grant to her devotees the gifts of success in love, blessing or cursing, conversing with spirits, finding hidden treasure, compelling spirits of priests to reveal hidden treasure, understanding the voice of the wind, changing water into wine, fortune-telling using the hand or cards, curing sickness, making ugly people beautiful, taming wild animals, and having their wishes fulfilled by choosing the right formula for addressing her.

In a parallel text Tana is presented as the first act of creation. The first darkness, she divided herself into darkness and light, which became her brother Lucifer. His matchless beauty caused Tana to tremble with desire for him, and her desire was the Dawn. Brother and sister descended for the creation of the earth. Tana assumed the form of a cat, crawled into bed with Lucifer, then changed back into

41

human form and seduced him in the darkness, conceiving Aradia. After spinning the lives of men while Lucifer turned her wheel, Tana changed mice into stars and became Queen of Heaven, of witches and rain.

Arathon
In works on magic, Arathon is listed as one of the seven Olympian Spirits. He is the celestial spirit of Saturn.

Arbatel
A sixteenth-century handbook of magic. It deals with the nature and functions of the spirit that pervades the cosmos.

Arcanum, the Great
This is the Great Secret that was the essence of the alchemical art. The secret, it is asserted, was not the transmutation of metals. It was actually the transformation of man's character to a higher plane.

Archaeus
In Greek, the word means The Ancient One. It is used by cabalists to name the oldest manifested deity.

Archer-Wizards
Makers of spellbound images. They often tried to insert into their waxen figures objects which had been parts of the intended victim—hair or the parings of nails. They flourished in the sixteenth century.

Ardat-Lile
In Semitic legend, a female demon who copulated with human males.

Argentinum Astrum
Society founded by Aleister Crowley after he was expelled from the Order of the Golden Dawn. The name Argentinum Astrum (Silver Star) was generally not used. Instead, members of the society used the designation A.˙.A.˙..

Ari

See Ashkenazi, Isaac.

Aries

In astrology, the Ram. The first, northern sign of the zodiac. In Egyptian religion, the deity Amon-Ra was represented with ram's horns.

Arithmancy

Divination by numbers. The Greeks, Chaldeans, and Jews all practiced arithmancy. See Numerology.

Armor, Yann D'

Pseudonym of Pierre Bourieux, French occultist.

Arnold of Villanova

He was a physician who belonged in the thirteenth century. He traveled in Europe and Africa, displaying interest in the interpretation of dreams, alchemy, and similar occult areas. He was reputed to have made transmutations of metals. Even as a physician he relied to a great extent on cabalistic symbols, occult invocations, and herbal concoctions of magic import. There was also a belief that he could communicate with the Satanic agencies.

Arnuphis

Egyptian sorcerer. In the second century A. D., he is supposed to have saved Marcus Aurelius' army by inducing a downpour of rain.

Arphaxat

An ancient Persian sorcerer. He met his death by a thunderbolt.

Art

Term used by British witches to designate their activities. See Witchcraft.

Artemidorus

A Greek writer of Ephesus, who belongs in the late second century A. D. He traveled widely for the purpose of collecting, classifying, and interpreting dreams. He is the author of a treatise on this subject, entitled *Oneirocritica*, which is extant. He also produced a work on palmistry, under the name of *Cheiroscopia*.

Artephius

A twelfth-century occultist, he reputedly lived more than a thousand years, with the help of demons. He wrote *The Art of Prolonging Life,* according to tradition, at the age of 1025.

Aruspex

Divination based on the patterns formed by birds in flight. The hour, the number of birds in the formation, and the direction of flight are significant factors.

Asafetida

Resin obtained from the members of the carrot family and worn about the neck as protection against evil spirits and disease. The foul-smelling substance is also used as an anti-convulsant.

Asch Metzareph

A Hebraic expression meaning The Cleansing Fire. It is the title of a cabalistic work dealing with alchemy.

Asclepius

A treatise purporting to describe the religion of ancient Egypt and to record the magic rites used by the Egyptians to draw the cosmic powers into their statues. The work probably dates from the second or third century A. D. and contains few genuine Egyptian elements.

Ascletarion

Sorcerer who predicted that the Roman Emperor Domitian's body would be devoured by dogs. After Domitian's death the prediction was fulfilled.

Ashkenazi, Isaac Loria

Mystic and cabalist (1534-1572). He was also known by his combined initials, Ari, of which the Hebrew meaning is appropriately Lion. Born in Jerusalem, he spent most of his brief life on the shores of the Nile but won for himself during the 23 months he remained at Safed in Israel a reputation little short of angelic. At desolate burial grounds in Galilee, in the company of numerous pupils who would easily have accepted him as their new redeemer, he would prostrate himself over the tombs of the hallowed dead and by means of special acts of concentration unite with their souls and absorb their wisdom. One such union occurred over the tomb of Simeon ben Yohai, the 2nd-century mystic and reputed founder of the Cabala.

The Ari united with Simeon at Meron, near Tiberias, and gained an understanding of the obscure passages of the Zohar, which he dictated to Hayyim Vital. His apostle in turn passed on to posterity the hidden wisdom entrusted to him. The direct chain, embracing both written and oral traditions, numbered among its earliest links Benjamin Levi, Moses Zacuta, Benjamin Vita, and Moses H. Luzzatto.

The Ari's soul was supposed to have ascended nightly to heaven for enlightenment. The prophet Elijah tutored him regularly.

Ashmedai

In talmudic tradition, king of the shedim and tutor of Solomon.

Ashtar Vidya

The most ancient Hindu work on magic, preserved only fragmentarily.

Asmodeus

In Jewish demonology, an evil spirit sometimes credited with causing matrimonial happiness. His cradle is the Avesta, the sacred book of the Zoroastrian religion. The Persians added the word daeva to the name Aeshma. Aeshma daeva, "demon of lust," later was identified as the king of demons. The genie of the concupiscence became a satellite of Satan in Christian theology. Asmodeus was the name of the chief demon who possessed the body of Jeanne des Anges. He filled her mind with "shameful things."

Aspects

In astrology, the aspects of the planets in relation to each other. These aspects determine the significance, whether favorable or not, of the planet. The more important aspects are:

Trine, marked △ when two planets are four signs apart. Sextile, marked * when two planets are two signs apart. Quintile, when two planets are 72 apart.

These three aspects are favorable.

Conjunction ☌ when two planets or stars are of the same sign. This aspect may be favorable or unfavorable. Opposition ∞ when two planets are six signs apart. Quartile ☐ when two planets are three signs apart. Semi-quartile ½☐ when two planets are 45 apart. These last three aspects are unfavorable.

Aspilcuetta, Marie D'

French witch. She was arrested during the reign of Henri IV. She confessed that she had attended the Sabbat.

Assaput

In ancient Chaldean divination, Assaput was a prophetic sound pregnant with prediction. Insects and natural phenomena such as rain and thunder were similarly used to interpret coming events. Among the Romans, practices of the same type were in force.

Assyrian Incantations

The Assyrians used magic formulas to cast spells and to remove them. One exorcism, recited over sick people, contains the names of their ancient deities. Ea was the god of wisdom, Marduk the son of and Dumkina the consort of Marduk.

> The man of Ea am I,
> The man of Damkina am I,
> The messenger of Marduk am I,
> My spell is the spell of Ea,
> My incantation is the incantation of Marduk,
> The circle of Ea is in my hand,
> The tamarisk, the powerful weapon of Anu,
> In my hand I hold,
> The date-spathe, mighty in decision,
> In my hand I hold.

Asthar Vidya

The oldest Hindu work on magic. Only fragments survive.

Astral Body

A spiritual essence composed of matter fine enough to penetrate the physical body and remain detached from it. It contains emotions, passions, and desires. These qualities may depart from the physical body and return, depending on the whereabouts of the astral body. In dream states, for example, a person may receive impressions over great distances through his roaming astral body, as when he dreams of a friend who warns him of some impending danger, awakens, discovers the danger, and learns that the friend had sensed trouble and was trying to warn him of it. Those who believe in the existence of the astral body say that it can detach itself from the physical body, through conscious projection or as the result of an accident, and remain invisible or take on the physical appearance of the host body. Detached, it can travel freely throughout the physical and astral worlds.

Modern occultism teaches that the astral body leaves the corpse of a dead man and moves on to the astral plane of existence. His soul eventually moves on to higher planes, leaving the body of light on the astral plane as an astral corpse or body. The astral body retains a faint spark of life. It retains a desire to live again and can be drawn back to the ordinary world, where it can prolong its existence indefinitely by absorbing life-energy from living creatures.

Astral Corpse
See Astral Body.

Astral Light
The Astral Light is an ocean of unconsciousness interlinking all things and all minds. It makes possible telepathy, clairvoyance, and prophecy. It lies beyond the range of our senses. It is the plastic medium which the magician, by the power of his will, manipulates from the safety of a consecrated circle. Its fluidity makes it so susceptible of influence that it can transmit the most tenuous ideas. By directing the flow of his will, the magician with his rituals is able to cause changes in the Astral Light.

The existence of Astral Light is suggested by psychology, mysticism, and the new physics.

Astral World

The world that lies beyond the ordinary physical world. It is the second lowest in a hierarchy composed of seven worlds, of which the upper five are for the most part incomprehensible to mortals. Some adepts claim to have inhabited the astral world for brief periods and to have provided descriptions of their experiences. Some people claim that they have stumbled into it through astral projection and learned to pass at will between the lower two worlds. Though the concept is mainly a Theosophical explanation of the destiny of the astral body, which is supposed to move into the astral world at the death of the physical being and to have the opportunity for further advancement (that is, to develop a more spiritual approach to the higher worlds by performing good deeds), it has its counterparts in many primitive religions.

Astrampsychos

Ancient Chaldean sorcerer.

Astroite

A precious stone said by Zoroaster to help one to appease the terrestrial demon, summon benevolent spirits, and obtain answers to questions put to them.

Astrolatry

The cult of the stars as a means of divination. This type of cult was predominant in the Near East and in Mesopotamia. It was also in force among the Aztecs, in the pre-Columbian period.

Astrological Anatomy

In astrology, the Sun operates through the anterior pituitary gland. The Moon is the substance of the body. Mercury is associated with the thyroid gland. Venus, with the thymus gland. Mars, with the cortex. Jupiter, with the posterior pituitary gland. Saturn affects the medullary portion of the adrenal gland. Uranus, the parathyroid gland. Neptune, the pineal gland. Pluto, the pancreas.

Astrological Colors
In astrology, the colors of the spectrum are associated with specific planets.

The Sun—orange, gold, yellow.
The Moon—white, pearl, opal, iridescent hues.
Mercury—slate color.
Venus—sky blue, pale green.
Mars—red, carmine.
Jupiter—purple, deep blue.
Uranus—streaked mixtures.
Neptune—lavender, sea-green.
Pluto—luminous pigments.

Astrological Correspondences
The study of astrology is based on the influences exerted by the seven planets on each other and on the universe and everything contained in it. Robert Fludd defined astronomy as "the science of divination by the aspect of the celestial harmony and the pattern of the sublunar elements. It studies the influence of the different heavens on the elements and the influence of these elements on terrestrial things, including plants and animals as well as human beings.

The sun, considered (like the moon) as one of the seven planets, has the following planetary correspondences: element—fire; color—yellow, gold, orange; musical note—do; metal—gold; number—six; gem—diamond, onyx, ruby, amber, topaz, chrysolite; natural perfume—heliotrope, lavender, rose; compounded perfume—orange peel, marshmallow, Parma violet, lavender; quadruped—horse, ram, lion, cynocephalus; bird—cock, swan, canary—fish—grayling, seal.

Magical hours do not correspond to solar hours. The day

begins at sunrise and ends at sunset. Night begins at sunset and ends at sunrise. Thus the value of each of the hours varies from day to day. The planet that governs a particular day also governs the first hour of that day. On Tuesday, for example, Mars governs the first hour, then come the sun, Venus, Mercury, the moon, Saturn, Jupiter, after which the cycle begins anew. Wednesday begins with Mercury in control, then come the moon, Saturn, Jupiter, Mars, the sun, Venus, etc.

Albert the Great classified the parts of plants according to astrological correspondences:

Venus......Flowers
Mercury.. Seeds and bark
Moon   Leaves
Saturn   Roots
Jupiter   Fruits
Mars ..   Stem.

Astrological Flavors
In astrology, planets are associated with certain flavors.

The Sun—sweet, pungent.
The Moon—odorless.
Mercury—astringent.
Venus—warm, sweet.
Mars—astringent, pungent.
Jupiter—fragrant.
Saturn—cold, sour.

Astrological Jewels
In astrology, certain planets are associated with particular jewels and precious stones.

Sun—diamond, ruby, carbuncle.
Moon—pearl, opal, moonstone.
Mercury—quicksilver.

Venus—emerald.
Mars—bloodstone, flint.
Jupiter—amethyst, turquoise.
Saturn—garnet, all black stones.

Astrological Pathology

In astrology, certain ailments are associated with planetary influences.

Sun—ailments of heart and spine, fevers, spleen.
Moon—endocrine imbalance, catarrhal infections.
Mercury—nervous disorders.
Venus—blood impurities.
Mars—infectious diseases.
Jupiter—maladies resulting from surfeit.
Saturn—skin diseases, rheumatism, melancholia.

Astrological Vegetation

In astrology, herbs are classified according to planetary influences:

Sun: almond, celandine, juniper, rue, saffron.
Moon: chickweed, hyssop, purslain, moonwart.
Mercury: calamint, endive, horehound, marjoram, pellitory, valerian.
Venus: artichoke, foxglove, ferns, sorrel, spearmint.
Mars: aloes, capers, coriander, crowfoot, gentian, ginger, honeysuckle, peppers.
Jupiter: aniseed, balm, myrrh, wort, lime, linden, nutmeg, jessamine.
Saturn: aconite, fumitory, ivy, medlar, moss, sloes, senna.

Astrology

The great magical doctrine of "as above, so below" is the foundation of the great art of astrology. Man and events on earth are the counterpart of God and events in heaven since the microcosm and the macrocosm depend on the workings of the same force, the mysterious One which reconciles all diversity in unity. Developed first in Mesopotamia, where each city-state had its own god and shifts in the balance of power between city-states was interpreted as changes in the relationships of the gods, astrology is linked to the names of gods and to the names of planets. The Babylonians and Assyrians linked their principal gods with the planets, and modern astrology has retained the practice.

Events in the sky are interpreted as signals of events on earth. Thus the conjunction of salubrious Jupiter with malevolent Saturn and Mars signaled the terrible Black Death of 1348. At a later date the conjunction of these three planets signaled an epidemic of syphilis in Europe. Napoleon's tendency to overeat is explained by the fact that Venus, symbolizing love, was in the sign of Cancer, which rules the stomach, when he was born. Similarly, a man born when Venus (femininity) is too close to the sun (personality) is likely to be effeminate.

In many pagan religions astrology played an important role in rituals and ceremonials and in the general beliefs of the people. This was particularly the case among the Egyptians, the Romans, and the Assyro-Babylonians. The movements of the heavenly bodies, the rising and setting of the sun, eclipses were studied in order to discover the arrangement of the cosmic system and its influence on the lives of men.

The Babylonians were the pioneers in this science. Their observations, from the third millennium on, were gradually systematized into formal prognostications, based on astrological and astronomical calculations, regarding the effectiveness of any human undertaking. The interpreters were the priests attached to a particular temple, and their decisions were accepted not only by the people at large but by the rulers themselves.

The Assyro-Babylonian deities, to whom were assigned in the divine scheme special areas of the heavens, were the arbiters of human fate as manifested by astrological science.

Among the Romans, astrology was carried to even greater lengths and greater exactitude. The entire cosmic system was put under minute observation. The orderliness of the heavenly bodies suggested to the professional astrologers the possibility of mathematical precision in forecasting human events. For the gods themselves had now become identified with heavenly bodies. During the period of the Roman Empire, astrology exerted a powerful influence in major national policies and in the imperial decisions and decrees of the ruling emperor.

From Mesopotamia and the temples where astrological practices were in force, the science spread to Egypt. Greece was not greatly affected until after the death of Alexander the Great in 323 B. C., when Oriental influences imposed themselves on Hellenistic life.

In Rome, every level of society felt the force of astrological predictions. In one particular direction, in medicine, astrology exercised a powerful influence that lasted for centuries. See Aquarius.

Astrology, Branches of
These are distinct branches of astrology: natal or genethliacal, dealing with the birth Figure. Horary: a Figure cast for the birth-moment of an idea or an event.

Electional: choosing the propitious moment for an undertaking.

Mundane or Judicial: referring to the influences of the planets on populations or countries or cities.

Medical: application of astrology to health.

Meteorological: application of astrology to weather conditions.

Agricultural: application of astrology to planting and harvesting of crops.

Astronauts

Erich Von Daniken posed the theory that the ancient gods actually were astronauts who reached various points on the surface of the earth, instructed men in the arts and sciences, and departed, leaving behind the impression that they would one day return. His views were set forth in his book *Chariots of the Gods* and were widely publicized in a 1973 television presentation, *In Search of Ancient Astronauts,* which reviewed his evidence: ancient carvings in Africa, South America, and Italy depicting men apparently dressed in space suits; Biblical passages suggesting space travel; great structures revealing vast astronomical knowledge (Stonehenge, Mayan pyramids, etc.); huge statues cut from hard stone and transported, according to surviving legends of the natives of Easter Islands, by the mana of two men who subsequently disappeared; and a series of roads leading nowhere on the Plain of Nazca in Peru but forming a coherent pattern when seen from the sky, as if intended to serve as an airfield.

Astrum Argentinum

A secret society founded by Aleister Crowley. The scandalous behavior of those who entered his Abbey of Theleme in Sicily discredited the society.

Asuramaya

Ancient Hindu occultist and astrologer. Occult tradition makes the lost continent of Atlantis his birthplace.

Ataraxia

Greek word designating a state of serenity and physical well-being. The word also designates a sleep-inducing drug, such as Miltown (Meprobamate). In occultism, adepts try to induce ataraxia before communicating with spiritual forces.

Atavism

In occultism, the reappearance in human beings of characteristics associated with pre-human forms of existence. Frederick Kaigh in *Witchcraft and Magic of Africa* describes a ritual dance of a witch-doctor whose frenzied performance caused a young couple to transform their bodies into the likeness of jackals and indulge in repeated copulations far beyond the capacity of normal human beings. Kaigh explained the atavistic phenomenon as the result of a combination of spiritual ecstasy and possession of the dancers by the projected double or astral body of the witch-doctor.

Egyptian priest-magicians identified themselves with powers represented by animals and may have known how to call forth atavistic energies buried in man's subconscious. The ancient system of Chinese magic transmitted in *I Ching* may also involve atavism. William Seabrook, a collector of occult experiences, once experimented with the *Ko* hexagram, which in *I Ching* denotes transformation or change. Adepts believe that by visualizing a hexagram and mentally impressing it upon the surface of an imaginary door, one can open the door and gain access to a part of the astral world. When one of Seabrook's friends superimposed the *Ko* hexagram on an imaginary door, she projected her consciousness across the threshold and soon began to assume the characteristics of a wolf speeding across a desolate tract of ice. Her features began to change. She frothed at the mouth and snarled. Her trance state had enabled her to experience an event based on an urge she had once had as a child to join a pack of wolves she had seen speeding over the snow in Russia.

Athame

A knife with black handles, used by modern witches to draw a magic circle. See Coven, Admission into.

Athanor

Derived from an Arabic word meaning oven, the term is used by alchemists to designate the furnace in which the elixir is prepared. Generally depicted as a small domed tower, it contains an egg-shaped glass vessel lying in a sand-bath placed immediately above the fire. In its symbolical meaning the athanor is the human body, a simplified image of the cosmos.

Atlantis

According to Plato, Atlantis was a great sea power that launched an attack on Egypt and Athens. A natural cataclysm destroyed the Athenian army and Atlantis. Plato's account of the lost paradise appears in two of his dialogs, in the *Timaeus* and, in greater detail, in the *Critias*. The description of Critias, a real person, is based on documents possessed by his family and a family tradition concerning what Egyptian priests had told Solon, the Athenian lawgiver.

Atlantis was ruled by a federation of ten kings, led by the descendant of Atlas, the eldest of ten sons of Poseidon, god of the sea, and a mortal woman. The Ancient Metropolis of the extremely advanced empire was a small island. Most of its territory lay beyond the Pillars of Hercules. The inhabitants of the empire practiced a bull-cult and worshiped a number of gods besides Poseidon, whose temple was in the Ancient Metropolis. Such was the account given by Plato of a civilization which was destroyed more than 9,000 years before Solon's conversations with the priests.

In 1967 Professor Marinatos of Athens led an expedition that uncovered evidence identifying the island of Santorini, 70 miles north of Crete, as Atlantis. By eliminating the final zero of the date assigned by Plato, one finds that the destruction of Atlantis corresponds roughly with the archeologically attested destruction of the great empire of Minoan Crete late in the 16th century B. C.

Archeological findings have not lessened the enthusiasm of occultists, whose method of research into the history of Atlantis is called astral clairvoyance, pioneered by W. Scott-Elliott in the 1890s. In *The Story of Atlantis,* reissued by the Theosophical Society in 1962, he revealed that in deep meditation he had managed to reach the astral plane on which all events are recorded and determine that a million years ago Atlantis occupied most of what is now the Atlantic. Its black inhabitants, the Rmoahals, stood more than ten feet high and were ruled by the Toltecs, averaging eight feet in height. The practice of black magic brought about their downfall, but not before some of the Toltecs emigrated to Egypt. Their descendants built the pyramids of Egypt and Central America as well as Stonehenge. From them sprang the civilizations of the Middle East and Europe. See Bernard, Raymond; Bimini; Cayce, Edgar; City of the Condors.

Atman
In esoteric philosophy, the one unchanging reality behind surface appearances. It is the inmost link with the Unutterable, the universal selfhood, the feeling or consciousness of selfhood that is the same in every human being.

Attila
The 5th-century leader of the invading Huns and Scourge of God was also the lord of sorcery to the Goths, who viewed all Huns as the children of sorceresses and unclean spirits. Before the battle with Actius, Attila brought his sorcerers together in a great tent lit by torches. One magician plunged his hands into a victim's entrails and watched their palpitations; another put his divination sticks inside a white flag, shook them, and studied their arrangement in

order to determine their prophecies; still another whirled round beating a drum and evoking the spirits of the dead until he became exhausted, rolled over, and grew rigid. Attila watched their activities from his stool and listened to every sound.

Auch
In 551 the Council of Auch attacked witchcraft and "those who, under the influence of the Devil, pronounce magical incantations."

Augury
The taking of omens among the Romans, usually to determine whether the gods looked with approval or disapproval on a proposed course of action. The augurs sat in a special tent in taking omens from birds. The pitching of the tent was a closely guarded professional secret. The rules were very complicated, and the augurs kept precise records of their activities. Not all birds were significant. Those whose flight was significant included the eagle, buzzard, and vulture. Those whose cries were ominous included the crow, raven, and owl. The crow's cry was a favorable omen if it was heard on an augur's left, the raven's if heard on the right. Sacred chickens also were used in augury. Most of our information on Roman augury comes from Cicero's work *On Divination.*

Auldearne Witches
A group of Scottish witches. Isabel Gowdie, the most famous of them, confessed in 1662, without torture, that they had ridden through the air on pieces of straw, visited fairyland, killed people with elf-arrows, and worshiped the Devil. After she was hanged, her body was burned and her ashes scattered.

Aumgn
Aleister Crowley's expansion of the Buddhist Om. It is "a

mantra of terrific power by virtue whereof (the magician) may apprehend the Universe."

Aura

An emanation surrounding the physical body. The cloudlike light, made up of layers of color, is always present, according to occultists, but is visible only to those who have advanced to the stage of clairvoyance, mediumship, etc. Theosophists hold that it consists of five layers of divisions, each keyed to a specific personality trait: health, vitality, character, karmic nature, and spiritual nature. The radiation or luminous emanation has also been called Od, Odyle, or Odic Force. It is related to the halo or aureole surrounding the bodies or heads of religious figures painted by artists.

Aurobindo, Sri

Indian seer and patriot (1872-1950). He renounced politics in 1910 to devote his life to discovering how the universe might be made divine. Sri Aurobindo founded an ashram which is distinguished by having no creed or ritual except the practices of meditation. He has been acclaimed as the hierophant of the new age, that of the God-man—the gnostic being who excels man in things of the spirit.

Educated in Europe, he explained Hindu concepts in terms comprehensible to Westerners. His idea of "Supermind" and the doctrine of Shakta won him many followers. Supermind offers a technique for achieving moral and psychological perfection. Shakta anticipated the development of atomic energy.

Australian Magic

See Dreaming.

Austromancy

A form of divination by observation of the winds.

60

Automatic Art

The production of writing, painting, and drawing without conscious direction of the performing hand. It is associated with other manifestations of subconscious layers of personality, such as hysterical tics, somnambulism, loss of memory, mediumship, prophecy, multiple personality, and glossolalia. Automatic writing has recorded events unknown by the waking self and to manifest what seems to be flashes of telepathy. The automatist is likely to claim that the writing has its source in a supernatural being, a dead person, or another person who is still alive. It has been an important influence on modern spiritualism and has provided accounts of the nature of the supernatural realm. Notable examples of automatic writing are W. Stainton Moses' *Spirit Teachings* (1873), the Bible of British spiritualism; K. Wingfield's Guidance from Beyond (1923); and Geraldine Cummins' Beyond Human Personality (1935).

Automatic paintings and drawings may excel those produced under ordinary conditions. Emily A. Tallmadge, before her death in 1956 at the age of 82, produced thousands of intricate pictures. She believed that her work was inspired by spirit guides and conveyed symbolism that had been "handed down through aeons of time."

Auxonne Nuns

From 1658 to 1663 nuns in the Ursuline convent of Auxonne were allegedly possessed by demons. The nuns made accusations of Lesbianism against their Mother Superior, who later was found innocent. Physicians testified that the nuns had never displayed any convincing signs of true demoniacal possession.

Avarus

A demon summoned by the French sorcerer Soubert.

Avicenna

Alchemist (c. 980-1036). Born at Bacara in Persia, he achieved such fame that magical rituals frequently appeal to him as the authority for their supernatural secrets. According to A. E. Waite:

> Six or seven treatises on Hermetic philosophy are ascribed to Avicenna; some of them are undoubtedly spurious. There is a treatise on the "Congelation of the Stone" and a *Tractatulus de Alchimia,* which may be found in the first volumes of the *Ars Aurifera,* Basle, 1610. In 1572 the *Ars Chimica* was printed at Berne. Two Hermetic tracts are also attributed to Avicenna by the compilers of the Theatrum Chimicum.

Ayman, Jacques

A seventeenth-century French dowser who was able to uncover crimes and find the guilty perpetrators by means of his divining rod.

Azaradel

Fallen angel who taught mortals the secrets of the moon. See Book of Enoch.

Azilut

In the Cabala, the world of emanations. It is the great and highest prototype of the other worlds, the Great Sacred Seal by means of which all the worlds are copied.

Azoth

In alchemy, mercury, treated as the creative principle in nature. It is symbolized by a cross bearing the letters TARO. Each combination of these letters has an occult meaning. Paracelsus owned a talismanic jewel in which a powerful spirit was supposed to dwell. His jewel was called the Azoth.

Azriel
A Spanish-Jewish cabalist (1160-1238). He was the author of works on cabalistic mysticism.

B

Ba

In Egyptian religion, the soul that leaves the body at death and wings its flight to the gods in the form of a man-headed bird. It returns from time to time to the mummy to comfort it and reassure it. The *ba* is immortal.

Baaras

A miraculous plant known to the Arabs as the Golden Plant. It grows on Mt. Libanus, beneath the road leading to Damascus. It flowers in May, after the snow melts. Though invisible by day, it can be seen by torchlight. Alchemists used it in their attempts to transmute base metals into gold.

Baba, Meher

Modern occultist. Since 1925 he has kept a vow of silence, using a small letter board to communicate his teachings. He has promised his followers that when he speaks, he will utter "the word of words" that will penetrate men's minds and hearts. The Indian mystic claims to be the reincarnation of Krishna. His real name is Sathyanarayana Raju.

Babau

An ogre used by French nurses to frighten children. He devours naughty children in salad.

Babylonian Demonology

Belief in demons had a central place in Babylonian life. Strongly influenced by Sumerian ideas, the Babylonians recognized whole armies of demons, divided into several classes, such as demons of the field in the shape of an animal. Boundary stones topped by demonic figures protected the fields. Graveyard demons, half-man and half-animal, frequented the kingdom of the dead and were looked upon as the ghosts of men who had died.

The Babylonians had many different methods of protecting themselves against demons: putting certain plants, such as aloes and cacti, near the door; wearing rings and amulets bearing sacred texts; and seeking help from the physician-priest, who had the power of exorcism. The priest had to wait, however, until the stars were favorable. Then he called off the names of many demons, hoping to hit upon that of the offending one and thereby gain control over him. Whoever knew the demon's name had power over him. Then the priest called upon a powerful god for help, for each demon was subject to the power of a particular god. The most powerful god, Ea, was called The Lord of the Incantations. The priest tried to send the demon into an animal, which then was driven away or killed, or into a cauldron, which then was destroyed. The priest might also, if he suspected a witch of causing the trouble, burn a likeness of the witch or undo a knot. He had recourse to expedients such as meteorites, animal feathers and hair, plants, and human excrement. Exorcism was supposed to result in recovery from a disease, for demons were used to explain illnesses; they had no place in theology.

The stress on the relation between demons and sickness caused every type of ailment to be viewed as an act of possession by a particular demon. The demon could enter the body with the breath or food, through the mouth or ear.

Symptoms of possession included sleeplessness, anxiety, screaming, roaming about, behaving like an animal, senseless ranting and raving, and hallucinations.

Common designations for demons were Alu and Gallu, but the Babylonians also spoke of Lilu, Utukku, Etimmu, Rabisu, and Lamastu.

Lilu was simply a spook or ghost. The restless, aggressive ghosts of strong or prematurely dead men were called Lilu or Utukku. The Rabisu hid in the shadows and leaped forth to overpower their victims, while the Lamastu preyed on pregnant women and young children. Female demons included Ardat-Lili and Lilitu. Shedim in the form of winged bulls (mentioned in Psalms 106:37 as having the claws of a cock) stood before the temples. Babylonian demons often traveled in groups of seven.

Babylonian Incantations
Magic formulas used by the Babylonians still survive. One, addressed to the goddess Tasmitu, is intended to remove sickness and spells:

I, son of . . . , whose god is . . . , whose goddess is . . . ,
In the evil of an eclipse of the Moon, which in . . . month
    and on . . . day has taken place
In the evil of the powers, of the portents, evil and not
    good, which are in my palace and my land,
Have turned toward thee! I have established thee!
Listen to the incantation! Before Nabu thy spouse, the
    lord, the prince, the first-born son of Isagila, intercede
    for me!

May he hearken to my cry at the word of thy mouth.
May he remove my sighing, may he learn my supplication!
At his mighty word may god and goddess deal graciously
    with me!

67

May the sickness of my body be torn away!
May the groaning of my flesh be consumed!
May the consumption of my muscles be removed!
May the poisons that are upon me be loosened!
May the ban be torn away!

Another Babylonian incantation contains the names of Ea and Marduk, gods of magic:

Bright oil, pure oil, shining oil, the purifying oil of the gods, oil which softens the sinews of man.
With the oil of the incantation of Ea, with the oil of the incantation of Marduk
I have made thee drip; with the oil of softening which Ea has given for soothing
I have anointed thee; the oil of life I have put on thee.

The Babylonians also had special formulas for exorcism:

May the wicked demon depart. May the demons seize one another. The propitious demon, the propitious giant, may they penetrate his body.
Spirit of the heavens, conjure it!
Spirit of the earth, conjure it!

Babylonian Invocation

An invocation to the goddess Tasmitu to remove sickness and evil spells contains these words:

I, son of . . . , whose god is . . . , whose goddess is . . . ,

In the evil of an eclipse of the Moon . . . ,

In the evil of the powers, of the portents, evil and not good, which are in my palace and my land,

Have turned toward thee! . . .

May the consumption of my muscles be removed!

May the poisons that are upon me be loosened!

May the ban be torn away!

Bacchic Mysteries

Greek mysteries centered round the cult of Bacchus and said by some to have been brought to Greece from Egypt by Melampus. Women, the Bacchantes, were the chief attendants of the god of the vine and vegetation. See Greek Mysteries.

Bachelor

Name given to the Devil when he appeared in the form of a goat to have intercourse with women at the Sabbat.

Bacis

Famous soothsayer of Beotia. After he died, many other persons claiming to have the power to foretell the future adopted his name.

Bacon, Roger

Franciscan scholar (1214-1294). Legend credits him with the creation of an android. His scientific writings led to his imprisonment on the charge of witchcraft. His studies of alchemy led him to a belief in the philosopher's stone and the elixir of life. His name became popular in the 16th century, as the study of magic was pursued with increased zeal. Most of the magical exploits attributed to him probably derive from a play written by Robert Green and the book on which he based his play, *The History of Friar Bacon.*

The application of alchemy to the extension of life was another subject of study with Bacon. The grand secret of this science, he assures us, may be used to prolong life. The operation that purges most inferior metals from the corrupt elements they contain and exalts them into the purest gold and silver can eradicate the corrupt particles of the human body and extend the life span to several centuries.

Bacoti
Among the Tonkinese, this name is applied to sorcerers and diviners.

Bad
A Persian spirit who is said to command the winds and tempests. He presides over the 22nd day of each month.

Badb

One of the great Irish goddesses. She was said to have had many names—Brigid, Macha, Morrigan, Cailleach, Danu, Graney, Ma Gog, The Mother Goddess. In the Mediterranean countries, in classical times, she was called Baubo.

Bael
Head of the infernal powers. Wierus begins his inventory of the famous Pseudonomarchia Daemonum with this demon, whose estates are situated on the eastern regions of hell. The monarch of hell has three heads: a crab's, a cat's, and a man's. He commands 66 legions.

Bagahi Laca Bachabe
An ancient formula for invoking a demon.

Bagoe
A Tuscan sibyl. She judged all events by the sound of thunder. She is said to have been the first woman to practice the art of divination.

Bahir
A Hebrew term meaning luminous. The *Book Bahir* is a source book on the mystic Judaic Cabala. The *Book Bahir* and the *Zohar*, the *Book of Splendor*, together constitute the

70

two most important works in the mystic Cabala. It belongs in the 12-13th century.

Bailey, Alice
A little-known figure whose books on astrology and cosmology were supposedly inspired by higher sources.

Bailey, Charles
A famous apport medium of Melbourne. He began his mediumship in 1889 and was for many years the private medium of Thomas Welton Stanford, who collected apport materials now preserved at Leland Stanford University. Bailey was repeatedly charged with fraud.

Balaam
One of the evil demons who possessed Sister Jeanne des Anges. Balaam's passion was "all the more dangerous because it seemed less evil." The *Lemegeton* identifies Balaam (Balan or Balam) as a three-headed devil who rides a bear, carries a hawk on his wrist, and predicts the future. He is said to have one head like a bull's, another like a man's, and a third like a ram's. He is often shown naked. In the Old Testament, a symbol of avarice, immorality, and idol-worship.

Balak and Balaam
Occultists mentioned in the Bible. Balak was a king who had mastered the 28 degrees of enchantment by birds and was known as the Son of the Bird. According to the *Zohar*, he sent for Balaam and asked him to divine the hour and method of attacking Israel. The greatest of diviners, Balaam had learned his magic from two of the Watchers, and he later gave the book of Asmodai to Solomon. The unity of the children of Israel thwarted his attempts, and he was slain. His bones became serpents; whoever finds them can learn enchantment. But evil magic (Goetia) is such "that

he who follows it is killed by it, and it is with his soul when it departs from him."

Balasius
A purple or rose stone that overcomes vain thoughts, relieves infirmities, and reconciles quarrels among friends. If a person touches the four corners of a building or plot of ground with the stone, it will protect the entire building or plot against lightning, tempest, and worms.

Balberith
A demon who possessed Sister Madeleine, at Aix-en-Provence. He also listed the other demons possessing Madeleine, and he gave the special saints opposing these demons.

Ballanche, Pierre Simon
French philosopher (1776-1847). His peculiar blend of illuminism, social philosophy, and prophecy had an enduring appeal to successive generations of romantic writers. He believed in palingenesis, or regeneration of fallen man through ordeal, expiation, and initiation. Society originated through language, and history is a succession of rebirths designed to prepare mankind for freedom. The great initiators, from Orpheus to Jesus, worked to achieve the designs of Providence. Jesus set forth the master plan for all future rebirths.

Ballou, Adin
Nineteenth-century Universalist minister. In 1842 he founded the Hopedale Community, which helped the advance of spiritualism.

Balor
Mighty king of the Formorians. In Irish mythical tales he was usually styled Balor of the Evil Eye. His angry glance could destroy an enemy. When he grew old, he used ropes to keep his eyelid raised. Lugh crept near him one day and

slew him when the eyelid drooped momentarily. The great stone wielded by the sun-god sank through Balor's eye and brain.

Bamberg Witch Trials

Hundreds of persons accused of practicing witchcraft were burned in Bamberg, beginning with the administration of Bishop Johann Gottfried von Aschhausen (1609-1622) and continuing through that of Bishop Johann Georg II, who died in 1632.

Banishing Demons

A spell for banishing demons sent to extract human hearts was used by King Solomon.

> Lofaham,
> Solomon,
> Iyouel,
> Iyosenaoui.

Baphometic Statues

The Templars apparently worshiped certain figures to which they attributed talismanic powers. According to Jean Marquès-Rivière (*Amulettes, Talismans et Pantacles*, 1938), there is evidence to support the view that these statues or human heads were used in the rites of the Templars and treated as if they possessed magical properties. The French scholar suggests a connection between these figures and the ancient Hebraic tephilin, secret Asian divinities imported by the order as a result of their activities in the Near East, or certain Manichean sects that evolved from the Gnostic schools. He sees the statues as simple symbols unifying the speculative concepts that emerged from the contact between Christianity and Islam.

Baraduc, Hyppolite

A noted French psychical researcher who claimed to have

proved by photographic means that something misty leaves the body at the moment of death. He described his experiments in several books, among them *The Human Soul*, published in Paris in 1913.

Barbanell, Maurice

A well-known spiritualistic investigator who for some thirty-seven years has had visual evidence of certain psychic phenomena and manifestations that led him to conclude that such manifestations were caused by non-corporeal beings no longer living.

Barclay, Margaret

A Scottish housewife convicted of witchcraft, strangled, and burned at the stake in 1618. At her public trial, she recanted everything that she had confessed under the influence of a "most safe and gentle torture."

Bard

The chanted spells of the Celtic poet or singer were supposed to give him superhuman powers. He combined the offices of singer, genealogist, and custodian of tribal lore.

Barddas (Triads)

Welsh traditions recorded in triads and published in 1862 by the Welsh Manuscript Society. Purportedly taken from old manuscripts stored in a house destroyed by the Roundheads two centuries earlier, the *Barddas* describe the immigration of the Cwmry about 450 B. C. and suggest a connection between Druidic (Bardic) and Hindu beliefs regarding the transmigration of souls. That the *Barddas* actually do give an account of the Druidic faith seems plausible since the classical writers often called attention to parallels between Celtic beliefs and Pythagorean theories. The purest form of Druidism, according to Caesar, who kept a Druid priest at his headquarters, existed in Britain. Disciples had to devote twenty years to the task of committing to memory the verses embodying their ancient lore. Large portions of the *Barddas*, the Triads, are in verse. They are recorded in several versions and seem to have been collected in different parts of Wales. Though they would not require twenty years for mastery, they probably contain the essentials of Druidism. The witch cult now incorporates a belief in reincarnation that may date from the arrival of the Cwmry.

Bardesanian System
A system worked out by Bardesanes and called by some a Cabala within a Cabala. A very old Gnostic system, the so-called "Codex of the Nazarenes" contains doctrines formulated before Bardesanes as well as the ancient names of good and evil powers.

Bardo Thodol
The Tibetan Book of the Dead, according to Kazi Dawa Samdup, a lama who prepared an English version of the book, is a handbook of occultism. It describes the agony of death experienced by an initiate into the secret tradition. It guides the dead initiate's spirit through terrifying infernal visions. Hell, devils, torments are creations of the spirit itself. Then come transmigration and the choice of material factors (parents, sex, etc.) that condition reincarnation. The book uses the symbolism of Bonism and Buddhism to cloak the mystical teachings of the ancient Tibetan gurus. Interpreted esoterically as an account of the life and rebirth of the ego, the book teaches that the attainment of freedom dpends on remembrance of certain things heard on the after-death plane.

Barguest
A goblin whose name derives from his habit of sitting on bars or gates. He can make himself visible in the day time.

Bari
Among the Bororos of Brazil, the bari is a sorcerer associ-

ated with terrifying spirits that control wind and rain, sickness and death. He mediates between human beings and the evil spirits.

Barkaial
Fallen angel who taught mortals the secrets of astrology. See Book of Enoch.

Barkers
Demoniacs who bark like dogs. Famous examples include the barkers of Jocelyn, in Brittany, France, and Spanish nuns of the seventeenth century.

Barnaud, Nicholas
A physician who belongs in the sixteenth century. He is the author of a number of treatises on alchemy.

Baron
A demon who signed a pact with Gilles de Rais (1404-1440). To him Gilles de Rais sacrificed the hands and hearts of children to obtain the secret of the philosopher's stone.

Barqu
Demon responsible for guarding the secret of the philosopher's stone.

Barre, Margot de la
Central figure in a trial held by secular authorities in Paris in 1390. Margot de la Barre, called Coingnet, was accused of simple maleficium. She helped Marion la Droituriere to even the score with the lover who had jilted her by using magic to make him impotent. Both women confessed after torture that they had caused the demon to appear before them by uttering these words: "Enemy, I command you in the name of the Father, Son, and Holy Ghost to come to me here." Both women were burned at the stake.

Barrett, Sir William Fletcher

British scientist and occultist (1845-1926). In *The Magus* (1891) he describes, with illustrations, demons, conjurations, spells and necromancy: Mammon is the prince of tempters; Asmodeus, the prince of evil vengefulness; Belzebuth, chief of the false gods. He also introduces new attributes for five demons: Pytho is the prince of the spirits of deceit; Belial, prince of iniquity; Merihim, prince of war and evil; and Astaroth, prince of accusers and inquisitors. He believed in the existence of a spiritual world, survival after death, and the possibility of communicating with the dead.

Basque Witchcraft

In the 17th century witches in the Basque country of northwestern Spain and southwestern France were accused of inducing sterility, blighting crops, and worshiping the Devil. Many of them confessed to having made ointments with babies' hearts and toads' blood. They also admitted that they had trafficked with the Devil in the form of a man, but with a horn in his forehead and long teeth protruding from his mouth. There are also indications of a cult of "La Dama" or "La Señora" similar to that of Aradia in Italy. Witches were known as *brujos* and *xorguinos*. See Aradia.

Details of the wholesale burnings that occurred in the Basque regions of France in 1609 are reported in Pierre de Lancre's *Tableau* (1612).

Bat

Its uncanny ability to hunt its prey in total darkness may account for the frightening reputation the bat has acquired over the centuries as a creature of occult power. In folklore it has been represented as a witch and familiar, ghost and devil. It has the attributes of a bird when it symbolizes the soul and of a demon when it is associated with darkness.

Medieval witch enthusiasts were certain that the Devil often appeared as a bat.

Bataille, Doctor

Fictitious name of Leo Taxtil, author of sensational revelations published in *Le Diable au XIXe siecle,* beginning in 1892. Dr. Bataille claimed to have traveled widely, to have witnessed spirit manifestations, satanic initiation rites, and modern worshipers of Bahomet, and to have learned the secrets of Albert Pike's occult powers, Sophie Walder's conversion, etc. In 1897 Leo Taxil admitted publicly that he had fabricated all of Dr. Bataille's sensational revelations.

Batsaum-Pasha

A Turkish demon or spirit, invoked to produce good weather or rain.

Bearded Demon

The demon who teaches the secret of the philosopher's stone, so called on account of his remarkable beard.

Beckford, William

Eighteenth-century English writer. He was interested in demonology and Oriental magic. He wrote *Vathek.*

Behemoth

One of the seven demons who possessed Sister Jeanne des Anges. Behemoth often filled her mind with blasphemies and gave her "a very strange aversion" to her vocation.

Bekker, Balthasar

In *De Betoverde Weereld* (The World Bewitched), published in 1691, Dr. Balthasar Bekker attacked the doctrines of witchcraft then prevalent and charged that they were invented by the papacy "to warm the fires of purgatory and to fill the pockets of the clergy."

Belephantes

According to the Greek historian Diodorus Siculus, Belephantes was a Chaldean astrologer. He rightly predicted that Alexander the Great's entry into Babylon would be fatal to the Emperor.

Beliefs of Occultists

Among the major tenets of contemporary occultism are: that man is evolving to higher degrees of spiritual life; that the entire cosmos is governed by a hierarchy of Intelligence; that the cosmos is constituted totally of energy.

Belin, Albert

A Benedictine monk who flourished in the seventeenth century. Author of treatises in alchemy, astral figures, talismans.

Bell, Book, and Candle

The resources of the Church for excommunicating heretics were summed up in the phrase "to curse by bell, book, and candle." The sound of bells forces demons to abandon the witches that they are taking to the Sabbat.

Belli Paaro

Secret African society stressing fraternal relations with departed spirits. Those who join the cult, centered in Liberia, desire to be regarded as having died and been brought to life again.

Belloc, Jeanne

A French sorceress who, at the age of 84, was indicted and persuaded to confess that she had attended a Sabbat in the winter of the year 1609 and been presented to the Devil. He bestowed upon her a kiss, the mark of approbation reserved for the greatest sorcerers.

Belomancy

Divination by arrows. This form of divination was practiced by the Chaldeans, Greeks, and Arabians.

Belphegor

In obscene worship, a demon with a gaping mouth and a phallic-shaped tongue.

Beltane

May 1(old style) is linked to one of the four major sabbats celebrated by witches. Modern English witches celebrate May Eve. The Mayday festival probably originated as a sun or fire rite. On this occasion the druids drove cattle between two bonfires to protect them against murrain.

Benedict, Mrs.

The official medium of the Apostolic Circle, known simply as Mrs. Benedict, was associated with the spiritualists known as the Katie Fox Circle in Auburn, New York, in the 19th century.

Benedict IX

A child pope who excelled in sorcery. A wealthy and ambitious family placed the throne in his hands when he was 12. According to one story he made the Roman matrons follow him everywhere by the charm of his magic.

Benemmerinnen

Hebrew witches. They haunt women in childbirth and steal their newborn children.

Beng

In Gypsy superstition, the Devil.

Benge

Poison used by the Azande in divination. The red paste is administered as a supernatural agent in such a way as to provide a yes or no answer, depending on whether the animal that consumes it lives or dies. About half of the animals used in this form of divination live.

Bensozia

According to Don Martin's book on the religion of the Gauls (*Religion des Gaulois*), she was the Diana of the Celtic tribes. She was also called Nocticula, Herodias, and "The Moon." See Aradia.

Beowulf

An Anglo-Saxon saga based on events that occurred about the fifth century. Probably one of the Sons of Light whose business it was to fight the powers of darkness, he defeated the monster Grendel and eventually became king of Gothland. He was poisoned by the fangs of a dragon in the course of a mighty struggle.

Berean Society

An English society that flourished in the nineteenth century. It studied theoretical occultism.

Berigard, Claude

Italian philosopher and alchemist. A. E. Waite writes:

> The following account of a transmutation performed by himself, is recorded by the celebrated Italian philosopher, Claude Berigard, and will be found on the twenty-fifth page of his *Circulus Pisanus,* published at Florence in 1641.

> "I did not think that it was possible to convert quicksilver into gold, but an acquaintance thought proper to remove my doubt. He gave me about a drachm of a powder nearly of the colour of the wild poppy, and having a smell like calcined sea-salt. To avoid all imposition, I purchased a crucible, charcoal, and quicksilver, in which I was certain that there was no gold mixed. Ten drachms of quicksilver which I heated on the fire were on projection transmuted into nearly the same weight of good gold, which stood all tests. Had I not performed this operation

in the most careful manner, taking every precaution against the possibility of doubt, I should not have believed it, but I am satisfied of the fact."

Bernard, Raymond

Head of the French Rosicrucians. The Grand Master set forth in his book *L'Empire Invisible* (The Invisible Empire) a description of the lost continent of Atlantis and its inhabitants. (The library of the Rosicrucians is supposed to contain secret documents showing that Plato was the depository of the Atlantean tradition.) The Grand Master is believed to have imparted a portion of the teachings of the Rosicrucians to the members of the association in his book. According to him Atlantis was a highly civilized continent. Its inhabitants had at their disposal advanced techniques of transportation and communication unknown to the modern world. They were the rulers of widely dispersed colonists to whom they revealed only as much of their secret wisdom as the colonists were capable of assimilating and employing. In some instances a direct line was set up between a country and the College of Sages, made up of the wisest of the initiates, who were the guardians of the secret wisdom. A pyramidal temple modeled on the supreme temple where the College of Sages presided, symbolized the link between the colony and the heart of the world. The pyramid of Cheops is the only one that preserved Atlantean wisdom in its wholeness; the others revealed it only partially.

The Atlanteans knew the nature and power of certain cosmic forces, which they applied in achieving an ecological balance and preventing geological catastrophes. The pyramids had a part in this scheme of things, as did the dolmens and menhirs that marked the spots where cosmic energies could be collected and focused, and where magical rituals and ceremonies could best be conducted.

Ambitious and ignorant men brought about changes in the supreme pyramid. The planetary catastrophe that caused Atlantis to disappear beneath the ocean and altered the face of the earth was erroneously remembered as the Flood.

The wisdom of the Atlanteans is perpetuated fragmentarily in the teachings of the secret African societies. The sages who settled in Africa after the cataclysm that destroyed Atlantis communicated only a part of their wisdom to selected groups. They did not try to reconstruct the empire that had been destroyed, for they were acting according to a universal plan, and it is the whole world that is destined to become the New Atlantis. The sages have directed our evolution through the centuries, revealing their wisdom to us as we reach the stage where we can use it without again endangering the world. Their knowledge came from another galaxy. It was brought by those who became the first leaders of the Atlanteans. Some of them remained on the earth to continue their instruction; others returned to their point of origin. The Grand Master of the French Rosicrucians is convinced that contemporary Atlanteans, who will take the place of the College of Sages, act in concert with the supreme council of his organization. He expects Atlantis to reappear, populated by Atlanteans who will spread across the earth and take the initiative in uniting our world with other worlds and galaxies.

Berosus

A Babylonian priest of Bel. In the third century B. C., he authored a history of Babylon from its beginnings to the death of Alexander the Great. In 280 B. C. he founded a college for the study of astrology on the Greek Island of Cos. To him are attributed many manuals on witchcraft and magic.

83

Bes

In Egyptian religion, an ancient phallic god, represented as standing on a lotus ready to devour his own progeny. Later, his image was widely used as an amulet, throughout the Greco-Roman world down to the Middle Ages.

Besant, Annie

English theosophist (1847-1933). A pupil of Mme. Helena Petrovna Blavatsky, she proposed to make Jiddu Krishnamurti, her own protégé, a Messiah. After Mme. Blavatsky died, she became president of the Theosophical Society. She was founder of the Central Hindu College at Benares and a strong advocate of nationalism in India.

The most famous of British Theosophists and self-styled "servant of the great Brotherhood" believed that the great Sages exist today and that they "wield powers and possess knowledge before which our control of Nature and knowledge of her ways is but child's play." She wrote of her occult experiences in *Man: Whence, How and Whither* (1913). Two excellent books by A. H. Nethercot deal with her career: *The First Five Lives of Annie Besant* (1960) and *The Last Four Lives of Annie Besant* (1963).

Beth Elohim

A cabalistic treatise on angels, demons, and souls. The Hebraic expression means House of God.

Beuther, David

Seventeenth-century alchemist. He was reputed to possess the secret of making gold. He was imprisoned by those eager to extract his secret. Released from prison, he poisoned himself to guard his secret.

Bewitch

To cast a spell over a person or gain power over him by

charms or incantations. To injure by witchcraft. To seduce with erotic or evil intent.

Beyrevra
A Hindu demon, master of souls that roam through space.

Bezoar
A concretion found in the alimentary organs of human or animals. Such concretions are widely supposed to have medicinal and magical applications. Those taken from serpents are supposed to be effective in combating the effects of cobra venom. Medieval handbooks contain many descriptions of bezoars.

Bhutas
In Oriental mysticism, these are astral entities of deceased human beings. They are equated with ghosts or spirits.

Bibliomancy
Divination from a book, generally the Bible. The Koran is used by Moslems. Virgil's *Aeneid* was used in the Middle Ages, the poet having acquired fame as a magician. The diviner opens the book at random, touches blindly a certain spot, and reads the text to determine its content.

Billis
African sorcerers who are credited with the power to prevent the growth of rice.

Bilson Boy
One of a number of young impostors who made false accusations that caused others to be suspected of witchcraft. His real name was William Perry. In 1620 he accused an old woman of bewitching him. Later it was discovered that he had been trained by a priest to feign possessions.

Bimini
Edgar Cayce is supposed to have predicted the discovery of

the submerged walls of a city dating back to the disappearance of Atlantis. His prediction was made in 1940. Later the head of the French Rosicrucians published similar views in a book titled *L'Empire Invisible* (The Invisible Empire). Subsequently many strange events were reported in the Magic Triangle and along the 35th parallel. French diver Dimitri Rebikoff was the first to report the presence of huge geometric masses off the western coast of Bimini.

In Cayce's vision of Atlantis, the great continent was exposed to three great catastrophes.

The first two cataclysms occurred more than 15,000 years B. C. and divided the continent into islands. The third occurred around 12,000 years ago and resulted in the disappearance of Atlantis. Before the last catastrophe, when the continent stretched from the Sargasso Sea to the Azores, the superior race that governed the great empire emigrated to Peru, Egypt, Mexico, New Mexico, and Colorado, where their descendants, the Mount Dwellers, still reside. The brilliant civilization of the Atlanteans was made possible by the discovery of a means of utilizing solar energy. The Atlanteans used a large cylindrical crystal placed in a dome-shaped structure to capture solar energy and use it to power vehicles of various types.

Their last migrations resulted in intermarriages that produced the Egyptians in Africa and the Incas in America. The epicenter of the shock waves that destroyed Atlantis was near Bimini. The three main islands that were submerged in that area were called Poseidia, Aryan, and Og.

Binah

The third sephira, represented in the first triangle of the Tree of Life. In the cabalistic system, it is the passive, female principle in God. It is called the Mother, the Throne, the Great Sea. It is the passive Understanding of God. Binah is symbolized by the cteis, cup, circle, diamond, and oval. Its deities include Hecate, goddess of witchcraft and sorcery.

Binseld, Peter
German authority on witch-hunting (1540-1603). He incited many trials for witchcraft and was widely quoted.

Biscar, Jeannette
A French sorceress, reputed to have been conveyed to a Sabbat in goat form by the Devil himself. She was rewarded by being suspended in midair, head downward.

Bishop, Bridget
A black servant tried and convicted of practicing witchcraft in Massachusetts in 1692. She and several other servants implicated in the Salem affair may have been practicing a cult resembling voodoo.

Black Books (Grimoires)
Manuals of magic, pseudepigraphically ascribed to Solomon, Albertus Magnus, certain Popes, and other karcists or wizards. Highly popular during the Middle Ages, they describe many occult practices, rituals, and ceremonies. Among the most notable: *Liber Spirituum;* the Hebrew manual called *Shemamphoras; Oupnekhat,* a Sanskrit manual translated into Persian and later into Latin (1802); *Grimoirium Verum,* by Alibeck the Egyptian (1517); *The Constitution of Honorius,* attributed to Pope Honorius III; *Little Albert; Red Dragon; Arbatel; Tonalamatl,* an ancient Mexican manual; *Y-Kim,* an obscure Chinese work assigned to the fourth millennium B. C.; *Red Book of Appin; Hell's Coercion,* attributed to Johannes Faustus; *The Black Hen; The Great and Powerful Sea Ghost,* by Faustus; Lemegeton, or the *Lesser Key of Solomon,* which describes the demonic hierarchy; *The Key of Solomon,* ascribed to King Solomon; *The Testament of Solomon,* a tenth-century account of the

building of the Temple by Solomon with the aid of demons; *Liber Pentaculorum; The Sage of the Pyramids; The Almadel;* and *The Book of Raziel,* reputedly derived from *The Book of Signs,* a handbook on magic attributed to Adam.

Black Cat

Like the black pullet, the black cat plays an important role in magic. Long associated with the Devil and credited with having nine lives, the cat was worshipped by the ancient Egyptians. A maleficent companion of the Devil and witches who participate in Sabbat dances, the black cat is a harbinger of bad luck. Those who see him crossing the street before them must take defensive steps. The heretical Stadinghians were said to worship a black cat, kissing its genitalia as they did in the case of the Devil at the Sabbat.

Black Dog

In many cultures the black dog is associated with sorcery. The black demon Cernobog was represented by the Slavs as a black dog. Among the Wallachians there is a horrible vampire-like creature called Priccolitsh, or Priculics, who appears as a man in fine healthy condition, but by night he becomes a dog, kills people by the mere touch, and devours them. (Charles Leland.)

Black Dragon

A popular grimoire. Attributed to Honorius, it contains instructions for summoning demons and making pacts. Each day of the week calls for a different procedure. On Monday, Lucifer is invoked; on Tuesday, Frimost; on Wednesday, Astaroth; on Thursday, Silcharde; on Friday, Bechard; on Saturday, Guland; and on Sunday, Surgat.

Black Glance

Another name for the Evil Eye.

Black Hen

Like the black dog, the black hen or pullet has long been associated with the Devil and witchcraft. A medieval grimoire bearing this title tells how magic words may be used with a talisman to obtain knowledge and cure sickness:

This talisman and this ring will give you knowledge of all minerals and all vegetables, their virtues and properties, and you will possess universal medicine. There is no sickness that you will not be able to cure, no remedy that you cannot successfully undertake. Aesculapius and Hippocrates will be but schoolboys compared with you.

Just pronounce these words: Reterrem, Salibat, Cratares, Hisater, and when you are at a sick bedside, carry the talisman on your stomach and the ring attached to a red ribbon round your neck.

Black Magic

As practiced in medieval times, black magic was the use of supernatural knowledge for the purposes of evil, the invocation of infernal powers obedient to man's will, a perversion of mystical science of the true adept. It was in many ways the perpetuation of the popular rites of paganism. In the Middle Ages the ancient gods had become devils, their mysteries orgies, their worship a perverted form of magic.

The simplest ailments or most revolting diseases were traced to the power of black magic in the form of spells and conjurations. Cures were predicated on fantastic incantations and exorcisms, talismans and amulets, philtres and weird medicaments. Practitioners and believers swarmed everywhere. The hierarchy of the fraudulent fraternity embraced various grades, from the pretenders, charlatans and diviners of the common people to the secret societies and orders of initiates. Grimoires were filled with weird rites, formulas, conjurations, evocations, charms, and spells, all clothed in incomprehensible jargon. K. Nixey, writing in Lewis Spencer's *Encyclopaedia of Occultism,* gives the following account of medieval magic:

The deity who was worshipped, whose powers were invoked in the practice of Black Magic, was the Source and Creator of Evil, Satanas, Belia, the Devil, a direct descendant of the Egyptian Set, the Persian Ahriman, the Python of the Greeks, the Jewish Serpent, Baphomet of the Templars, the Goat-deity of the Witches' Sabbath. He was said to have the head and legs of a goat, and the breasts of a woman.

To his followers he was known by many names, among these being debased names of forgotten deities, also the Black One, the Black He-Goat, the Black Raven, the Dog, the Wolf and Snake, the Dragon, the Hell-hound Hell-hand Hell-bolt. His transformations were unlimited, as is indicated by many of his names. . . . The signs by which he might be identified, though not invariably, were the cloven hoof, the goat's beard, cock's feathers, or ox's tail.

In all his grotesquery are embedded ancient mysteries and their symbols, the detritus of dead faiths and faded civilizations. . . .

Beneath the Devil's sway were numberless hordes and legions of demons and spirits, ready and able to procure and work any and every evil or disaster the mind of man might conceive and desire. . . .

According to the Grimoires, the rites and rules are multifarious, each demon demanding special invocation and procedure. . . .

90

These rites fell under the classification of divination, bewitchments and necromancy. The first named was carried out by magical readings of fire, smoke, water or blood; by letters of names, numbers, symbols, arrangements of dots; by lines of hand or finger nails; by birds and their flight or their entrails; by dice or cards, rings or mirrors.

Bewitchments were carried out by means of nails, animals, toads or waxen figures and mostly to bring about suffering or death. In the first method nails were consecrated to evil by spells and invocations, then nailed crosswise above the imprint of the feet of the one who is destined for torment. The next was by selection of some animal supposed to resemble the intended victim and attaching to it some of his hair or garments. They gave it the name and then proceeded to torture it, in whole or part according to the end desired, by driving nails, red-hot pins and thorns into the body to the rhythm of muttered maledictions. For like purpose a fat toad was often selected, baptised, made to swallow a host, both consecrated and execrated, tied with hairs of the victim upon which the sorcerer had previously spat, and finally buried at the threshold of the bewitched one's door, whence it issued as nightmare and vampire for his undoing.

The last and most favoured method was by the use of waxen images. Into the wax was mixed baptismal oil and ash of consecrated hosts, and out of this was fashioned a figure resembling the one to be bewitched. It was then baptised, and next subjected to curses, torture by knives or fire; then finally stabbed to the heart. . . .

For paraphernalia and accessories the sorcerers scoured the world and the imagination and mind of man, bending all things, beautiful or horrible to their service. The different planets ruled over certain objects and states and invocations. . . . Mars favoured wars and strife, Venus love, Jupiter ambition and intrigue, Saturn malediction and death. . . .

The history of the Middle Ages is shot through with the shadows cast by this terrible belief in Black Magic.

Black Mass

Some authorities hold that the Black Mass was largely a literary invention of 19th-century occultists. As performed in the Chambre Ardente affair by degenerates of the court of Louis XIV, the obscene travesty of the Christian Mass attracted widespread attention. Earlier, toward the end of the 15th century, such a performance was reported in the trial records of Brescia in Lombardy. These records detail the first and only instance of the celebration of a Black Mass in medieval times. There the witches were alleged to have celebrated masses in honor of their god Lucibel.

Traditional accounts of occult practices indicate that the mysteries of witchcraft are inextricably interwoven with occult pagan cults which, despite unceasing attacks by Christianity, have flourished through the centuries. Pagan cults allegedly stress the distinction between Christian tenets and the beliefs of the "Old Religion," or witchcraft. The Black Mass, which attracted much attention during the Middle Ages, is an obscene travesty of Christianity. Its inverted rituals, lascivious formulas, and weird pronouncements raise and exalt the Archfiend. Long associated with the Witches' Sabbat, the Black Mass probably overlapped into its ceremonials, merging with it to produce one unit with the sole aim of forming an alliance with the dark forces of the universe and rejecting all tenets in conflict with the "Old Religion."

As it evolved during the Middle Ages, the Black Mass became a parody of the Christian Mass. Satan was the object of worship. The altar was dominated by an obscene figure of Christ or an infernal goat; candles were black, the chalice contained blood or human fat. Sometimes a nude woman was used as an altar, with the mass being celebrated on her buttocks or stomach. Presiding over the mass was a defrocked priest. The celebrants were nude except for a cassock adorned with Satanic symbols. The host was black.

Finally the Black Mass acquired a sinister importance of its own, becoming an independent ritual with its own locale and devotees, bound by their common interest in Satanism. People from all walks of life—lowly peasants and high-born ladies, priests and prelates, nobles and servants, were drawn by curiosity or avarice, by lust or hope, to worship the Archfiend, the Devil, Diabolus. At the height of the ceremonial, with the priestly officiant taking the leading role, an unbridled sexual orgy occurred. Brocken Mountain and the church of Blokula, in Sweden, were famous as meeting places for Black Mass participants.

Many paintings, etchings, and sculptures have tried to capture the wild, orgiastic nature of the rites, often involving sacrifices of crops and animals.

Black Pullet
Title of a book printed in France in 1740, purporting to be a narrative of an officer serving in Egypt. The officer had become acquainted with a magician who revealed to him the secret of making a black pullet capable of discovering gold. A black hen should be hooded or placed in a box lined with black material and allowed to hatch her own egg. The resulting chicken will be able to detect places where gold is hidden. The book contains many illustrations of magical rings and talismans. It is also called the *Black Hen.*

Black Shaman

A shaman who is associated with malignant and magic forces.

Blake, William

English mystic poet and artist (1757-1827). Influencing his writing and painting was the belief that each entity contains all things within itself and that the "world of the Imagination is the world of Eternity." He is supposed to have received from his dead brother his peculiar technique of illuminated painting. His gods (Zoas) and their progeny are the emanations of the Platonists, the archetypes of C. G. Jung—"self-portraits of the instinct," evocations of the collective unconscious, basic mental patterns common to all men. His famous painting, *The Ancient of Days*, shows Urizen (the power of reason) creating the material world and dividers symbolizing both rational creation and the divisive nature of reason. His genius probably derived from his acute perception of the content of the collective unconscious and his illuminated vision of nature. He said that his visions came to him faster than he could set them down. "To me," he said, "this world is all one continued vision of fancy or imagination." Rejecting the materialistic teachings of Bacon, Newton, and Locke, he studied the writings of Swedenborg, Jacob Boehme, Paracelsus, Plato, and Plotinus. Following the cabalistic tradition of identifying four worlds corresponding to four states of consciousness, he saw in his vision Eden, Beulah, Generation and Ulro. His Four Zoas, the "living creatures" in Ezekiel's vision of the Chariot, are named Luvah, Tharmas, Urizen, and Urthona. They correspond to Jung's four functions of feeling, sense, reason, and intuition. A central theme in Blake's mythology is the supremacy of "Jesus the Imagination" over reason. In "Auguries of Innocence," he wrote:

To see a World in a Grain of Sand

And a Heaven in a Wild Flower,
Hold Infinity in the palm of your hand
And Eternity in an hour.

A good introductory book to the life and works of the English mystic is Bernard Blackstone's *English Blake* (1949).

Blanckenstein Trials

Chatrina Blanckenstein was acquitted of the charge of bewitching a small child. Her trial was held in Saxony in 1676. In 1689, her daughter confessed to a series of crimes, under torture, and was condemned to be burned alive.

Blarney Stone

In Irish legend, the Blarney Stone is some twenty feet from the top of a wall in a castle and accessible only with great difficulty. Those who journey to the village of Blarney in County Clark receive the gift of free-flowing speech if they succeed in kissing the stone.

Blavatsky, Helena Petrovna

Russian-born spiritualist and theosophist (1831-91). She founded the Theosophical Society, traveled widely, and wrote Isis Unveiled, The Secret Doctrine, and The Key to Theosophy.

She married, at the age of seventeen. . . . Her married life was of short duration. . . . The next year or so she occupied chiefly in travelling, Texas, Mexico, Canada and India, were each in turn the scene of her wanderings, and she twice attempted to enter Tibet. On one occasion she managed to cross its frontier in disguise but lost her way, and after various adventures was found by a body of horsemen and escorted homewards. The period between 1848 and 1858, she described as the "veiled" time of her life, refusing to divulge anything that happened to her in these ten years, save stray allusions to a seven years' stay in Little and Great Tibet, or in a "Himalayan Retreat." In 1858 she returned to Russia, where she soon achieved distinction as a spiritualistic medium. Later on she went to the United States where she remained for six years, and became a naturalised citizen. She became prominent in spiritualistic circles in America about 1870. The idea occurred to her of combining her spirtualistic "control" with Buddhistic legends about Tibetan sages, and she professed to have direct "astral" communication with two Tibetan mahatmas.

With the aid of Col. Henry Olcott, she founded in New York, in 1875, the Theosophical Society with a threefold aim: (1) to form a universal brotherhood of man; (2) to study and make known the ancient religions, philosophies and sciences; (3) to investigate the laws of nature and develop the divine powers latent in man. In order to gain converts to Theosophy she was obliged to appear to perform miracles. This she did with a large measure of success, but her "methods" were on several occasions detected as fraudulent. Nevertheless her commanding personality secured for her a large following, and when she died, in 1891, she was at the head of a large body of believers in her teaching, numbering about 100,000 persons. (Lewis Spence.)

Isis Unveiled is a survey of the literature of magic and its interconnections with western science and eastern mysticism. While writing it and smoking hashish, she said she caught a glimpse of the goddess herself. She set forth the doctrine of Astral Light, calling it Akasha, and a secret science known to the ancients and transmitted through the ages by a secret brotherhood of adepts. The Secret Doctrine, based on her examination of the Akashic Records, gives an account of the root knowledge out of which all religion, philosophy, and science have grown. Her biography was written by John Symonds, *Madame Blavatsky, Medium and Magician* (1960).

Blood

From time immemorial blood has been regarded as a vitalizing agent and has figured prominently in ritual sacrifices. In paleolithic times the bodies of the dead were put in pits containing ocher. The reddish ore may have been intended to provide the deceased with a substitute for the vitalizing agent.

The Greeks poured blood into graves to revive the spirits of the dead. In certain mystery cults, as in Mithraism, blood baptism was used to purify both body and soul. Demons are said to love blood. Whenever a necromantic act is performed, according to Gratian, author of the twelfth-century *Decretum*, "blood is mixed with water so that they may be exorcised more readily by the color of the blood."

Bocor

A voodoo adept. Unlike the *hungan*, who is endowed with supernatural powers, the bocor buys his gods. He relies on magic alone, not on prayers.

Bodin, Jean

Demonologist (c. 1530-96). The author of one of the earliest essays on the philosophy of history was also a student of demonology. His *Démonomanie des sorciers* (1580) is a defense of witchcraft. It demonstrates that spirits have communication with mankind, explains diabolic prophecy, and sets forth the characteristics of sorcerers.

Boehme, Jacob

German mystic and clairvoyant (1575-1624). Also known as Böhm, Böhme, and Behmen. An untutored cobbler, he wrote *Aurora* (1612), a study of the deity, which circulated in manuscript and drew attention to his original mind; four great works in which he explored the manifestation of the divine in the structure of the world and of man; and a number of other speculative works, such as the treatise on eternal nature which may have anticipated Sir Isaac Newton's formulas.

Alchemist or not himself, *Boehme's* writings demonstrate that he studied Paracelsus closely. . . . At the same time, he seems to have felt a curious and constant intimacy with the invisible world, he appears to have had a strangely perspicacious vision of the *Urgrund,* as he calls it, which is, being literally translated, primitive cause; and it was probably his gift in these particular ways, and the typically German clearness with which he sets down his ideas and convictions, which chiefly begot his vast and wide influence over subsequent people inclined to mysticism. (Lewis Spence.)

Boehme anticipated Swedenborg in the doctrine of correspondences, inspired by mystical revelations. During the first such experience, he was "surrounded with a divine light for seven days, and stood in the highest contemplation and kingdom of joys." At the age of 25 he was again "surrounded by the divine light, and replenished with the heavenly knowledge, insomuch . . . , viewing the herbs and grass of the field, in his inward light, he saw into their essences, use, and properties, which were discovered to him by their lineaments, figures and signatures." Afterwards he wrote a book on the subject, titled *Signatura Rerun,* The Signature of All Things. In another of the 32 volumes that he composed before his death at the age of 50, he stated:

I saw and knew the Being of all Beings, the Byss and the Abyss, and the eternal generation of the Holy Trinity, the descent and original of the world, and of all creatures through the divine wisdom. I knew and saw in myself all the three worlds—namely, the divine, angelical, and paradisiacal; and *the dark world,* the original of the nature of the fire; and then, thirdly, the external and visible world, being a procreation or external birth from the inner and spiritual world. And I saw and knew the whole working essence, in the evil and the good, and the original and existence of each of them; and likewise how the fruitful-bearing womb of Eternity brought forth.

The chaotic universe of his vision was revealed to him by degrees over a twelve-year period, and the things which at first were couched and concealed were opened to him as in a young plant. In his highest and truest clairvoyance he glimpsed gems of truth, but when his inspiration departed he was, according to his own testimony, unable to understand his own writings. See Correspondences.

Boguet, Henri
French jurist. His *Discours des sorciers* (1602) examines the Sabbat, the powers and the marks of witches, and punishments to be meted out. The appendix presents in seventy articles many different statutes and court decisions concerning witchcraft. The book is supposed to have resulted in the burning of more than six hundred witches in Burgundy.

Bokor
A Haitian necromancer. He exercises control over the spirits of the dead.

Bolingbroke, Roger
Fifteenth-century English wizard. He was hanged in London for trying to kill Henry VI by witchcraft.

Bolos of Mendes
Author of the oldest known book on alchemy, *Physika kai Mystika* (The Physical and the Mystical), about 200 B.C.

Bona-Oma

In Roman religion, a goddess of fertility who was also patroness of female occultists.

Bonatti, Guido

An Italian astrologer and adept in the Black Arts, who flourished in the thirteenth century. He wrote prolifically on these subjects. He was reputed to have made an apothecary wealthy by fashioning a wax figure of a ship and endowing it with magic properties.

Like Michael Scot the occultist, he was consigned to Hell by Dante.

Bonewits, Isaac

An occultist and serious student of magic; Isaac Bonewits was the first person to receive a college degree based on the study of the supernatural. In 1970 he received his bachelor of arts degree for "studies in the field of magic" from the University of California in Berkeley. His expressed aim is to translate magic "into modern terms that can be used in a parapsychological laboratory."

Boniface VIII

Pope who was regarded by many as an adept in black magic and has a place in Dante's *Inferno*. A noted jurisconsult, he was born about 1228, elected pope in 1292, accused of heresy and sorcery in 1303, and cleared of these charges in 1312.

Bonifarce

One of the demons who possessed Elisabeth Allier, a seventeenth-century French nun.

Bonnevault, Pierre

Seventeenth-century French sorcerer. Arrested on his way

to the Sabbat, he confessed that his parents had dedicated him to the Devil, who had helped him to perform magical acts. He acknowledged that he had killed several persons but denied that he had bargained away his own soul. Pierre's brother Jean told how he had been transported through the air to the Sabbat and had received orders to kill certain people. He was also condemned.

Book of Enoch

Apocryphal book of the Old Testament, written in Hebrew and preserved partially in an Etheopic version of a text known to the early Greek Fathers. The book deals with the foundations of magic.

> There were angels who consented to fall from heaven that they might have intercourse with the daughters of earth. . . . They took wives with whom they had intercourse, to whom also they taught Magic, the art of enchantment, and the diverse properties of roots and trees. Amazarac gave instruction in all secrets of sorcerers; Barkaial was the master of those who study the stars; Akibeel manifested signs; and Azaradel taught the motions of the moon.

The apocryphal book also gives an account of the characteristics of demons:

> Demons have their own peculiarities, their physical distinctiveness, their functional activities. Some dwell in mines and forests, on mountain tops. Some copulate with humans. Some display beneficent attitudes to humans, teaching crafts, astrology, enchantments. Others have skill in herbs.

Book of Formation

In Hebrew, this is the *Sefer Yezirah*. It is a treatise of great

101

antiquity. In its six chapters, by means of mystical numerical calculations based on the values of letters of the alphabet, it expounds the creation of the world. A legend declares that by studying the text several cabalistic occultists were able to create a calf, deer, and fawns.

Book of Moses
The standard magicians' code of the Middle Ages. It contained a complicated ritual for the induction of neophytes.

Book of the Dead
See Egyptian Book of the Dead.

Book of the Measuring Rod
The title of a mystic cabalistic treatise dating in the fourteenth century. Its contents are traditionally ascribed to the revelations of the prophet Elijah.

Books on Witchcraft
The first book on witchcraft was Johannes Nider's *Formicarius,* written in 1435 and published in 1475. The first printed work was Alphonsus de Spina's *Fortalicium Fidei* (1845). Jean Vineti, in a work written in 1450, *Tractatus contrademonum invocatores,* described witchcraft as heresy. The idea of the Sabbat was developed in *Errores Gazariorum,* also written in 1450. The first work written in French was *La Vauderie Lyonoise,* compiled by the inquisitor of Lyon. J. Spenger and H. Kramer compiled the *Malleus Maleficarum,* which became the handbook of the inquisitors.

Bordelon, Laurent
Demonologist (1635-1730). Author of some thirty works on witchcraft, he has been called the Don Quixote of demonography. The French writer ridiculed both witchcraft and the harsh measures used to repress it.

Borley Rectory
"The most haunted house in England." See Price, Harry.

Bos, Francoise

French witch accused of having sexual relations with an incubus disguised as the "Captain of the Holy Ghost." She was burned on July 30, 1606.

Bosch, Hieronymus

Mysterious Dutch painter (c. 1450-1516). His fertile imagination enabled him to create a universe of hallucination; paintings mingling alchemical symbolism, sorcery, and diabolism; fantastic visions of a supernatural dimension. In works like "The Concert in the Egg," he reveals man's inner fears, his fantasies, dreams, longings, obsessions.

Boston Society for Psychic Research

The Boston society was founded in 1925 by Walter Franklin Prince, who had served previously as research officer of the American Society for Psychical Research. The Boston society published bulletins and books on subjects of interest to its members.

Botanomancy

A form of divination by observation of certain herbs.

Botocudo

A primitive tribe of South America, more properly called the Kaingang. They have evolved elaborate techniques of imitative magic, closely related to animism, in their attempts to control the weather. The fundamental religious outlook of the Kaingang is animistic. Their religion is not the expression of an inner need but a naive projection of a peculiar psycho-physical orientation which focuses attention on the fundamental distinction between one's own body and all other bodies. Death sets in motion awesome forces of destruction, causing the Kaingang to mobilize all their emotional resources. When death is momentarily actualized in the form of the *kupleng* or ghost-soul of the deceased, the most elaborate ritual forms are used to protect the liv-

103

ing. The spouse or *thupaya* stands in greatest danger and must remove all traces of old contacts with the deceased. The thupaya must free himself from the kupleng quickly, and he performs rites designed to rid him of his personal fear as well as to protect the community. He leaves camp alone, abstains from eating cooked food, and sleeps alone at night. When he kills an animal, he opens its belly and rubs the blood on himself to "wash off" the hunting formerly done for his wife.

Bottle Imps
German spirits akin to familiars. Also, imps contained in bottles, like the jinns described in *Arabian Nights*.

Boullan, Abbe
Leader of the Work of Mercy, a mysterious sect founded by Pierre Vintras, and central figure of the great "battle of bewitchment" that raged in the 1880's and 1890's. Prior to his affiliation with the Work of Mercy, the Abbé Boullan and a nun called Adèle Chevalier had founded the Society for the Reparation of Souls. A defrocked priest, Boullan had a pentagram tattooed at the corner of his left eye and celebrated Mass in vestments displaying an inverted crucifix. He specialized in exorcism and recommended consecrated hosts mixed with feces for nuns possessed by demons. On December 8, 1860, he ceremoniously sacrificed his and Adèle Chevalier's child, as the high point of a Mass. He announced in 1875 that he was a reincarnation of John the Baptist and the new head of the Work of Mercy. He taught nuns to enjoy sexual intercourse with his own astral body and to hypnotize themselves into thinking that they were having intercourse with Christ and the saints. Stanislas de Guaita claimed that the practical result of Boullan's belief in union with God through the sex act was unlimited promiscuity. Guaita and Oswald Wirth broke with Boullan and

initiated the battle of bewitchment by announcing that they had judged him and condemned him. Huysmans, one of the partisans of Jean-Antoine Boullan, called him "a very learned and intelligent priest" in his novel *La Bas*. The Abbé was also known as Dr. Johannes. The Satanic orgies that he proposed to his parishioners were called "Life Union." One of his co-workers as the Supreme Head of the Church of Carmel was the Head Priestess, Mme. Thibault.

Bourieux, Pierre
Breton magician who wrote many articles on occultism under the name of Yann d'Armor. His mysterious death in 1949, exploited by the press, drew thousands of visitors to Ker Guy, the manor in which he had lived. The next year Ker Guy was destroyed by a fire that was unanimously attributed to the Devil.

Bouvet, Lesieur
Seventeenth-century provost general of the French armies in Italy. On the basis of his personal experience, he wrote *Manières admirables,* a technical manual for witch-hunters.

Bozano, Ernesto
Psychical researcher (1862-1945). The dean of Italian psychical researchers wrote numerous books and articles, collected a unique library on psychic and spiritualistic phenomena, and concluded after many years of research that the survival of the spirit is beyond question.

Bragadini, Marco Antonio
An Italian Rosicrucian who was also an occultist and alchemist. He was executed in 1595 for transmuting base metal into gold.

Bragga
In 563 the Second Council of Bragga branded as heretical

the belief that the Devil "by his own power created thunder, lightning, storm and drought."

Bran
In Celtic tradition, the magician king. He traveled through mysterious regions toward the west and into the next world on a chariot that never touched the water. Some occultists interpret legends about Bran as evidence of the appearance on the earth of astronauts or alien beings possessed of superior knowledge and power.

Brigid
Great Mother Goddess worshiped in Ireland and England and made a Christian saint under the dictum of Pope Gregory.

Brigue, Jehanne de
Diviner, imprisoned for a year by the Bishop of Meaux for practicing magic and indicted in 1390 by the secular court of Paris on the charge of bewitching Hennequin de Ruilly in an attempt to cause him to marry Macète, then using magic to inflict upon him a grave illness after Mme. de Ruilly expressed her dissatisfaction with the marriage. Jehanne used wax figures and toads to work her magic. She claimed that Macète had actually performed the rites and, under torture, told the court her grandmother, also named Jehanne, had instructed her in magic as a child. She had learned to summon a demon called Haussibut by refraining during one day from making the sign of the cross, using holy water, and washing her hands. To summon the demon she called upon the Trinity, drew a circle around her, and said "Haussibut, come to me." She admitted after torture that she had also summoned Lucifer by reciting a passage from St. John three times. The secular courts, after transforming maleficium into heresy, condemned Jehanne and Macète to be burned at the stake on August 19, 1391.

Brinvilliers, Marie-Marguerite de
Famous French demoniac. She was possessed by the Devil at the age of seven.

British National Association of Spiritualists
The first meeting of the association was held on April 16, 1874. The name was changed in 1882 to The Central Association of Spiritualism, which published three successive organs: W. H. Harrison's *Spiritualista* (1879-81), *The Spiritual Notes,* and *Light* (from 1882 onward). The association was founded largely through the efforts of Dawson Rogers. It was recognized in 1884 as The London Spiritualist Alliance.

Brocken
Highest mountain peak in Harz Mountains in central Germany. Long associated in popular legend with Walpurgis Night or witches' sabbat. One scene in Goethe's *Faust* has its setting here.

Brothers of the Shadow
In the occult arts this expression refers to the adherents of the Left-hand Path. They were the adepts in Black Magic. This is particularly the case in Tibet, where sorcerers are known as Dugpas, wearers of the Red Cap.

Brownies
Friendly male household spirits of Scottish origin. The small long-nosed creatures, though msichievous at times, protect a house from strange spirits.

Bruno, Giordano
Italian philosopher (1548-1600). His belief in magic contributed to his condemnation and burning at the stake as an "impenitent and pertinacious heretic." Behind all movement (the earth around the sun and the sun's movement) he saw a world soul manifesting itself in every particle of

the universe and human souls capable of merging with God. He compared the magical arts to a sword. In the hands of a wicked person it can wreak havoc, but a good man can use it to produce much good. He identified ten kinds of magic, including necromancy, mathematical magic, natural magic, and sympathetic magic. He fashioned various images of the sun and believed that by meditating on them he could capture the sun's influence.

A good account of his life and work was written by F. A. Yates, *Giordano Bruno and the Hermetic Tradition* (1964).

Bruxa

In Portugal the bruxa, the witch or sorceress, is far from extinct. In isolated country districts she still plies her occult trade, particularly the concoction of love philtres. In 1968 a bruxa was brought to trial in Lisbon. She was an illiterate peasant, age fifty-four. There was, however, not enough evidence to convict her of the illegal practice of medical treatments.

In Oporto another bruxa, known to have performed wonders, was brought to trial on a charge of extortion. But her refutation was that she had heavy expenditures in her efforts to drive out the evil spirits that assailed her clients.

BT

In parapsychology, these letters are the initials of Basic Technique. This is the clairvoyance technique in which cards are laid aside by the experimenter as they are called by the subject.

Buchanan, J. Rhodes

American psychologist (1814-1899). A pioneer in psychometric research, he claimed the discovery of phrenomesmerism. He believed that all substances threw off an emanation perceptible to mediums, that "the past is entombed in the present," and that he had received a communication from St. John.

Buddhism

The religion founded by Siddhartha Gautama (c. 530-575 B. C.) affirms man's ability to acquire superhuman wisdom, compassion, and power. Six super-knowledges are among the fruits of meditation: the mundane, concentration-centered magical powers (transvection, shape-shifting, projecting a mind-made body, walking on water), clairaudience, clairvoyance, and memory of former lives; and the supramundane power of extinction of the outflows, attained by arhants, through insight.

Bugatis, Pierina de'

Central figure in a trial conducted by the secular court of Milan in 1390. In her first confession she described the meetings of a society whose members worshiped Oriente (Diana), who ruled them as Christ ruled the world. Pierina reported one incident that may have been a remnant of an ancient fertility cult: Oriente resurrected animals that had been consumed by members of the society with a touch of her wand. In a second deposition, this time to the Inquisition, she confessed that she called upon Lucifer whenever she wished to attend a meeting. He appeared before her in the form of a man, instructed her, and took her to the meeting. She had attended the revels of the society since she turned 16 and at the age of 30 had signed a pact with the Devil, using blood drawn from her body. Her trial and that of a woman named Sibillia suggest that the Inquisition confused ancient fertility rites with witchcraft and coerced the accused into contributing elements of diabolism to their confessions.

Bull Roarer

A whistle used almost exclusively by male members of primitive tribes in Africa, New Guinea, and the South Pacific. It is made of wood or stone and produces its eerie sound when thrown into the air or whirled around the head on a tether. Its sound represents the voices of various deities or spirits, who are summoned by its use.

Bulls, Papal

The basis for witchhunts in Europe was laid by papal bulls issued by John XXII, Eugene IV, Innocent VIII, Alexander VI, and Leo X. In *Super illius specula* (1326) John XII censured those "who worship demons and make offer sacrifices to them." Eugene IV (1437) criticized those who "make ill use of the Eucharist and the elements of baptism." In *Summis desiderantes affectibus* (1484) Innocent VIII charged that "many people of both sexes . . . turn away from the Catholic faith and indulge in orgies with incubi and succubi." In *Cum acceperimus* Alexander VI charged the Lombards with practicing "diabolical incantations and superstitions."

Bulwer-Lytton, Edward

English novelist and occultist (1803-1873) His many writings include a collection of fantastic tales, *The Pilgrims of the Rhine* (1834); *Zanoni* (1842), dealing with occultism; and *The Haunted and the Haunters* (1861), a series of ghost stories.

Bune

One of Satan's powerful lieutenants. He manifests himself as a man but does not speak. He haunts places associated with death and confers persuasive powers on those who serve him.

Bunot, Leon

A hunchback regarded as a witch by the people of Saint-Andre-de-Briouze and killed by Victor Delorme on November 26, 1948. Delorme accused him of threatening to loose "the red dog."

Burckhardt, Titus
Writer and scholar (b. 1908). In addition to translating important works from the Arabic and writing books on art and philosophy, he has published an important work relating alchemy to some of the great psychospiritual teachings and discrediting the conventional notion that alchemists were primitive chemists who tried to convert lead into gold. Published in German in 1960, the book was translated into English under the title *Alchemy, Science of the Cosmos, Science of the Soul* (1967). Hermetism is to him "a branch of the primordial revelation which, having persisted throughout all ages, extends also into the Christian and Islamic worlds."

Burmese Magic
Charms and occult medicines figure prominently in Burmese magic. Medicinal preparations cause hallucination, induce second sight, and are supposed to confer on people invulnerability or invisibility. Necromancy and astrology are linked to magic.

Burton Boy
Thomas Darling, a disturbed English youth living in Burton, began making unsubstantiated charges against others in 1596. John Darrell staged a performance in which he exorcised the demon that was torturing the youth.

Bwaga'u
Among the Trobriand Islanders, these are male sorcerers.

C

Caacrinolaas
In medieval demonology, a powerful demon generally identified as the grand president of Hell.

Caapi
A mind-expanding agent used by South American Indians in ritual activities. Sorcerers have used it for centuries as an adjunct in casting spells, settling disputes, and making predictions. They believe that the ingestion of the god-like substance confers upon them supernatural powers that enable them to communicate with the gods.

Cabala
A Judaic mystic esoteric body of lore, based on occult interpretations of the Bible. The Cabala, which is variously translated as "tradition" or "acceptance," dates in the fourteenth century. It consists of ancient doctrines dealing with the mystic symbolism of numbers and letters. There are different views on the sources of the Cabala. It is referred to the Greeks and the Pythagorean interpretation of numbers. Again, it is associated with the Gnostics, an ancient esoteric sect.

The Cabala stresses light, its emanations, letter-mysticism, space and time, good and evil, man in the cosmos, angels and demons. These themes in the Cabala coincide in many

113

directions with ancient Persian beliefs, especially the two opposing principles of good and evil, Ahura Mazda and Ahriman respectively.

The central area associated with the study of the Cabala was the Holy Land. Subsequently the centre was transferred to Mesopotamia, where it was developed systematically. In Babylonia it was studied intensely between the sixth and the eleventh century. The Cabalistic system was cultivated in particular in the Academy of Pumbeditha. In the nineteenth century the Cabala became widely known in Europe, especially in Italy, Germany, and France. Those who were deeply versed in the text and its interpretation were known under various names, as Bearers of the Secret, Men of Action, Gnostics. Among the most noted Cabalists were Aaron ben Samuel, Isaac the Blind, and Azriel.

The most sacred of all Cabalistic writing was the Zohar, which was revealed to the public by Moses de Leon in 1300. With the appearance of the Zohar, the study of the Cabala spread, thereby losing something of its exclusively esoteric import.

The influence of the Cabala on modern magicians is unmistakable. Eliphas Levi, Aleister Crowley, and others see the Tree of Life as a diagram of the emanation of the universe from the One, the hidden unity behind all things, and a plan to enable man to climb the ladder of the ten sephiroth and unite with the One. The Tree of the ten sephiroth is a cosmic diagram, revealing the structure of the universe and the interpenetrations of its multiple phenomena, and the 22 major trump cards of the Tarot, linked to the 22 Paths connecting the sephiroth, are the mystical courses followed by the magician. Believing that man is a miniature replica of the universe and God, and that he can expand himself spiritually to become God, the magician sets out on his journey, not in the ordinary physical body, but in the astral body. Along his route he is guided by a complicated system of correspondences. Rising through the spheres, he dominates the power of each individual sephira, for the master of the occult arts must experience and master all things if he is to achieve supreme perfection and power.

The magical side of the Cabala is explored in W. E. Butler's *Magic and the Qabalah* and in Richard Cavendish's *The Black Arts* (1967). Professor G. G. Scholem placed the study of the Cabala on a sound linguistic and historical footing in *On the Kabbalah and Its Symbolism* (1961) and *Major Trends in Jewish Mysticism* (1969).

Cabalistic Symbols
Hebraic mysticism has four secret symbols associated with the four letters comprising the name of God: the wand is associated with I, the cup of libation with H, the sword with V, and the shekel of gold with H.

Cabiri
Minor deities of Greek origin. Their cult was prominent in Lemnos, Samothrace, Thessalia, and Boeotia. The elder was originally identified with Dionysus, the younger with Hermes. After their worship was fused with that of Demeter and Ceres, two sets of Cabiri came into being. The Romans identified them with the Penates. Greek and Roman writers refer to them as powerful magicians.

Cacodaemons
Lesser demons, capable of serving as messengers between mortals and the gods. They are generally hostile, finding their pleasure in revenge and injury.

Cactus Tree Worship
Some African tribes believe that certain trees in the cactus

family are worthy of veneration because they are endowed with souls that gave birth to the human race.

Cadiere, Catherine

Principal figure in the last formal trial for witchcraft in France. Born at Toulon in 1709, Catherine was brought up in a religious atmosphere and longed to become a saint. She went so far as to tell Father Jean-Baptiste Girard, whom she later accused of seducing her, that God had recommended him to her in a vision. He had doubts about her religious vocation after working with her for several months and recommended that she enter the convent of Ollioules. There she showed signs of hysteria and insanity. She was sent home, and Father Nicholas attempted exorcism. She claimed that Father Girard had bewitched her and seduced her. Two other women charged that they had been seduced by the Jesuit priest. The Parlement of Aix undertook to hear the controversial case on January 10, 1731. The trial intrigued the whole of western Europe, generating excitement comparable to that surrounding the Dreyfus affair two centuries later.

Catherine explained how Father Girard had bewitched her. The event is narrated in the *Case of Mistress Mary Catherine Cadiere* (1732):

> Then stooping down and putting his mouth close to hers, he breathed upon her, which had such a powerful effect upon the young lady's mind that she was immediately transported with love and consented to give herself up to him. Thus did he bewitch the mind and inclinations of his unhappy penitent.

Catherine explained how he seduced her, claiming step by step that he was doing God's will. The other allegations included flagellation and abnormal sex acts.

The judges listened to the evidence for nearly a year. Twelve

116

of them held that Father Girard should be burned, twelve that Catherine should be hanged. President Lebret cast the deciding vote, returning Father Girard to the ecclesiastical authorities and putting Catherine back into the hands of her mother. The mob was less evenly divided. Father Girard was manhandled, Catherine's lawyer lifted up triumphantly. The priest was cleared by the church authorities.

Caduceus

Hermes' magic wand. The entwined serpents, one black and the other white, represent good and evil, disease and health.

Caduceus

A winged staff encircled by two serpents. Carried by the Greek God Hermes, who later passed it on to Aesculapius, it was supposed to have remarkable healing powers.

Cagliosto, Count Alessandro

This was the assumed name of one Giuseppe Balsalmo (1743-95), a Sicilian alchemist and occultist. One of the most famous occult figures of all time, he practiced fraud and blackmail on a grand scale, but his greatest talent seems to have been in keeping the good will of those he deceived. Some of his feats have defied explanation. His most ambitious undertaking was the formation of the Egyptian Masonic Rite Temple, open to both men and women. He acquired his fortune largely by selling love potions and elixirs. He is credited with manufacturing a diamond by alchemical means, conjuring up a dead woman's spirit, and performing numerous miraculous feats.

Cahagnet, Alphonse

Nineteenth-century French student of somnambulic phenomena. His analyses of the trance utterances of somnambules were published in three volumes, beginning in 1848, titled *Arcanes de la vie future dévoilées*.

Cailleach

Scottish goddess similar to the Indian Kali. She has a dark face and a monstrous eye in the middle of her forehead. In the witch cult she represents the Great Mother in her old aspect, as a killer of men. She corresponds to Black Annis in England and the Danu or Annu of Ireland. She seems to have required a new husband every seven years. As the Lady of the Forest she carried a thunderbolt and raised storms. The church raised her to sainthood under the name of Anne.

Cake, Worthington

Founder of the Society of the Mystic Spiral. The 18th-century Irish occultist staged lavish seances and demonstrations of levitation. He claimed that an adept moved spiritually along a diminishing spiral until he reached a point of infinity and merged with the supreme spiritual force.

Calalu

A herb used by the *obeah* man in the West Indies. Jamaican slaves were induced to join a secret society in the belief that after their initiation they would be beyond the control of the white man. After receiving an infusion of the herb, the slave danced until he collapsed and fell into a profound sleep. The obeah men then rubbed him with another substance that removed the effects of the calalu and the memory of all that had happened to him after he stopped dancing.

Calendar of Leti

See Leti's Calendar.

Calmecac

In ancient Mexico, an institution where the occult arts were studied.

Calmet, Dom Augustin

Benedictine occultist (d. 1757). He is chiefly remembered

for his writings on angels, demons, ghosts, and vampires.

Calundronius
A stone endowed with magic properties. It can be used for apotropaic purposes against demons, enchantments, and spells.

Cambions
The offspring of succubi and incubi.

Cambodian Sorcery
Two kinds of sorcerers operate in Cambodia: soothsayers, ap thmop, who forecast future events, and sorcerers who are also medicine men, kru. The latter are also exorcists.

Cambriel, Francois
Author of a French treatise on alchemy, published in 1943 under the title of *Cours de Philosophie hermétique*.

Campanella, Tomaso
Italian occultist (1560-1639). He wrote treatises on alchemy, magic arts, and astrology. He had been a Dominican friar. After being imprisoned on charges of heresy, he turned to the occult arts.

Cancer
In astrology, the Crab. The fourth, northern sign of the zodiac. In the mystery cult of Orpheus, it is the entrance of the soul into incarnation. In occultism, this sign stands for tenacity to life. Cabalistically, it signifies the vital organs of the grand old man of the skies and therefore the life forces.

Canewdon
A parish in Essex, England, renowned as the "witch country" and reputed to have had, until well into the 20th century, six witches under a master of witches. George Pickingale, a farm laborer who died in 1909, was the last "Master

of Witches." He was supposed to have the power to halt farm machinery with a glance, to charm warts, and to compel his imps to do most of his work for him.

Canidia

A sorceress often mentioned by Horace. She cast spells, using wax figures, and succeeded in making the moon descend from the heavens.

Cannabis

A genus of herbs, regarded as a holy plant in Hindu tradition. It is said to have been brought from the ocean by the god Shiva. Some Moslems look upon it as an embodiment of the spirit of Mahomet. Cannabis indica, or Indian hemp, has been used for centuries as an aphrodisiac. Its dried flowering tops, when smoked, produce a feeling of euphoria. Cannabis, hashish, ganja, and marihuana, whether smoked or consumed orally, have hallucinogenic properties and have been used as adjuncts in mystical, magical, and religious practices.

Cannabis sativa (or cannabis indica, as the Indian variety is called) grows in Central and Western Asia and the Western Himalayas, in India, Africa, and North America. The resin extracted from the plant is called *cannabinon,* from which cannabinol stems, a red oily substance found in the flowering tops of the female plant. Extracted from the plant in pure form, it is known in India as *charas.*

Charas is smoked and eaten. The powdered and sifted form of this resinous substance is *hashish.*

Another, weaker form is known as *bhang,* which is used as a drink. In Mexico, it is known as *marihuana.* Another form is ganja, made from the cut crop of the female plant and used for smoking.

Cannabis Indica produces some 150 different preparations

120

of the drug. For some 5000 years this hemp plant has been known and used from China to Egypt, and is now so used in the cities of the world.

In the second millennium B. C. the Chinese were already acquainted with the properties of the hemp plant. In 800 B. C. it was introduced into India, and from that time on it has been cultivated extensively and continuously. In the seventh century B. C. the Assyrians began to use the drug for its narcotic powers. In the second century A. D. the ancient Chinese physician Hua Tu administered a narcotic draught to his patients before an operation. The drug was known as *Ma Fu Shuan*. It was also used by Dioscorides, the Greek army physician, in the first century A. D., to relieve cases of earache.

Cantrip
A spell cast by a witch. Of uncertain origin, the word generally refers to a playful or mischievous act.

Capnomancy
Divination by observation of fumes rising from poppies thrown on live coals.

Capricorn
In astrology, the goat. The tenth, southern sign of the zodiac. It represents the dual movement of life plunging into the depths and reaching toward the heights. Esoterically, it is viewed as the scapegoat of the Israelites. Cabalistically, this sign stands for the knees of the grand old man of the heavens and is the emblem of material servitude.

Carcassonne Trials
In 1335 two important series of trials for heresy, witchcraft, and sorcery were held, one at Carcassonne and the other at Toulouse. In his detailed summary of the Latin documents reporting in detail on the trials, Étienne de Lamothe-Langon

used for the first time the word *sabbat,* perhaps as the equivalent for the Latin *synagoga.* The original documents have disappeared, but Lamothe-La Lamothe's summary offers the most detailed account of the witch cult in the fourteenth century.

At Carcassonne 74 men and women were brought before the Inquisition on May 16, 1335. Some of the 14 who were eventually executed by the secular arm were found guilty of maleficium, others of witchcraft.

To summon the demonic powers who helped him to prepare a sacrificial offering of bread and wine, a shepherd named André Cicéron disrobed completely and said Mass, as he claimed Adam had done before him. That he was guilty of heresy was obvious to the Inquisitors since Adam did not say Mass. Catala and Paul Rodier, two other shepherds, were accused of sacrificing a black hen to cause war and of invoking the Devil at crossroads in order to procure poison to be put in wells.

Going a step further, the Inquisitors accused four women of boasting that they had attended a sabbat. Matheline Faure, Armande Robert, Pierrille Roland, and Paule Viguier were confronted by witnesses who said that they had heard the women boast of going by night to a sabbat held on Mount Alaric, near Carcassonne. The women escaped burning by proclaiming their hatred of Satan and their loyalty to God.

In June of the same year Pierre Gui and two vicars conducted a trial at Toulouse. Among the 63 cases heard were those of two middle-aged women, Catherine Delort and Anne-Marie de Georgel.

Angela de Labarthe was burned at Carcassonne in 1274, charged with giving birth to a monstrous child, offspring of

122

the Devil. The Inquisition found 74 persons in the vicinity guilty of practicing black magic between 1330 and 1335. In the latter part of the fourteenth century, six hundred persons living in Carcassonne and Toulouse were burned as witches.

Cardan, Jerome

French occultist (1501-1576). He claimed to have his own familiar demon, called Scaliger.

Éliphas Lévi called Cardan one of the boldest students and most skilful astrologers of his time. He was a martyr to his faith in astrology, if we accept the legend of his death. He left a calculation by means of which anyone can foresee the good or evil fortune attached to all years of his life. His theory was based upon his own experiences, and he assures us that the calculations never deceived him. To ascertain the fortune of a given year, he sums up the events of those which have preceded it by 4, 8, 12, 19 and 30; the number 4 is that of realization; 8 is the number of Venus or natural things; 12 belongs to the cycle of Jupiter and corresponds to success; 19 has reference to the cycles of the Moon and of Mars; the number 30 is that of Saturn or Fatality. Thus, for example, I desire to ascertain what will befall me in this present year, 1855. I pass therefore in review those decisive events in the order of life and progress which occurred four years ago; the natural felicity or misfortune of eight years back; the successes or failures belonging to twelve years since; the vicissitudes and miseries or diseases which overtook me nineteen years from now, and my tragic or fatal experiences of thirty years back. Then, taking into account irrevocably accomplished facts and the advance of time, I calculate the chances analogous to those which I owe already to the influence of the same planets, and I conclude that in 1851 I had employment which was moderately but sufficiently remunerative, with some embarrassment of position; in 1847 I was separated violently from my family, with great attendant sufferings for mine and me; in 1843 I travelled as an apostle, addressing the people, and suffering the persecution of ill-meaning persons: briefly, I was at once honoured and proscribed. Finally, in 1825 family life came to an end for me, and I entered definitely on that fatal path which led me to science and misfortune. I may suppose therefore that this year I shall experience toil, poverty, vexation, heart-exile, change of place, publicity and contradictions, with some eventuality which will be decisive for the rest of my life: every indication in the present leads me to endorse this forecast. Hence I conclude that, for myself and for this year, experience confirms fully the precision of Cardan's astrological calculus, which connects furthermore with the climacteric years of ancient astrologers.

Carmen
A Latin word designating magical formulas used in incantations. See Incantatio.

Caro, Joseph Ben Ephraim
The most outstanding scholar of his generation and great codifier of Jewish law (1488-1575), he was second only to Maimonides in his knowledge of the laws and customs of Judaism. Seventy-one years after his death, his admirers were shocked by the appearance of a small book titled *Maggid Mesharim* (Lublin, 1646), for it was the secret diary kept for more than half a century by the great sage and included verbatim reports of visitations by a divine mentor or familiar spirit, known to him as Maggid.

Caro (or Qaro) was known throughout the Jewish world as the author of two great works, a commentary on the *Turim* and the *Shulhan Arukh*, a four-part code published in 1565, which gradually won acceptance as the authoritative guide to ritual, ethics, and law. According to his secret diary, much of his work was inspired by his familiar spirit.

In the early morning hours, particularly on the Sabbath, the Maggid would enter his mouth, articulate his tongue, and unveil to him future events. The Maggid appeared when Caro was troubled by great fears, obsessed by vaulting ambitions, or lost in deep thought as he tried to penetrate the hidden meaning of a sacred text. His divine mentor would disclose to him the triumphs and honors that awaited him here and in heaven and warn him of the pitfalls prepared for him by Satan and his dark legions. See Hirsch Loeb Gordon, *The Maggid of Caro* (1949).

Carrington, Hereward

English spiritualist (1881-1959). He has written many books on psychic phenomena. He founded the American Psychical Institute and Laboratory in 1921. After investigating Mrs. Eileen Garrett at the Institute, he concluded that there are indeed mental entities that exist apart from the conscious or unconscious mind of the medium.

Carus, Paul

Demonologist, author of the classic scholarly work on demonology (*A History of the Devil and the Idea of Evil,* 1900). Among his ideas:

This world of ours is a world of opposites. There is light and shade, there is heat and cold, there is good and evil, there is God and the Devil.

The dualistic conception of nature has been a necessary phase in the evolution of human thought. We find the same views of good and evil spirits prevailing among all the peoples of the earth at the very beginning of that stage of their development which . . . is commonly called Animism. . . .

Belief in witchcraft was only the main result of the established authority of a religion of magic, involving the belief in a personal Devil. There are other consequences which, though less important, are sometimes bad enough in themselves. We mention a few of them: (1) There were persons who actually tried to make contracts with the Devil. (2) People possessed of a lively imagination began to dream that they stood in all kinds of relations to the Evil One. . . . (3) Soldiers entertained the hope of rendering themselves bullet-proof. (4) Many methods were devised to predict the future. (5) There were plenty of fools who tried to become rich by magic; and (6) worst of all, men who knew better than the self-constituted guardians of the right faith, were relentlessly persecuted even unto death.

The Devil was believed to hold court and to celebrate witches' sabbaths, on which occasions homage was paid him and the Christian sacraments were travestied with diabolical malice. . . . The religion of miracles had in the natural course of evolution become the religion of magic. The religion of magic had proved to be a belief in witchcraft, and the belief in witchcraft had brought forth the terrible fruit of witch-prosecution with all kindred superstitions, among which the hatred of science was not the least injurious to true religion and the highest interests of mankind. . . . Evil personified appears at first sight repulsive. But the more we study the personality of the Devil, the more fascinating it becomes. In the beginning of existence the Evil One is the embodiment of everything unpleasant, then of everything bad, evil, and immoral. He is hatred, destruction, and annihilation incarnate, and as such he is the adversary of existence, of the Creator, of God. . . . Now, let us look at the mythical figure of Satan as represented in theology, folklore, and poetry. Is he not really a most interesting man? . . . Satan is the father of science, for he induced Eve to make Adam taste of the fruit of knowledge, and the Ophites, a gnostic sect, worshipped the serpent for that reason. Satan produces the unrest in society, which . . . makes the world move onward and upward; he is the patron of progress, investigation, and invention. Giordano Bruno, Galileo, and other men of science were regarded as his offspring and persecuted on his account by the Church. . . .

Indeed, we must grant that the Devil is the most indispensable and faithful helpmate of God. To speak mystically, even the existence of the Devil is filled with the presence of God.

Cassandra
Trojan sorceress, daughter of King Priam. Apollo first endowed her with prophetic powers, hoping to obtain her favors, then decreed that no one would believe her predictions because she refused to give herself over to him.

Cassendi, Geraud
French notary. In 1410 the Inquisition at Carcassonne prosecuted him for invoking demons.

Castaneda, Carlos
Anthropologist who spent several years in the company of a Yaqui Indian from Sonora, Mexico, learning from him the uses of hallucinogentic plants in achieving mastery of a world of "nonordinary reality." His initiation into the plan to be followed by a "man of knowledge" and the art of "seeing" is detailed in two remarkable books, *The Teachings of Don Juan; A Yaqui Way of Knowledge* (1968) and *A Separate Reality; Further Conversations with Don Juan* (1971).

Castaneda concluded from his studies that what he had experienced was the orderly presentation of a coherent system of beliefs, with particular stress on the uses of hallucinogenic plants known to Indians since before their contacts with Europeans. Don Juan knew the properties of peyote (Lophophora williamsii), Jimson weed (Datura inoxia), and a mushroom (probably Psilocybe mexicana). He believed that a man of knowledge had to be a man of courage, that a man had to be either victorious or defeated and, consequently, a persecutor or a victim, until he learned to "see." The illusion of victory, or defeat, or suffering was dispelled by "seeing." He believed in shape-shifting, spells, and spirits. One type of spirit he identified as an ally, a giver of secrets. The ally dwells in a lonely, abandoned, almost inaccessible place, and must be wrestled to the ground and forced to share its power.

In his most recent book (*Journey to Ixtlan,* 1972) he relates how Don Juan (Juan Matus), in sharing the secrets of his sorcery, led him to the heart of ordinary reality, showed him that the ordinary world is a product of a social consensus, and enabled him to grasp the paradoxical unity of opposites and enter into the sorcerer's higher state of consciousness.

Castaneda's experiences recall those of Jacob Boehme and Emanuel Swedenborg. See Man of Knowledge.

Castelmezzano
A mountainous region of southern Italy, reputed to be the present capital of sorcery. Earlier capitals were Toledo, Loudun, and Prague.

Catabolignes
Demons who abuse and kill their agents, generally magicians and sorcerers.

Catherine de Medici
Queen of France and noted astrologer (1519-1589). Her enemies accused her of enlisting the aid of demons.

Cato

Roman statesman and writer (234-149 B. C.). He used the following incantation for a dislocated bone:

Huat hanat huat
Ista pista sista
Domiabo damnaustra.

Catoptromancy

A method of divination by means of magic mirror. This technique was known by the ancients. It is mentioned by Apuleius the Roman philosopher and novelist, Pausanias the Greek traveler, and St. Augustine the Church Father.

Cats

The "first pet of civilization" has long been associated with sacred rites, superstitions,, and magic. The cat was held sacred in ancient India. As an Egyptian deity, it was supposed to have oracular powers. The entire city of Bubastis was dedicated to feline worship, and a festival honoring the sacred animal was attended each May by more than half a million pilgrims.

The most prominent of the feline goddesses was Ubasti, represented in bronze as a cat-headed woman. Prayer and sacrifice were elements of the cult. Dead cats were embalmed and sent to Bubastis for burial.

The cat also had great prestige in Britain, where sacred rites were held in its honor. In Scandinavian countries, Freya was the cat-goddess, and her chariot was said to be drawn by two cats.

Cat's Eye

A semiprecious stone reputed to have the power to protect the wearer against the evil eye and assure him a long life.

Cathars (Catharists, Catharites)

A widespread movement, closely linked with witchcraft,

prominent over most of Europe from the tenth to the four-teenth century. It originated in eastern Europe and included a belief in the Manichaean principle of a God of good and a God of evil. Satan, the God of evil, ruled over the world, which was the same as Hell. Pope Innocent III organized a crusade against the Cathars in southern France. They were charged with worshiping the Devil in the form of a goat or a cat at meetings labeled "synagogues of Satan" by Catho-lics. Under torture some of them confessed to flying through the air on broomsticks or greased poles, slaughtering and eating stolen children, etc.

Caul
A portion of the thin membrane that envelops the foetus. A caul that covers the head of a newly born child is an omen of good fortune and has powerful magical properties. As late as 1944, a sailor tried to buy a caul, believing that it would keep him from drowning at sea.

Cauldron of Regeneration
A witch ceremony, also called "Drawing down the Moon," practiced in England on or about December 12. Spirit is poured over leaves thrown into a cauldron set in the middle of a magic circle. The spirit is lighted and Bacchus, the god of wine and fertility, is invoked by a chant led by a witch-priestess.

Cayce, Edgar
Clairvoyant and psychic healer (d. 1945). Before his death at the age of 67, he had treated some 30,000 patients and earned the distinction of being perhaps the most remarkable healer who ever lived. Born in Hopkinsville, Kentucky, he became known as "The Man of Miracle." As a child he was boxed on the ear by his father. The incident established a pattern: whenever he had difficulties, he simply went to sleep; on awakening, the situation would be remedied. As

a child he also spoke with an angel and saw visions of his dead grandfather. Shy and deeply religious, he had a great love for reading although he never finished school. He discovered that if he put a book under his pillow before going to sleep, the next morning he knew it by heart.

Cayce was only 16 when he became aware of his power to heal. Bedridden as a result of an accident, he ordered his mother to apply a poultice to the injured spot. She did so, and by morning, though he knew nothing of what had taken place, he had recovered completely. Later, after he had contracted a throat disease and put himself to sleep in the presence of a hypnotist named Al Layne, he spoke in a clear voice, saying, "Yes, we can see the body." He prescribed the treatment necessary to restore circulation to the affected area, Layne gave the appropriate instructions, and Cayce awoke, completely healed. He began to help others in difficulty. He had no medical knowledge, but he would induce a trance state, hear a voice saying, "Yes, we can see the body," and prescribe medical procedures that were highly successful.

The sick and suffering began to come to him from every direction. Layne was present in the early days, but later Cayce had the help of a medical man. Much of his treatment of those who had been given up as incurable by medical doctors was based on diagnosing spinal lesions and prescribing osteopathic and homeopathic remedies. During most of the healing sessions he was assisted by an osteopath. Though he was opposed by the ranks of orthodox medicine, Dr. Wesley Ketchum, a homeopath, vindicated his methods of treatment. His reputation was tarnished in medical circles when he had recourse to folk remedies such as bed bug juice for dropsy and his ventures into electrotherapy and patent medicines (he marketed cures for hemorrhoids and pyorrhea). In 1931 the Association for Research and Enlightenment began to accumulate records of the thousands of medical cases treated in his fully-staffed hospital at Virginia Beach, Virginia.

His clairoyant powers enabled him to identify a murderer. Relatives of servicemen listed as missing in action in World War I frequently sought his help. Questions submitted to him while he was in a trance state were the basis of an occult philosophy combining many of the elements of theosophy, pyramidology, and Christianity. His reputation among occultists was enhanced by *The New Tomorrow*, a journal published by his followers, and by the pamphlet *Aura*, which he published in 1945 and in which he claimed the ability to see the human aura. In the same pamphlet he predicted that color therapy would become an approved form of medicine.

Cayce's astoundingly accurate readings (in trance) on scientific, personal, and social matters, and his long-range predictions about geological change and world events have made him the center of much speculation. The Cayce Foundation of America continues to honor the memory of the man whose unquestioned powers defy a rational, conclusive explanation. See Bimini.

Cazotte, Jacques

French occultist and seer (1720-92). He is supposed to have written a prophetic work, the famous *Prophétie de Cazotte*, in which he foretold the deaths of many leading figures of the French Revolution, including his own. He was the author of the famous occult romance titled *Le Diable Amoureux* (The Lovesick Devil).

Cellini, Benvenuto

In his classic autobiography the celebrated Italian artist Benvenuto Cellini (1500-71) gives a detailed account of his association with occultists and demons.

I made acquaintance with a Sicilian priest. . . . Happening one day to have some conversation with him . . . on the subject of necromancy, I . . . told him that I had all my life felt a curiosity to be acquainted with the mysteries of this art. The priest made answer, "That the man must be of a resolute and steady temper who enters upon that study." I replied, "That I had fortitude and resolution enough, if I could but find an opportunity." . . . Thus we agreed to enter upon a plan of necromancy. . . . We repaired to the Colloseo, and the priest, according to the custom of the necromancers, began to draw circles upon the ground with the most impressive ceremonies imaginable: he likewise brought hither asafoetida, several precious perfumes and fire, with some compositions also which diffused noisome odors. As soon as he was in readiness, he made an opening to the circle . . . and began his incantations.

The priest was not successful in bringing him into the company of his Sicilian mistress Angelica but did convince him, on this and subsequent occasions, that hosts of demons had been summoned at their ceremonies—demons which would raise both of them "to opulence and power."

Celts
In ancient times magic among the Celtic peoples was closely identified with Druidism. The Druids possessed a large share of transcendental knowledge and were supposed to be able to change their bodily shape, produce an enchanted sleep, utter charms and spells that could cause death, control the elements, and make themselves invisible.

Ceromancy
A form of divination by dropping melted wax into water and observing the results.

Chain, Forming a

Spiritualists join hands to strengthen and reinforce the magnetic current generated as they sit at a table. Baron de Guldenstubbé gives these directions for forming a chain:

> The twelve persons each place their right hand on the table, and their left hand on that of their neighbour, thus making a circle round the table. Observe that the medium or mediums if there be more than one, are entirely isolated from those who form the chain.

Chain, Magic

See Magic Chain.

Chakras

In Oriental mysticism the seven chakras are the organs of the astral body. Chakras are usually called Lotus flowers. The word itself signifies wheel, but esoteric speculation has resulted in extensions of the original meaning. A Chakra now means a period during which the wheel of time turns once, or certain centers of the body which collect streams of pranic energy.

Along the spine, according to occultists, the chakras are spherical loci of the body in which streams of pranic energy collect. The chakras are associated with the spine and occur along the following levels: base of the spine, organ of generation, navel, heart, throat, and between the eyebrows. See Kundalini.

Chaldean Invocations

Long associated with sorcery, the Chaldeans and the Akkadians are credited with composing the oldest extant magic texts. The royal library at Nineveh contains incantations dating from the second millennium B. C. One Chaldean incantation involves sympathetic magic, the Evil Eye, and the casting of spells:

134

He who forges the image, he who enchants—
The spiteful face, the evil eye,
The mischievous mouth, the mischievous tongue,
The mischievous lips, the mischievous words,
Spirit of the Sky, remember!
Spirit of the Earth, remember!
They are the enemies of En-Kin, the God.
They who have revolted cause the gods to tremble.
They spread terror over the highways, and advance
    with whistling roar.
They are evil, they are evil.
They are seven, they are seven, and again they are
    twice seven.
Spirit of the Sky, remember them!
Spirit of the Earth, remember them! Conjure them!
Conjure these evil spirits, spirit of Ramanu, King
    of the luminous Word, conjure them!
Spirit of Samas, King of Justice, conjure them!
Spirit of Annunas, mighty god, conjure them!
Incantations of these evil spirits.

A Chaldean text preserved in the British Museum contains
a bilingual incantation against evil spirits:

They are seven, they are seven.
In the valley of the abyss, they are seven.
In the numberless stars of heaven, they are seven.
In the abyss, in the depths, they grow in power.
They are not male, they are not female.
They dry up the moistness of the waves.
They do not love women, they have not begotten
    offspring.
They scorn consideration and justice.
They hearken to neither request not prayer.
They harken to neither request nor prayer.
Like the horses of the mountains, they are big.

135

A Chaldean formula for curing a headache was also recorded:

Knot on the right and arrange flat in regular bands, on the left of a woman's diadem:

> divide it twice in seven little bands;
> gird the head of the invalid with it:
> gird the seat of life with it:
> gird his hands and his feet:
> seat him on his bed:
> pour on him enchanted waters.

The Chaldeans had a special talisman to keep demons, such as Utuq, Alal, Gigim, and Maskim, from entering their houses:

> Talisman, talisman, boundary that cannot be taken away, boundary that the gods cannot pass, barrier immovable, which is opposed to malevolence! whether it be a wicked Utuq, a wicked Alal, a wicked Gigim, a wicked god, a wicked Maskim, a phantom, a spectre, a vampire, a succubus, a nightmare, may the barrier of the god Ea stop him!

Chaldeans (Chaldaei)
An ancient Semitic tribe occupying the estuaries of the Tigris and Euphrates. They became the learned Cabalists of Babylonia. In Roman times they were the interpreters of astrological phenomena until their great power caused them to be banished from Rome.

Chambre Ardente
Star chamber established by Louis XIV to investigate poisoning among the French nobles, between 1679 and 1682. Witchcraft was a pervasive theme. The name is also applied to other tribunals that conducted witchcraft trials. Certain degenerates of the court of Louis XIV were alleged to have

taken part in the celebration of the Black Mass. Mme. de Montespan is reputed to have taken part in such obscene ceremonies, having been persuaded to appear nude as the central performer on at least one occasion.

Cham-Zoroaster
Reputed to be the first sorcerer to appear after the Flood. His four sons were Cush, Mizraim, Phut, and Canaan, lords of magic, respectively, over Africa, Egypt, the desert tribes, and Phoenicia.

Changeling
In Scottish superstition, a child secretly removed from its crib and replaced by a mannekin of the elf race. Though old in spirit and age, it has the shape of the stolen child. As it grows up, however, it becomes ugly, cranky, and a source of grief for the entire household. If the substitution is discovered in time, the child will be returned. The mannekin may be stabbed, dropped into a river, or forced to sit on a hot oven.

Charlemagne
Also called Charles I and Charles the Great, Charlemagne (742-814) ordered bishops to make their rounds each year and "to prohibit pagan practices." These included divination, sorcery, and incantations.

Charms and Amulets
In many pagan religions verbal charms, in the form of spells and incantations, were employed in rituals and ceremonies associated with religious cults. Amulets or talismans, material charms, were similarly in use, for protection against disease, disaster, or evil forces. Such amulets consisted of animal teeth or claws, roots of plants, human hair or bones, arrow heads, phallic objects, tusks, feathers, written magic formulas, and inscribed objects.

Chelas
See Adepts.

Chelidonus
In Celtic lore, a small stone found in a dead bird and used to cure melancholy, rheumatism, and other afflictions. When placed in a yellow cloth and worn around the neck, it cures a fever.

Chelmsford Witches
One of the first trials for witchcraft in England, following enactment of Queen Elizabeth's Statute of 1563, was held at Chelmsford in the summer of 1566. The proceedings were published in a sensational chapbook: The Examination and Confessions of Certain Witches. . . . Highly imaginative stories of children were accepted as evidence against three defendants, Elizabeth Francis, Agnes Waterhouse, and Joan Waterhouse.

Chemical Wedding of Christian Rosenkreutz
A Rosicrucian work, published in 1469, by Johannes Valentinus Andreas. It is an account of a man's pilgrimage in terms of alchemy and the spiritual teaching of Rosicrucianism. Symbolically, it represents man's power to transcend the physical world.

Cheops
Egyptian king (c. 2,900 B. C.). Well versed in magical arts, he supposedly included various mystical features in the great pyramid which he built near Gizeh.

Cheu Kyongs
In Tibetan mysticism, a group of beings of diabolical origin controlled by a magician.

Chevalier, Adele
French nun, co-founder of the Society for the Reparation of Souls. Adèle Chevalier claimed to have heard super-

natural voices and to have been miraculously healed of a disease by the Virgin Mary. She bore a child to Abbé Boullan, who sacrificed it ceremoniously, as the high point of a Mass, on December 8, 1860.

Children and Witches

During the judicial reign of terror that descended upon Europe in the middle of the fifteenth century and lasted until the middle of the eighteenth, children played a predominant role. In suspending the common rule regarding children as witnesses in all other forms of judicial proceedings (no witness below the age of 14 could testify), the judges must have taken their cue from the Biblical pronouncement, "Out of the mouths of babes cometh forth truth." Moreover, it was assumed that innocent children could easily identify a corrupt witch who had made a pact with the Devil, and that children could easily be persuaded to inform against the accused. The role of children in the history of witchcraft is detailed in Ronald Seth's *Children Against Witches* (1969).

Seth divides the children who set themselves against the witches into two categories: those who were not affected by maleficia but had seen a relative commit an act of witchcraft or had personal knowledge to support the accusation; and those who feigned the accepted results of maleficia. Among these were the Bilson Boy, the Nottingham Boy, and the Burton Boy, who feigned symptoms that led others to conclude that they were victims of maleficia.

Chinese Talismans

Chinese thought has always closely linked man and the universe, the microcosm and the macrocosm. Vast systems of correspondences are assumed to exist between man and his surroundings: the elements, the heavens, society.

The Chinese talisman is generally very simple, consisting of

139

a series of characters informing the gods and spirits as to what is expected of them. The words are engraved on a seal. The classic collection of talismans is that of the first great Taoist, Chuang Tzu. Talismans are based on two great principles: (1) that like evokes and produces like (law of correspondences); and (2) the part is equivalent to the whole (the totality of a person or thing resides in each of its parts).

Chiromancy
Divination based on the lines and mounts (small protuberances) of the hand. In this form of astral physiognomy, the lines and the seven mounts at the base of fingers and thumbs, named for the Greek and Roman gods, are analyzed for dominant traits and relationships. For instance, a person with a well-developed mount of Jupiter (the protuberance at the base of the index finger) connotes ambition, honor, happiness, and religion. Depending on their depth and length, the lines are associated with the heart, head, life, and fortune.

Choronzon
The Demon of Chaos evoked by Aleister Crowley and Victor Neuburg. He appeared in the Algerian desert in 1909, following a dangerous magical ceremony which they had conducted.

Choronzon
A mighty demon conjured up by Aleister Crowley in the Algerian desert. Some occultists claim that he was possessed by the demon for the rest of his life. Choronzon appeared, shouting the words that will open the gates of hell: *Zazas, Zazas, Nasatanada, Zazas.*

Chou Kung
The authorship of the Hsiao-T'ze was traditionally attributed to Chou Kung, son of King Wen, author of the T'uan.

The Hsiao-T'ze and T'uan became the basis of occultism as set forth in *I Ching*.

Chwezi

A pantheon of mythical hero-gods forming the basis of divination cults among the Nyoro people of Uganda. They are believed to have ruled the country for some time before disappearing as mysteriously as they had appeared. These spirits are identified with the well-being of the various clans of the Nyoro.

Chyndonax

A magician-priest of the Druids.

Ciceron, Andre

See Carcassonne Trials.

Circe

A sorceress whose attempts to keep Odysseus and his men under her spell are recounted by Homer. The mandrake, a frequent ingredient in love-philtres, is also called the plant of Circe since her witch-brew is traditionally thought to contain infusions of mandrake.

Circle

Sorcerers protected themselves from the fury of evil spirits by retreating inside a magic circle. Generally, there were two circles, a smaller one inscribed in a large one. In the East the outer circle was seven feet square, elsewhere about nine feet square. Between the parallel lines marking off the larger circle and between the two circles were inscribed the holy names of God and other occult characters.

The circle is more than a symbol of perfection, unity, and completeness. It is a reminder of the pattern exhibited by nature in the visible production of round trees, planets, shells, bodies, and eyes, and of the invisible cycles of the seasons and events. It was used in the construction of sacred places, such as Stonehenge. Since prehistoric times it has been considered as a means of evoking and preserving power.

Circle, Magic

See Magic Circle.

Circles of the Seven Planets for the Seven Days of the Week

The sorcerer who draws a magic circle should choose the circle that corresponds to the day of his enterprise: the circle of Saturn for Saturday, the sun for Sunday, the moon for Monday, Mars for Tuesday, Mercury for Wednesday, Jupiter for Thursday, and Venus for Friday.

SATURN   SUN

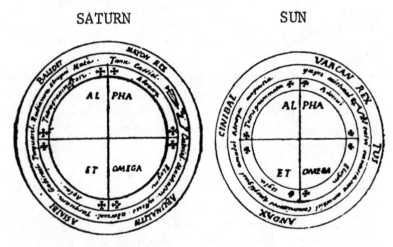

City of the Condors

A huge Andean city discovered in the region of Payatea in 1965 and linked by occultists with the lost continent of Atlantis. Numerous representations of the condor appear on the walls of the city, along with beings whose heads are encircled by hexagonal halos and great solar rays. Some occultists make the City of the Condors an advanced colony of the empire of the Atlanteans.

142

Clairaudience

A faculty for hearing sounds and words that are not normally heard by others at the same time. Many medieval saints were reputed to have spiritual clairaudience. Joan of Arc, who heard "voices" is another instance.

Clairvoyance

The power of discerning things not present to the senses. The spiritual faculty is supposed to enable a person to see objects and persons across great distances. Emanuel Swedenborg, among many others, is supposed to have had such power. He claimed to have direct intercourse with the spiritual world after his spiritual senses were opened, in 1745.

Cleromancy

Divination by casting small objects: beans, bones, dice, stones, etc.

Coca

Known as the divine plant of the Incas, coca is the only source of Cocaine. Peruvians since the time of the Incas have chewed the leaves of the plant in order to acquire the endurance of the gods.

Cock

An occult bird much appreciated in ancient augury and symbolism. According to the Zohar, the cock crows three times before the death of a person. The bird was sacred to Aesculapius. The cock's crow made the demons flee and brought the Sabbat to an end. To delay or stifle the sound the witches rubbed the cock's head with olive oil and put a garland of wine-branches around its neck.

Coffin-Rite

The final rite of initiation in the ancient mysteries of Egypt, Greece, and elsewhere. The last and supreme secrets of occultism could be revealed to the adept only after he had passed through an allegorical ceremony of death and resurrection into new light.

Cohobo
A drug found in the West Indies and South America. Endowed with hallucinogenic properties, the pods and seeds of the plant are inhaled through a tube and produce wild excitements and strange visions, followed by a period of calm. Prophetic visions often involve the user himself, his clan, and one or more spirits.

Coingnet
See Barre, Margot de la.

Cold Remedy
The Gypsies treat chills or colds by attacking the evil spirits that cause them. Charles Leland offers this recipe:

Three lungs and three livers of frogs are dried and powdered and drunk in spirits, after which the sick man or woman says:—

"Cuckerdya pal m're per
Cáven save miseçe!
Cuckerdya pal m're per
Den miseçeske drom odry prejiál!"

"Frogs in my belly
Devour what is bad!
Frogs in my belly
Show the evil the way out!"

Coleridge, Samuel Taylor
English poet and mystic (1772-1834). He has been credited with introducing the occult into verse with a mastery that has not been surpassed in English literature and producing the two most beautiful poems in which the supernatural plays an important part, "Christabel" and "The Rime of the Ancient Mariner."

144

College of Sages
See Bernard, Raymond.

College of Sorcery
See Salamanca.

Combe, George
Scottish lawyer (1788-1858). He migrated to the U. S. A. He promoted the study of phrenology. He was a follower of the phrenologist Spurzheim. Combe was the founder, in 1820, of the Phrenological Society. He also established the Phrenological Journal, in 1823. A brother, Andrew Combe (1797-1847), was also a phrenologist as well as a physiologist. At one time he was physician to Queen Victoria.

Concentration
The sorcerer must have a powerful imagination and intense powers of concentration. He must use his imagination to magnify his inner impulses until they merge with the great moving forces of the universe, then subject them to his will through his powers of concentration and direct them toward a specific goal. See Imagination and Great Work.

Condors
See City of the Condors.

Cone of Power
The witches of England claim credit for the destruction of the Spanish Armada as well as for stopping Napoleon's and Hitler's invasions of the island. According to Gerald Gardner, anthropologist, folklorist, and sorcerer, an invasion seemed imminent following the German conquest of France, Belgium, and Holland. The old lady who had initiated him into the Craft alerted all the covens of England. They met nightly in New Forest and drew the Great Circle reserved for emergencies. The Great Cone of Power was directed toward Hitler and this message was sent out: "You must

not cross the sea. You must not come." Numbers of those involved died a few days following the last of the four meetings, but Hitler's forces were stopped.

The cone of power, according to R. C. Lethbridge, is an auric emanation, a cone of invisible but demonstrable force surrounding every animate or inanimate form.

Congo

One of the three great rites or divisions of Voodoo, the Congo division includes a group of wicked gods. Those known to noninitiates include Savanne, Maussai, and Moudongue. These gods may take possession of a Voodooist and demand that he make sacrifices to them.

Conjunction

A demonic spell which prevents the consummation of marriage. The means of effecting conjunction, also called the witches' knot, vary according to the authority consulted. The *Petit Albert*, a medieval handbook of magic, prescribes the killing of a wolf and removal of its organ. When the person to be bewitched is near, he should be called by name. When the victim answers, the "organ is to be tied with a lace of white thread and the bewitched will be as impotent in the marriage act as if he had been castrated." See Ligature.

Conjuration

The *Great Key of Solomon* gives the following directions for invoking a spirit for the purpose of making a pact with him. Here the pact is to be made with Lucifuge.

Emperor Lucifer, Master of all the rebellious spirits, I beg you to be favorable in the invocation that I make to your great Minister Lucifuge Rofocale, as I wish to make a pact with him. . . .

O great Lucifuge! I beg you to leave your abode . . . and to speak to me. Otherwise I shall constrain you by the power of the great living God, his dear Son, and the Holy Spirit.

Obey promptly, or you will be tortured eternally by the force of the potent words of the Great Key of Solomon that he himself used to bind the rebellious spirits to accept his pact.

So come forth instanter! or I shall torture you endlessly by the force of these powerful words from the Key: Agion, Telagram, vaycheon stimulamaton y ezpares retragrammaton oryoram irion esytion existion eryona onera brasim moym messias soster Emanuel Saboot Adonai, te adoro at invoco.

Conjuration Against an Enemy
An ancient book of magic first published by M. Gaster under the title of *Sword of Moses* (1896) contains a a formula for conjuring spirits to be used against an enemy:

I call thee, evil spirit, cruel spirit, merciless spirit. I call thee, bad spirit, who sittest in the cemetery and takes away healing from man. Go and place a knot in N's head, in his eyes, in his mouth, in his tongue, in his throat, in his windpipe: put poisonous water in his belly. If you do not go and put poisonous water in his belly, I will send you the evil angels Puziel, Guziel, Psdiel, Prziel. I call thee and those six knots that you go quickly to N and put poisonous water in his belly and kill N because I wish it. Amen. Amen. Selah.

Conjuration, Great
See Great Conjuration.

Conjuration of a Demon
Having entered the magic circle with his assistants and started exorcizing his lighted fire, the magician utters the following words:

I conjure thee,   , in the name of the living Great God, who made heaven and earth and all contained therein, and his only son, redeemer of the human race, and by the holy spirit, the merciful consoler, and by the power of the heavenly empyrean, instantly and without delay to appear unto me in comely shape, without noise or hurt done to my person or to my companions, and to reply to all that I shall command thee. Hereto I conjure thee by the living God, El, Ehome, Ertha, Ejel, Aser, Ejech, Adonay Iah Tetragrammaton Saday Agios other Agla ischiros athanatos amen amen amen!

The conjuration must be written on parchment and repeated three times. When the spirit named in the conjuration appears and does the magician's bidding, he must be dismissed in these words:

Because thou hast come in answer to the name of God in whose name I called thee, I return thanks to God. Go now in the peace of God to the place destined thee for all eternity and let peace be between thee and us, and every time and so many times as I shall call thee see thou come in the name of the Father and of the Son and of the Holy Ghost. Amen!

Conjuration of Lucifuge

The Great Grimoire gives the formula for summoning Lucifuge Rofocale:

I conjure you, O spirit, to appear within a minute by the power of Great Adonai, by Eloim, by Ariel, Johavam, Agla, Tagla, Mathon, Oarios, Almouzin, Arios, Membrot, Varvis, Pithona, Magots, Silphae, Rabost, Salamandrae, Tabost, Gnomus, Terrae, Terreae, Coelis, Godens, Aqua, Gingua, Anua, Etituamus, Zariatnctmik.

Conjuration of the Seven

An incantation used in consecrating talismans.

In the name of Michaël, may Jehovah command thee, and drive thee hence, Chavajoth!

In the name of Gabriel, may Adonai command thee, and drive thee hence, Belial!

In the name of Raphaël, begone before Elchim, Sachabiel!

By Samuel Zebaoth, and in the name of Eloïm Gibor, get thee hence, Adrameleck!

By Zachariel and Sachiel-Meleck, be obedient unto Elvah, Samgabiel!

By the divine and human name of Shaddaï, and by the Sign of the Pentagram which I hold in my right hand; in the name of the angel Anaël, by the power of Adam and of Heva, who are Jotchavah, begone, Lilith! Let us rest in peace, Nahemah!

By the holy Eloïm and by the names of the genii Cassiel, Sehaltiel, Aphiel and Zarahiel, at the command of Orifiel, depart from us, Moloch! We deny thee our children to devour.

Conjurations

One desiring to summon the Devil must adhere to certain rules. Lucifer may be invoked on Monday at dawn, provided the conjurer wears a new stole and surplice and offers a live mouse as a pledge. Frimost can be summoned only between nine and ten p. m. on Tuesday; he requires as a pledge only a pebble found during the day. Astaroth will appear between ten and eleven on Wednesday if he is invoked in the name of the Father, Son, Holy Ghost, and the Virgin Mary.

Conscience
The mystical and mysterious instrument of preparation in the work of alchemy, according to Hitchcock, is called by a thousand misleading and confusing names, but it is really the conscience. Quickened into vital activity under the awareness of God's presence, this instrument purges and purifies the matter of the stone (Man) and makes possible the inner realization of Truth.

> By a metonymy, the conscience itself is said to be purified, though, in fact, the conscience needs no purification, but only the man, to the end that the conscience may operate freely. . . . The still small voice is in alchemy, as in Scripture, compared to a *fire*, which prepares the way for what many of the writers speak of as a Light. . . . The repentance which in religion is said to begin conversion, is the "philosophical contrition" of Hermetic allegory. It is the first step of man towards the discovery of his whole being.

Contemporary Witchcraft
Angoon, on Admiralty Island off the coast of Alaska, has a population of a few whites and some four hundred Tlingit Indians. In 1957 the death of a Tlingit Indian child was the occasion for a sequence of magic rites. Cats and dogs were burnt in sacrificial ceremonies, while two young Indian girls, "mediums for the witches," were beaten with "devil clubs"—bundles of thorns. Several villagers too were denounced to the United States authorities for practicing witchcraft.

Control
In spiritualism, the spirit who controls the medium.

Convulsionaries of St. Medard
An outbreak of convulsions and religious ecstasy occurred

150

in the cemetery of St. Medard, Paris, during the first half of the 18th century. The Jesuits were the victims of the outbreak, which began with a few isolated cases of miraculous healing. Following news of cures effected at the tomb of St. Francis de Paris, people of all ages thronged to the cemetery and were witnesses to a violent outburst of convulsive behavior. Though the cemetery was closed by royal decree in 1759, appalling scenes persisted until 1787.

Cook, Florence
Nineteenth-century English medium. She is credited by some spiritualists with being the first to present the phenomenon of materialization in its complete form.

Coral
It is supposed to have the power to ward off the evil eye, stop bleeding, and reveal the presence of poisons in foods. In Italy it is worn as a talisman or as a charm to protect one's virility.

Cordiere, La
See Brigue, Jehanne de.

Corelli, Marie
English novelist (1855-1924). Her works on occult themes include the following: *The Secret Power, The Sorrow of Satan,* and *The Soul of Lilith.*

Corn Witchcraft
A powerful spell utilizing a kernel of corn. The Yaqui sorcerer puts a kernel inside a yellow flower or a fresh bud, places it on a spot where the intended victim will step, and waits for it to produce its effect. All the power of the kernel enters the victim's body.

Corpus Hermeticum
Pseudo-Egyptian philosophical writings dating from the sec-

151

ond century A. D. The collection is a blend of Platonic, Stoic, Judaic, and Persian doctrines dealing with the ascent of the soul, regenerative processes through which the soul frees itself from the material world, etc.

Correspondences

St. Paul anticipated neo-Platonists and mystical truth-seekers bent on establishing relations between the microcosm and the macrocosm by declaring that everything on earth is made after the pattern of things in the heavens. Jacob Boehme held that Adam, before the fall, was in Paradise.

> That in that condition his body was little removed from spirit. That, had he continued in that state, men would have descended from him alone without woman, who would have been a superfluity; his descendants proceeding from each other in succession, just as men's thoughts flow from them. He contends that it was only after the fall that Adam and Eve's bones became solid, and their flesh gross and corruptible. His theory is, that man, withdrawing himself from God, had lost the divine life in his soul, and that all communication between him and his Maker was nearly lost. In order to reopen the intercourse between the Deity and the soul of man, the second person in the Trinity became man.   (William Howitt.)

The uneducated German shoemaker spoke from the direct experience of an *Ungrund,* God, who produces and reconciles all opposites.

Magicians in their desire to classify all the features of the universe in terms of the forces which which they are associated have evolved an extremely detailed system of correspondences. The oldest part of the system is perhaps that detailing the correspondence between planets, metals, colors:

Planets	Metals	Colors
Mercury	Quicksilver	Grey
Venus	Copper	Green
Mars	Iron	Red
Jupiter	Tin	Blue
Saturn	Lead	Black
Sun	Gold	Yellow
Moon	Silver	White

The magician uses these correspondences to gain control over supernatural forces. The logic behind such associations, is fairly obvious. Mercury, the fast-moving planet that shoots across the sky, pairs with quicksilver, the most mobile of the metals. Venus under her Greek name of Aphrodite may have been identified with copper because Cyprus, the world's chief source of supply of copper, was also a focal point of her cult. Mars is associated with the horse, war, iron, and red. The Hittites, who used horses and iron weapons, proved their superiority over forces equipped with bronze weapons. Red, recalling bloodshed as well as the reddish tinge of what the Egyptians called "the red planet," also symbolizes life, energy and vitality. Jupiter's association with blue, the color of the sky, and with tin, which resembles its silvery glow, may hark back to the ancient Sumerian designation of tin as "metal from heaven." Saturn, the dimly seen planet that moves slowly around the sun, was regarded as the ruler of life and lord of death. The darkest and heaviest of metals, lead, and the color black were naturally assigned to the planet which in the old cosmology was the most distant from the sun. Gold and yellow are associated with the sun because of its color. The moon, which like the sun was distinguished from the other planets as being sources of light and of most benefit to men, was likewise associated with silver and white. Gold and silver were of course the two most important metals.

It is not surprising to find that these and many other correspondences worked out by occultists in ancient times have the ring of truth today. With respect to colors, for instance, green is traditionally linked with love (Venus), peace, and harmony; psychologists have demonstrated that green does exert a calming, peaceful influence. B. J. Kouer found that people associate with red, the color of mighty Mars, passion, rebelliousness, sexuality, etc. The red lights associated with the modern brothel recall Ovid's "red Priapus," the god of the phallus.

Cory, Giles
The most courageous of those tortured at the Salem witchcraft trials. He died under torture in 1692.

Cosmic Consciousness
A phenomenon discussed at length by Richard M. Bucke (1837-1902) in his book, *Cosmic Consciousness: A Study of the Evolution of the Human Mind.* Consciousness of the order of the universe, described by Walt Whitman as "ineffable light . . . lighting the very light beyond all signs, descriptions, languages," appears in exceptional males between the ages of thirty and forty. Cases cited by Bucke include Buddha, Jesus, Plotinus, Dante, Boehme, Balzac, and Whitman. The man who experiences sudden awareness of the meaning of life in the cosmos loses all fear of death, as he sees that life is eternal, the soul is immortal, and the whole universe is grounded on love.

This is one of the tenets of Rosicrucianism, which is, according to its announcements, the application of simple, natural laws. It offers to expound the method of indulging in the privacy of one's own home in the mysteries of life as known to the ancients: how to throw off the shackles of the body, how man's mind may be attuned to the Infinite Wisdom, how to experience cosmic consciousness. This is achieved through momentary flights of the soul, resulting in man becoming one with the universe.

Cosmic Diagram
The Tree of Life, with its ten sephiroth, is viewed by cabalists and modern magicians as a cosmic diagram, showing structure and functioning of the universe. See Cabala.

Cosmic Memory
A repository of all that has been thought or done. It is constituted or contained by the Astral Light. It is also called the Akashic Records, which are open to a competent medium or skryer. Madame Blavatsky and Rudolf Steiner claimed to have discovered in the Cosmic Memory information concerning Lemuria and Atlantis.

Coven
A term that first appeared in 1662, when one of the Auldearn Witches, Isobel Gowdie, confessed that "there are thirteen persons in each coven." Various theories have been proposed: that the coven is a survival of the Stone Age religion of the Horned God, thirteen being the maximum number of men and women who can dance inside a nine-foot circle; that it appeals to women who cherish the survival of the matriarchal society that once was dominant; and that heretical Catharists, under the influence of mystery religions of the East, used the coven to parody Christianity.

The notion of a coven of twelve witches headed by a devil or leader disguised as a devil has been upheld by Margaret Murray. Alex Keiller has found in a number of instances that the prevalence of thirteen is unfounded.

In modern English covens magic is of secondary importance. When practiced, magic requires total concentration. For this reason all the members of a coven must be in complete sympathy with each other. Sometimes a postulant is refused admission to a coven because the leader realizes that his personality conflicts with that of another member. Witches are reluctant to reveal the secrets of their magical practices, but they are known to prefer simple rhymes and jingles that seem natural or spontaneous and can be repeated effortlessly. One general rule seems to be that one can not employ magic to obtain money if the money is to be used for bad purposes. Another is that magic cannot be used to injure another person.

Coven, Admission Into

As a general rule the first question a would-be witch has to answer is this: "Why do you want to become a witch?" If the answer to that question or to other preliminary questions is unsatisfactory, according to Justine Glass (*Witchcraft*, 1965), the candidate for admission to a modern coven is simply told that his request cannot be considered. The best answer to the first question, says one High Priestess, is simply, "I don't know." Such an answer may indicate the awakening of the sixth sense or the presence of a link with an earlier incarnation.

The candidate is also questioned about his belief in reincarnation, his life style and ambitions, his hobbies and beliefs. His psychical powers are evaluated and his aura is subjected to analysis. After a preliminary screening comes a 13-month probationary period, devoted to the study of the properties of plants, the Cabala, telepathy, clairvoyance, mediumship, comparative religions, numerology, and archeology. As he progresses the candidate receives help in developing fully different forms of psychical perception: intuition, astral projection, precognition, and memory of previous incarnations. He learns how to make use of hypnosis and trance states. He also learns something about levitation and exorcism.

The rite or initiation follows a general pattern to which

156

each coven may add its own features. A nine-foot circle is outlined with a sacred black-handled knife. An altar placed in the center of the circle contains a knife symbolizing the air, a cauldron symbolizing water and the Great Mother, a wand symbolizing the phallus and fire, and the pentacle symbolizing the earth. Other instruments may include a sword, a burin, a white-handled knife for use in making talismans, and a cord symbolizing the unifying spirit that links all the elements together. The altar has on it lighted candles, incense burners, a vase filled with salt and water, and a whip symbolizing purification.

The circle is consecrated, using ritual instruments, salt, and water. An incantation, repeated over and over, asks the ancient gods of the four cardinal points to appear. During this part of the ceremony the postulant stands outside the circle. The leader of the coven touches his chest with the point of the blackhandled knife and warns him that it is better to die by the knife than to enter the coven with fear in his heart. The postulant replies with the password "Perfect love and perfect faith," enters the circle, and has his feet and hands ceremoniously bound with the cord. The leader presents him to the gods of the east, the south, the west, and the north, brings him back to the altar, forces him to kneel, grasps his feet firmly, and asks: "Are you prepared to swear to remain faithful to the Art forever?" When the postulant states that he is ready, the leader tells him that he must first be purified, and applies first three, then seven, then nine, and finally 21 lashes. Flagellation is followed by further interrogation. "Are you prepared always to protect, help, and defend your brothers and sisters of the Craft?" the leader asks. If the answer is yes, the postulant takes an oath: "In the presence of these Powers I freely and solemnly swear to keep secret and never reveal the secrets of the Art unless it is to a worthy person who has prepared himself to receive them and has entered a circle such as this one, and that I shall never refuse to reveal these secrets to such a person if he has the support of a brother or sister of the Art. I swear this in the expectation of a future life, mindful of the fact that I have been put to the test and that my arms will turn against me if I fail to keep my solemn oath."

Oil, wine, and a ritual kiss follow. Then the new member of the coven receives the arms of the Craft: Athame (the black-handled knife), the white-handled knife, the sword, cauldron, incense burner, whip, wand, and white cord. The spirits of the cardinal points are dismissed and the members of the coven, seated in a circle, have their ritual meal of cakes and wine. The white cord presented to the neophyte is an indication that he has been admitted to the first degree of the Craft. A red card is the sign of the second degree. Formerly a third degree involved a sexual rite, practiced only by two people who loved each other. The interval separating the first two degrees varies with the individual.

The ceremony itself resembles the initial ceremony. This time he receives a secret name and takes this oath: "I swear by my mother's womb and my honor, surrounded by my brothers and sisters, never to reveal any secret of the Art except to a worthy person who enters such a circle as this. I swear this by my hope for salvation, my past lives and hope for future lives, and I wish to die if I fail to keep my oath."

Then the candidate is instructed in the use of instruments and arms. He receives the cords for binding the High Priestess, lashes her as he was lashed when he was a neophyte, but using three times as many blows. Then comes his consecration to the Powers of the four cardinal points and the separation of the group.

Craft

Term used by British witches to embrace science, religion, philosophy, and profession.

Critomancy

A method of divination by observation of the paste of cakes and the barley flour sprinkled over a sacrificial victim.

Croiset, Gerard

A noted Dutch clairvoyant. He is called the Seer of Holland, and has achieved remarkable results in finding missing persons and in solving crimes by means of his clairvoyant and telepathic powers.

Crollius, Oswald

Follower of Paracelsus and author of the *Book of Signatures.* The introduction to his book gives a good account of hermetic philosophy. Crollius tries to show that God and Nature have signed all their works and that a person who is initiated in the occult writings is able to read the sympathies and antipathies of things, the properties of substances, and all other mysteries of creation.

Cross-Correspondences

Correspondence found in the script of two or more automatic writers performing under conditions that rule out any possibility of communication by normal means. Mrs. Piper was brought to England in 1906 so that the phenomenon of cross-correspondences could be studied to better advantage. The experiments seemed to prove the operation in all the writings of an intelligence other than the automatist's.

Crowley, Aleister

Scottish Satanist (1875-1947), founder of a cult violently opposed to Christianity, and editor and author of many works on the occult. His numerous magical writings include many

159

articles published in The Equinox (a journal which he founded), contributions to a number of obscure magazines, *The Kabbalah Unveiled, Magick in Theory and Practice,* and *Moonchild,* an occult suspense tale.

Crowley claimed to be a reincarnation of Edward Dee. After he died at Hastings in 1947, his orgiastic "Hymn to Pan" was recited during the funeral services held for him in the chapel of the Brighton crematorium and a Black Mass was administered at his grave by his passionate disciples. Unlike his teacher MacGregor Mathers, he neither created nor stilled thunderstorms, but he did invoke by magical means, and with fateful consequences to himself, forces hidden in the depths of that reality that underlies the world of appearance. His writings are largely responsible for the revival of magic today and of an attitude toward man that was almost thrust aside by the rise of science in the 17th century. He faced the new age with ancient instruments— the mystic names of power, the wand, the magic circle. See Great Beast.

Crystalomancy
See Crystal Gazing.

Crystal Gazing
Divination by a clear globe, pool of water, mirror, or any transparent object. The crystal favored by most modern crystal gazers is a spherical or oval globe, free of any speck or flaw. The object of the performer is to induce a hypnotic state in which he may project his visions into the crystal.

Curandero
In Mexico, a medicine man or witch doctor with a reputation for working evil as well as casting beneficial spells and effecting cures. He may use his knowledge of herbs, folk medicine, and human psychology to promote cures. He may direct his efforts toward appeasing the gods and may also

preside at religious ceremonies where peyote and mushrooms are ritually ingested.

Current Literature

The tremendous current interest in psychic, supernatural, and occult phenomena is widespread and continuous, at all levels of society and sophistication. Popular novels, films, monthly magazines and newspapers produce a constant stream of occult episodes, Satanic encounters, first-hand accounts of presumably inexplicable situations involving spirits, witchcraft, and occult practices in their widest applications. The mystery of the flying saucers has created an intense concern about outer space possibilities. Dark beliefs that have haunted men for centuries have sprung into new life. There is a passionate eagerness to discover and test whatever phenomena have been hidden in the heavens, under the dark spaces of the earth, in traditional legends of remote ethnic communities. The scientific mind in these latter years began to take a determined and serious interest in all such phenomena. The urgency to probe is desperate. The desire for assurance in what has been for centuries mere untested beliefs and attitudes based on hearsay and unverified records has created a vast almost universal challenge. The secrets of the earth, invisible as well as material, are subject to prolonged and minute investigations. Man is thus continuously questing and what he has already accomplished in this respect is merely a fore-runner of his advancing pilgrimage.

Cybele

Anatolian nature goddess in whose honor orgiastic rites and revelries were celebrated. Like Hecate, she was venerated by sorcerers. Phrygia was an early center of her cult. The Greeks identified her with the Great Mother of the Gods. The Romans introduced her cult direct from Asia Minor in 204 B. C. Her eunuch priests, called Galli, sacrificed their virility to her on her sacred day, March 24. Her day was called *sanguis,* or feast of blood, since she was thought to thirst for human blood, an important element in magic. The Galli mutilated themselves, using stone implements or pottery. Their organs were carefully collected, washed, embalmed, and deposited in the Thalamus, or bridal chamber of the goddess. The Galli were experts in the fabrication and use of amulets, talismans, and magic philtres. They practiced telluric divination and were familiar with astrology. They rivaled the Chaldeans as talismanic specialists.

Cynocephalia
A herb used to protect the possessor against evil enchantments. If plucked out of the ground, however, it may cause instant death. Such was the view of Pliny the Elder.

D

Dactylomancy

A method of divination by means of various arrangements and positions of finger rings. One method resembles table-rapping as practiced by spiritualists. A ring is suspended above a round table on which are inscribed the letters of the alphabet. The letters indicated by the ring spell out a message.

Dactyls

Magicians, exorcists, and soothsayers who are supposed to have come from Phrygia and to have discovered the notes of the musical scale.

Daemon (Daimon)

In Greek, a general term for a supernatural power or being. Homer used the word *daemon* almost interchangeably with *theos,* "god." Theos stresses the personality of the supernatural power, daemon his activity, regularly applied to a sudden supernatural intervention not ascribed to a particular deity. The word daemon came to mean the power determining the fate of an individual. Like Socrates, a man could have his own personal daemon. The dead of the golden age were regarded first as demons, then as a little lower than the gods but higher than mankind.

Dalai Lama
See Lama.

Damnum Minatum
A threat of evil made by a sorcerer or witch. See Maleficia.

Dana
Irish goddess. Like Diana, she instructed her people in the art of magic. Also known as Annu, she was probably worshiped by the Irish as the great Mother Goddess.

Danaans
One of the three Nemedian families who lived through the Formorian victory and returned to Ireland. They were the people of the goddess Dana, and they represented to the authors of medieval romance power and beauty, science and poetry. To the common people they were gods. Though subject to death in battle, they were able to use their magical powers to conquer their mortal enemies. From Falias they were said to have brought the Stone of Destiny, from Gorias an invincible sword, from Finias a magical spear, and from Murias the Cauldron of the Dagda. They were thought to have arrived in Ireland on a magical cloud. This legend has persuaded some modern occultists to view them as astronauts from another world.

Daniken, Erich von
See Astronauts.

Dark Moon
Symbolizing the forbidden or the unattainable, the Dark Moon is known astrologically as the demoniac Lilith, the legendary first wife of Adam.

Darrell, John
England's only exorcist (c. 1562-1602). His activities provoked Canon 72, prohibiting exorcism in the Church of England (1603). His first efforts to achieve exorcism failed

when Catherine Wright admitted that she had faked her fits and visions. His encounters with Thomas Darling (the Burton Boy) and William Somers (the Nottingham Boy) brought him notoriety and, after both of them had been revealed as impostors, a jail sentence.

Dauphine Witches
See Witches of Dauphiné.

Davanni
In Gypsy mythology, these are beneficent spirits.

Davis, Andrew Jackson
Nineteenth-century spiritualist. In 1843, before the Fox sisters had heard their first rappings, he became a clairvoyant, drew attention to his powers of seeing into and curing diseases, and acquired the name of the Poughkeepsie Seer. Almost illiterate, he had been apprenticed to a shoemaker in Poughkeepsie.

> In his clairvoyant state Davis not only declared that the power of seeing into and healing diseases was given; but he prescribed for scores who came most successfully, stating their symptoms in a manner that surprised the patients and equally so several accomplished physicians who attended the *séances*. . . . He beheld all the essential natures of things; saw the interior of men and animals as perfectly as their exterior; and described them in language so correct that the most able technologists could not surpass him. . . . Everything appeared to him, as to all clairvoyants, clothed with its peculiar atmosphere; not only living forms, but every grain of salt or sand, the minutest bones and tendrils, mineral and earthy substances, had the coloured atmosphere. As George Fox and Swedenborg before him, he declared that the whole of creation was opened to him; that he saw the names of

all things in their natures, as Adam saw them. (William Howitt.)

Death by Sorcery

In many parts of the world individuals are said to have died by exorcism and casting of spells. Standing aloof from others in his community, the doomed individual finds that everyone else accepts his impending departure. Sacred rites are performed to hasten his journey to the land of the dead. Banished, obsessed, and terrified, the victim of the sorcerer's art accepts his fate.

Dee, John

English scholar, mathematician, and occultist (1527-1608). He was imprisoned for practicing enchantments against Mary, Queen of England. He wrote *Liber Mysteriorum* (Book of Mysteries).

Dee lived in solitude, practicing astrology to earn his subsistence but studying alchemy for pleasure. He also studied Cabalistic mysteries and Rosicrucian theories. He reached a state of mystic exaltation in which his visions seemed like realities. He believed that the bright angel Uriel appeared before him one day, gave him a piece of crystal, and told him that he had only to examine it intently in order to communicate with beings of another world. These beings would appear to him and reveal to him the mysteries of the future. Even after his enthusiasm for crystal-gazing began to subside, he enlisted the help of a clever rogue named Edward Kelly, who pretended to hold conferences with the spirits of the dead. Dee and Kelly gained a reputation that extended to the continent, but Dee's enthusiasm and credulity eventually degraded him into the tool and slave of Kelly. At Trebona, in Bohemia, they resided for two years, pursuing their alchemical studies and, for a time, sharing all things, including their wives. Dee returned to England with a splendid train, soon sank into poverty, and became known as a mere "conjurer, a caller, or invocator of devils."

Defenses Against Demons

The sign of the cross is the most powerful weapon against the Devil. Next comes holy water, then bells, the relics of saints, and certain natural objects—gems such as chrysolite and agate, plants such as garlic and rue, salt, the cock, and a herb called by the French *permanable,* which can enchant demons.

Delort, Catherine

One of 8 persons burned at the stake at Toulouse in 1335. The pressure applied by the Inquisitors to persuade her to implicate others became standard procedure in later witch trials. At her trial she confessed that a shepherd had inveigled her into signing a pact with the Devil. The shepherd took her at midnight to a crossroads, where they built a fire and burned the remains of corpses they had stolen from a graveyard. Uttering strange words, she spilled a few drops of her blood over the embers. Berit, a demon shaped like a purplish flame, appeared and seemingly bestowed on her the power to work different kinds of maleficium.

After she had made her pact with the Devil, Catherine was able to fall into a deep sleep and be transported to the sabbat, where she copulated with the Devil. Every Saturday night, at assemblies held in different locations, she took part in a general orgy with other cult members, drank foul potions, and ritually consumed flesh from the bodies of children conceived on such occasions.

Her testimony includes the first mention in witch trials of the lack of salt at the sabbat. The tradition that salt could dispel evil spirits was deep-rooted, and it was maintained in the practice of applying salt at the baptism of a child in the Church.

Like Anne-Marie de Georgel, she equated Satan with God and outlined a doctrine containing some distorted elements of Joachite millenarianism. Also like Anne-Marie, she was handed over to secular authorities for burning.

Del Vaux, Jean

Confessed sorcerer and monk. When he was 15, he agreed to serve a man he had met in some woods, in return for a promise of honor and progress in a field of his own choosing. The man then revealed himself in monstrous form, carried Jean to the Sabbat, marked him twice on the shoulders, provided him with deadly poisons, and urged him to take the religious vows, and gave him poison to kill the Abbot of his monastery so that he, the demon, could fill the post. In 1596 Del Vaux implicated over 500 others in witchcraft, named the nine main societies of sorcerers in the districts of Stablo, Cheren, Houfalis, Malmedy, Salm, Tafgnies, Trier, and Vaux, together with their meeting places, described magical routines, gave a detailed account of a witches' Sabbat. He steadfastly maintained that he had spoken only the truth even though he was tortured and every attempt was made to turn up contradictions in his testimony. His accusers would read excerpts from his previous depositions, changing certain details or names, in an attempt to convince themselves of the truth of his statements. Repeatedly, he corrected these contrived errors and returned "to the original order and facts." Del Vaux was beheaded and his body returnd to the Abbey of Stablo, near Liége, Belgium. Strangely, none of those whom he implicated seems to have been brought to trial.

De Magis

An occult treatise (1591) in which Johann Georg Godelman defines sorcerers as those who by evil spells, dire curses, and the sending of foul spirits, by potions prepared by the

Devil or through illicit arts from corpses of hanged men, harm and destroy the health and lives of men and beasts.

Demiurge

In Greek, the word means "artisan." It was used by Plato to designate the creator of the universe. The Gnostics, Marcionites, Paulicians, and the other heretical sects used it to designate the evil power responsible for matter. Also called Demiurgus or Demiurgos.

Demonology

That branch of learning dealing with malevolent spirits. The Greek term *daimon* meant genius or spirit, but the word demon today means a wicked spirit. According to Michael Psellus, demons are grouped in six great classes: (1) demons of fire; (2) demons of the air; (3) earth demons; (4) those inhabiting the waters of the earth; (5) subterranean demons who cause earthquakes and volcanic eruptions; and (6) shadows. See Hierarchy of Hell. See also under separate headings: Babylonian Demonology, Greek Demonology, Jewish Demonology, Persian Demonology, Roman Demonology.

Demons

A lower order of supernatural beings, generally thought to be hostile to mankind. Belief in such beings is widespread. The ancient Mesopotamians lived in fear of demons, commonly represented in their art with human bodies and animal heads. Both the Babylonians and the Assyrians thought the demons were evil spirits who came from beneath the earth or ghosts of the unburied dead. In Greece, the word *daimon* had a good as well as a bad connotation. Socrates had a familiar demon who warned him when he was on the point of making a wrong decision. The rise of Christianity, with its condemnation of the spirits of the pagan world, assumed to be in league with the Devil, transformed demons into malevolent spirits.

Since the first stirrings of consciousness men have sought through sorcery to protect themselves against these supernatural powers and gain control over them. Ancient peoples and religions were generally convinced of the reality and, in most instances, malefic deeds of demons. Demonology had a strong and lasting influence on the thoughts, beliefs, and cultures of men scattered across the surface of the globe.

The great forces of the unified magical world have a positive and a negative aspect, an angelic and a demonic side. The magical universe is like an ocean in which men are moved by invisible tides which they are sometimes capable of manipulating and controlling. Sinister creatures lurk in the cold depths of the ocean—malignant elementals, the shells or husks cast off by the universal organism, hideous things spawned by the malice of sorcerers, zombies, astral corpses. Many primitive peoples believe that diseases are caused by evil spirits or demons. These are the universal forces corresponding to the waste products, impurities, and viruses associated with the human body. Psychologically, they are the dark, instinctive, evil impulses of the mind. Fear of demons and ghosts, of creatures that lie in wait for their hapless victims still persists, as if belief in the existence of evil supernatural beings were instinctive. The Babylonians designated as *maskim* the seven terrible demons which they identified as being the evil counterparts of the gods of the seven planets. Those beings, like the Arab *ghul*, lurked in ambush.

Like Roman Catholic theologians, modern occultists accept the existence of demons. One magical tradition makes the Devil the sorcerer's god, as in witchcraft; the sorcerer wins his favor by doing his will and worshiping him. The other tradition treats demons as powerful evil intelligences which

170

the sorcerer can learn to dominate by the force of his will and by carrying out extremely dangerous operations involving curses, symbols, perfumes, and rituals of blood and sacrifice. See Jewish Demonology.

Dervishes
Several Dervish sects practice prolonged dancing. The Maulawi Dervishes, a Sufi order founded in 13th-century Persia by Jalaluddin Rumi, practice a series of complicated dances designed to educate the body and mind in certain cosmic laws. The dances imitate the revolutions of the planets. Inwardly, the dancers achieve a state of ecstasy by carrying on mental exercises.

D'Espagnet, Jean
Sixteenth-century Hermetic philosopher. He wrote two treatises: one on the secret of Hermetic philosophy (*Arcanum Philosophiae Hermitacae*) and an *Enchiridion* dealing with the physical possibility of transmutation. The *Arcanum* has been claimed as a treatise on mystical alchemy.

D'Esperance, Elizabeth
A medium (1855-1919) whose experiences are recounted in William Oxley's *Angelic Revelations* and in her own *Shadow Land*. The strangest phenomenon of her mediumship relates to dematerialization. The lower part of her body is supposed to have dematerialized.

Destroying Angel
A white-stalked, red-capped fungus which grows in fairy rings. Its scientific name is amanita phalloides. The deadly fungus may cause intense hallucinations.

Devil
The word derives from the Greek *diabolos* (from *diaballein*, to slander) through the Latin *diabolus*. In the Septuagint and for most Christian writers the *diabolos* is the supreme

spirit of evil. Both demons and the Devil figure prominently in sorcery and witchcraft.

The Devil is the rebel of the cosmos, the independent in the empire of a tyrant, the opposition to uniformity, the dissonance in universal harmony, the exception to the rule, the particular in the universal, the unforeseen chance that breaks the law; he is the individualizing tendency, the craving for originality, which bodily upsets the ordinances of God that enforce a definite kind of conduct. . . .

Milton's Satan is a grand character, a noble-souled rebel, who would rather undergo an eternity of torture than suffer humiliation. Consider but the fact that, taking the statement of his adversaries alone, the Devil is the most trustworthy person in existence. He has been cheated by innumerable sinners, saints, angels. . . . The Devil is the father of all misunderstood geniuses. It is he who induces us to try new paths; he begets originality of thought and deed. He tempts us to venture out boldly into unknown seas for the discovery of new ways to the wealth of distant Indias. He makes us dream of and hope for more prosperity and greater happiness. He is the spirit of discontent that embitters our hearts, but in the end often leads to a better arrangement of affairs. In truth, he is a very useful servant of the Almighty, and all the heinous features of his character disappear when we consider the fact that he is necessary in the economy of nature as a wholesome stimulant to action and as the power of resistance that evokes the noblest efforts of living beings. (Paul Canus.)

Devil and Theology
Pope Paul VI, anxious to correct Catholic theologians who deny the reality of the Devil, in a sermon delivered at St. Peter's in June, 1972, warned that "the smoke of Satan has entered the temple of God through a fissure in the church."

Later, in November, he devoted an entire sermon to the wiles of Satan, arguing that "this obscure and disturbing being really exists . . . a perfidious and astute charmer who manages to insinuate himself into us by way of the senses, of fantasy, of concupiscence, of utopian logic, of disorderly social contracts."

The Pope's concern for Satan caused the secular press to predict a return of "bright and profitable days for the occult scientists, magicians, and witches all celebrating the unexpected but authoritative return, after many years, of His Highness, the Prince of Darkness."

Devil of the Tarot
In the Tarot, the Devil is the fifteenth mystery, combining the four primal elements of fire, air, water, and earth.

Devils
Alphonsus de Spina identified ten varieties of devils:

1. Fates
2. Poltergeists, who create mischief by night.
3. Incubi and succubi, who pollute nuns by night.
4. Marching hosts, who sound like hordes of men.
5. Familiar demons, who eat and drink with men.
6. Nightmare demons, who disturb men's dreams.
7. Demons formed from semen and the odor accompanying copulation. These demons cause men to have erotic dreams so that they can "receive their emission and make the reform of a new spirit."
8. Deceptive demons, who appear now as men, now as women.
9. Clean demons, who assault only holy men.
10. Demons who cause old women to believe that they fly to sabbats.

Devil's Girdle
Matical girdles were commonly worn in medieval times.

Witches often were accused of wearing them, probably as a mark of allegiance to the Devil.

Devil's Mark

A small birthmark, scar, or other disfiguration presumed to have been left by the Devil's talon upon the victim's body. As early as the 15th century witchhunters began to accept it as proof of guilt. In later centuries stripping and shaving witches in search of such a mark became standard practice. Sometimes the Devil's mark was confused with the witch's mark, a pimple, wart, or other protuberance from which the familiar was supposed to receive nourishment.

The Devil's mark was allegedly imprinted of the victim's body by the Devil to prevent betrayal of the pact. According to the Italian demonologist Ludovico Sinistrari,

> The Devil makes a mark on them, especially those whose allegiance he suspects. The mark varies in shape and size; sometimes it is like a hare, sometimes like the foot of a toad, sometimes like a spider, a puppy, or a dormouse. It is imprinted on the most secret parts of the body; men may have it under their eyelids or armpits, on the lips or shoulders, on the anuse or elsewhere; women generally have it on their breasts or private parts. The stamp that makes these marks is nothing less than the Devil's talon.

Diablero

Term used by the Yaqui Indians to denote an evil person who practices sorcery and is able to assume the appearance of an animal.

Diabolic Pact

Though a pact between the Devil or one of his henchmen and a man or woman may vary in detail, it always includes:

1. Preparation for the pact (abstinence from meat, etc.).

174

2. An invocation in the form of a ritual accompanied by the sacrifice of a black fowl, fire, etc.
3. A complex set of formulas.
4. The appearance of the devil.
5. Signing the pact with blood drawn from the left arm. On signing the pact, the individual "loses his double" —that is, he casts no shadow and his image cannot be seen in a mirror.

Diakka

In occultism, these are astral bodies or spirits which, though defective, may achieve redemption through education following the physical death of their host bodies.

Diana

Throughout the Roman world Diana had many different names and attributes. As the chaste huntress she carries a bow and often is accompanied by a stag. Her Greek name was Artemis, corresponding to the Etruscan Tana, Egyptian Isis, Palestinian Ashtoreth, Irish Danu (or Badb, Cailleach, Macha, Morrigan, or one of 26 other names), and the Carthaginian Tanit. As Triformis, she was Diana, Proserpina, and Hecate. She was also designated as Agrotera, Aricia, Cybele, Cynthia, Delia, Luna, Orthia, Lucina and Selene. As Hecate she was considered the goddess of magic and was represented as having three heads: that of a horse, a dog, and a boar. Crossroads were sacred to her in her role as Trivia, the goddess of the three ways. Though she was the goddess of chastity, her love affairs included one with the horned god Pan, and statues recovered from her temple at Ephesus show her as the great fertility goddess with at least three tiers of bare breasts. In an earlier form she may have been a totem bear. Intermingling of cultures through many centuries produced a composite Diana-Artemis-Isis figure known by a bewildering mass of names and endowed with many attributes: the great mother goddess, creator of the universe, supreme deity of life and death, peace and war, love and fertility. Men worshiped her to obtain her favors.

Dibbuk

In Jewish occultism, the belief that a person possesses two souls at one time, the second soul being that of a sinner returned from beyond to expiate its sins by sharing in the good deeds of the pure soul belonging to its host. A person possessed of two souls could not control the intruder, whose voice and behavior were at odds with true self. The dibbuk shouted, cursed, slandered noted personalities, and could be expelled only by frightening rituals performed in a dark synagogue to the accompaniment of shrill blasts from a ram's horn. A skilled rabbi could expel the refractory dibbuk through the little finger of the possessed.

The dibbuk served as the theme of a play by S. Anski, presented in Yiddish in 1920 and subsequently in other languages.

Diodorus of Catania

Ancient sorcerer, burned alive in an oven.

Dionysus (Bacchus, Liber)

In classical mythology, the god of wine and fertility. His cult was widespread in Thrace, where the Thracian women were particularly dedicated to his orgiastic rites. The women, Maenads, in their ecstatic frenzy, abandoned their homes, roamed the fields and hillsides, dancing, swinging their flaming torches. In their passion they caught and tore apart animals, sometimes even children, and devoured the flesh, thus acquiring communion with the divinity. Dionysus himself at times appeared to them in the form of some animal, usually a bull. Celebrations, of a milder type, were also held on Mount Parnassus.

176

In the mystic cult, Dionysus was associated with the Lower Regions. This cult became highly popular in Hellenistic and later on in Roman times. The cult of Dionysus as practiced by his devotees is presented dramatically in Euripides' tragedy *The Bacchae.*

Modern scholars surmise that memories of the cult of Dionysus survived and influenced the Sabbat. In animal form, the Greek deity sometimes appeared as a goat. At Eleutherai he was called Melanaigis, "he with the black goatskin." Like other fertility deities, he was associated with the underworld. He was attended by satyrs, lustful goat-spirits, for whom he served as the object of orgiastic rites.

Dismissing a Spirit
True Grimoire, a medieval book, gives the formula for discharging a spirit once its task is accomplished.

I am pleased and contented with thee, Prince Lucifer, for the moment. Leave thou in peace now, and go in quiet and without trouble. Do not forget our pact, or I shall blast thee with my Wand. Amen.

Dittamy
An aromatic plant growing on Mount Dicte and Mount Ida in Crete. It possesses occult and mystical properties. The evergreen shrub was sacred to the moon goddesses and had a place in many magical performances. Occultists claim that it cures somnambulism. Pharmacy attributes to the plant strongly sedative and quieting properties.

Divination
Divination, the technique of presumably gaining knowledge of future or otherwise unknown events, was practiced from the earliest times on record, through the Biblical period down to the immediate present. Divination is prevalent in all countries, and at all intellectual levels. It assumed a great

variety of forms. In the eleventh century B. C. (I Sam. 2.8.3), Saul prohibited divination by necromancy. All kinds of diviners, including interpreters of dreams, sorcerers, necromancers, were condemned by the major prophets.

Just as the great magical doctrine of "as above, so below" is the foundation of astrology, its converse, "as below, so above" is the basis of many forms of divination. By studying events on earth the sorcerer can discover the conditions in heaven. He may inspect a sheep's liver, for instance, to determine whether celestial conditions are favorable for a particular terrestrial undertaking. This and other highly eclectic methods of predicting the future are based on the assumption that apparently random events are in reality parts of the great design of the universe and indicate the direction in which the universe as a whole is moving.

Among the branches of divination are:

amniomancy, or observation of the caul on a child's head at birth;

anthropomancy, or consultation of the intestines of sacrificed children (the Emperor Julian the Apostate was believed to have practiced this method of divination);

apantomancy, or observation of objects that appear haphazardly;

armomancy, or observation of the shoulders of an animal that has been sacrificed for the purpose;

aspidomancy, or divination by sitting on a shield, within a magic circle, and falling into a trance while pronouncing occult formulas;

belomancy, or divination by means of the flight of arrows;

bibliomancy, or consultation of a passage or line in a book, selected at random;

178

botanomancy, or divination by burning branches of brier and vervain, on which were inscribed questions to be answered;

catoptromancy, or divination by means of a lens or magic mirror—a practice in vogue in antiquity, and mentioned by Apuleius, the Roman philosopher and novelist, Pausanias, the Greek traveler, and St. Augustine;

causimomancy, or divination by fire (when an object cast into a fire did not burn, the omen was propitious);

chiromancy, or evaluation of the lines of a person's hand with a view to interpreting character and fate (palmistry);

cubomancy, or divination by thimbles (an ancient Greek technique, practiced by the Romans also, among them the Emperors Augustus and Tiberius);

daphomancy, or observation of the way in which a laurel branch burns and crackles in a fire;

empyromancy, or observation of objects placed on a sacrificial fire;

gastromancy, or divination by means of ventriloquism;

geloscopy, or observation and interpretation of a person's laughter;

gyromancy, or circumambulation of a chalked circle and observation of the position of the body in relation to the circle;

hepatoscopy, or observation of a sheep's liver;

hippomancy, or observation of a horse's pace;

ichthyomancy, inspection of the entrails of fish;

lampadomancy, divination by means of the flame of a lamp;

libanomancy, observation of the smoke of incense;

margaritomancy, divination by means of pearls;

metoposcopy, an occult procedure that evaluates a person's life and fate from the lines of the forehead;

oeonisticy, observation of the flight of birds;

ovomancy, divination by means of putting eggs on a fire and observing how they break;

and xylomancy, observation of the position of twigs lying on the ground.

Divine Names
See Names, Divine.

Doctrine of Correspondences
See Boehme, Jakob; Correspondences; and Swedenborg, Emanuel.

Doctrine of Signatures
See Signatures; Laws of Magic.

Dog
The Devil's accomplice. Dogs are also faithful companions of necromancers. The Devil assumes the shape of a dog to help the necromancer without arousing suspicion, but his presence is betrayed by his black hair. Early magicians believed that demons appeared as dogs. Plutarch relates that a black dog came to Cimon to announce his impending death. Early Christians drove dogs away from their churches. The Furies were called the dogs of hell, and black dogs in ancient times were sacrificed to infernal deities.

Don Juan
See Castaneda, Carlos.

Doppleganger
A double or ghost closely resembling a living person. The

word is derived from German and means Double Walker. A doppelgänger is visible to the person he resembles and to others as well. He often floats along the ground.

Dowsing

The practice of using a dipping or divining rod to search for water, treasure, lost items, etc. A green Y-shaped hazel, willow, or peach twig or branch is most commonly used in dowsing. Generally the divining rod is gripped by its inverted branches as the dowser, his fists turned outward, walks across the surface concealing the item to be discovered. The tip of the Y turns downward immediately above the concealed item.

Dowsing to locate underground sources of water is also called divining, water witching, and rhabdomancy. There have been attempts to show a relationship between the forces that cause the divining rod (the Y-shaped twig) to move downward and the forces that cause tornados to strike the earth.

The Book of Numbers in the Old Testament contains an account of a rod which Moses used to strike a rock and produce water for his people. Dowsers have used the incident to support the view that rhabdomancy is a god-given talent. Herodotus reported its use by the Medes, Persians, and Scythians, and Marco Polo wrote that it was used in the Orient.

Dreaming

The Eternal-Now of the Aborigines of Australia. Like the Akashic Records, the myths, rituals, and symbols exist in a timeless past and are accessible to the initiated. The sacred dances and chants of the Aborigines preserve the racial heritage and reveal the supernormal powers of the heroes of the past. These heroes could move through the air or under the ground, change into other shapes, and act as men or animals.

In Eastern Australia, the leader and culture giver of old appeared, his origin unknown, and went up into the sky when he had finished his work. The sky world is the stage on which human and animal heroes of the Dreaming perform. The old guardians of their secret knowledge ("past-masters") are reluctant to disclose what they know to outsiders or even to young men of the tribe who have not proven their loyalty to their tradition.

Dreams

To the ancients, particularly the Greeks, dreams were a link between the actual immediate state and the future. Dreams were regarded as prognostications of coming events, and were so interpreted, especially by the Greek priest-physicians. Dreams were recorded in temples so that use might be made of them when identical dreams occurred. A famous dream book, which included interpretations, was produced by Artemidorus Daldianus, who belongs in the second century A. D. In Biblical literature, dreams are tantamount to prognostications. References to such dreams occur in Genesis (20.3, 31.23, 37.5); Job (33.15); Numbers (12.6); and I Kings (3.5).

The Greek historian Xenophon discusses dreams as a means of divination.

According to Sigmund Freud in *The Interpretation of Dreams,* the dream is the fulfillment of a wish. The supernatural character of dreams is suggested by J. W. Dunne's experiences. Dunne kept a careful record of his dreams and found that many of them anticipated future experiences. See Jung, Carl Gustav.

Dream Soul

Like the astral body, the dream soul may leave the body during sleep and travel over great distances. The dream soul is assumed to be a part of a man's spirit. If it fails to return before he awakens, the man may sicken and die unless he has the help of a sorcerer in restoring the unity of his spirit.

Druids

In Celtic religion, priests gifted with the power to predict the future. Adept in the magical arts, the Druids used many incantations and spells to appease the gods, control the elements, and promote fertility. They were skilled in astrology, medicine, and psychology.

The druids believed in the indestructibility of matter, the immortality of the soul, and metempsychosis. Their concept of the life beyond seems to have been based on fragmentary memories. They imagined three life circles: the inner circle where all things have their source (*abred*); the center circle of consummate bliss (*gwenved*); and the outer circle where God alone holds sway (*keugant*). They believed in five elements: solid bodies and the earth, water, air, heat and light, and the divine spirit or emanation, whose union with the other elements produces all life.

Druids and Sorcerers

Both the Druids and European sorcerers believed in the power of the magic circle to call up and collect supernatural energies such as those involved in extrasensory perception. Both believed in reincarnation, recognized the importance of stone circles as centers of worship, and celebrated four great sabbats.

Dukun

A Malay shaman. He specialized in spells and charms.

E

Earth Movers

Powerful goddesses worshiped under various names—Demeter, Erda, Frey, Hel, Ishtar, Kali, etc.—as embodied manifestations of the female principle or the creative principle of Earth.

Easter Island

Gigantic statues found on this island in the South Pacific have caused occultists to link it to the legendary continent of Mu and the theory that astronauts from another planet were the source of secret wisdom transmitted by stages to earthlings. The inhabitants of the island attribute magical properties to the first egg laid each year by a migratory bird. Each chief designates a swimmer to represent him in the race to retrieve the egg, generally from a swallow's nest on the islet of Motunui. The man who finds the egg and swims back safely with it becomes for a year a sorcerer or demigod possessed of a terrible mana. Whoever touches him is in danger of receiving a mortal charge. The bird-man motif appears in Jewish and Christian legend (angels), in Egyptian writings (the falcon-kings), and in many mythologies investing men with the ability to fly. Some occultists hold that the motif is a survival of the belief that Great Initiators appeared from some distant planet long ago and imparted their secret wisdom to men on this earth.

Eckankar (Eck)

Soul travel. According to Paul Twitchell, who since 1964 has brought his message to thousands of converts, spiritual freedom is most readily achieved through travel in the soul body. This means that the soul body is projected out of the physical body and that the essential soul can have perfect freedom to visit at will any plane or level of existence. A vast spiritual hierarchy is assumed to operate throughout the universe. The adept or *chela* masters the mysteries of the universe.

Ectenic Force

A supernatural force emanating from a medium and enabling him to move physical objects.

Ectoplasm

A spiritually generated, luminescent substance said to emanate from the medium's body during a trance and to provide proof of the existence of the spiritual world.

Edmonds, John Worth

A distinguished jurist and influential American spiritualist (1816-1874). He investigated the mysterious rapping sounds heard near Rochester, New York, by the Fox sisters, developed the gift for mediumship, and received communications from Bacon, Swedenborg, and others.

Egbo (Esik)

Secret society of Calabar. The African society is divided into 11 grades, of which the first three are not open to slaves.

Egg, Orphean

See Orphean Egg.

Egyptian Book of the Dead

A collection of the inscriptions found on papyrus, the walls of buildings, monuments, and tombs. These ancient Egyptian writings embody the rituals and magic associated with the burial of the dead and their passage into the afterlife.

The work abounds in magical references since its main purpose is thaumaturgical protection against the dangers faced by the dead seeking to reach the other world. The dead had to undergo judgment by Osiris before being allowed to enter the next world. The recitation of various magical formulas and spells was supposed to ward off the evil influences along the way. Every Egyptian of means had a papyrus buried with him. On this were written the information that would help him to travel safely and to reply well during his ceremony of justification. Paramount among the spells contained in the papyrus were "words of power" in the form of names or attributes of gods. Pictorial representation also played a considerable part in the magical ritual of the papyrus. Budge, in his *Egyptian Magic,* explains how preparations are to be made:

> On a piece of clean papyrus a boat is to be drawn with ink made of green *abut* mixed with *anti* water, and in it are to be figures of Isis, Thoth, Shu and Khepera, and the deceased; when this had been done the papyrus must be fastened to the breast of the deceased, care being taken that it does actually touch his body. Then shall his spirit enter into the boat of Ra each day, and the god Thoth shall take heed to him, and he shall sail about with him into any place that he wisheth. Elsewhere it is ordered that the boat of Ra be painted "in a pure place," and in the bows is to be painted a figure of the deceased.

The importance of pictorial representation is indicated in Chapter 133 of the Book of the Dead:

> This chapter shall be recited over a boat four cubits in length, and made of green porcelain (on which have been painted) the divine sovereign chiefs of the cities; and a

figure of heaven with its stars shall be made also, and this thou shalt have made ceremonially pure by means of natron and incense. And behold, thou shalt make an image of the spirit which thou dost wish to make perfect (and place it) in this boat, and thou shalt make it to travel about in the boat (which shall be made in the form of the boat) of Ra; and he shall see the form of the god Ray himself therein.

Many spells included in the book were intended to preserve the mummy from decay. Except for the weighing of the heart by Thoth in the presence of Osiris, the deceased who had absolute knowledge of the book could face all the dangers of the afterlife with confidence, knowing that he had control over the powers of Amenti.

One Egyptian incantation from *The Book of the Dead* is intended to keep the Apshait (a beetle) away from the dead:

Depart from me, O thou that hast lips which gnaw, for I am Khnemu, the lord of Peshennu, and I bring words of the gods to Ra, and I report my message to the lord thereof.

The book currently enjoys considerable popularity with users of mind-expanding drugs because they consider it to be a useful agent in enhancing the effects of psychedelic substances and deepening their mystical-religious experiences.

Egyptian Incantations
Magic tablets of ancient Egypt contain charms and incantations for various purposes. An incantation against dangerous animals reads:

Come to me, O Lord of Gods!
Drive far from me the lions coming from the earth, the

188

crocodiles issuing from the river, the mouth of all biting reptiles coming out of their holes!

Stop, crocodile Mako, son of Set!
Do not wave thy tail:
Do not work thy two arms:
Do not open thy mouth.
May water become as a burning fire before thee!
The spear of the seventy-seven gods is on thine eyes:
The arm of the seventy-seven gods is on thine eyes:
Thou who wast fastened with metal claws to the bark of Ra,
Stop, crocodile Mako, son of Set!

Another contains a series of names referring to magically transfigured names of the gods Osiris and Seth:

O Oualbpaga!
O Kammara!
O Kamalo!
O Karhenmon!
O Amagaaa!

An Egyptian spell to counteract the effects of the bite of any snake was recorded on papyrus. The spell is to be recited over a hawk with two feathers on its head, made of isy-wood and painted. Open the hawk's mouth and offer it incense, bread, and beer. Place the hawk on the face of the person bitten by the snake and recite the words of the spell, which refers to Ra, the sun-god, Osiris, god of the dead, and his son Horus. N-N means the name of the person affected by the spell:

Flow out, thou poison, come forth upon the ground. Horus conjures thee, he cuts thee off, he spits thee out, and thou risest not up but fallest down. Thou art weak

189

and not strong, a coward and dost not fight, blind and dost not see. Thou liftest not thy face. Thou art turned back and findest not thy way. Thou mournest and dost not rejoice. Thou creepest away and dost not appear. So speaketh Horus, efficacious of magic! The poison which was rejoicing, the hearts of multitudes grieve for it; Horus has slain it by his magic. He who mourned is in joy. Stand up, thou who wast prostrate. Horus has restored thee to life. He who came as one carried is gone forth of himself: Horus has overcome his bites. All men, when they behold Ra, praise the son of Osiris. Turn back thou snake, conjured is thy poison which was in any limb of N the son of N. Behold, the magic of Horus is powerful against thee. Flow it out, thou poison, come forth upon the ground.

Another spell from the *Book of the Dead* is addressed to the dead and intended to make all the good features of the spell apply to them:

Thou hast carried thy hands into the house of eternity, thou art made perfect in gold, thou dost shine brightly in sun metal, and thy fingers shine in the dwelling of Osiris, in the sanctuary of Horus himself.

A demotic papyrus contains a formula for making a love knot:

You take a band of linen of sixteen threads, four of white, four of green, four of blue, four of red, and make them into one band, and stain them with the blood of a hoopoe, and you bind it with a scarab in its attitude of the sun-god, drowned, being wrapped in byssus, and you bind it to the body of the boy who has the vessel and it will work magic quickly.

The Egyptians placed an incantation addressed to Ra around the neck of the deceased:

190

O thou that cleavest the water as thou comest forth from the stream and dost sit upon thy place in thy boat as thou goest forth to thy station of yesterday, and do thou join the Osiris, the overseer of the seal, Nu, triumphant, the perfect Khu, unto thy mariners, and let thy strength be his strength. Hail, Ra, in thy name of Ra, if thou dost pass by the eye of seven cubits, which hath a pupil of three cubits, then verily do thou strengthen the Osiris Nu, triumphant, the perfect Khu and let him be among thy mariners, and let thy strength be his strength. Hail, Ra, in thy name of Ra, if thou dost pass by those who are overturned in death then verily do thou make the Osiris Nu, triumphant, the perfect soul, to stand up upon his feet, and may thy strength be his strength. Hail, Ra, in thy name of Ra, if the hidden things of the underworld are opened unto thee and thou dost gratify the heart of the cycle of thy gods, then verily do thou grant joy of heart unto the overseer of the house of the overseer of the seal, Nu, triumphant, and let thy strength be his strength. Thy members, O Ra, are established by this Chapter.

The series of names in the following invocation refers to magically transfigured names of the Egyptian gods Osiris and Seth.

O Oualbpaga!
O Kammara!
O Kamalo!
O Karhenmon!
O Amagaaa!

Egyptian Mysteries

First at Thebes and then at Memphis, the Egyptian mystery cults flourished. As in the Greek and Mithraic cults, the candidate for admission into the Egyptian mysteries had to prove himself worthy of the honor. A long series of tests awaited him, and failure on a particular test of intelligence, character, or courage meant total failure. Before being allowed to undertake to pass the first test, he had to have authorization from the congress of sacred colleges. The initial test seems to have been one that only a man of exceptional strength of character could pass. The candidate could decide at this stage to abandon the attempt to win admission or to continue at the risk of being killed if he learned the first occult symbols and then failed to pass any one of the subsequent tests.

Plato is supposed to have been one of the foreigners who passed the tests and was initiated into the mysteries of Hermes-Thoth at Memphis. Proclus says that he devoted 13 years to the effort, working with four Magi. Thales and Pythagoras were also initiates. In his book on the mystery cults, Iamblichus, the Syrian Neoplatonist, gave a description of the tests. They took place in sacred caves entered through a bronze door set between the front paws of the Sphinx of Gizeh. The door was opened by means of a secret spring. The candidate was met at the door by two elderly initiates, the Thesmothetes, or guardians of the rites, and conducted, blindfolded, past a second bronze door and along a winding stairway to a circular room.

There a trapdoor opened on creaking hinges, revealing a figure holding a scythe. As the candidate's blindfold was removed, he heard these words: "Damned be he who comes to disturb the peace of the dead." The Thesmothetes stood beside him, dressed in white garments; one wore a gold belt symbolizing the sun, the other a silver belt symbolizing the moon. One had his face covered with the mask of a lion, the symbol of the throne of the sun; the other wore the mask of a bull, symbolizing the zodiacal sign in which the moon is most powerful. The inner symbolism signified that the

192

study of the laws of nature is the first step toward supreme illumination and that these laws must be understood and respected before they can be manipulated.

The scythe crossed the candidate's head seven times, grazing his hair, before the figure wielding it disappeared. If the candidate had shown no fear up to this point, the Thesmothetes removed their masks, congratulated him, and told him that he was now to undergo a test of the moral quality of humility. Touching a hidden spring in the wall, one of them opened a door leading to a passageway so low and narrow that a man could enter it only by lying flat on the floor. They gave the candidate a lamp and told him that the passageway led to an inner sanctuary where he would receive knowledge and power in exchange for humility. They told him that the passageway symbolized the tomb through which mankind must pass before awakening from the night of material life to the life of the spirit. They offered words of encouragement, telling him to go and triumph over the horrors of the tomb. If the candidate was unable to endure the test, they bound his eyes and led him back to the starting point. If he elected to continue the tests, they gave him the kiss of peace. A door closed behind him as a distant voice proclaimed: "All fools who covet knowledge and power perish here!" An acoustical arrangement caused the message to be repeated seven times.

The hierophants who organized the tests were masters of psychology. Solitude, ominous echoes and repetitions, the terror of darkness, crawling through a strange, narrow tunnel—all of these factors could create a state of mind resembling the anguish of death.

The candidate who continued crawling through the narrow passageway realized that he was going deeper and deeper under the ground. Then he came to the mouth of a huge crater. An iron ladder consisting of 78 rungs took him deep into the crater. When he reached the last rung, he looked down upon a gaping black well and faced a hard choice. Should he continue his course toward total oblivion or again face death in the tunnel? The successful candidate climbed back up the ladder and discovered along the way an opening large enough for him to pass through and follow a 22-step spiral stairway to a bronze lattice through which could be seen a gallery lined on each side with 17 sculptured sphinxes. The walls were painted with symbols and representations of strange creatures. Oil and incense burned in 11 sphinx-shaped crystal lamps placed on 11 bronze tripods in the center of the gallery. He went into the gallery and was welcomed by a Magus, who assured him that he had passed the well test and discovered the way of wisdom. He received the key to power in the form of an explanation of the meaning and symbolism of the paintings and hieroglyphs in the gallery. The key to knowledge and the source of all power, the magus told him, are contained in the 22 hieroglyphs or Arcana. The letters of the sacred language and the numbers linked with them form correspondences with the arcana and represent a spiritual, physical, or intellectual reality. Expressed in visual images, the arcana constitute the law that governs human activity in accordance with certain spiritual, mental, and material forces. The sun of these forces is called life.

Other tests awaited the candidate who had learned the meaning of the arcana. He was led into a long, narrow cave. At the end of the cave was a burning furnace. If he retreated in the face of what seemed to be certain death, the Magus told him that death frightens only imperfect beings and asked him, "If you are afraid, what are you doing here?" The door between the candidate and the gallery closed with a loud noise as he moved toward the flames and discovered that they were only an optical illusion, created by placing small piles of wood on an iron grating. He had still to pass through deep water that threatened to drown him and to grasp a metal ring held between the jaws of a sculptured lion. He was again blindfolded and led through passageways underneath the Sphinx to the Great Pyramid, where the members of the Sacred College awaited him. On the walls of a crypt in the middle of the pyramid were painted symbols of the teachings of Hermes-Thoth, the Illuminated. Above each symbol was its explanation, in a language known only to the initiates. These were the keys to all knowledge and wisdom.

On a silver throne in the middle of the semicircle formed by white-robed priests was the Hierophant or Master, and behind him, a huge statue of Isis, the Mother Goddess of Egypt. On a huge silver table in the center of the crypt was a complicated planisphere. The candidate had to be able to cast a horoscope with absolute accuracy before becoming an initiate. Before undertaking this supreme test, however, he had to swear never to reveal what had happened on that night. After he had taken the oath, his blindfold was removed and he saw himself surrounded by the Magi, their drawn swords symbolizing human justice. The Hierophant explained to him that human justice is often fallible and that an initiate should be assured of divine justice. Consequently the next test was one in which only divine intervention could save him. He was offered two cups, one containing wine and the other poison, he was told. If he was unable to choose between the two, he was locked up for seven months in a cell inside the pyramid and given materials to study (maxims of Hermes-Thoth). If he passed the test when given another opportunity, he became a Zealot but could never rise above that grade. If he failed again, he went back to his cell for seven more months. The pro-

195

cedure continued until he passed the test or died. The candidate who succeeded in making a choice the first time was told that neither cup contained poison.

The final and most dangerous test was carried out in sensuous surroundings. The beautiful daughters of the Magi danced provocatively and tried to entice him to choose one of them. If he showed any sign of weakness, he was judged to have profaned the sacred mysteries and killed on the spot. If he resisted the temptation of the flesh, he was told that he could return to the outer world or live with the Magi. If he chose to remain with them, he might rise through the nine grades of the hierarchy: Zealot, Theoricus, Practicus, Philosophus, Adept Minor, Adept Major, Liberated Adept, Master of the Temple, and Magus of the Rosy Cross.

Eheieh
One of the Mystic Names used to summon demons.

Eight
The number associated with regeneration. The Old Testament specifies circumcision on the eighth day of a child's life. Many baptistries are eight-sided. In astrology, the eighth house is the house of death.

Eight Trigrams (Pakua)
The arrangements of divided and undivided lines forming the basis of *I Ching*. These trigrams symbolize the eight fundamental elements of the universe and the attributes associated with them: Ch'ien is Heaven, father, strength; K'un is Earth, mother, docility; Chen is thunder, the eldest son, movement; Sun is wood and wind, the eldest daughter, penetration; K'an is water and the moon, the second son, danger; Li is fire and sun, the second daughter, brightness; Ken is the mountain, the youngest son, stand-still; Tui is the marsh, the youngest daughter, pleasure.

El

Before the Mosaic period the Hebraic tribes used the term *el* to designate the holy power. Similar terms in other languages: *ilu* in Babylonian, *ilah* in Arabic, corresponding to Latin *numen* and the *mana* of Polynesians.

El

One of the Nine Mystic Names used to summon demons.

El Adonai Tzabaoth

One of the Nine Mystic Names used to summon demons.

Elder

A plant long associated with sorcery. Gypsies use its bark in preparing a remedy for erysipelas, mixing it with the blood of a bullfinch and putting the mixture on a cloth which then is used to bind the eyes.

> From the earliest times among the Northern races the Lady Elder . . . had an unearthly, ghostly reputation. Growing in lonely, gloomy places its form and the smell of its flowers seemed repulsive, so that it was associated with death, and some derived its name from Frau Holle, the sorceress and goddess of death. . . . The ancestors of the Poles were accustomed to bury all their sins and sorrows under elder, thinking that they thereby gave to the lower what properly belonged to it. . . . On the other hand, Elder had certain protective and healing virtues. Hung before a stable door it warded off witchcraft, and he who planted it conciliated evil spirits. And if a twig of it were planted on a grave and it grew, that was a sign that the soul of the deceased was happy. In a very curious and rare work, entitled "Blockesberge Berichtung" (Leipzig, 1669), by John Praetorius, devoted to "the Witch-ride and Sorcery-Sabbath," the author tells us that witches make great use of nine special herbs. . . . Among these is *Elder,* of which the peasants make wreaths, which, if they

wear on Walpurgis night, they can see the sorceresses as they sweep through the air on their brooms.—(Charles Leland.)

Elder Tree
Many operations involving sorcery are associated with the elder tree. A Gypsy expression, *yakori bengeskro*, means "Devil's Eye" and applies to the berries of the tree.

Elementals
In occultism, four classes of beings: undines who inhabit water, gnomes who dwell in the earth, salamanders who live in fire, and sylphs who inhabit the air.

Eleusinian Mysteries
The greatest of the Greek mysteries. Though the secret rites are not known in detail, they probably symbolized the myth of Demeter, the goddess of grain. They were held in spring and September, following a long period of enforced purification and preparation, and became an allegory of the soul of man as he came to birth, lived, and died. Following the descent of the soul into Hades and its release came the climactic viewing of secret symbols. Also embodied in the festival was the depiction of the rape of Persephone, her mother's sorrow, and the final reconciliation. See Greek Mysteries.

Elixir of Life
Alchemists and mystics searched for a universal medicine and the renewal of youth. They called the object of their search the elixir of life. Trithemius as he lay dying dictated a formula for concocting the elixir. Among its ingredients are calomel, gentian, aniseed, nard, cinnamon, tartar, coral, nace, and wine or brodium. Eugenius Philalethes also offered a recipe:

Ten parts of coelestiall slime; separate the male from the

female, and each afterwards from its own earth, physically, mark you, and with no violence. Conjoin after separation in due, harmonic vital proportion; and straightaway, the Soul descending from the pyroplastic sphere, shall restore, by a mirific embrace, its dead and deserted body. Proceed according to the Volcanico magica theory, till they are exalted into the Fifth Metaphysical Rota. This is that world-renowned medicine, whereof so many have scribbled, which, notwithstanding, so few have known.

Eliphas Levi's own death casts doubt on the recipe which he copied from Cagliostro:

A retreat of forty days, after the manner of a jubilee, must be made once in every fifty years, beginning during the full moon of May in the company of one faithful person only. It must also be a fast of forty days, drinking Maydew—collecting from sprouting corn with a cloth of pure white linen—and eating new and tender herbs. The repast should begin with a large glass of dew and end with a biscuit or crust of bread. There should be slight bleeding on the seventeenth day. Balm of Azoth with a dose of six drops and increasing by two drops daily till the end of the thirty-second day. At the dawn which follows thereafter renew the slight bleeding; then take to your bed and remain in it till the end of the fortieth day.

On the first awakening after the bleeding, take the first grain of Universal Medicine. A swoon of three hours will be followed by convulsions, sweats and much purging, necessitating a change both of bed and linen. At this stage a broth of lean beef must be taken, seasoned with rice, sage, valerian, vervain and balm. On the day following take the second grain of Universal Medicine, which is Astral Mercury combined with Sulphur of Gold. On the next day have a warm bath. On the thirty-sixth day drink a glass of Egyptian wine, and on the thirty-seventh take the third and last grain of Universal Medicine. A profound sleep will follow, during which the hair, teeth, nails and skin will be renewed. The prescription for the thirty-eighth day is another warm bath, steeping aromatic herbs in the water, of the same kind as those specified for the broth. On the thirty-ninth day drink ten drops of Elixir of Acharat in two spoonsful of red wine. The work will be finished on the fortieth day, and the aged man will be renewed in youth.

Elves

Scandinavian fairies. They live underground, work mischief, and cause sickness and accidents. The elf king who rules them is extremely ugly.

The Danes consider the elves to be rebel angels who were cast out of heaven, or the offspring of Lilith and Adam. The Irish believe that they cause cattle to sicken by shooting into them small arrows.

Embalming

The ancient Egyptians believed that the gods would visit a mummy and assure the deceased of everlasting life. Convinced that the body must be kept intact if a man was to achieve eternal life, they preserved bodies by baking them, at first, in the sun or near a small fire. Later they used spices, honey, and sweet-smelling ingredients to embalm bodies.

Emerald Table

A tablet of emerald on which are engraved Phoenician characters. It is said to have been discovered by Abraham's wife Sarah (or by Alexander the Great) in a cave, where it was held by the lifeless fingers of Hermes Trismegistus. Hermes Thrice Greatest was reputed to be the grandson of

200

Adam and the builder of the Egyptian pyramids. The Emerald Table is supposed to be extremely mysterious. No two translations of the Latin version which has been known since the eleventh century, or of the earlier Arabic versions, seem to agree. The opening sentence of the Latin version states the occult doctrine of "as below, so above," which is the foundation of astrology and a key element of cabalistic lore: quod superius est sicut quod inferius et quod inferius est sicut superius ad perpetranda miracula rei unius ("that which is above is like that which is below and that which is below is like that which is above, to achieve the wonders of the one thing").

The brief document, unanimously accepted as being in accord with the spirit of the Hermetic tradition and first mentioned in an eighth-century text by Jâbir ibn Hayyân, summarizes the meaning and structure of the alchemical work. The following translation is from the Latin version (*Tabula Smaragdina*).

> Without doubt that which is above is like that which is below and that which is below is like that which is above, to achieve the wonders of the one thing. All things proceed from One alone by meditation on One alone; similarly, by adaptation they are born from this one thing. The sun is its father, the moon its mother; the wind has carried it in its body, the earth has nursed it. It has fathered every wondrous work in the whole world. Converted into earth, it acquires perfect power.

Divide the earth from the fire, the subtle from the gross, gently and carefully. It ascends from earth to heaven and descends again from heaven to earth, taking on the power of that which is above and that which is below; that is how you will acquire the glory of the whole world and rid yourself of all darkness. This is the greatest of all powers, for it vanquishes all that is subtle and penetrates all that is solid. Thus the microcosm is created on the model of the macrocosm. Many wondrous applications of this principle are made. That is why I am called Hermes Trismegistos, for the three parts of the wisdom of the world are mine. I have called the operation of the sun *(operatione solis)* perfect.

Empedocles

Greek philosopher and thaumaturgist (c. 493-33 B.C.). He believed in the Pythagorean doctrine of metempsychosis (transmigration of souls or reincarnation) and is quoted as having said, "I remember well the time before I was Empedocles, when I was once a boy, then a girl, a plant, a glittering fish, and a bird that cut the air." He is said to have addressed these words to a number of would-be students: "You shall learn medicines powerful enough to cure disease and rejuvenate; you shall have the power to claim the savage winds . . . , send forth the tempests . . . , cause the skies to be fair . . . , draw down refreshing showers . . . , recall the strength of the dead when he has already become Pluto's victim."

Empusa

A terrifying creature with a vampire's appetite. See Lamia.

Encausse, Girard

Better known as Papus, he was a serious student of occultism. His *Traité élémentaire de Magie Pratique,* published in Paris in 1893, was intended as an introduction to Eliphas Lévi's *Ritual.* Papus also wrote on the Cabala, the Gypsies, and hypnosis. He is said to have predicted the failure of the German attack at Verdun in World War I. He founded a theosophical group known as Isis.

Enchiridion of Pope Leo

A collection of charms, cast in the form of prayers, published at Rome in 1553. A treatise on practical magic, the enchiridion also contains exorcisms, conjurations, and prayers for preparing magical instruments. Most of the symbols it uses are of oriental origin.

Ennemoser, Joseph

German philosopher and student of magic (1787-1854). His monumental *History of Magic* was translated into English by William Howitt in 1854. A physiologist and physician, he set forth the theory that thinkers of all ages have accepted the existence of a spiritual world and power linked with the physical nature of man and showing itself above it. Clairvoyance is a positive condition of the inner life. "In the higher steps of clairvoyance," he wrote, "soars the winged spirit wholly in the super-sensuous region."

Enoch

The seventh of the ten antediluvian patriarchs mentioned in Genesis. The Biblical record relates that he lived three hundred and sixty-five years. This record furnished the motif for two Jewish, post-Biblical, non-canonical, apocalyptic books. Both of them describe the travels of Enoch, under divine guidance, through entire earth and the seven heavens. The divine revelation came to him regarding all the mysteries of heaven and earth. He in turn would reveal them to mankind. The older and larger book, usually designated I Enoch, was of composite authorship, written in Palestine, probably in Aramaic, between the third and first century B.C. It is preserved complete in an Ethiopic translation only, though some fragments of the ancient Greek version likewise exist. II Enoch was probably written in Egypt, in Greek, during the first half century A.D. It has survived only in a Slavonic translation.

In occultism, Enoch is identical with the Egyptian Thoth, the Phoenician Cadmus, and the Greek Palamedes.

Enoch, Book of
See Book of Enoch.

Envoutement
A French word meaning spell. It is used to decribe the magical practice of pricking the wax image of a person in order to injure him in some way. A wax figurine is fashioned, then abused with needles, pins, flames, etc., in the hope that the human victim will suffer pain or death. Special rituals and incantations accompany the sorcerer's actions.

Envy
Like jealousy, envy is strongly linked to the evil eye and may serve as the pathway through which evil spirits enter the body.

Epimenides
Mystical philosopher (fl. 600-400 B.C.). Traditionally Cretan by birth, he may have inspired the verse quoted by St. Paul (Titus 1.12): "One of themselves, even a prophet of their own, said, The Cretans are always liars, evil beasts, slow bellies." About 596 B.C. the Athenian senate once called for the great sage Epimenides to purify their city by religious rites after a plague had ravaged the city and rumors spread that the dead had come to life and spectres were walking the streets. He sacrificed sheep, and possibly human beings, to halt the plague. Years later, about 500 B.C., he again appeared at Athens to perform rites and utter prophecies. He is supposed to have slept in a cave for 57 years and to have discovered on awaking that he had become a superlative philosopher.

Equinox
Magazine published by Aleister Crowley. In 1910 Mac-

Gregor Mathers got a court order to stop publication of the secrets of the Order of the Golden Dawn in Crowley's magazine. Using a talisman from the Sacred Magic of Abramelin, which Mathers had translated, Crowley successfully appealed the order. The talisman he chose was one recommended for just such an occasion. See Gaining the Affection of a Judge.

Ergot
A substance closely related to LSD and known to produce hallucinations. See LSD.

Erichtho
In Lucan's *Pharsalia,* a witch "who had kept on good terms with the infernal powers by squatting in tombs" and who succeeded in making a ghost enter the body of a corpse and provide answers to questions posed by Pompey.

Called the Crone of Thessaly, Erichtho dwelt in deserted tombs, knew the Stygian abodes, and was counseled by the infernals. She withered the fruits of the earth wherever she passed, and she poisoned the air with her breath. She could slay the living and revive the dead.

Errores Valdensium
An early 15th-century treatise which alleged that the Waldensians rubbed a staff with magical salve, flew to the Sabbat on the staff, and kissed the backside of a demon in the shape of a cat.

Esbat
See Sabbat.

Eskimo Souls
An Eskimo belief is that spirits or sorcerers cause disease. In the Polar regions and in Greenland and Canada, the belief is that sickness is caused by the loss of a man's soul. It is assumed to have been stolen or by torment extracted out

of the patient. The shaman then proceeds on a spirit-flight to recover the soul.

Eskimos

Among the Eskimos, the angakok or shaman, the medicine man, performed the functions of tribal adviser, sorcerer, and prophet. With the help of spirits he foretold weather conditions, predicted future events. He could also fashion a figure of human form, composed of bones, fragments of corpses, and endow it with supernatural powers of levitation and malevolence.

In a general sense, the Eskimo believes that Nature is whimsical and unreliable and hence he accepts the concept of "supernatural" phenomena more readily. Hence, too, mountains are endowed with evil intentions: a walrus may have sinister anti-human attitudes. Everything has a soul-spirit— the living form as well as an inanimate object.

Esoteric Doctrine

Occultists claim to possess a body of mystical teachings known to the highly evolved adepts in all ages. They believe that the esoteric doctrine, which incorporates elements of truth found in the aggregate of all the world's religions but only partially in any one religion, has been held since time immemorial by exalted seers who promulgate parts of it to the world when the need arises. See Secret Tradition.

Esoteric Fiction

Imaginative works incorporating esoteric themes include: L. Adams Beck, *The House of Fulfillment;* Algernon Blackwood, *The Garden of Survival;* E. G. Bulwer-Lytton, *The Coming Race, Zanoni;* Rider Haggard, *She, Ayesha;* Lafcadio Hearn, *Karm;* Arthur Machen, *Tales Strange and Supernatural;* Talbot Mundy, *Winds of the World.*

Espanto

Magic fright. It has no serious psychological consequences and no effect on the soul.

Espiritismo

A cult rooted in African and Voodoo practices. It is widespread among black and Spanish-speaking people in the United States. This form of spiritism deals heavily in curses and charms. Master Gambling Oil is used to anoint the armpits of gamblers, essence of Bendover to control minds, and Chango candles to achieve evil purposes.

Ethlinn

Daughter of Balor in Irish magical legend. Believing that he would be killed by his grandson, the king of the Formorians had his only daughter imprisoned in a tower. Balor stole a magic cow from Kian, causing the latter to sire three children by Ethlinn. One of these was rescued from drowning, after Balor had ordered their deaths, and carried to Kian by the druidess Birog. The child, named Lugh, eventually killed his grandfather, Balor.

Eusebius

Ecclesiastical historian (d. 309 A.D.). He credited evil angels with the origination of magic and sorcery, in *Praeparatio Evangelica:*

> The evil angels had sown the seeds of that strange art among men and had introduced every kind of sorcery and magic among them.

Evil

The sacred Persian texts known as the *Avesta* contain a charm against evil. The charm refers to Zarathustra, founder of the cult of Zoroastrianism.

Get thee a feather of the widefeathered bird Varenjana,

O Spitama Zarathustra. With that feather thou shalt rub thy body: with that feather thou shalt curse back thine enemy. He who hath a bone of the mighty bird or a feather of the mighty bird gaineth divine favor. No one, however magnificent, smiteth him or turneth him to flight.

Evil Eye

Superstitions prevalent almost universally attribute to certain peculiarly endowed individuals a baleful influence which brings bad luck to those on whom they cast their eyes. The common people often try to counteract the Evil Eye by wearing special charms or amulets.

Execution of Witches

The number of persons executed as witches is unknown. G. Lincoln Burr estimated in 1914 that at least one hundred thousand victims had been executed in Germany. A sixteenth-century authority told Spina that he had used ten executioners to put an end to a thousand witches in one year. The last witches were executed in Holland in 1610; in England in 1684; in America in 1692; in Scotland in 1727; in France in 1745 (although the death penalty for witchcraft had been outlawed in 1731, isolated executions occurred in 1826 and 1856); in Germany in 1775; in Switzerland in 1782; in Italy in 1791; and in Poland in 1793.

Exorcism

The act or process of expelling evil spirits by means of magical or religious ceremonies, regularly practiced by the ancient Egyptians, Assyrians, and Babylonians. Methods used to drive out evil spirits include words or incantations, flagellation, and sacrificial acts. According to Catholic doctrine, exorcism must be performed by a priest and with the permission of a bishop. The rite is prescribed in the *Rituale Romanum*. Foreign missionaries are still asked in some instances to use the rite.

Methods of exorcism have varied considerably during the centuries. One method, used in the case of a Median princess possessed by the demon Asmodeus, was to mix incense with the heart and liver of fish and to set fire to the mixture, while the smoke fumes routed the demon. In early Christian centuries, priests were the official exorcists, but later on learned laymen were permitted to practice.

The sacred books of the Hindus, the Vedas, contain magic prayers designed to exorcise evil spirits from the bodies of those so possessed.

The Dybbuk is a famous contemporary dramatization of a medieval case of possession and exorcism.

The medieval priest, following prescribed ritualistic ceremonies and formulaic utterances calls upon the spirit by name. Threats too are used, also prayers and maledictions and magic expressions. In the Middle Ages anchorites, saintly men and others were frequently the victims of possession by demons. A large body of hagiographical material, in Latin, is extant, in which many cases of possession are cited and described in great detail. Caesar of Heisterbach, a Cistercian monk who belongs in the thirteenth century, produced a voluminous corpus, still extant, dealing with miraculous exorcisms. His collection, known as *The Dialogue of Miracles,* is full of accounts of many paranormal occurrences: visions, apparitions, diabolic interventions.

In *Antiquities of the Jews,* Josephus, the early historian (first century A.D.), reported a case of exorcism that occurred in the presence of the Roman Emperor Vespasian.

Eleazar put a ring that had a root of one of those sorts

mentioned by Solomon to the nostrils of the demoniac, after which he drew out the demon through his nostrils: and when the man fell down, immediately he abjured him to return into him no more, still making mention of Solomon, and reciting the incantation which he composed. And when Eleazar would persuade and demonstrate to the spectators that he had such a power, he set a little way off a cup or basin full of water, and commanded the demon as he went out of the man to overturn it, and thereby to let the spectators know that he had left the man. And when this was done, the skill and wisdom of Solomon was shown very manifestly.

Exorcism, The Rite of

As prescribed in the *Rituale Romanum,* the rite of exorcism begins with the litany of the Saints, the Pater Noster, two prayers for the demoniac, and a warning to the unclean spirit. Then the exorcist reads one or more passages from the Gospels, puts his right hand on the head of the possessed, invokes the name of God in a short prayer, and pronounces three long exorcisms of the demon, accompanying them by signs of the cross.

All the forms of adjuration and conjuration were laid down in what came to be called *Pheumatologia Occulta et Vera.*

The exorcist was, in a well-washed and cleansed room, or under the open sky, having the preceding morning well-washed his body all over, to enter a circle, but not before midnight. He must be newly and purely clad in a sort of surplice, having a consecrated band falling in front, hanging from the neck, and written over with sacred characters. He must wear on his head a tall, pointed cap of fine linen, on the front of which is attached a paper label, having written upon it in Hebrew the holy name TETRA-GRAMMATON: a name not to be spoken. The ground

210

must be purified from all uncleanness, and well fumigated. He must fumigate the sacred name on his cap, the letters of which must be written with a never-before-used-pen, dipped in the blood of a white dove.

When the exorcist wishes to release a miserable spirit which haunts some spot on account of its hidden treasure, he is recommended to take one or two other persons, properly purified, into the circle with him; so that, whilst he exorcises the spirit, the others may make two different kinds of smoke, one to allure the spirit, and the other to drive it, or any evil spirits, away when necessary. They are to carry each a piece of chalk, and on the four outsides of the circle draw as many pentacles. One of the associates must hold in one hand a glass of holy water, in the other a cup containing the mixed blood of a black lamb, not a year old, and of a white pigeon, not two months old. The exorcist must hold in his right hand a crucifix, and four wax-lingts must be lit within the circle; the staff Caroli standing in the centre. They must then sprinkle the mingled blood and water, all round the circle, and, kneeling down, each must cross himself on the forehead, the mouth, and the heart, in the name of the Father, of the Son, and the Holy Ghost. The exorcist then makes a prayer for the success of their attempt. Scarcely shall this be done when the wicked spirits will begin to torment the unhappy soul which they seek to release; and the adjuration must recommence, saying, 'All good spirits, praise the Lord with us.' At this the poor soul will sigh and complain, and say, 'With me too.' The incense is at the same time to be waved, and the associates to repeat 'Amen!' to all the prayers of the exorcist, which are made in succession. The poor soul will sigh and complain, and say, 'With me, too.' The incense is at the same time to be waved, and the associates to repeat, 'Amen!' to all the prayers of the exorcist, which are made in succes-

211

sion. The poor soul reaches the outside of the circle, but its gaolers hold it fast, and when the exorcist bids it depart to its eternal rest, in the name of the Father, the Son, and the Holy Ghost, the devils set up a horrible raven-cry, croak like frogs, and fly like ravens around the exorcists' heads, but they must not be alarmed. They must have three bits of bread, and three bits of paper, on which the name of Jesus is written, and the instant the demons are compelled to deliver into the circle the treasure, the exorcist must lay a piece of bread and the inscribed paper upon it, that it may not be whisked away again, or changed for something else, as will be the case if this is not promptly done.

Then the exorcist must adjure the evil spirits and princes of hell, Acheront, Ashteroth, Magoth, Asmodi, Beelzebub, Belial, Armagmon, Paymon, Eggson, with their subordinates and aiders, and all present spirits, keepers, and damned souls, in the all-mighty name Jehovah, Adonay, Elohah, Saday, and Saboiath, which is and was the God of Abraham, Isaac, and Jacob, who appeared face to face with Moses on Mount Sinai, who dwelt in the Urim and Thummin—to depart, and that in the strength of Tu Hagiu, Hagiotatu, which the holy angels adore in heaven with singing and cries of 'Holy! holy! holy! Lord God of Sabaioth!' And as the rebellious spirits left their seats in heaven, never to return, so shall these evil ones evacuate the earth in the name of Jesus, Amen!

Then the damned souls will fling in the face of the exorcist that he is a sinner, and in no condition to force the treasure from them, and will mock and insult him; but he shall answer that all his sins are washed out in the blood of Christ, and he shall bid them depart as cursed ghosts and damned flies, and, though they shall still resist, the exorcist shall utter fresh prayers and bannings in all the holy names, cross himself and his companions, who shall

212

during the same, make fresh consecrated smoke, and he shall point to the pentacles and extacles described on paper with various sacred names:—Hel, Heloym, Sotter, Emmanuel, Sabaioth, Agla, Tetragrammaton, Agyros, Otheos, Ischyros, Athanatos, Jehovah, Va, Adonai, Saday, Homousion, Messias, Eschereheye, Uncreated Father, Uncreated Son, Uncreated Holy Ghost, Christ conquers, Christ rules, Christ triumphs.

Still fresh adjurations and prayers are necessary before the cursed spirits will relinquish the poor soul and depart; but the exorcist adds fresh and more terrible adjurations, and banishes them, as cursed hellhounds, into dark woods and fetid pools, and into the raging floods of hell, by the name of Christ and all the Evangelists. He holds up the cross before them, and fresh and stronger fumigations are made till they are compelled to depart, and the poor tormented soul is comforted in the name of the Saviour, and the rescued treasure, of course, is secured for the church, and then all is concluded by hymns of praise and the singing of Psalm xci.

Certain days are laid down in the calendar of the church as most favourable for the practice of exorcism; and, if the devils are difficult to drive, a fume of sulphur, asafoetida, bear's gall, and rue, is recommended, which, it was presumed, would outstench even devils. (William Howitt.)

Exorcist

In the Catholic Church, the second of the minor orders. The duties of the exorcist are "to cast out devils, to warn the people that noncommunicants should make room for the communicants, and to pour the water needed in divine service." Today the order is only a step to the priesthood. In the early Church, anyone who had the gift of exorcism could use it.

Eye of Balor

Term used by the Irish to denote the Evil Eye.

Eye of Horus

Amulet worn by Egyptians to protect themselves against evil forces. Also called *utchat*.

Eyes

A stock popular belief is that a magician can be recognized by the fixed stare of his eyeballs. Adepts hold that rigorous training will develop the powers of concentration to the abnormal degree of efficiency required for the performance of magical operations. See Concentration.

Eymeric, Nicolas

Late fourteenth-century Dominican inquisitor, author of the *Directorium Inquisitorium*. He collated civil and ecclesiastical documents dealing with witchcraft. The handbook states:

> Any magical operation involves abandonment of the faith, apostasy, *by virtue of a pact with the Devil* . . . , so that those who practice magic must be treated as heretics.

Ezra

A famous Cabalist whose full name was Rabbi Azariel ben Manahem. Also known as Azareel and Azriel, he is the author of a work on the Ten Sephiroth. He lived in Spain in the twelfth century.

F

Fabre D'Olivet, Antoine
Eighteenth-century French occultist who attempted to revive the Pythagorean mystical system.

Fakir
A Hindu dervish or worker of miracles.

Falk, Cain Chenul
First-century cabalist, reputed to have communicated with spirits.

Familiars
Attendant demons attached to a witch. They sometimes assumed the shape of a human being but appeared more frequently as animals: goats, lizards, ferrets, moles, birds, dogs, apes. They are identified by names in demonological writings: Phrin, Rapho, Robin, Zewuiel. Agrippa von Nettesheim had a black dog called Monsieur. Jehanneret Reynal-le-Boiteux, a French warlock of the fifteenth century, had a familiar named Josaphat. Oliver Cromwell is supposed to have had a familiar called Grimoald.

In 1303 King Philip IV of France accused Pope Boniface VIII of being a sorcerer and having a familiar spirit. The notion that sorcerers had commerce with demons is deep-rooted, but the concept of a familiar demon who counsels, advises, follows, and helps a particular person to perform magic did not become popular until the 14th century. The concept of the pet demon appeared at the same time as pet names like Berit and Robin. Thus the kobold or fairy of folklore was associated in the 14th century within the popular imagination with witchcraft. By the end of the century the familiar spirit had become a routine accusation in witch trials.

In many instances the familiar was said to exist only as a spirit. When given a material shape, it was described almost always as an animal. The Devil and his demons had long been ascribed animal shapes, perhaps recalling the ancient hunting cults, and as well as the even more primitive notion, prevalent in many societies, that the sorcerer is gifted with the power of metamorphosis.

Leopold, brother of Duke Frederick III of Austria, tried to use Truwesniet, a certain sorcerer's familiar spirit, to free the Duke from prison. In 1326 Truwesniet appeared before the prisoner as a poor scholar but was banished by the sign of the cross.

Familiar spirits mentioned in a number of witch trials had many pet names: Bara, Federwisch, Galifas, Josaphat, Krutli, Oberycom, Raphas, Ragot, and Robin. As worship of the Devil became important in witchcraft, familiar spirits were confused with the Devil. Antoine of Annecy worshiped a spirit named Robinet, who presided over witches' revels.

Fascination
The Evil Eye. Persius, a Roman satirist of the first century A.D., offered a charm against fascination:

> A grandmother or a superstitious aunt has taken the baby from the cradle and is charming its forehead and slob-

ABOMINATION DES SORCIERS

Est il rien qui soit plus damnable,   Ils tirent de leurs noirs mysteres   C'est la que ces maudites ames
Ny plus digne du feu d'enfer,   L'horreur, la hayne le debat.   Se vont preparer leur tourment.
Que cette engeance abominable   Et font de sanglans caracteres   Et qu'elles attisent les flammes.
Des ministres de Lucifer: Dans leur execrable Sabat.   Qui bruslent eternellement.

THE ABOMINATION OF THE SORCERERS

Jaspar Isaac (sixteenth century).

DR FAUSTUS
Etching by Rembrandt.

bering lips against mischief by the action of her middle finger and her purifying spittle: for she is skilled in checking the evil eye.

Fascinum
A phallic-shaped amulet that protects the wearer against the Evil Eye.

Fates
In Greek and Roman tradition, the three goddesses in control of human life. In Greek they were known as the Moirai and in Latin as the Fata: Clotho (Spinner), who spins the thread of human life; Lachesis (Disposer of Lots), who fixes the length of life; and Atropos (Inflexible), who cuts the thread of life.

Fatihat
A prayer found at the beginning of the Koran and used like the sign of the cross to protect a person against evil. It may be written on a slip of paper and carried as an amulet.

Faure, Matheline
See Carcassonne Trials.

Faust
Whether legendary or real, Faust is the prototype of the man who has sold his soul to the Devil in exchange for youth and honors. He practiced magic in Prague, invoked spirits in Wittemberg, and claimed to have ridden through Hell astride Belzebuth. He performed miraculous cures, flew through the air, was cursed by Luther, and was imprisoned. At the end of the pact, the Devil caused him to suffer a horrible death. Afterwards he appeared several times to his faithful servant Christopher Wagner.

217

Febris
In Roman religion, an evil spirit, worshiped in order to prevent her from doing harm.

Feldspar
When worn as an amulet, this hard green stone protects its possessor against sunstroke and headache.

Fern
In European folklore, the fern seed is used to acquire treasures from the powers of darkness.

Fetch
In Irish folklore, a wraith or apparition resembling in every detail the individual whose death it portends. It may be seen by more than one person, including the one who is to die.

Fetish
A material object with magical powers. It may contain a powerful medicine like the urine of a virgin or the gall bladder of a crocodile. It may be a carving, a figurine, or a part of a material object (the tooth or claw of an animal, for instance), and it is supposed to protect its possessor against evil, help him to recover his health, promote fertility, etc.

Fetishism
Any form of belief in fetishes, which are material substances or objects assumed to be the abode of supernatural spirits or powers. The essential idea of fetishism, that spiritual powers reside in material objects, finds expression in the reverence of primitive and advanced peoples for sacred places, trees, relics, etc. The mistletoe of the Druids, the Cross, and great numbers of amulets and charms attest to the tendency to adopt fetishistic beliefs.

The word fetishism is derived from Portuguese *feitico*,

218

which first meant a charm and was applied to relics, rosaries, and images thought to possess magic qualities. Portuguese explorers applied the word to objects worshipped by the natives of West Africa. Fetishism was used by Auguste Comte to explain his theory of early religion. He believed that primitive men could reach the stage of star worship without priesthood. Fetishism, according to him, allowed free exercise to man's innate tendency to attribute to all external bodies "a life analogous to his own with a difference of mere intensity."

Fever Cure
The Gypsies recommend the following cure for a fever: The sufferer goes in the forest and finds a young tree. When the first rays of the rising sun fall on it the patient shakes it with all his might and exclaims:

"Shilályi, shilályi prejia
Káthe tu beshá, káthe tu beshá!"

"Fever, fever, go away!
Here shalt thou stay. Here shalt thou stay!"
(Charles Leland.)

Fever Spell
An ancient Hebraic incantation is intended to banish fever:

Ochnotinos
Chnotinos
Notinos
Tinos
Inos
Nos
Os

Fifteen
In the Kaballah, a sacred number with the power of the

name of God. It has a numerical value of one of the names of God, YH.

Fifty
In the Kabbalah, the number of the Holy Spirit. It was on the fiftieth day following Israel's exodus from Egypt that Moses wrote down the Law on Mt. Sinai.

Finger Amulets
Usually made of the little finger of the right hand, these charms offer protection against evil and attract strong benevolent powers.

Finicella
Witch burned at Rome in 1424. The secular authorities accused her of working with the Devil to slay children. One day she took the shape of a cat and tried to kill a neighbor's child, only to be driven away by the child's father, who stuck a knife into her. Later Finicella was found to have a stab wound in the corresponding part of her body.

Finn MacCummal
In Irish romance, the central figure of the Ossianic tales. The druid who taught Finn science and poetry had been unable to catch the salmon of knowledge until he met his pupil. Finn ate the salmon and acquired the wisdom of the ages.

Fire Invocation
Russian Gypsies invoked fire to punish an enemy. Facing the burning hearth, the speaker recited these words:

> Fire, you punish the evil-doer, you hate falsehood, you scorch the impure, you destroy offenders; your flame devours the earth. Devour ———— if he says what is not true, if he thinks a lie, and if he acts deceitfully.

Fire-walking

In India, Japan, Dutch Guiana and other Oriental countries ritual fire-walking forms part of mystic religious ceremonials. In the South Seas, too, there are regular rites involving walking barefooted over live coals and flaming fires. Monks, priests, villagers are credibly reputed by travelers and observers to have come unscathed from these performances. The practice was known as early as Roman antiquity. A tribe belonging to Sora, a Volscian town, performed this rite twice annually. Authorities and eyewitnesses differ markedly concerning the alleged immunity from burns of participants in the ritual ceremony of fire-walking, common to many peoples and prevalent in all ages. Hagiographic and mediumistic accounts of fire ordeals are found in Oliver Leroy's *Les Hommes Salamandres*, published in Paris in 1932.

First Festival of Occult Arts

In April, 1970, a rock-music center, New York City's Fillmore East, hosted the "First Festival of Occult Arts." Witches and mediums, according to news reports, were among those present.

Five

A lucky number symbolizing completeness. The Seal of Solomon has five points. The five wounds of Christ are known as the Wells of Comfort, Everlasting Life, Grace, Mercy, and Pity.

Flamel, Nicolas

In his pursuit of perfection or spiritual mastery of the human universe, he had recourse to the language of the Christian faith. He claimed that alchemy cleansed him of his sins and made him mild, pious, and generous, "continually filling him with the grace and mercy of God."

Having failed as a public scrivener, poet, and painter, he

221

succeeded as an astrologer. He began to study the magic arts in earnest, particularly alchemy.

In 1297 he lighted upon a manual of the art which would have been invaluable if it had been intelligible. He bought it for two florins. It contained three times seven leaves written with a steel instrument upon the bark of trees. . . . The author of this mysterious book purported to be "Abraham, the patriarch. . . ." He had included within these precious pages a complete exposition of the art of transmuting metals. . . . In fact, the book would have been perfect, but for one deficiency; it was addressed not so much to the tyro as to an adept, and took it for granted that its student was already in possession of the Philosopher's Stone. This was a terrible obstacle. . . . For thrice seven years he pored over these perplexing pages, until at length his wife (Perrenelle) suggested that a Jewish Rabbi might be able to interpret them. From one of the Hebrew sages (in Spain) he obtained some hints which afforded a key to the patriarchal mysteries, and returning to Paris he recommenced his studies with a new vigour.

In his own book *On the Hieroglyphic Figures which He Had Depicted in the Cemetery of the Holy Innocents in Paris,* he relates:

Finally I found the object of my search, and I knew it by its strong smell; and with it I accomplished the magistery. I had learned the preparation of the first agent and had only to follow my book word by word. The first time I carried out the operation, I worked with quicksilver and transmuted about one and a half pounds of it into pure silver, better than silver from a mine. I put the results to the test several times. The event occurred on January 17, 1382, about midday, in my house. Only Perrenelle and I were there. Later . . . I accomplished the operation with the red stone on a similar amount of quicksilver . . . on the 25th day of April of the same year . . . when I transmuted the quicksilver into about the same amount of gold. This gold was clearly superior to ordinary gold. . . . I accomplished the magistery three times with Perenelle's help.

Thus a man and a woman, incarnating in natural fashion the two poles of the alchemical work (Sulphur and Quicksilver) by their spiritually heightened and internalized love developed the power of the soul or cosmos that brings about dissolution and coagulation (alchemical *solve et coagula*). Critics claimed that Flamel used his alchemical studies to disguise the usurious practices that made him immensely wealthy. His followers considered him a great magician and believed that he would live in seclusion for six centuries.

Flammarion, Camille
Famous French astronomer who originated the word psychic (1842-1925). He believed that unknown natural forces "as real as the attraction of gravitation and as invisible as that" were responsible for levitation, telepathy, clairvoyance, and related phenomena.

Fludd, Robert
The chief of the fire-philosophers was generally known by his Latin name, Robertus de Fluctibus (1574-1637). A celebrated English Philosopher and Hermetist, he was a voluminous writer on mystic and occult subjects.

He wrote Mosaical Philosophy and Summum Bonum, treatises in defense of necromancy.

Flying Ointment
Medieval witches frequently confessed to flying to the Sabbat. They rubbed themselves with flying ointment and ut-

223

tered appropriate spells in order to prepare for the flight. Some of the ingredients of their flying ointment were capable of inducing delusions. Recipes frequently included aconite, belladonna, hellebore root, hemlock, soot or baby's fat, and bat's blood. Flying ointment may be traced back to classical times. Apuleius' *Golden Ass* contains the account of a witch who smeared her body with ointment and recited a spell in order to turn herself into a bird. Prierias, Luther's adversary, thought that flying ointment was made from boiled, unbaptized children.

Fontaine, John

Medieval alchemist. A. E. Waite writes:

> The life of this artist is buried in the obscurity of his closet or laboratory, where he divided his time between attention to his furnaces and the composition of curious verses. He was alive in Valenciennes in the year 1413. His Hermetic poem, *Aux Amourex de Science*, has been printed several times. The author announces that he is an adept, and describes in allegorical manner, after the fashion of the "Romance of the Rose," and in the same quaint and beautiful tongue, the different processes which enter into the art of transmutation.

Ford, Arthur

A Philadelphia medium, reputed to be the world's greatest clairvoyant (b. 1896). A televised seance with James A. Pike in which the medium allegedly made contact with the late Episcopal bishop's son, brought Ford into the national limelight. Ford helped to found Spiritual Frontiers Fellowship, an association that boasts membership of more than five thousand leaders from every major faith.

Formicarius

A fifteenth-century Dominican preacher and writer, Joseph Nider, wrote one of the best treatises on the practice of witchcraft in his day. The title means "The Book of Ants."

Forming a Chain
See Chain, Forming a.

Fort, Charles
American occultist (1874-1932) who established his reputation with *The Book of the Damned*. He reported many supernatural incidents and convinced his followers that he was in direct communication with the spiritual world.

Fortune, Dion
Modern English occultist. The founder of the Society of the Inner Light, she thinks that magic is a good way to achieve divine union. A serious student of the Cabala, she has written *Psychic Self-Defence* (1930) and *The Mystical Qabalah* (1935).

Fortune-telling
Using palmistry, crystal-gazing, dream interpretation, etc. to predict the future is a grave sin, according to the teachings of Catholicism, if the aid of spirits is invoked.

Four
Numerologists make four the number of solidarity. It is associated with dullness, hard work, and failure. It is the number of the earth. Because of its connection with lifeless matter, it is an unlucky number.

Four Cardinal Points, Angels of
See angels of the Four Cardinal Points.

Four Elements
In alchemy, the qualitative determinants of matter. Earth, water, air, and fire point to matter's solid, liquid, aerial, or igneous mode of existence. To these four elements the Hindus add ether *(akasha)*, which alchemists treat as the quintessence *(quinta essentia,* fifth essence).

Four Magical Elements

In the words of Éliphas Lévi, the four magical elements are:

in alchemy, Salt, Sulphur, Mercury and Azoth; in Kabalah, the Macroprosopus, the Microprosopus and the two Mothers; in hieroglyphics, the Man, Eagle, Lion and Bull; in old physics, according to vulgar names and notions, air, water, earth and fire. But in magical science we know that water is not ordinary water, fire is not simply fire, etc. These expressions conceal a more recondite meaning. Modern science has decomposed the four elements of the ancients and reduced them to a number of so-called simple bodies. That which is simple, however, is the primitive substance properly so-called; there is thus only one material element, which manifests always by the tetrad in its forms.

Four Secret Sciences

Éliphas Lévi summarized transcendental magic under the rubric "Summary and General Key of the Four Secret Sciences":

Analogy is the final word of science and the first word of faith. Harmony consists in equilibrium, and equilibrium subsists by the analogy of contraries. Absolute unity is the supreme and final reason of things. . . .

Analogy is the sole possible mediator between finite and infinite. . . .

The analogy of contraries is the relation of light and shade, of height and hollow, of plenum and void. Allegory, the mother of all dogmas, is the substitution of impressions for dies, of shadows for realities. It is the fable of truth and the truth of fable. . . .

Analogy is the key of all secrets of Nature and the sole

fundamental reason of all revelations. That is why religions seem to be written in the heavens and in all Nature, which is just as it should be, for the work of God is the book God, the expression of Whose thought should be seen in that which He writes, and so also of His being, since we conceive Him only as supreme thought. . . .

Analogy yields all forces of Nature to the Magus; analogy is the quintessence of the Philosophical Stone, the secret of perpetual motion, the quadrature of the circle, the Temple resting on the two pillars JAKIN and BOAZ, the key of the Great Arcanum, the root of the Tree of Life, the science of good and evil. To find the exact scale of correspondence in things appreciable by science is to fix the bases of faith and thus become possessed of the rod of miracles. Now, there exists a principle and a rigorous formula, which is the Great Arcanum. Let the wise man seek it not, since he has already found it; let the profane seek forever: they will never find.

Metallic transmutation takes place spiritually and materially by the positive key of analogies. Occult medicine is simply the exercise of the will applied to the very source of life, to that Astral Light the existence of which is a fact, which has a movement conformed to calculations having the Great Magical Arcanum for their ascending and scale. This Universal Arcanum, the final and eternal secret of transcendent initiation, is represented in the Tarot by a naked girl, who touches the earth only by one foot, has a magnetic rod in each hand, and seems to be running in a crown held up by an angel, an eagle, a bull and a lion. . . .

Why are these simple and pure truths for ever and of necessity concealed? Because the elect of intelligence are always few on earth and are encompassed by the foolish and wicked, like Daniel in the den of lions. Moreover, analogy instructs us in the laws of the hierarchy, and absolute science, being an omnipotence, must be the exclusive possession of the most worthy.

Fox Sisters

Katie and Margaretta are believed to be the first spiritualistic mediums in the United States. Rappings which they began to hear in 1848 were alleged to be responses from intelligent spiritual beings. Using information gleaned through these rappings, the girls discovered that a former occupant of their house, Charles Haynes, had been murdered. Charges of fraud were brought against them and the wave of interest in spiritualism which they had initiated in America began to subside. Psychic researchers have speculated that the two girls, because of their age, attracted poltergeists. With the help of their sister Lea, they initiated a groundswell of interest in spiritualism.

Fox Tail

Traditionally used as an amulet to protect animals against the evil eye, the fox tail frequently makes its appearance on modern automobiles.

Fragarach

A sword to which the Irish attributed magic properties.

Frazer, Sir James George

Scottish anthropologist (1854-1941). His vast knowledge of primitive customs and traditions resulted in the publication of many works, including his masterpiece, *The Golden Bough,* first published in two volumes (1890) and later enlarged into twelve (1911-1915). He was the first to apply the comparative method to the study of totemism and taboo. His studies are based on the "psychic unity" of man throughout time.

Freemasonry

The history of the fraternal organization now disseminated over the civilized world is attested only since the 14th century but is closely interwoven with the trails of other mystical brotherhoods and linked to a legend that credits its foundation with the construction of the Temple of Jerusalem. Most modern authorities associate its beginnings with the lodges of medieval cathedral builders. The early masons of Britain may have been influenced by Egyptian and Roman mystical societies. The later British masons may have borrowed extensively from continental secret societies, such as the Rosicrucians. The history of modern freemasonry begins, however, with the formation of the Grand Lodge of England in 1717. Though the tenets of modern freemasonry are mystical and lofty, only a few of the higher officials understand these transcendental teachings.

Freya

In Scandinavian demonology, goddess of love and queen of the Underworld. Witches held their meetings on Friday, her sacred day.

Frimost

One of the demons who can be invoked by mortals. He can be summoned only between nine and ten o'clock on Tuesday night. He requires as a pledge the first pebble that the conjurer has found during the day.

Frogs

Associated with witchcraft and black magic, but less important in these practices than toads.

Frogs

Universally associated with fecundity and fertility, in Coptic traditions frogs symbolize resurrection. Frog-shaped amulets help women to conceive.

229

Frum, John

See John Frum Movement.

Fuchsin

A demon succubus known to Johannes Junius.

Furfur

Count of Hell. He reveals himself as an angel or a winged stag with human arms and a flaming tail. He commands twenty-six legions and controls storms. He lies unless confined in a magic triangle.

G

Gabirol, Solomon Ibn

Famous Spanish-Jewish philosopher and poet (c. 1021-58). In his major work, *Fons Vitae* (The Fountain of Life), a Neoplatonic treatise, he discusses form and matter, and establishes a hierarchy of all beings, a graduation which, on each level, shows a more perfect relation between form and matter.

Gaining the Affection of a Judge

A talisman, successfully used by Aleister Crowley in appealing an order directing him to stop publishing secrets of the Order of the Golden Dawn. Directions for making the talisman are contained in the *Sacred Magic of Abramelin*. The following letters are written on parchment:

```
A L M A N A H
L
M A R E
A A L B E H A
N
A R E H A I L
H           A
```

Galactides (Galaricides)

A precious stone, perhaps a species of emerald utilized by

magicians for its power to promote love and friendship as well as its power to make magical writings heard.

Gallgai, Leonara

French sorceress (d. 1617). She was said to have bewitched the queen. Her trial established that she had three volumes full of magic characters, charms, and amulets. She confessed that she and her husband, the Maréschal d'Ancre Concino Concini, had brought sorcerers from Nancy to sacrifice cocks and had consulted magicians and astrologers. She was beheaded and burned.

Galli

Eunuch priests of Cybele, patroness of sorcerers. See Cybele.

Gardner, Gerald

British authority on witchcraft, author of *The Meaning of Witchcraft* and *Witchcraft Today*. He tried to bring together available information on the surviving members of what he considered to be a fragmented cult that had existed since the Stone Age. He maintained that some modern covens stress theology, others ritual, and others occultism. He dressed ostentatiously, cultivated a devilish appearance, and was frequently seen on the television screen. He died in 1964.

Garinet, Jules

French writer on occultism. In 1818 he published a curious book on the history of magic in France. In his book he offered a description of the Sabbat, an account of demons, and a discourse on magical superstitions.

Garlic

Worn as an amulet, garlic provides protection against vampires, witches, and the evil eye.

Garnet

Worn as an amulet, this semiprecious stone wards off evil dreams and helps stop excessive bleeding.

Gaufridi, Louis

French wizard, executed in 1611. He was known as the Prince of Sorcerers. An anonymous writer has provided a copy of the pact which he was supposed to have made with the Devil:

> I, Louis, a priest, renounce each and every one of the spiritual and corporal gifts which may accrue to me from God, from the Virgin, and from all the saints, especially from my patron John the Baptist, and the apostle Peter and Paul and St. Francis. And to you, Lucifer, now before me, I give myself and all the good I may accomplish, except the returns from the sacrament in the cases where I may administer it; all of which I sign and attest.

Lucifer, in return, was said to have signed this agreement with Gaufridi:

> I, Lucifer, bind myself to give you, Louis Gaufridi, priest, the faculty and power of bewitching by blowing with the mouth, all and any of the women and girls you may desire; in proof of which I sign myself Lucifer.

Geber

(fl. eight century A.D.). The first and, by consensus of Hermetic authorities, the prince of the alchemical adepts of the Christian era. His true name was Abou Moussah Djafar al Sofi, but he was also known as Giaber, or Yeber. A native of Mesopotamia, he wrote many treatises which were widely acclaimed. Only a few fragments of his colossal achievements survive. No less than 500 treatises were attributed to the Arabian adept, and enthusiasts have credited him with being for the history of chemistry what Hippocrates is for the history of medicine.

Gematria
A division of the practical Cabala, showing the numerical values of letters and analogies between words and phrases.

Gemini
In astrology, the Twins. The third, northern sign of the zodiac. It is of dual significance, creative and destructive. In occultism it symbolizes the twin souls. Cabalistically, the signs represent the arms and hands of the grand man of the universe, and accordingly the executive principle of humanity.

Genethlialogy
In astrology, the branch that deals with the birth of individuals, whereby a judgment is formed of a person's characteristics from a map of the heavens cast for his given birth moment.

Geomancy
Divination from the configuration of the earth's surface, or from markings and patterns. Topography, crevices, etc. once were the basis for divination. Patterns formed by sand or objects thrown on the ground were also studied, as were markings made on the sand. Geomantic figures constitute an important category of talismanic signs. Sixteen such figures are used in making talismans, each designated by a Latin name: VIA, POPULUS, CAUDA DRACONIS, PUER, PUELLA, CARCER, CONJONCTIO, FORTUNA MINOR, FORTUNA MAJOR, RUBEUS, ALBUS, TRISTITIA, LOETITIA, AMISSIO, ACQUISITIO. They are formed by a series of 16 lines of dots, constructed on paper or sand. Each of the 16 squares formed by the dots has a

234

definite meaning. Each square contains from four to eight dots. The four squares containing four dots are the "mothers." The subject is treated in detail in E. Caslant's Traité élémentaire de Géomancie (1935). VIA, for instance, consists of four dots in a straight line. It corresponds to seeds, streams, July, Monday, and the intestines. It cures diarrhea, anemia, and boils. It protects vagabonds, travelers, letters, everything having to do with roads.

Georgel, Anne Marie De

Fourteenth-century French witch. Catherine Delort and Anne Marie de Georgel, two elderly witches of Toulouse, gave the earliest accounts of the Sabbat. In 1335 they confessed that they had served Satan for the past twenty years. They described the he-goat worshiped by those who attended the Sabbat and many of the excesses associated with his worship. They believed that the Devil was God's equal; he ruled the earth while God ruled the sky.

Before she was burned at the stake, along with seven other witches, Anne Marie said that she had been forced to enter a cult by a giant who approached her one morning while she was doing the laundry. The black-skinned creature had flaming eyes and wore an animal hide. Terrified, she offered to give herself to him, whereupon he blew his breath into her mouth. Subsequently by a simple act of will she was able to transport herself through the air over vast distances to the sabbat, where she would give her body over to a huge goat in return for his teaching her how to work maleficium. Though sexual orgies had previously been mentioned in connection with witchcraft, Anne Marie's testimony is the first recorded evidence of ritual copulation with Satan. The notion of ritual copulation with the Devil, who as president of the assembly and lord of the sabbat assumed the shape of a goat, later caused women in particular to be accused of witchcraft more often than men even though both were present at assemblies.

The Devil taught Anne Marie to prepare ointments and poisons by using ingredients from the bodies of the dead, including hanged criminals. Here again, her testimony mentions for the first time in the history of witchcraft specific ingredients and their preparation, including the use of fat, nails, and hair from the bodies of criminals.

Under questioning by the Inquisitors she revealed that God and the Devil are co-equals, one ruling in heaven and the other on earth. After death the Devil's followers stayed on earth or in the air; as wandering ghosts they tried to lure children into Satan's fold. She claimed that she had hoped to share in Satan's ultimate triumph but now wanted to be reconciled to the Church. Her confession and pleas were to no avail. She was handed over to the secular arm for burning.

Gerbert (Sylvester II)
Consecrated Pope Sylvester II in 999, Gerbert reigned until 1003. A great statesman and scholar, he collected manuscripts of the classical scholars. His fame led Cardinal Benno to designate him as the first of a long line of magician popes. William of Malmesbury added a compact with the devil and the story of a bronze head that gave oracular responses.

Ghirlanda Delle Streghe
The Italian words for ligature.

Ghost
A general name for the visible spirit of a person who has died.

Ghost-dance Religion
An American Indian cult founded on divinations reported

236

by sorcerers. The destruction of the buffalo herds and the harshness of several successive winters caused Indian shamans to have recourse to the spirits and to decree that a return to the days of plenty depended on the slaying of the white oppressors of the Indians. Many of the Plains Indians took up the new cult, which included ritual fasts and the practice of ritual medicine. They participated in secret rituals, dressed in white shirts and buffalo skins. By the time the cult reached the Navahos of Arizona in 1890, it had incorporated the belief that nonbelievers would die while believers would return to life after they died.

Gift of Tongues
See Glossolalia.

Gilgul
In talmudic and cabalistic tradition, the process of transmigration which results in the reincarnation of the soul of a dead person. Though the Talmud describes such a phenomenon, belief in transmigration did not become prominent in Jewish thought until the eighth century. By the end of the 13th century it had found a place of honor in the classical works of Jewish mysticism, which stressed the animation of old bodies by new souls. See Dibbuk.

Gilles De Rais
A murderous pervert (1404-1440). Tried in 1440 in an ecclesiastical court and a secular court, he confessed under torture that he had practiced alchemy and murdered children. A wealthy man and powerful Marshal of France, he was charged with practicing alchemy and magic, of invoking demons, of making a pact with the Devil, and murdering over a hundred children. Demons appeared in the form of serpents or under the names of Barron, Beelzebub, Belial, Orion, and Baron. He sacrificed to the Devil the organs of children or powder made from their bones. Though

many of the charges brought against him were motivated by jealousy and desire for vengeance, Gilles de Rais probably did derive pleasure from the sexual abuse and slaughter of children.

Girard, Jean-Baptiste
One of the protagonists in the last formal trial for witchcraft in France. See Cadière, Catherine.

Girdle, Devil's
See Devil's Girdle.

Glanyil, Joseph
English clergyman and philosopher (1636-80). He served as chaplain to Charles II and defended the belief in the supernatural in *Sorcerers and Sorcery* (1666) and other works.

Glas Ghairm
Scottish spell of particular value to young men engaged in courting young ladies. It was supposed also to open locks and keep dogs from barking.

Glosopetra
A stone to which magic properties were attributed. It is said to have fallen from heaven during a waning moon. It was shaped like a human tongue.

Glossolalia
The gifts of tongues, a phenomenon known to early Christians and widely observed today. In New Testament times ecstatic utterances frequently were unintelligible to the hearers and even to the speakers until they were interpreted by someone with special knowledge or sensitivity. In modern times Friends, Jansenists, and Methodists experienced glossolalia.

Some spiritualists view glossolalia as a means of spirit communication through a human agency. Mediums report the delivery of messages in ancient and modern languages and dialects unknown to the speaker. Some messages are said to come from spiritual adepts in the astral world, others from living gurus, mahatmas, and swamis.

It is possible that the mechanism underlying glossolalia is identical with or similar to that responsible for coprolalia, or an almost irresistible urge to use obscene or scatological language.

Gnomes

A fabled race of small creatures inhabiting the inner parts of the earth. Paracelsus designated as gnomes those beings endowed with the ability to move as freely through the earth as fish through water. They dress exclusively in gray and guard underground mines, caves, and tunnels. Skilled in woodwork and metalwork, they cannot endure light, which turns them into stone.

Gnosticism

A religious system centered in Alexandria and embracing some seventy esoteric sects. The Gnostics took their name from the Greek term for knowledge. Absolute, complete knowledge was at the core of their doctrine. They also posited a series of emanations from the One Supreme Being. Matter was evil. Later, Gnostics adopted magic practices. Notable adherents included Marcion, Bardesanes, Valentinus, and Carprocrates.

Goat

According to popular legends, the Devil's creation, symbolic of lechery. The goat in medieval folklore appears as the symbol of Judaism and the Jewish God. The goat's beard or goatee, a supposedly characteristic feature of the Jewish physiognomy, was also considered to be a physical token of the Jew's Satanism. The Devil, frequently represented as having goat's horns, often took the form of a goat. In this shape he was worshiped by his devotees, who often sacrificed a goat to him.

Satan appears at the Sabbat in diverse forms, but as the Devil himself and as Leonard, patron of witches and wizards, he appears in the form of a three-horned goat. The middle horn serves as a torch to illuminate the area. The sight of the black-crowned beast inspires terror. His long tail covers a face-like rump on which the faithful bestow their kisses.

Goblins
Helpful spirits who protect the English household against alien spirits.

Goethe, Johann Wolfgang
German writer (1749-1832). His interest in the occult manifested itself at an early age. As a child at Frankfurt he made symbolical drawings of the soul's divine aspirations. Later his leanings in the direction of oriental mysticism were evidenced in works such as *West-östliche Divan*. One of his early notebooks indicates that he had more than a passing interest in the life and work of Giordano Bruno. He was also versed in the literature of alchemy, particularly the writings of Welling, Van Helmont, Basil Valentine, and Paracelsus. It may have been while working in his own laboratory that he conceived the idea of *Faust*, the great drama whose immortal theme gives it a preeminent place in the realm of mystical literature.

Goety
Derived from a Greek word meaning "witchcraft," the archaic term designates the black arts or magic.

Golden Dawn
See Order of the Golden Dawn.

240

Golem

In Jewish legend, a red-clay statue brought to life by the famed Rabbi of Prague, Judah Loew ben Bezaleel (1520-1609); hence, an artificial man. Loew brought the statue to life by uttering certain formulas and writing on its forehead the word "Emet," the magic term for Truth or Life-God. The statue returned to dust when the inscription was erased or replaced by "Death."

Golem

See Homunculus.

Gourd

An *obeah* man uses a gourd or calabash containing grave dirt, bones, teeth, etc. to cast a spell. He places the container near the intended victim. If the victim fails to succumb to fear, the obeah man may resort to poison.

Govinda, Lama

A German mystic who became a Tibetan monk. He lives in India and is acquainted with the Great Eastern religious leaders. He has written extensively on Tibetan mysticism.

Gowdie, Isobel

A Scottish witch whose four confessions in 1662 provide a basis for the notion of a thirteen-member coven. She confessed to having met the Devil in the church at Auldearne in 1647, made a pact with him, received his mark on her shoulder, and been rebaptized in her own blood which the Devil had sucked from her.

Sir Walter Scott devoted considerable space to her case in his book *Demonology and Witchcraft:*

Metamorphoses were, according to Isobel, very common among them, and the forms of crows, cats, hares, and other animals, were on such occasions assumed. In the

241

hare shape Isobel herself had a bad adventure. She had been sent by the devil to Auldearne in that favourite disguise, with some message to her neighbours, but had the misfortune to meet Peter Papley of Killhill's servants going to labour, having his hounds with them. The hounds sprung on the disguised witch, "and I," says Isobel, "run a very long time, but being hard pressed, was forced to take to my own house, the door being open, and there took refuge behind a chest." But the hounds came in and took the other side of the chest, so that Isobel only escaped by getting into another house, and gaining time to say the disenchanting rhyme:—

> "Hare, hare, God send thee care!
> I am in a hare's likeness now;
> But I shall be a woman even now—
> Hare, hare, God send thee care!"

Such accidents, she said, were not uncommon, and the witches were sometimes bitten by the dogs, of which the marks remained after their restoration to human shape. . . . The ceremonial of the Sabbath meetings was very strict. The Foul Fiend was very rigid in exacting the most ceremonious attention from his votaries, and the title of Lord when addressed by them. Sometimes, however, the weird sisters, when whispering amongst themselves, irreverently spoke of their sovereign by the name of Black John; upon such occasions the Fiend rushed on them like a schoolmaster who surprises his pupils in delict, and beat and buffeted them without mercy or discretion, saying, "I ken well eneugh what you are saying of me." . . . There were attendant devils and imps, who served the witches. . . . The witches were taught to call these imps by names, some of which might belong to humanity, while others had a diabolical sound. These

BEASTS OF THE BLACK ARTS
Fantastic creatures, half animal and partly human, characteristic of Goya's interest in
magic subjects. A possible reminiscence of Circe's magic animal transformations.
(Painting by Goya, 18th century Spanish artist)
Courtesy of The Metropolitan Museum of Art, N. Y.

The Four Witches
Albert Dürer engraving, 1491.

were Robert the Jakis, Saunders the Red Reaver, Thomas the Feary. . . .

The devil, who commanded the fair sisterhood, being fond of mimicking the forms of the Christian church, used to rebaptize the witches with their blood, and in his own great name. . . .

Isobel took upon herself, and imputed to her sisters, as already mentioned, the death of sundry persons shot with elf-arrows, because they had omitted to bless themselves as the aeriel flight of the hags swept past them. . . . Such was the singular confession of Isobel Gowdie, made voluntarily, it would seem, and without compulsion of any kind, judicially authenticated by the subscription of the notary, clergymen, and gentlemen present. . . .

It only remains to suppose that this wretched creature was under the dominion of some peculiar species of lunacy, to which a full perusal of her confession might perhaps guide a medical person to judgment and experience. Her case is interesting, as throwing upon the rites and ceremonies of the Scottish witches a light which we seek in vain elsewhere.

Gram
In Norse legend, a sword to which magic powers were attributed.

Grandier, Urbain
Catholic priest and accused sorcerer. In 1634 he was tried for sorcery and convicted, according to the authorized account of the trial, upon the evidence of Astaroth, chief of the possessing devils and a member of the Order of Seraphims, Easas, Acaos, Cedon, Celsus, Alex, Zabulon, Naphthalim, Cham, Asmodeus of the Order of Thrones, and two

members of the Order of Principalities, Uriel and Achas. As a result of the indictment and conviction based upon the testimony of these notorious demons, the priest was burned alive.

Grandier was a popular preacher in the town of Loudun, France, but he was not without enemies or jealous rivals. He had been accused of scandalous activities involving women before he was charged with sending devils to possess the Ursuline nuns of Loudun. These nuns had been attacked with a disease which gave rise to the notion that they had been possessed. A rumor was spread that Grandier was responsible. According to some accounts, Father Mignon, his archenemy, conspired with the Mother Superior to discredit him. Grandier was suspected of a leaning toward Protestantism, and a "pious fraud" might enrich and glorify the Ursuline Order. Magistrates came to observe the rite of exorcism. Urbain was identified as the one who had caused the Mother Superior to be possessed by a devil. Despite the fact that much of the court proceedings had been a mere farce, he was convicted after twelve nuns, claiming to be the devils possessing them, named him as the cause of their bewitchment. He was tortured and burned alive. The pact that he reputedly made with Satan is preserved in the Bibliothèque Nationale in Paris.

Great Albert

Magical textbook published at Lyon, France, in 1791. Purporting to reveal "the admirable secrets of Albert the Great, the small treatise contains some instructions for magical operations and some popular superstitions. Noteworthy are certain observations on embryology and astral influences, a discussion of magical correspondences among plants, stones, and animals, along with a table of planetary influences; a book of secrets relating to witchcraft and magic;

244

and an appendix containing some notions about physiognomy.

Great Arcanum
See Arcanum, the Great.

Great Magical Arcanum
According to Éliphas Lévi, the Great Magical Arcanum depends

> on an incommunicable axiom and on an instrument which is the grand and unique athanor of the highest grade of Hermetists. The incommunicable axiom is enclosed kabalistically in the four letters of the Tetragram . . . , in the letters of the words Azoth and Inri written kabalistically; and in the monogram of Christ as embroidered on the Labarum, which the Kabalist Postel interprets by the word Rota, whence the adepts have formed their Taro or Tarot, by the repetition of the first letter, thus indicating the circle, and suggesting that the word is read backwards. All magical science is comprised in the knowledge of this secret. To know it and have the courage to use it is human omnipotence; to reveal it to a profane person is to lose it.

Great Beast (The)
Title of John Symond's biography of Aleister Crowley. *The Great Beast* describes Crowley's attempt to take over the leadership of the Order of the Golden Dawn. Samuel Mathers, the Visible Head, sent a vampire to attack Crowley, who "smote her with her own current of evil." Crowley's bloodhounds were all killed, but he retaliated by summoning up Beelzebub and forty-nine demons to attack Mathers.

Great Conjuration
To help him in the performance of his magical operations,

the magician summons "Uriel Seraphim." One manuscript notes that the demons will tremble from the very moment the conjuration begins.

Uriel Seraphim, potesta, Io, Zati, Zata, Abbati, Abbata, Agla, Cailo, Caila, I pray thee and conjure thee in the name of the Living God and by Him, thy Master and mine; by all the might of the Holy Trinity; by the virginity of the Holy Virgin; by the four sacred words which the great Agla said with his own mouth to Moses, Io, Zati, Zata, Abbata; by the nine heavens in which thou dwellest; and by the virtue of the character said before, that thou appear to me visibly and without delay in a fair human form, not terrifying, without or within this phial, which holds water prepared to receive thee, in order that thou mayest answer what I desire to ask thee, and fetch and bring the book of Moses, open it, put thy hand upon it and swear truth while making me see and know clearly all that I desire to know; appear then, I conjure thee in the name of the Great God, Almighty Alpha, and be thou welcome in galatim, galata, cailo, caila.

Dismissal of the obliging spirit takes this form:

Go, beneficent genie; return in peace unto the places destined for thee, and be thou always ready to come and to appear when I shall call upon thee in the name and on behalf of the great Alpha.

Great Magical Agent
The key to all power, according to Eliphas Levi, is variously termed the Astral Light, Azoth, Magnesia, and the Great Magical Agent.

The Great Magical Agent, by us termed the Astral Light, by others the soul of the earth, and designated by old chemists under the names of AZOTH and MAGNESIA, this occult, unique and indubitable, is the key of all empire, the secret of all power. It is the winged dragon of Medea, the serpent of the Edenic Mystery; it is the universal glass of visions, the bond of sympathies, the source of love, prophecy and glory. To know how to make use of this Agent is to be the trustee of God's own power; all real, effective Magic, all occult force is there, and its demonstration is the sole end of all genuine books of science. To have control of the Great Magical Agent there are two operations necessary—to concentrate and project, or, in other words, to fix and to move.

Great Mother

In *Prehistoric Religions* (1957) Edwin O. James outlines the scope of the doctrine of the Great Mother and describes innumerable objects that testify to her worship throughout the whole of the ancient world, from India and Asia Minor over the Mediterranean world and beyond the Channel Islands, not simultaneously in all places but at some stage in the development of man. Her cult began before the Age of Bronze and continued under the Roman occupation of Britain. Thousands of tiny statuettes with unmistakable pairs of breasts suggest the predominance of the Great Mother cult throughout much of Europe, as do menhirs. These ivory figurines have been found in many different places and indicate that people had many different names and epithets for one central figure that dominated their religious life. The worship of Diana (Artemis, Tana, etc.) is at the root of the witch cult and is a development of the worship of the ancient fertility figure whose true name was held sacred.

In *Witches* (1962) T. C. Lethbridge presents the theory that there was at one time only one Great Mother who, over a period of some four thousand years and an area encompassing all of the ancient world, acquired so many different names and epithets that the essentials of her cult are obscured. The main elements are these: The Great Mother of All made everything. At first she was both Darkness and Light, then she made Light her consort. Though she might choose to show herself only dimly as the Moon and allow her husband, the Sun, to give off more light, she remained always the source of life. She presided over love-making, birth, growth, and death. She was the goddess of life and death, of fertility and destruction. Later she was seen in three aspects—the New Moon, the Full Moon, and the Waning Moon, and worshiped under three distinct names. Conquests, migrations, and fusions of tribes resulted in a proliferation of names and attributes.

In Britain she was called Macha ("Lady of the Fertile Plain") and Cailleach ("Lady of the Forest").

Great Secret
See Arcanum, the Great.

Great White Brotherhood
See Adepts.

Great Witch of Balwery
The name popularly given to Margaret Aiken, a 16th-century Scotswoman who, in order to save her own life, went about the country detecting other so-called emissaries of the Devil.

Great Work
The supreme magical operation. It can be accomplished in one or many lifetimes only by the complete man who has experienced and mastered the totality of the universe. The magician assumes that the universe and everything it contains constitute God, that man is a miniature of the universe, and that man can by a process of spiritual expansion mystically extend his own being until it covers the

macrocosm and subjects it to his will. In completing the Great Work the sorcerer must master the great moving forces of the universe (ten according to the Cabala, 9 for numerologists, seven or more for astrologers) by experiencing and absorbing them into his own being. These forces are magnifications of his own impulses. He requires a powerful imagination, intense powers of concentration, and extraordinary self-discipline. He sets his imagination to work and focuses the whole force of his being on a single idea. According to Éliphas Lévi, "To affirm and will what ought to be is to create; to affirm and will what ought not to be is to destroy."

According to Éliphas Lévi, the Great Work is described in the Emerald Table and is

> before all things, the creation of man by himself, that is to say, the full and entire conquest of his faculties and his future; it is especially the perfect emancipation of his will, assuring him universal dominion over Azoth and the domain of Magnesia, in other words, full power over the Universal Magical Agent. This Agent disguised by the ancient philosophers under the name of the First Matter, determines the forms of modifiable substance, and we can really arrive by means of it at metallic transmutation and the Universal Medicine. . . .

> Now, there are two Hermetic operations, the one spiritual, the other material, and these are mutually dependent. For the rest, all Hermetic science is contained in the doctrine of Hermes. . . .

> "Thou shalt separate the earth from the fire, the subtle from the gross, gently, with great industry. It rises from earth to heaven, and again it descends from heaven to earth, and it receives the power of things above and of things below. By this means shalt thou obtain the glory

of the whole world, and all darkness shall depart from thee. It is the strong power of every power, for it will overcome all that is subtle and penetrate all that is solid. Thus was the world created."

To separate the subtle from the gross, in the first operation, which is wholly inward, is to liberate the soul from all prejudice and all vice, which is accomplished by the use of Philosophical Salt, that is to say, wisdom; of Mercury, that is, personal skill and application; finally, of Sulphur, representing vital energy and fire of will. By these are we enabled to change into spiritual gold things which are of all least precious, even the refuse of the earth. . . .

When the masters in alchemy say that little time and money are needed to accomplish the works of science, above all when they affirm that one vessel is alone needed, when they speak of the great and unique Athanor which all can use, which is ready to each man's hand, which all possess without knowing it, they allude to philosophical and moral alchemy. As a fact, the strong and resolute will can arrive in a short time at absolute independence, and we are all in possession of the chemical instrument, the great and sole Athanor which answers for the separation of the subtle from the gross and the fixed from the volatile. This instrument, complete as the world and precise as mathematics, is represented by the sages under the emblem of the Pentagram or five-pointed star, which is the absolute sign of human intelligence.

Grecian Magic
The theogony and mythology of the Greeks, as well as their literature, sculpture, and history, are imbued with magic. The natural features of the country were dedicated to the gods: Apollo, the sun god lived on Parnassus; Adonis had

as his abode the lovely vale of Aphaca; Zeus favored the oak
groves of Dodona; the Oracle of Trophonius was characterized by the roar of underground waters. Their stories contain many references to magical events.

The power of transformation is shown in a multitude of
cases, among them those of Bacchus who, by waving a
spear, could change the oars of a ship into serpents . . . ;
in those wrought by Circe who by her magic wand and
enchanted philtre turned her lovers into swine. The
serpent-staff of Hermes gave, by its touch, life or death,
sleep or waking; Medusa's head turned its beholders into
stone; Hermes gave Perseus wings that he might fly and
Pluto a helmet which conferred invisibility. Prometheus
moulds a man of clay and to give it life steals celestial
fire from heaven; Odysseus to peer into the future descends to Hades in search of Tiresias the Soothsayer;
Achilles is made invulnerable by the waters of the
Styx. . . .

Medea, the arch-sorceress of later times . . . , became the
witch par excellence, her infamy increasing from age to
age. The same may be said of Hecate, the moon-goddess,
at first sharer with Zeus of the heavenly powers, but later
become an ominous shape of gloom, ruler and lover of the
night and darkness, of the world of phantoms and ghouls.
Like the Furies she wielded the whip and cord; she was
followed by hell hounds, by writhing serpents, by lamae,
strygae and empusae, figures of terror and loathing. She
presided over the dark mysteries of birth and death; she
was worshipped at night in the flare of torches. She was
the three-headed Hecate of the cross-roads where little
round cakes or a lizard mask set about with candles were
offered to her in propitiation, that none of the phantom
mob might cross the threshold of man. . . . Leaden tablets
were buried inscribed with the names of foes and victims,

251

pierced through with a nail in order to bring disaster and death upon them. At this time it became the law that none who practiced sorcery might participate in the Eleusinian Mysteries. (Lewis Spence.)

Greek Demonology

In Homeric times the word demon (*daimon*) was almost synonymous with the word god (*theos*), but the former word was more often used to explain events not attributed to a particular god. After Homer particular gods were called demons even though fate and *daimon* were used interchangeably. This situation led to the use of *daimon* to designate supernatural powers not definitely linked with particular gods. After Hesiod applied the term to those who had died during the Golden Age, *daimon* designated the souls of the dead. Then the term acquired the meaning of intermediate beings—beings halfway between gods and men—some good, some bad. Through the influence of Christianity and Oriental thought, *daimon* came to signify bad spirits only.

Greek Mysteries

The most famous of the Greek mysteries, held at periodic intervals in connection with the worship of different deities, were the Samothracian, the Bacchic, and the Eleusinian. Their origin is to be traced mostly to a pre-historic natureworship and vegetation-magic. All these mysteries had three trials or baptisms by water, fire and air, and three specially sacred emblems, the phallus, egg and serpent, generative emblems sacred in all secret rites.

See Eleusinian Mysteries.

Gregory VII

Eleventh-century Pope. Following a series of political quarrels, Henry IV, Emperor of Germany, had him sentenced as a sorcerer. His fame as a magician rests mainly on his public prophecy that Rudolph would defeat Henry IV. Actually, Rudolph died on the battlefield the sixth time he tried to fulfill the prophecy. Other accounts credit the Pope, whose original name was Hildebrand, with the power of causing thunder to roll from his sleeve and lightning to strike when he shook his sleeve. On one occasion he sent his servants to find a magical book that he had left behind. Though he had warned them not to look into the book, one of them opened it and uttered some words. A band of demons appeared and offered to do his bidding. The servants escaped harm by telling the demons to cast down the wall that obstructed their passage.

Gremlins
Like their female counterparts, the fifinellas, the Gremlins plagued airmen during World War II, impishly causing malfunctioning of planes flown by pilots of all the warring nations.

Gresel
One of the demons who possessed Sister Jeanne des Anges. She managed to drive him out as soon as she understood what he was doing with her.

Grillandus, Paulus
Author of *Tractatus de Hereticis et Sortilegiis* (Treatise on Heretics and Witches), one of the most influential works on witchcraft published in the sixteenth century.

Grimoire
In his *Treasury of Witchcraft* (1961) Harry E. Wedeck writes:

> A grimoire is a manual of magic. Such handbooks, pseudepigraphically ascribed to King Solomon, certain Popes, Albertus Magnus, and other karcists or putative wizards, were highly popular during the Middle Ages.

Among the most notable of such Black Books were: *Liber Spirituum,* the Book of Spirits; *Shemhamphoras,* Hebrew Manual of Magic; *Oupnekhat,* Sanskrit magic manual translated into Persian and, in 1802, into Latin; *Grimoirium Verum,* published by Alibeck the Egyptian in 1517; *The Constitution of Honorius,* attributed to Pope Honorius III, whose floruit was the thirteenth century. This book, first published in Rome in 1629, describes the ritual of conjuration and other occult ceremonials; *Little Albert; Red Dragon; Arbatel, Tonalamatl,* ancient Mexican Book of Fate, containing magic rituals and formulas; *Y-Kim,* ancient and obscure Chinese text on mysticism attributed to fourth millennium B.C.; *Red Book of Appin; Hell's Coercion,* attributed to Dr. Faust; *The Great Grimoire; Sanctum Regum; The Black Hen or Pullet; The Great and Powerful Sea Ghost,* by Dr. Johann Faustus; *Lemegeton,* also known as the *Lesser Key of Solomon.* This is a manuscript, now in the British Museum, describing the demoniac hierarchy. *The Book of Death,* is a volume in which the Devil, during the Sabbat, listed the names of the participants. *The Book of the Sacred Magic* of Abramelin the Mage as delivered by Abraham the Jew unto his son Lamech was a sixteenth century text dealing with magic adventures in a picaresque, novel form. *The Key of Solomon,* ascribed to King Solomon, was one of the most popular grimoires in the Middle Ages, dealing with rituals, the operations of magic, and the requisite preparations for effective consummation. *The Sword of Moses* is a tenth century guide to magic formulas and prescriptions. *The Testament of Solomon* is based on the Old Testament and describes the building of the Temple by King Solomon with demoniac aid and the names and functions of the demoniac powers. *Zekerboni,* a seventeenth century grimoire, gives directions for incantations, spells, and conjurations. Other popular manuals were *Liber Pentaculorum; The Sage of the Pyramids; The Almadel. The Book of Raziel,* still extant, is a grimoire, reputedly derived from the *Book of Signs,* a magic manual attributed to Adam.

Grimoire of Honorius
One of the most diabolical handbooks on magic ever written. It overflows with impassioned appeals to God and pious statements, yet prescribes the most ruthless steps for summoning the Devil: slaughtering a lamb, tearing out the eyes of a black cock, etc. The grimoire probably dates from the sixteenth century. It was first published in Rome in 1670.

Grimoirum Verum
An eighteenth-century French grimoire based on the *Key of Solomon.* It purports to have been published by Alibeck the Egyptian in 1517.

Gris-Gris
Charms sold by many Hoodoo doctors in New Orleans. They are supposed to do almost anything the purchaser desires them to do.

Grossetete, Robert
English prelate (c. 1175-1253). Known as Robert of Lincoln, he is supposed to have numbered among his many accomplishments some proficiency in the art of magic. He was credited with making a brazen head which could answer questions and foretell the future.

Guaita, Stanislas De
Morphine addict and founder of the cabalistic Order of the Rose-Cross in Paris. Stanislas de Guaita (1861-1897) engaged in the celebrated "battle of bewitchment" with the Abbé Boullan. Huysmans became convinced that he, too, was an intended victim of Guaita's witchcraft. After Boullan

255

died, on January 4, 1893, both Huysmans and Jules Bois, another of Boullon's supporters, believed his death had been caused by Guaita. Bois published violent attacks on Guaita and fought a duel with him. Bois' supporters believed that his gun had fired and that they had magically kept Guaita's bullet from leaving the pistol. Guaita died of an overdose of drugs.

Guazzo, Francesco Maria
Early 17th-century friar, author of the encyclopedic *Compendium Maleficarum* (1608). His handbook was intended to expose and classify the practices of witchcraft.

Gui, Bernard
A Dominican inquisitor responsible for classifying types of heresy and witchcraft. Between 1307 and 1323 he burned 632 heretics in Toulouse, France. His guide, *Practica contra infectos labe hereticae pravitatis,* recommends the use of torture in the event all other means of saving a lost soul fail.

Guillaume De Postel
French occultist (1510-81). He became professor of Oriental languages and mathematics in Paris. He was imprisoned by the Inquisition. He wrote *The Key of Things Kept Secret from the Foundation of the World.*

Guna-Guna
Black magic as practiced by the Indonesians, especially at Java.

Gurdjieff, George
Modern occultist. He taught that the body, emotions, and minds may be brought into proper balance through a technique of physical movements, self-observation, and activation of a sleeping conscience.

256

Gwenved
In Celtic religion, the center circle of life. See Druids.

Gypsy Incantation
See Skin Remedy.

Gypsy Sorcery
Charles Godfrey Leland, late president of the Gypsy-Lore Society, wrote in 1891:

> There is not a town in England or in Europe in which witchcraft is not extensively practiced—instead of yielding to the progress of culture it seems actually to advance with it—next to the Bible and the Almanac there no *one* book which is so much disseminated among the millions, as the fortuneteller in some form or other.

Cosmological excitement had sparked a revival of interest in occult arts in general and in Gypsy sorcery in particular. Leland's thesis was that for centuries the Gypsies had been the international purveyors of witchcraft, assimilating and transmitting the accumulated lore of the world's peasantry as they moved westward in their long trek from India through Afghanistan, Persia, Syria, Egypt, the Caucasus, the Balkans, Greece, medieval Europe, and the New World:

> As their peculiar perfume is the chief association with spices, so sorcery is allied in every memory to gypsies. And as . . . there is something more strangely sweet and mysterious in the scent of cloves than in that of flowers, so the attribute of inherited magic power adds to the romance of these picturesque wanderers.

Both the spices and the Romany come from the far East— the fatherland of divination and enchantment. The latter have been traced with tolerable accuracy . . . back to the threshold of history, or well-nigh into prehistoric times, and in all ages they, or their women, have been engaged, as if by elvish instinct, in selling enchantments, peddling prophecies and palmistry, and dealing with the devil generally in a small retail way. As it was of old so it is to-day—

Ki shan i Romani
Adoi san' i chov'hani.

Wherever gypsies go,
There the witches are, we know.

See Davanni, Mule, Nivashi, Pcuvushi, and Zracne Vile. See also Fire Invocation, Love Charm, Quail, Salamanca, and Skin Remedy.

Gyromancy

A form of divination based on spinning and falling to the ground. A person who spins in circles, chants the proper incantations, and falls to the ground may experience an oracular vision. The diviner may divide a circle into 24 segments marked according to astrological signs and Hebrew letters corresponding to parts of the Cabala, then use the information contained in the segment where he falls to make predictions.

Gyud

In Tibetan mysticism, this term denotes ritual magic, a phase in the initiatory progress of a mystic.

H

Haborym

Duke of Hell. He has three heads: that of a cat, man and snake. He sits astride a viper, holding a torch. He commands twenty-six legions and is the demon of holocausts.

Hailstorms and Tempests

Witches confessed that they could raise hailstorms and tempests by enlisting the help of demons who resided in the clouds. The *Formicarius* gives the details of one such undertaking.

A certain man . . . was asked by the judge how they proceeded in raising up hailstorms and tempests, and whether it was easy for them to do so. He answered: "We can easily cause hailstorms but we cannot do all the harm that we wish, because of the guardianship of good Angels. . . . We can only injure those who are deprived of God's help; but we cannot hurt those who make the sign of the Cross. . . . First we use certain words in the fields to implore the chief of the devils to send one of his servants to strike the man whom we name. Then . . . we sacrifice to him a black cock at two crossroads, throwing it up into the air; and when the devil has received this, he performs our wish and stirs up the air, but not always in the places we have named, and with God's permission, sends down hailstorms and lightnings.

Hair

In occult philosophy, hair is considered to be the natural receptacle of the vital essence which often escapes with other emanations from the body. With various sects, cutting of the hair and beard has been regarded as a sign of defilement.

In many religions, hair is given deep significance. Shaving the head signifies humiliation, punishment, or penance. The tonsure dates from the beginning of Christianity and signifies renunciation of the world. In Greece, youths offered hair to the gods at the initiation rites.

Recently, a play titled *Hair* popularized the notion of the advent of the Age of Aquarius.

Haitian Voodoo

Combining portions of magical rites borrowed from Ashanti cults and religious rites borrowed from the Roman Catholic church, Haitian Voodoo is characterized by erotic dance rhythms, occult chants, and the sacrifice of chickens and goats. Until the early part of this century, snake worship, human sacrifice, and cannibalism were also practiced in Haiti.

First divided into two sects, the red and the white, Haitian practitioners now are often merged into one body. The white sect believed in sacrificing only white fowls and goats, whereas the red sect stood for human sacrifice. The former sect was allowed to practice its rites freely. The sacrifice of human beings, "goats without horns," has been suppressed, and adherents of the red sect must let symbolism replace physical acts.

A huge collection of gods and spirits, know as *loa,* participate in different ways in the Voodoo ritual.

Haizmann, Christoph

Bavarian painter who confessed in 1677 that he had twice sold himself to Satan. Through exorcism he managed finally to regain possession of both pacts. In his autobiography he illustrated the seven appearances of the Devil: Satan had appeared to him first as a man with a black dog and last as a dragon. Freud used Haizmann's confession to illustrate his theory of schizophrenia.

Hand of Glory

A human hand especially prepared for use in necromantic practices. The sorcerer took the hand of a hanged man, wrapped it in a shroud, and pickled it in a jar. Two weeks later it was exposed to the sun or dried in an oven.

Hansa

In Hindu mythology, the white goose (or swan), the vehicle of the Asvins and, later, of Brahma. The mystical bird is analogous in occultism to the pelican of the Rosicrucians.

Hartley, Edmund

Sixteenth-century occultist. First called upon to exorcise evil spirits, he was later suspected of casting spells and convicted of practicing sorcery. Convinced that a strange ailment affecting his children was related to sorcery, Nicholas Starkie, who lived at Cleworth Hall, in Lancashire, England, turned to Hartley, the "Kissing Magician." Hartley successfully treated the two surviving Starkie children, but an argument with his patron caused him and all the others involved with him to develop convulsions. One woman accused Hartley of bewitching her, and a preacher concluded that Hartley kissed his victims and breathed the Devil into their bodies.

Hashish

Also known as bhang, kef, and marijuana (marihuana).

Derived from the hemp plant, *Cannabis sativa*, it was studied by J. J. Moreau in 1845. Moreau reported that its effects included feelings of excitement and pleasure as well as the heightening of all sense perceptions and hallucinations.

Hauffe, Frederica

German somnambule who came under the observation of Dr. Justinius Kerner early in the 19th century. Better known as the "Seeress of Provost," she spent the greater part of her life in trance, displaying all the usual somnambulic phenomena and conversing directly with spirits. She had gone to Dr. Kerner as a patient to be treated medically. Failing to effect a cure for her convulsive states, he resorted to magnetism. She developed remarkable clairvoyant faculties, constructed a primitive language purporting to be that of the ancient patriarchs, and described an intricate symbolical circle-system, based on the principle that every person has two numbers connected with his life.

Haunted Sites

In Ireland and in country houses in England, in remote farms and in houses in old European towns, from Vienna to Italy, the traditional ghost is still active. The apparition appears in various guises, sometimes ectoplasmically, or as a dark shape. On occasion only the being's voice is heard, uttering groans or lamentations or curses. The apparition may appear to more than one person at a time, at a specific hour, usually of the night. But in most cases scientific investigators and parapsychologists have exposed the phenomenon publicly as illusions or as circumstances that admit of sober rational and earthly explanation. But there is despite all this an almost continuous flow of accounts that appear to disprove the non-existence of the ghost. Day and hour are given, along with other evidences of the actuality of such manifestations. Such evidence, in most of these latter instances, assume some form of psychic operation.

Questions still remained unsolved regarding the objective validity of all such spirit calls and spirit appearances. What connection is there, for example, in the opening of Egyptian tombs and in the doom that often awaits those who violate these ancient tombs? What relation is there between the opening of Tutankhamen's tomb in 1922 and the fate of the Earl of Carnarvon and Howard Carter? Was it a case of cause and effect? Or were the two situations merely sequential?

Hawaiian Magic
Necromancy, spiritualism, in its essential significance, and other occult arts were practiced for centuries by the Hawaiians. Divination and astrology were also in force.

Hawkweed
A plant that is supposed to ward off demons. It must be gathered by old women walking backwards on St. John's Eve.

Hazel
A tree associated with the god Thor and believed by occultists to possess divinatory properties. The hazel rod, considered the badge of authority of fairies, is popular with dowsers.

Heart Transplants
Some occultists link the lost continent of Atlantis with the first great magicians (Initiators, Superior Ancestors, Magi) whom they credit with knowing the secrets of heart transplants, electricity, nuclear energy, etc. Excavations carried out by Soviet scientists in 1969 uncovered 30 well preserved skeletons dating back almost 100,000 years. Experts from the universities of Leningrad and Ashkhabad reported evidence of thoracic intervention and trepanation. Their reports led occultists to believe that a patient had lived as long as five years after recovering from the operation that

resulted in a successful heart transplant. The library of Alexandria in Egypt is said to contain a papyrus on which is recorded, in Coptic, an account of another successful heart transplant. A calf's heart was said to have been substituted for the heart of a wounded soldier.

Hebrew Alphabet

The Hebrew alphabet consists of twenty-two letters. Much Cabalistic speculation was tied to this alphabet and its three "mother" letters, Aleph, Mem, and Schin. Aleph, for example, corresponds to the number 1, the sign of fire, the heavens, summer, and the head. The seven double letters of the alphabet correspond to the seven planets, the seven days of the week, and the seven orifices of the head. The twelve simple letters correspond to the zodiac signs, the months, and various organs of the body.

Hecate

In classical mythology, a triple goddess, patroness of witchcraft. She is mentioned by Hesiod, the Greek poet. She is depicted as being accompanied by the souls of the dead. Dogs howl at her approach. Her statues were in three forms: as Selene, the moon, in heaven; as Artemis, the huntress, on earth; and as Persephone, Queen of the Underworld. Her name is associated with sinister rites and sacrifices. Her emissaries were a ghastly ghoul called Mormo and Empusa.

Hecate's Circle

See Psellus, Michael Constantius.

Hekakontalithos

A stone used in demonic offerings in occult rites.

Hekau

In Egyptian religion, a magic formula used to achieve the

wishes of the spirit of the deceased. Used as a word of power in sorcery, it protects the sorcerer against the evil intentions of spirits outside the circle around which it is inscribed.

Helena
Companion of Simon Magus. According to his enemies, Helena was a prostitute whom he had met at Tyre. She was the first conception (the Ennoea) of God, but through her conjunction with matter, she had become enslaved to its evil influence and had been in a constant state of transmigration. She had occupied many bodies, including that of Helen of Troy.

Hell, Hierarchy of
See Hierarchy of Hell.

Helmont, J. B. Van
Physician, scientist, and alchemist (1557-1636). A. E. Waite writes:

> This author, so illustrious throughout Europe for his scientific knowledge, and no less celebrated for his noble rank than by the probity of his character, testifies in three different places that he has beheld, and himself performed, transmutation. In his treatise, De Vita Eterna, he declares himself as follows:—"I have seen and I have touched the philosophers' stone more than once; the colour of it was like saffron in powder, but heavy and shining like pounded glass. I had once given me the fourth part of a grain—I call a grain that which takes six hundred to make an ounce. I made projection therewith, wrapped in paper, upon eight ounces of quicksilver, heated in a crucible, and immediately all the quicksilver, having made a little noise stopped and congealed into a yellow mass. Having melted it in a strong fire, I found within eleven grains of eight ounces of most pure gold, so that a grain of this

powder would have transmuted into very good gold, nine-teen thousand one hundred and fifty-six grains of quick-silver."

Helvetius, Jan F.

Seventeenth-century Dutch physician. In 1667 he published a remarkable account of metallic transmutation.

On the 27th December 1666, in the afternoon, a stranger, in a plain, rustic dress, came to my house at the Hague. . . .

Having read some of my small treatises, particularly that against the sympathetic powder of Sir Kenelm Digby, and observed therein my doubt of the Hermetic mystery, it caused him to request this interview. He asked me if I still thought there was no medicine in Nature which could cure all diseases, unless the principal parts, as the lungs, liver, etc., were perished, or the time of death were come. To which I replied, I never met with an adept, or saw such a medicine, though I read much of it, and often wished for it. Then I asked if he was a physician. He said he was a founder of brass, yet from his youth learned many rare things in chemistry, particularly of a friend—the manner to extract out of metals many medicinal arcana by the use of fire. After discoursing of experiments in metals, he asked me, Would I know the philosophers' stone if I saw it? I answered, I would not; though I read much of it in Paracelsus, Helmont, Basil, and others, yet I dare not say I could know the philosophers' matter. In the interim he drew from his breast pocket a neat ivory box, and out of it took three ponderous lumps of the stone, each about the size of a small walnut. They were transparent and of a pale brimstone colour, whereto some scales of the crucible adhered when this most noble substance was melted. The value of it

I since calculated was twenty tons weight of gold. When I had greedily examined and handled the stone almost a quarter of an hour, and heard from the owner many rare secrets of its admirable effects in human and metallic bodies, also its wonderful properties, I returned him this treasure of treasures, truly with a most sorrowful mind, like those who conquer themselves, yet, as was just, very thankfully and humbly. I further desired to know why the colour was yellow, and not red, ruby colour, or purple, as the philosophers write. He answered, that was nothing, for the matter was mature and ripe enough. Then I humbly requested him to bestow a little piece of the medicine on me, in perpetual memory of him, though but of the size of a coriander or hemp seed. He presently answered, "Oh no, this is not lawful, though thou wouldst give me as many ducats in gold as would fill this room, not for the value of the metal, but for some particular consequences. Nay, if it were possible," said he, "that fire could be burnt by fire, I would rather at this instant cast all this substance into the fiercest flames." He then demanded if I had a more private chamber, as this was seen from the public street. I presently conducted him into the best furnished room backward, not doubting but he would bestow part thereof or come great treasure on me. He entered without wiping his shoes, although they were full of snow and dirt. He asked me for a little piece of gold, and, pulling off his cloak, opened his vest, under which he had five pieces of gold. They were hanging to a silk green ribbon, and were of the size of breakfast plates. This gold so far excelled mine that there was no comparison for flexibility and colour. The inscriptions engraven upon them he granted me to write out; they were pious thanksgivings to God, dated 20th August 1666, with the characters of the Sun, Mercury, the Moon, and the signs of Leo and Libra.

267

I was in great admiration, and desired to know where and how he obtained them. He answered, "A foreigner, who dwelt some days in my house, said he was a lover of this science, and came to reveal it to me. He taught me various arts—first, of ordinary stones and crystals, to make rubies, chrysolites, sapphires, etc., much more valuable than those of mine; and how in a quarter of an hour to make an oxide of iron, one dose which would infallibly cure the pestilential dysentery, or bloody flux; also how to make a metallic liquor to cure all kinds of dropsies most certainly and in four days; as also a limpid, clear water, sweeter than honey, by which in two hours of itself, in hot sand, it would extract the tincture of garnets, corals, glasses, and such like." He said more, which I, Helvetius, did not observe, my mind being occupied to understand how a noble juice could be drawn out of minerals to transmute metals. He told me his said master caused him to bring a glass of rain-water, and to put some silver leaf into it, which was dissolved therein within a quarter of an hour, like ice when heated. "Presently he drank to me the half, and I pledged him the other half, which had not so much taste as sweet milk, but whereby, methought, I became very light-headed. I thereupon asked if this were a philosophical drink, and wherefore we drank this potion; but he replied, I ought not to be so curious." By the said master's directions, a piece of a leaden pipe, being melted, he took a little sulphurous powder out of his pocket, put a little of it on the point of a knife into the melted lead, and after a great blast of the bellows, in a short time he poured it on the red stones of the kitchen chimney. It proved most excellent pure gold, which the stranger said brought him into such trembling amazement that he could hardly speak; but his master encouraged him saying, "Cut for thyself the sixteenth part of this as a memorial, and give the rest away among the poor," which the stranger did, distributing this alms, as he affirmed, if my memory fail not, at the Church of Sparenda. "At last," said he, "the generous foreigner taught me thoroughly this divine art."

As soon as his relation was finished, I asked my visitor to show me the effect of transmutation and so confirm my faith; but he declined it for that time in such a discreet manner that I was satisfied, he promising to come again in three weeks, to show me some curious arts in the fire, provided it were then lawful without prohibition. At the three weeks end he came, and invited me abroad for an hour or two. In our walk we discoursed of Nature's secrets, but he was very silent on the subject of the great elixir gravely asserting that it was only to magnify the sweet fame and mercy of the most glorious God; that few men endeavoured to serve Him, and this he expressed as a pastor or minister of a church; but I recalled his attention, entreating him to show me the metallic mystery, desiring also that he would eat, drink, and lodge at my house, which I pressed, but he was of so fixed a determination that all my endeavours were frustrated. I could not forebear to tell him that I had a laboratory ready for an experiment, and that a promised favour was a kind of debt. "Yes, true," said he, "but I promised to teach thee at my return, with this proviso, if it were not forbidden."

When I perceived that all this was in vain, I earnestly requested a small crumb of his powder, sufficient to transmute a few grains of lead to gold; and at last, out of his philosophical commiseration, he gave me as much as a turnip seed in size. saying, "Receive this small parcel of the greatest treasure of the world, which truly few kings or princes have ever seen or known." "But," I said, "this perhaps will not transmute four grains of lead,"

269

whereupon he bid me to deliver it back to him, which, in hopes of a greater parcel, I did; but he cutting half off with his nail, flung it into the fire, and gave me the rest wrapped neatly up in blue paper, saying, "It is yet sufficient for thee." I answered him, indeed with a most dejected countenance, "Sir, what means this? The other being too little, you give me now less." He told me to put into the crucible half an ounce of lead, for there ought to be no more lead put in than the medicine can transmute. I gave him great thanks for my diminished treasure, concentrated truly in the superlative degree, and put it charily up into my little box, saying I meant to try it the next day, nor would I reveal it to any. "Not so, not so," said he, "for we ought to divulge all things to the children of art which may tend alone to the honour of God, that so they may live in the theosophical truth." I now made a confession to him, that while the mass of his medicine was in my hands, I endeavoured to scrape away a little of it with my nail, and could not forebear; but scratched off so very little, that, it being picked from my nail, wrapped in a paper, and projected on melted lead, I found no transmutation, but almost the whole mass of lead sublimed, while the remainder was a glassy earth. At this unexpected account he immediately said, "You were more dexterous to commit theft than to apply the medicine, for if you had only wrapped up the stolen prey in yellow wax, to preserve it from the fumes of the lead, it would have sunk to the bottom, and transmuted it to gold; but having cast it into the fumes, the violence of the vapour, partly by its sympathetic alliance, carried the medicine quite away." I brought him the crucible, and he perceived a most beautiful saffron-like tincture sticking to the sides. He promised to come next morning at nine o'clock, to show me that this tincture would transmute the lead into gold. Having taken his leave, I impatiently awaited his return, but the next day he came not, nor ever since. He sent an excuse at half-past nine that morning, and promised to come at three in the afternoon, but I never heard of him since. I soon began to doubt the whole matter. Late that night my wife, who was a most curious student and inquirer after the art, came soliciting me to make an experiment of that little grain of the stone, to be assured of the truth. "Unless this be done," said she, "I shall have no rest or sleep this night." She being so earnest, I commanded a fire to be made, saying to myself, "I fear, I fear indeed, this man hath deluded me." My wife wrapped the said matter in wax, and cut half an ounce of lead, and put it into a crucible in the fire. Being melted, my wife put in the medicine, made into a small pill with the wax, which presently made a hissing noise, and in a quarter of an hour the mass of lead was totally transmuted into the best and finest gold, which amazed us exceedingly. We could not sufficiently gaze upon this admirable and miraculous work of Nature, for the melted lead, after projection, showed on the fire the rarest and most beautiful colours imaginable, settling in green, and when poured forth into an ingot, it had the lively fresh colour of blood. When cold it shined as the purest and most splendid gold. Truly all those who were standing about me were exceedingly startled, and I ran with this aurified lead, being yet hot, to the goldsmith, who wondered at the fineness, and after a short trial by the test, said it was the most excellent gold in the world.

The next day a rumour of this prodigy went about the Hague and spread abroad, so that many illustrious and learned persons gave me their friendly visits for its sake. Amongst the rest, the general Assay-master, examiner of coins of this province of Holland, Mr. Porelius, who with others earnestly besought me to pass some part of the gold through all their customary trials, which I did, to gratify my own curiosity. We went to Mr. Brectel, a silversmith, who first mixed four parts of silver with one part of the gold, then he filed it, put aquafortis to it, dissolved the silver, and let the gold precipitate to the bottom; the solution being poured off and the calx of gold washed with water, then reduced and melted, it appeared excellent gold, and instead of a loss in weight, we found the gold was increased, and had transmuted a scruple of the silver into gold by its abounding tincture.

Doubting whether the silver was now sufficiently separated from the gold, we mingled it with seven parts of antimony, which we melted and poured out into a cone, and blew off the regulus on a test, where we missed eight grains of our gold; but after we blew away the red of the antimony, or superfluous scoria, we found nine grains of gold for our eight grains missing, yet it was pale and silver-like, but recorded its full colour afterwards, so that in the best proof of fire we lost nothing at all of this gold, but gained, as aforesaid. These tests I repeated four times and found it still alike, and the silver remaining out of the aquafortis was of the very best flexible silver that could be, so that in the total the said medicine or elixir had transmuted six drams and two scruples of the lead and silver into most pure gold.

Hematite
An ore of iron, worn as an amulet to staunch bleeding or ground into a powder and applied directly to a wound. It also cures snake bite and soothes bloodshot eyes.

Henry III
The sixteenth-century French king was accused of partici-

pating in black masses at the Louvre. He was also accused of "sleeping with Terragon," his familiar spirit.

Hepatoscopy
A form of divination by observation of the liver of a sheep. This type of divination was practiced, among many nations, but largely by the Babylonians, Hittites, and Etruscans.

Her
Egyptian sky god whose twin eyes appear on ancient funerary rites. The likenesses of his eyes were supposed to protect the dead and serve as a reminder of the fact that the spirit of the departed was eternal.

Hermes
The Greek god of magic, guardian of herds and travelers, messenger of the gods, and conductor of the dead to the underworld. In Egypt he was identified with Hermanubis and Thoth; in Rome, with Mercury. During the Roman imperial period he was worshiped as a revealer of divine wisdom.

Hermes Trismegistus
Late name of Hermes (literally, "Hermes thrice greatest"), as identified with the Egyptian god Thoth. He was the reputed author of all sacred books—forty-two volumes subdivided into six groups, only parts of which have survived and been translated into English: *Poimandres* ("Perfect Sermon"), the basis of all later Hermetic literature; excerpts by Stobaeus; and fragments from Zosimus, Fulgentius, and the Church Fathers. His name is also assigned to many works on magic and alchemy. He is supposed to have written these magic terms in hieroglyphics: arbakoriph, obaob, abniob, baiax, chenor, ora, oresion, ousiri, pneuamousiri.

Hermetic Chain
The secrets of Hermes Trismegistus were allegedly handed down from pupil teacher to pupil in an unbroken succes-

sion. The ancient Greeks had a mystical tradition of a chain of living beings, reaching from the highest divinities downward through inferior gods, heroes, and sages to ordinary men and the beings below men. Each link in the Hermetic chain inspired and instructed the link below itself, communicating love, wisdom, and knowledge of the secrets of the universe.

Hermetic Egg

The microcosmic reflection of the world egg of Hindu mythology, which symbolizes the generative principle of the visible world and contains synthetically the ingredients from which the material world develops.

Hermetic Philosophy

See Alchemy.

Hermetic Writings

A body of writings, known as the Corpus Hermeticum, attributed to Hermes Trismegistus, who is identified with the Egyptian god Thoth. The writings are dialogues between Hermes and his son Tat or between Hermes and Asclepius. The first treatise in this corpus is called Poimandres. Together, these writings represent Hellenistic mysticism.

Hermetica

A body of literature attributed to the Egyptian god Thoth. See Hermes Trismegistus.

Herodias

One of the names of the divine patron of witchcraft. Herodias was the enemy of John the Baptist. Burchard, Bishop of Worms, says that the pagan goddess of the night-riders of the Middle Ages was also called Herodias and Holda. John of Salisbury says that the ignorant believed that the Queen of Night or Herodias summoned them to meetings by night.

Hesse, Hermann
German-born Swiss writer (1877-1962). Profoundly influenced by his early life in India, he charted a mystical course in a sequence of novels, from *Siddhartha* to *Magister Ludi*. He was awarded the Nobel Prize for literature in 1946.

Hexagram
A six-pointed figure used to control demons. Also known as the Shield of David.

Hexerei
German term for sorcery, first used at a trial held at Interlaken, Switzerland, in 1424.

Hierarchy of Demons
According to *The Key of Solomon,* the three principal infernal spirits are Lucifer, Beezlebub, and Astorath. They are, respectively, Emperor, Prime Minister, and Grand Duke. Then come the superior spirits that are subject to the above-mentioned demons:

Lucifuge, Prime Minister
Satanachia, Grand General
Agaliarept, Grand General
Fleuretty, Lieutenant General
Sargatanas, Brigadier
Nebiros, Field Marshal

These six demons just mentioned direct, by their power, the entire infernal might granted to the other demons.

They have at their service eighteen other spirits subordinate to them, as follows:

Baël	Bathim
Agares	Pursan
Marbas	Abigar
Pruslas	Loray
Aamon	Valefar

Barbatos	Foraü
Buer	Ayperos
Gusoyn	Nuberus
Botis	Glasyabolas

After listing these eighteen demons that are inferior to the six previously mentioned, it is advisable to inform you of what follows:
That Lucifuge is in command of the first three demons, Baël, Agares, and Marbas.

Satanachia controls Pruslas, Aamon, and Barbatos.

Agaliarept controls Buer, Gusoyn, and Botis.

Fleuretty controls Btathim, Pursan, and Abigar.

Sargatanas controls Loray, Valefar, and Foraü.

Nebiros controls Ayperos, Nuberus, and Glasyabolas.

Here are the exact powers, knowledge, arts, and skills of the above-mentioned demons, so that the initiate who wants to make a pact may find what he requires in each of the talents of the six superior demons. The first is the great Lucifuge Rofocale, infernal Prime Minister. He has the power assigned to him by Lucifer over all the wealth and treasures of the world.

Under him he has Baël, Agares, and Marbas, and several other thousands of demons or spirits who are subject to him. The second is the great Satanachia, Grand General. He has the power to make women and girls submissive to him and to do his will with them. He commands the great legion of demons. Under him he has Pruslas, Aamon, Barbatos, and others.

Agaliarept, also a general, has the power to discover the most hidden secrets in every royal court, in every cabinet in the world. He also unveils the greatest mysteries. He commands the second legion of spirits. Under him he has Buer, Gusoyn, Botis, and others.

Fleuretty, lieutenant general, has the power to perform any task required during the night. He also brings hail in whatever area he wishes. He commands a very considerable corps of demons. Under him he has Bathim, Pursan, and Abigar. Sargatanas, brigadier, has the power of conferring invisibility, transporting you anywhere, opening every lock for you, making you see what happens in every home, teaching you every shepherd's trick and wile. He commands many demoniac brigades. Under him he has Loray, Valefar, and Foraü.

Nebiros, field marshal and inspector general, has the power to inflict harm on whomever he wishes. He will find the hand of glory for you, he teaches all the properties of metals, minerals, and vegetables, and animals both clean and unclean. He can also predict the future, being one of the greatest necromancers of all the infernal demons. He goes everywhere, and supervises all the demoniac wiles. Un-

High Priestess

In modern occultism, the head of a witch sect. Mary Nesnick, a 26-year-old Ph. D. in psychology, claims to be the grand high priestess of a 1,000-member witch sect headquartered in New York City. "At this point my whole life is devoted to witchcraft," she told a newspaper reporter in June, 1973. She explained that fewer than one per cent of the applicants for membership in the Algard sect which she heads are permitted to join. She maintains that there is no connection between witchcraft and Satanism. She encourages members to worship the sun and the moon in the nude, concentrating their thoughts on the accomplishment of good deeds only since whatever they do will return to them threefold.

der him he has Ayperos, Nuberus, and Glasyabolas, and others.

Hildegard

German nun (c. 1100-79). Abbess of the convent of Ruperts-berg. She began to have visions at the age of three. She also became noted for her predictions.

Hindu Incantations

The *Atharva Veda,* a Hindu manual of magic, written in Sanskrit, contains many incantations and formulas for achieving desired goals. One spell gives instructions for achieving immortality:

> Immortality be upon this one! He is a sharer of the Sun's everlasting life. Indra and Agni have blessed him, and have taken him into immortality. Bhaga and Soma are with him, carrying him high, to prolong his days.
>
> There will now be no danger of death. This world will keep you, forever, rise up!
>
> The Sun, the Wind, the Rain, are all with thee!
>
> Thy body shall be strong and unaffected by disease. Life will be thine, I promise it; enter this ascending Never-perishing, age-old chariot.
>
> Savitar, the Saver, will guard thee, taking into converse The great Vayu, of the living, Indra; and strength and Breath shall be with thee; the spirit of life will Ever remain. No illness shall touch thee; all Powers are on Thy side.

Another Hindu spell tells how to arouse a woman's passion:

> With the all-powerful arrow of Love do I pierce thy heart, O woman! Love, love that causes unease, that will overcome thee, love for me!

That arrow, flying true and straight, will cause in thee burning desire. It has the point of my love, its shaft is my determination to possess thee!

Yea, thy heart is pierced. The arrow has struck home. I have overcome by these arts thy reluctance, thou art changed! Come to me, submissive, without pride, as I have no pride, but only longing! Thy mother will be powerless to prevent thy coming, neither shall thy father be able to prevent thee! Thou art completely in my power.

O Mitra, O Varuna, strip her of her will power! I, I alone, wield power over the heart and mind of my beloved!

One prescription for gaining a man's love is couched in these terms:

I am possessed by burning love for this man: and this love comes to me from Apsaras, who is victorious ever. Let the man yearn for me, desire me, let his desire burn for me! Let his love come forth from the spirit, and enter him. Let him desire me as nothing has been desired before!

I love him, I want him: he must feel this same desire for me!

O Martus, let him become filled with love. O Spirit of the Air, fill him with love. O Agni, let him burn with love for me!

Another calls upon the power and laws of Varuna, the supreme cosmic deity:

By the power and laws of Varuna I invoke the burning force of love, in thee, for thee. The desire, the potent love-spirit which all the gods have created in the waters, this I invoke, this I employ, to secure thy love for me!

Indrani has magnetized the waters with this love-force.

And it is that, by Varuna's Laws, that I cause to burn!

Thou wilt love me, with a burning desire.

Or a woman may use a spell to acquire a husband:

I seek a husband. Sitting here, my hair flowing loose, I am like one positioned before a giant procession, searching for a husband for this woman without a spouse.

O Aryaman! This woman cannot longer bear to attend the marriages of other women. Now, having performed this rite, other women will come to the wedding-feast of hers!

The Creator hold up the Earth, the planets, the Heavens.

O Creator, produce for me a suitor, a husband!

The husband may in turn use a spell to acquire virility:

Thou art the plant which Varuna had dug up for him by Gandharva, thou potent and lusty herb, which we have uprooted.

Ushas, Surya, Pragapati, all are with me; all will give me the potent force I seek! O Indra, give this material power; it has heat like that of the fire. Like the he-antelope, O Herb, thou hast all the force there is, as the brother of the great Soma.

Magic herbs are useful in banishing sickness and disease:

We invoke and address the magical plants; plants that are red, those that are white, and the brown and black herbs: all these do we invoke! Verily the spirits are in control of the infirmities. Herbs, rooted in the seas, mothered by the lands, fathered by the sky!

Plants and herbs of the Heavens! Illness and maladies coming from sinfulness do you exorcise! I call upon the

280

creepers, upon those plants that bear luxurious foliage. These are herbs that give us life: they multiply by division, they are vigorous, they have strong roots.

O plants and herbs! You have the power to rescue this sufferer! I call upon and adjure you to make the remedy that I shall prepare powerful and effective.

Another charm against sickness is chanted in connection with a talisman made from Gangida wood:

The seers, while speaking the name of Indra, gave to man the Gangida. It had been made a remedy by the gods from the beginning, and a destroyer of the Vishkandha.

Protect us, Gangida, for we look after his treasures, verily the gods and the Brahmanas made him a protection that nullifies evil forces!

I have approached the evil eye of the inimical: O thousand-eyed one, destroy all these! Gangida, thou art our refuge.

The Gangida will protect me from the heavens, from the earth, from plants, from the air; and from the past, and from the future. I am to be protected in every direction!

May the all-powerful, protective Gangida render all the magic of gods and men weak and powerless!

Hindu Talismans

A Hindu talisman is called a Kavac. It corresponds to the cabalistic pentacle. It is essentially a mantra inscribed in a geometric figure called a *yantra*. The mantra is based on the Sanskrit letters and the sounds they represent. The sound of the human voice originates in the secret center of a person and passes through three vibratory phases before it becomes audible as one of the 46 letters of the alphabet. The basic human sound is OM (AUM), the great Hindu

281

mantra, called the *Pranava*. The Brahmin who prepares the talisman first chooses a text (OM or a mantra consisting of any number of letters), then chooses its "support," which is generally a piece of bark from a birch-tree. The color of the bark matches the caste of the person.

Hindu Witchcraft

Even today witchcraft is practiced in some Hindu communities. By condemning socially undesirable traits in the individual, by putting blame for an unfortunate occurrence on an evil spirit rather than a person, and by upholding traditional values, witchcraft acts as a moralizing agent, sustains social equilibrium, and strengthens the traditional structure of society. Accusations of witchcraft usually involve persons who are on bad terms with each other. All accusations are against women and are intra-caste.

Hippomancy

Divination by horses. The ancient Celts kept white horses in consecrated groves. Their movements were observed as they walked behind the sacred car and used for drawing auguries.

Hitchcock, E. A.

An American who in 1857 wrote *Remarks on Alchemy and the Alchemists,* in which he postulated the mystical and allegorical significance of alchemy.

In his remarkable treatise he marshals an impressive body of evidence to refute the common notion that the goal of the alchemist was the chemical manufacture of material gold from commercially inferior substances.

The genuine alchemists were not in pursuit of worldly wealth or honours. Their real object was the perfection, or, at least, the improvement of man. According to this theory, such perfection lies in a certain unity, a living

282

sense of the unity of the human with the divine nature, the attainment of which I can liken to nothing so well as to the experience known in religion as the NEW BIRTH. The desired perfection, or unity, is a state of the soul, *a condition of Being*, and not a mere condition of KNOWING. This condition of Being is a development of the nature of man from within, the result of a process by which whatever is evil in our nature is cast out or suppressed, under the name of superfluities, and the good thereby allowed opportunities for free activity. As this result is scarcely accessible to the unassisted natural man, and requires the concurrence of divine power, it is called *Donum Dei.*

Hocus Pocus
First used by jugglers in mock incantations, the expression was probably derived from the Latin *hoc est corpus,* "this is the body," a phrase occurring in Catholic ritual in connection with the act of transsubstantiation.

Hodgson, Richard
Australian scholar and physical researcher (1855-1905). His major research efforts centered on the investigation of the mediumship of Mrs. Piper, whom he knew through William James. He is reported to have received communications from the controls of Mrs. Piper after her death and to have communicated after his death with James Hervey Hyslop.

Hokmah
The positive, active, thrusting, male force represented by sephira 2 on the cabalistic diagram of the Tree of Life and in Greek mythology by Uranus, the wise god who impregnated Earth, engendering Nature and man. The Hokmah corresponds to the spirit brooding on the waters in Genesis and to the Logos in the Gospel of St. John. Its symbols are

the phallus, the tower, and the straight line, which connects two points. It stands below Kether and opposite Binah in the first triangle of the Tree.

Hokmah Nistarah
These Hebrew words mean "the hidden wisdom" and designate a body of occult knowledge that has supposedly been handed down from generation to generation since the time of Abraham. Published materials do not contain its most profound secrets, which are closely guarded by initiates.

Holda
One of the names of the Queen of the Night, the divine patron of witchcraft. She was originally a Teutonic goddess.

Holly
Long associated with scenes of good will and rejoicing, the plant in ancient times was used to protect dwellings or sites against evil influence.

Home, Daniel Douglas
Famous English physical medium (1833-66). He produced almost every kind of materialization, ranging from rappings and levitation to ectoplasm and spirits. On one occasion he caused his accordion to float in the air and play exquisite music. He toured the United States and Europe, where he attracted many followers. Although he was frequently attacked, never once was he proved to be an imposter.

> Mr. Home is an exhibitor of what are called physical phenomena, but which are spiritual agencies acting on matter. Through him raps have been given and communications made from deceased friends; tables have been raised into the air, or have moved themselves, as it were, from one place to another in the apartment; his hand has been seized by spirit influence, and rapid communications

written out of a surprising character to those to whom they were addressed. . . . Mr. Home's mission seems to have been to go forth and do the preliminary work of restoring faith by the performance of these outward marvels. Till that foundation was laid there could be no faith in higher and more physical efforts. He was the herald of more interior truths. . . .

By circumstances that no man could have devised, he became the guest of the Emperor of the French, of the King of Holland, of the Czar of Russia, and of many lesser princes. . . . Mr. Home returned from this unpremeditated missionary tour amongst principalities and powers, endowed with competence, and loaded with testimonies of the thanks and approbation of emperors, kings and queens. At the Tuileries on one occasion, when the empress, a very distinguished lady, and himself only were sitting at a table, a hand appeared, took up a pen and wrote, in a strong and well-known character, the word Napoleon. . . . My concern only is to note his place in the history of spiritualism, as the herald of a coming restoration of faith in the indissoluble union of the natural and supernatural. (William Howitt.)

Homunculus

A Latin word designating a little man, manikin, or dwarf. The off-spring of the sun and the moon, he was conceived without any sexual union. The idea of man fashioned artificially, using sperm and blood, was popularized by Paracelsus.

Even learned men of the sixteenth century believed human beings with a will of their own could be created from inert matter. Names used to describe such creatures varied: machine-man, robot, golem, etc. In the first century B.C. Virgil wrote of a brass head that answered questions and predicted things to come. Roger Bacon (1214-1292) was reputed to have created an artificial being, and his contemporary, Arnaldus de Villanova, devoted much effort to the task of making one. Albertus Magnus (1200-1280) allegedly created a machine-man so garrulous that it was destroyed by his disciple Thomas Aquinas. Amatus Lusitanus (1511-1561) reported seeing in a jar a homunculus created by the alchemist Camillus.

The Talmud describes one event involving a robot. "Rabba created a man and sent him to Rabbi Zera. When the latter spoke to him and received no reply, he exclaimed, 'You, fashioned by the scholars! Return to dust!'

Solomon Rashi (1040-1105) believed that an accidental combination of letters in the Sefer Yezirah, which two rabbis were reading aloud one Sabbath eve, created a calf. Solomon Ibn Gabirol (1021-1058) was alleged to have created a woman who served as his maid and to have taken her apart to prove to the authorities that she was not a human being. Abraham Ibn Ezra (1092-1167) created a robot which, when ordered to turn about, returned to its material components.

The most important golem by far was the creation of Judah Loew (1512-1609), the chief rabbi of Prague, known as Maharal. Distressed by the hatred toward Jews aroused by the horrible accusation of a fanatical priest named Thaddeus (that the Jews used Christian blood in preparing the Passover mazzoth), Maharal sought guidance from heaven in a self-induced dream and was instructed to create a golem. He used magic letters to create from clay a golem named Joseph. Though he possessed neither articulate speech nor an independent will, Joseph was told that his task was to defend Israel. Maharal's son-in-law Isaac Cohen and trusted disciple Jacob Sassin Levi helped to create the Golem of Prague.

286

One Friday night, during the recital of Psalm 92 in a Prague synagogue, the golem went berserk and began to destroy everything around him. Maharal reduced him to a corpse by taking from his mouth the magic formula that had kept him alive. The giant's remains were placed in the attic of the synagogue. Maharal repeated Psalm 92 in the synagogue after he had recovered the magic formula, instituting a tradition that required the recitation of that psalm twice in the Friday night prayer entoned by Jews in Prague. The legend of the Golem of Prague has inspired several movies and stage plays.

Hoodoo
Name given in New Orleans and the Gulf Coast area to Voodoo or Afro-Haitian Juju after it had been transplanted and had incorporated elements of Roman Catholicism.

Hoodoo Formulas
Countless charms, curses, and spells play a part in the drama of Hoodoo (American Voodoo). To protect oneself against a spell, this formula is supposed to be effective: Bathe in water containing garlic, sage, thyme, geranium water, basil, parsley, and saltpeter, on Monday, Wednesday, and Friday. Then rub your body, first with bay rum and then with essence of verbena and jack honeysuckle. To cause disease in your lover, suck a copper penny while having intercourse with him. He will develop incurable syphilis. To make a man love you, take orange flower water, rose water, honey, sugar, and his name written with yours nine times. Burn a pink candle in the mixture every day for nine days.

Hopkins, Matthew
(d. 1646) Notorious witchfinder. Claiming that he had the Devil's list of all the witches in England, he brought hundreds of suspects to the point of confession by torturing them unmercifully. According to one report, from 1645 to

1646, over a period of fourteen months, he "sent to the gallows more witches than all other witch-hunters of England."

Horned Hand

A sign of recognition used by occultists. It is made by raising the index finger and the little finger while turning down the middle fingers and thumb. It is supposed to make the Devil powerless when held to the light.

Horns

Horns, associated mainly with the great goat of the witches' sabbat, and all forked or two-pointed objects recall the Devil. They deny the One (God) and proclaim the Two (God and the Devil).

Horoscope

Astrologically, the rising sign of the zodiac in which the degree of the ecliptic lies is called the horoscope. Popularly, a horoscope is a diagram showing the relative positions of the planets and signs of the zodiac and providing a basis for predictions concerning an individual. Hundreds of thousands of Americans now buy computer-produced "personal" horoscopes.

Horse

In the witch cult the horse is the symbol of the sun and closely associated with the Great Mother. In his 12th century account of the history of Ireland Giraldus Cambrensis describes the induction of one of the kings of Donegal, who had to walk on all fours like a stallion and later bathe in broth made from the carcass of a grey mare and eat its flesh. Thus magic was used to confer upon him the qualities of a stallion. In India the Kshatriyas practiced the asvamheda or horse sacrifice after the accession of a great rajah. On this occasion the wife of the rajah had to participate in a ceremony of semi-mating with a sacred stallion before it was killed. In Greek myth many gods took the form of a horse to seduce women. Epona, the Celtic equivalent of Artemis, bears a close resemblance to horse-headed Demeter and Hecate. The famous horse goddess, whose worship was introduced into Rome by the cavalry regiments recruited from Gaul, was believed to have been fathered by a man who mated with a mare. The hippogamous idea may have arisen with the domestication of the horse, and it appears in the records of witch trials of the 16th century. A man disguised as a horse was reported to have mated with the women of his coven.

Houses, Classification of

In astrology, Houses are classed as follows:

Individual or Life Houses: 1, 5, 9, representing respectively the body, soul, and spirit: the Trinity of Life.

Temporal or Possessive Houses: representing the temporal status of the native: 2, possessions and property: 6, comforts: 10, honor and credit, position in society: the Trinity of Wealth.

Relative or Association Houses: relating to human relationship: 3, ties of consanguinity: 7, conjugal ties: 11, friendship: the Trinity of Association.

Terminal or Psychic Houses: referring to eventualities, particularly the termination of conditions in the native's life: 4, environment in each period of life: 8, influence of others: 12, hindering influences: the Trinity of Psychism.

Houses, Grouping of

In astrology, Houses may be grouped by direction:

Eastern Houses: Those in the eastern half of the Figure, containing planets rising toward the Midheaven: that is,

289

the third, second, first, twelfth, eleventh, tenth. Of these, the three above the horizon—containing planets which, moving clockwise against the order of the signs, are passing away from the horizon toward their culmination at Midheaven—are considered to confer upon these planets added strength "by position."

Western Houses: Houses in the western half of the Figure—fourth, fifth, sixth, seventh, eighth, ninth. Posited in these Houses, malefic planets are said to be strengthened and benefic planets weakened—particularly regarding their influence on the native's health.

Oriental Houses: Houses which extend clockwise from the horizon to the meridian: the twelfth, eleventh, tenth, sixth, fifth, fourth.

Occidental Houses: Houses which extend clockwise from the meridian to the horizon: the ninth, eighth, seventh, third, second, first.

Howitt, William
Nineteenth-century scholar. He wrote a classic work on the supernatural (*The History of The Supernatural,* 2 vols., 1863).

Hrabanus Maurus
Ecclesiastic and philosopher (9th century). In *De Magicis Artibus* he developed the notion that only God can authorize magical operations:

> Nor for that reason ought anyone to believe that certain men can perform magic operations without the permission of God.

Hsien
Chinese mountain hermits who lived several centuries before the Christian era. They are said to have succeeded in

prolonging life far beyond the ordinary span by means of physical exercises, dieting, and mental cultivation.

The word *hsien,* derived from two pictographic elements, "man" and "mountain," was first applied to men who had retired from the world and confined their activities in the mountains to the gathering of herbs and roots, meditation, and cultivation of their physical and mental powers. They were often credited with supernatural powers besides the prolongation of life: control over the elements, rejuvenation, and the ability to move with great swiftness and to appear simultaneously in several places.

Later, hsien were classed according to their habitat: (1) celestial hsien, who dwelt in heaven; (2) terrestrial hsien, who remained on earth without aging; (3) aquatic hsien, purely *yin* or feminine; and (4) divine or spiritual hsien, demigods who dwelt on the Isles of the Blest.

Huacas
Among the Incas, places or objects worthy of veneration. They are associated with magical phenomena.

Huang Lao
A religious movement which involved divination and alchemy, and which provided Taoism with some of its essential features.

Huebener, Louise
The "official witch" of Los Angeles. Recently she led a witchcraft festival that drew thousands to the Hollywood Bowl. The purpose of the "world's largest spellcast," she said, was "to increase sexual vitality."

Hung Society
A Chinese secret society that has existed since 386 A.D. Closely associated with the White Lotus, it was founded by Eon or Hwui-Yin to spread the cult of Amitabha Buddha

and has the largest membership of any secret society in the world. The initiation ceremony symbolizes the soul's journey through the underworld and paradise to the City of Willows, which is the abode of the gods. Allegorically, the ceremony depicts the experiences of the mystic in seeking to unite with the Supreme Being. The importance attached to the triangle is reflected in the alternate name of the brotherhood, the Triad Society.

Hungan

A voodoo priest, endowed with supernatural powers. A typical ceremony within the confines of the family mingles African and Christian elements. Tables set up on a sacred place are laden with food for the gods. The hungan makes occult signs on the ground, using cornmeal as a marker. Then a bush priest conducts a lengthy ritual, based on the Catholic litany and designed to show that voodoo does not conflict with Christianity. The hungan invokes the loa, to determine the fee to be paid by those present. Sacrificial animals are offered to persuade the loa to take possession of the worshippers. Those possessed by the loa run, jump, roll on the ground, stamp out live embers with their feet, etc. Animals then are slaughtered, cooked, and placed in the house of worship. A calabash filled with their blood is set on the altar. The door is closed to allow the gods to enjoy their meal undisturbed. A few hours later, the hungan tells the worshipers that the loa have finished, and that they may have the food that remains. The whole ceremony lasts at least two full days and nights. A voodoo dance that follows the closed ceremony is open to the public. Observers have surmised that possession substitutes a second personality of the possessed, and that seizures result from innate neurotic tendencies as well as from a cultural tradition that stimulates seizures.

Huysmans, Joris Karl

French novelist (1848-1907). Author of *Là-Bas*, on a Satanic theme. Huysmans declared: The principle of Evil, and the Principle of Good, the God of Light and the God of Darkness, two streams contend for our soul. At the present time, it is quite evident that the God of Good is in eclipse, that Evil reigns over the world, as master. In *Là-Bas* he also describes a black mass celebrated in Vaugirard.

Hydeville

The town in New York made famous by the Fox sisters. In 1848 Margaret, Catherine, and Leah Fox caused their neighbors to believe that spirits were communicating with them by means of tappings—one tap for no, three for yes. These tappings marked the beginning of an upsurge of interest in spiritualism throughout America.

Hydromancy

Divination involving water. The water under examination may be contained in a dish, pond, lake, puddle, or other source.

Hyperboreans

In Greek mythology, a people linked to the worship of Apollo. Herodotus placed them in the extreme north, but legend associated them with a place beyond the north wind, in a region of perpetual sunshine. Some occultists say that before the Flood the world was ruled by the Atlanteans; after the cataclysms that destroyed Atlantis, history belonged to the Celts, Egyptians, and Hyperboreans. The latter have left in the memory of their descendants vague hints of the existence of a superior fair-skinned race that once lived in the polar region referred to as Thule. According to Diodorus Siculus (fl. 50 B.C.):

This northern island is inhabited by the Hyperboreans,

293

so named because they live beyond the source of Boreas (the north wind). The sun shines so perfectly on this island and the soil is so fertile that two crops are harvested every year. . . . The islanders worship Apollo. They are all priests of this god. . . . It is said that the moon, seen from this island, seems to be only a short distance from the earth and that one can distinctly see mounds on it. Apollo is supposed to visit the island every 19 years. It is also at the end of this period that the stars return to their original positions after completing their cycles.

Some occultists believe that Apollo was not a myth or a solar symbol but a hero or Initiator. He came from the north and was supposed by the early Nordic tribes to have the power to travel on a flying arrow, like Bran, or like the Irish magician Manannan. The Hyperborean capital of Thule, according to certain occultists, was a gateway to the terrestrial universe, a command post in the system of telluric currents. Guy Tarade, president of an esoteric French organization known by the letters CEREIC, believes that the two poles of the world were the gateways to the cosmos. The Van Allen belts can be penetrated at these points, which were known to Enoch. Like the biblical patriarchs, who came from outer space to serve as initiators of earthlings, he was an astronaut.

The space travelers known as Hyperboreans are supposed to have possessed knowledge still inaccessible to modern man. Their successors, the Celts, were great colonizers who established their spiritual dominion over the world. They reached the three Americas, Polynesia, and the Mediterranean Basin. In each region they imparted knowledge appropriate to the needs and stage of development of the indigenous peoples.

294

I

Ialdabaoth

In alchemy, the demiurge who lies captive in the darkness of the matter. He is that part of the deity that has been swallowed up in his own creation, the dark god who reverts to his original state of luminosity in the mystery of the alchemical transmutation. In Hebrew legend, he is the supreme archon. The Hebrew word means "child of chaos" and suggests a parallel between Ialdabaoth and Baal, Kronos, and Saturn. In the writings of the Gnostics, he is the evil spirit who created the Lower World.

Iamblichus

Syrian mystic philosopher (c. 250-325 A.D.). He stressed symbolism and ritual in magic in his great work, *The Mysteries of the Egyptians, Chaldeans and Assyrians:*

> Theurgic union is achieved only by observing ineffable ceremonies, ritually performed operations, worthy of the gods and surpassing all understanding, and by the inexplicable power of the symbols known only to the gods.

In Rome, he studied under Porphyry, also a Syrian, who was a pupil of the Neoplatonist Plotinus. Iamblichus founded a school of his own in his native Syria.

He initiated the attempt to construct on the basis of Neo-

Platonism a complete theology encompassing every myth, rite, and divinity associated with paganism.

Iao (I-Ha-Ho)

A mystic name embodying the symbols of the two generative principles. Clement of Alexandria said that it was worn by initiates of the mysteries of Serapis.

Ibn 'Arabi

Master of Islamic mysticism and the greatest enunciator of Hermetic principles (1165-1240), was born in Murcia, Spain, and educated in Seville; he traveled widely, then settled in Damascus, where he spent most of his life. His full name was Abu Bakr Mohammed Ibn 'Ali Muhyi Al-Din Al-Hatimi Al-Qai Al-Andalusi Ibn Al-'Arabi. He claimed to have had conversations with all the prophets and with God himself. The most extensive of his 150 extant works is his 12-volume encyclopedia of Sufistic beliefs and doctrines called Meccan Revelations. He conceived of universal nature as the feminine side of the creative act, the merciful "breathing-out" of God. Universal nature confers differentiated existence on the latent possibilities of non-being, which are longing for manifestation.

Ibn Gabirol

An 11th-century Jewish poet, philosopher, and Cabalist, Solomon Ben Judah Ibn Gabirol, also known as Avicebron, was born in Malaga and died in Valencia. His chief philosophical work Fons Vitae (Fountain of Life) introduced Neo-Platonism into Europe. In his system, universal matter emanates from the essence of God and universal form from His will. All beings are composed of matter and form. Fons Vitae is supposed to reveal some of the secrets of the speculative Cabala.

I Ching

In Confucianism, one of five books (Ching) in the canon

known as the Five Classics. The *I Ching* (Book of Changes, or Book of Divination), traditionally ascribed to Wen Wang in the twelfth century, B.C., is based upon the figures of divided and undivided lines known as trigrams and hexagrams. There are eight diagrams of triplet lines, undivided and divided. These are expanded and doubled to produce sixty-four hexagrams. Each hexagram is followed by a short, enigmatic explanation of each line.

The most ancient of the Chinese Classics is at once an oracle, a philosophy, and a work of art. Confucius is reported to have said, at the age of seventy, that he would spend extra years, if they could be added to his life, studying the I Ching. Hermann Hesse tells of his initiation to the work in *Magister Ludi*. The work originated in connection with a process of divination based on the manipulation of milfoil stalks.

Legend attributes the eight diagrams from which the work derives to Fu Hsi (2953-2838 B.C.). From the markings on the back of a turtle, Fu Hsi is said to have constructed the circular arrangement of the eight trigrams from which the whole system of *I Ching* was developed.

Ichthyomancy
Divination utilizing the entrails of a fish.

Icu
The Yoruba god of death. In Cuba, the *santero* conducts a mystic rite to protect a patient near death from Icú.

Igneous Demons
One of the six classes of demons identified by medieval theologians. They never descend to the earth from the air to have commerce with sorcerers.

Illuminati
An expression (literally, "the enlightened ones") applied

297

in the 15th century to certain occultists. In some instances the designation is restricted to those capable of manifesting sufficient power to produce a luminescent glow in their auras.

Ilomba

In Zambia and Angola, the familiar of a Ndembu man. The ilomba is a water-snake with a human head, like that of the sorcerer. People assume that when the ilomba is killed, the sorcerer dies.

Image Making

Bernardus Guilonis (1261-1331) described the fashioning of two images:

> He made and fashioned two images of wax with lead from fishing nets: moulded the lead: collected flies, spiders, frogs, snake skin, and a great many other items and placed them under the images along with conjurations and invocations of the demons. Then he drew blood from some part of his own body and mixed it with the blood of the frog and offered or gave it to the invoked demons.

Imagination

The channel between the sorcerer's inner impulses and the great moving forces of the universe. The magician must be able to magnify his impulses so as to experience the totality of the universe and subject these forces to his will. He uses many techniques to train his powers of imagination. If he wishes to turn the destructive force of Mars against an enemy, he uses his imagination to fashion a vivid mental picture of the force. He has recourse to incantations describing the attributes of Mars, gestures, dancing, intoxicants, stimulants, sex, visual images of blood and suffering, rage, and devastation. He may even slaughter or torture an animal or human being. As he unleashes his pent-up hatred

298

he becomes one with the force of Mars, controls it by his will, and directs it against his enemy.

Éliphas Lévi treated imagination as the eye of the soul:

Imagination, in effect, is like the soul's eye: therein forms are outlined and preserved; thereby we behold the reflections of the invisible world; it is the glass of visions and the apparatus of magical life. By its intervention we heal diseases, modify the seasons, warn off death from the living, and raise the dead to life, because it is the imagination which exalts will and gives it power over the Universal Agent. Imagination determines the shape of the child in its mother's womb and decides the destiny of men; it lends wings to contagion and directs the arms of warfare. Are you exposed to battle? Believe yourself to be invulnerable like Achilles, and you will be so, says Paracelsus. Fear attracts bullets, but they are repelled by courage. It is well known that persons with amputated limbs feel pain in the vicinity of members they possess no longer. Paracelsus operated upon living blood by medicating the product of a bleeding; he cured headache at a distance by treating hair cut from the patient. By the science of the theoretical unity and solidarity between all parts of the body, he anticipated and outstripped the theories, or rather experiences, of our most celebrated magnetics. . . .

There is one principle, there is one truth, there is one reason, there is one absolute and universal philosophy. Whatsoever is subsists in unity, considered as beginning, and returns into unity, considered as end. One is in one; that is to say, all is in all. Unity is the principle of numbers; it is also the principle of motion and consequently of life. The entire human body is recapitulated in the unity of a single organ, which is the brain. All religions are summed up in the unity of a single dogma, which is the affirmation of being and its equality with itself, and this constitutes its mathematical value. There is only one dogma in Magic, and it is this: The visible is the manifestation of the invisible, or, in other terms, the perfect word, in things appreciable and visible, bears an exact proportion to the things which are inappreciable by our senses and unseen by our eyes. The Magus raises one hand towards heaven and points down with the other to earth, saying: "Above, immensity: Below immensity still! Immensity equals immensity."—This is true in things seen, as in things unseen.

Imhetep

Ancient sorcerer-priest of Egypt. Also identified as Imhoteb, he was invoked whenever exorcism was attempted.

Imperator

A famous control who, according to Stainton Moses, announced his presence on September 19, 1872, and later claimed to be Malachias, leader of a band of spirits working toward the elevation of the human race. This band, or a similar band, is said to have taken over control of Mrs. Piper in 1897. Several later mediums claimed to receive communications through Imperator.

Impotence

Devils acting through witches can, according to the Malleus Maleficarum, obstruct procreation: intrinsically by preventing erection of the penis or the ejaculation or semen; extrinsically by means of herbs, images, cocks' testicles, etc. Acting through witches, the Devil can cause a man to be unable to copulate or a woman to conceive. Witches were likely to exert more power over the procreative act than anything else, and to have more power over serpents than other animals. Witches often used serpents, easily subject to the influence of incantations, to obstruct the procreative act.

> A wizard named Stadlin . . . confessed that in a certain house where a man and his wife were living, he had by his witchcraft successively killed in the woman's womb seven children . . . and caused all the pregnant cattle and animals of the house to be unable during those years to give birth to any live issue. And when questioned as to how he had done this, and what manner of charge should be preferred against him, he disclosed the details of his crime, saying: "I put a serpent under the threshold of the outer door of the house; and if this is removed, fecundity will be restored to the inhabitants." And it was as he said.

Incantatio

The Romans based their magic on the invocation of gods and spirits. The word *incantatio*, used to designate the direct invocation of supernatural powers, derives from a term meaning "to chant a magic formula." The magical formulas used in the incantation were also called *carmen*. Prayers could be addressed to the infernal gods if one who had violated the laws of equity was to be punished. The formula then was called a *devotio*. This was a curse containing the *nomen* (name) of the accused.

Incense

Symbolizing the breath of life, incense is an important element in ritual magic.

Incense of Abramelin

A mixture of cinnamon, myrrh, olive oil, and galingal. The fragrant mixture is used in summoning a spirit.

Incommunicable Axiom

The Incommunicable Axiom is a secret key to the occult.

It is found embodied in the four letters of the Tetragram, in cabalistic transcriptions of the words Azoth and Inri, and in the monogram embroidered on Constantine's standard (XP). One who succeeds in deciphering it is supposed to become omnipotent.

Incommunicable Name
The hidden name of a god or magician. It was carefully guarded by its owner to keep anyone else from gaining magical dominion over him.

Incubus
Many persons of both sexes, forgetful of their own salvation, have abused incubi and succubi.

Some Church Fathers maintain that an incubus is an angel whose lust for women brought about his fall. He corresponds to the succubus who appears to men. When associated with a particular witch, both are known as familiars. The incubus is called by other names: *follet* (French), *alp* (German), *folletto* (Italian), *duende* (Spanish).

Initiation
According to Éliphas Lévi, initiation into transcendental magic enables the adept to grasp the occult relations of things.

Initiation is a preservative against the false lights of mysticism; it equips human reason with its relative value and proportional infallibility, connecting it with supreme reason by the chain of analogies. Hence the initiate knows no doubtful hopes, no absurd fears, because he has no irrational beliefs; he is acquainted with the extent of his power, and he can be bold without danger. For him, therefore, to dare is to be able. Here, then, is a new interpretation of his attributes: his lamp represents learning; the mantle which enwraps him, his discretion; while his staff is the emblem of his strength and boldness. He knows, he dares and is silent. He knows the secret of the future, he dares in the present, and he is silent on the past. He knows the failings of the human heart; he dares make use of them to achieve his work; and he is silent as to his purposes. He knows the significance of all symbolisms and of all religions: he dares to practise or abstain from them without hypocrisy and without impiety; and he is silent upon the one dogma of supreme initiation. He knows the existence and nature of the Great Magical Agent; he dares perform the acts and give utterance to the words which make it subject to human will, and he is silent upon the mysteries of the Great Arcanum.

So you may find him often melancholy, never dejected or despairing; often poor, never abject or miserable; persecuted often, never disheartened or conquered. He remembers the bereavement and murder of Orpheus, the exile and lonely death of Moses, the martyrdom of the prophets, the tortures of Apollonius, the Cross of the Saviour. He knows the desolation in which Agrippa died, whose memory is even now slandered; he knows what labours overcame the great Paracelsus, and all that Raymond Lully was condemned to undergo that he might finish by a violent death. He remembers Swedenborg simulating madness and even losing reason in order to excuse his science; Saint-Martin and his hidden life; Cagliostro, who perished forsaken in the cells of the Inquisition; Cazotte, who ascended the scaffold. Inheritor of so many victims, he does not dare the less, but he understands better the necessity for silence. Let us follow his example; let us learn diligently; when we know, let us have courage, and let us be silent.

Initiation Into a Coven
One must be predisposed by nature to black magic, accord-

ing to Justine Glass (*Witchcraft*, 1965), in order to become a witch. Generally contacts with witches are made by questioning one's friends or relatives about the subject. After becoming acquainted with the members of a coven, the candidate has to answer questions concerning his reasons for wanting to join the coven. If his answers are satisfactory, he begins a trial period of 13 months. During this period he is instructed in what might be called external or superficial matters. He also undergoes a series of tests, which vary with the coven.

These tests may involve acts of vandalism committed in churches and cemeteries, grave-robbing, and other seemingly senseless acts. The price of admission is sometimes lowered from the standard sum of 75 pounds or so if the neophyte evidences an extraordinary aptitude in such matters as grave-robbing. In 1962 the London *Daily Sketch* reported the theft of an infant from its grave. The body was never recovered, and Glass attributes its disappearance to the actions of aspirants to membership in a black coven.

If at the end of the probationary period the candidate has proven to be worthy of admission into the order, and if he completes his assignments as a neophyte, he becomes a Zelator.

Then come several other stages, after which the candidate can become a Magus or even rise to the summit and be known as Ipsissimus.

The exact nature of the functions and responsibilities attached to the various stages is unknown, but Glass thinks that the basic rite of the modern black coven has changed very little since the Middle Ages. Animals, rather than unbaptized new-born children, are sacrificed today to avoid reprisals. Press reports suggest an upsurge of incidents involving the slaughter and mutilation of animals at the time the four Sabbats are supposed to be celebrated. See Coven, Admission Into.

Initiators

Name given by occultists to alien beings whom they credit with knowing the secrets of electricity, heart transplants, nuclear energy, etc. They are supposed to have come to the earth in the distant past and to have imparted their knowledge to terrestrial men. They are also called Superior Ancestors, Initiators, and Astronauts. They are credited with imparting the knowledge that resulted in the great achievements of the Mayas in Mexico, the Incas in Peru, the Assyro-Babylonians, the Phoenicians, the pyramid-builders of Egypt, and the architects of Stonehenge. See Astronauts; Hyperboreans.

Innocent VIII

Author of one of the key documents in the campaign of the Church against witchcraft. The papal bull which he issued on December 5, 1484, stressed the duty of men to combat the Devil and served as justification for the merciless persecution of those accused of sorcery.

Inquisition

The redoubtable institution for the suppression of heresy was developed under Innocent III (1227-1241). In 1223 Gregory IX entrusted its operation to the Dominicans. In 1451 Nicholas V allowed the Inquisition to move against those accused of witchcraft. Innocent VIII and his successors issued papal bulls reinforcing the decision of Nicholas V. Tortures, both physical and mental, were approved by most of the pontiffs. The excesses of the Inquisition, including the deaths of thousands of apostates, heretics, Jews, and presumed witches, came to an end long before the institution was formally abolished, in 1772 in France and in 1834 in Spain.

305

Intercourse with Demons

The pious authors of the *Maleus Maleficarum* held that demons or incubi in the form of human beings had carnal intercourse with women. The incubi are not always visible to onlookers, who nevertheless may infer what is going on when they see witches lying on their backs in the woods or fields, "naked up to the very navel," with their legs and thighs moving in a way suggesting the "venereal act and orgasm." The incubi infest not only those sired by their own efforts and those offered to them by midwives.

> They try with all their might, by means of witches who are bawds or hot whores, to seduce all the devout and chaste maidens in that whole district or town. For this is well known by the constant experience of magistrates; and in the town of Ratisbon, when certain witches were burned, these wretches affirmed, before their final sentence, that they had been commanded by their masters to use every endeavor to effect the subversion of pious maids and widows.

> If it be asked whether the venereal delectation is greater or less with incubus devils in assumed bodies than it is in like circumstances with men in a true physical body, we may say this: It seems that, although the pleasure should naturally be greater when like disports with like, yet that cunning Enemy can so bring together the active and passive elements . . . that he seems to excite no less degree of concupiscence.

Invocation of a Demon

Among the ancient formulas for invoking demons are these: Palas aron azinomas; Bagahi laca Bachabé; and utterance of the nine divine and mystic names—Eheieh, Iod, Tetragrammaton Elohim, El, Elohim Gibor, Eloah Va-Daath, El Adonai Tzabaoth, Elohim Tzabaoth, Shaddai.

Invocation of Spirits
In Haitian Voodoo this is a formula for invoking spirits: Go to a crossroads at midnight on Friday, taking a candle made of honey wax, ox tallow, and swallow's liver. Light the candle in the name of Belzebuth and say: "Belzebuth, I am calling you so that you can tell me about (such-and-such a thing) right now." Fire a shot from a gun loaded with dirt and incense. Fire toward the east and say: "As the thunder rumbles, may all the Kings of the earth kneel. May Puer, Agrippa, Berke, Astaroth, spare me. Amen."

Ipsissimus
The highest of the ten grades or ranks in Aleister Crowley's cabalistic system.

The first and highest sephira, the sphere of God, "is beyond all comprehension of those of lower degrees." The Ipsissimus is "free from all limitations." He wields the magical power which belongs to man as the potential God.

Iroquoian Witchcraft
The Iroquoian peoples attributed disease to the mind of the patient himself, to witchcraft, and to physical injuries. The human body was thought to be inhabited by a single soul with several functions or capacities: animation, knowledge, judgment, willing, desiring, and separation from the body. The soul occupied all parts of the body and had the power to leave the body during dreams or after death. Witchcraft was used to introduce foreign articles into a victim's body thereby producing sickness.

Irungu
One of several spirits involved in the Nyoro cult. When he is "in the head" of a medium, Irungu divines for clients willing to pay a fee for his services.

Isacaaron
One of the demons who possessed Sister Jeanne des Anges.

Isacaaron filled her imagination with strange, shameful notions. She describes his passion as violent and says that he "went to extremes and blinded reason."

Isis

In Egyptian religion, Isis is the supreme, the most widely worshipped goddess. Sister and consort of Osiris, mother of Horus, all three form the triad that was most dominant in Egyptian religious life.

The cult in time spread to Asia Minor and the entire Mediterranean world as well.

Isis is the daughter of Seb and Nut. She gave burial to the mutilated body of her consort Osiris. Her cult involved his death and his rebirth, accompanied with lamentation and jubilation respectively.

Identified with Demeter, who too represents a vegetation cult, Isis has man aspects, attributes, and functions.

She watches over sailors. She presides over magic arts, and she is the moon-goddess.

Isis was eagerly adopted into the Greek cities, and in Rome her temples were constantly filled with votaries. During the last four centuries B.C. and far into the fourth century A.D. her worship prevailed in the ancient world. She had temples in Egypt, Greece, Rome, and Asia Minor.

Isis had her official priests and her special festivals. Among the practices of her cult were the interpretation of dreams, lavish banquets, resplendent processions, and dances to the accompaniment of tambourines, cymbals, the sistrum, and other musical instruments.

Isis is identified with Aphrodite too, with Hathor, and with numerous other divinities, so that, to avoid offense, she was often addressed as "O Thou, of countless names." She was

Ceres and Juno, Diana the huntress and Bellona the ear-goddess, Hecate, of the Lower Regions, Cybele the Phrygian Mighty Mother of the Gods. In this polyform aspect she was known as Myrionyma, the deity of one thousand names. One inscription in Latin reads: To you, goddess Isis, who are one and all things. Isis is the eternal divinity, without beginning, without end.

The Roman philosopher and novelist Apuleius, who flourished in the second century A.D., describes the rites of the cult of Isis in his amazing novel the *Metamorphoses*. Isis is sometimes represented as a woman with cow's horns, and holding a sistrum. She is also depicted veiled, her head topped with flowers, with the earth at her feet. Again, she is winged, with a quiver over her shoulder, or holding a flaming torch or a cornucopia.

J

Jacinth

A stone worn as an amulet for protection against lightning and heart disorders, or for the attainment of honor, prudence, and wisdom. In powdered form it helps to control bleeding and internal disorders.

Jacob's Ladder

Cabalists hold that Jacob's Ladder was a metaphorical representation of the powers of alchemy, operating through visible nature. Jacob's dream implied a whole history of creation according to the hermetic tradition in which two colors, red and blue (representing spirit and matter) operated as the mystic rulers of the world and the source of all creation.

Jade

A green gem stone worn as an amulet to help women in childbirth and warriors on the battlefield. Chinese businessmen have used it in divination. The Mayans used a knife with a blade of jade in performing human sacrifices.

Jakin and Boas

Two symbolical pillars supporting Solomon's cabalistic temple. They were believed to explain all mysteries. One was black, representing good; the other white, representing evil. They also symbolized the need for two elements or forces: in the world, as in human reproduction.

Jalarupa

One of the most occult signs of the zodiac. The Sanskrit word means "water, body, form." It figures on the banner of Kama, god of love.

James, William

American psychologist and philosopher (1842-1910). He founded the American Society for Psychical Research and maintained a lifelong interest in the supernatural. James Hervey Hyslop discusses James' return after death, in a book titled *Contact with the Other World*.

Japanese Exorcism

A procedure practiced by the Japanese involves the use of lights and the recital of an incantation which is repeated one hundred times.

Jaquier, Nicolas

Dominican theologian who advanced the principle of the devil's mark. *Flagellum Haereticorum Fascinatorionum,* he tried to defend the actions of the inquisitors in forcing the learned Guillaume Edelin, professor at the Sorbonne, to confess in 1453 that he had traveled to a witches' sabbat on a broom.

Jawbones

The belief that the ghosts of the dead attached themselves to jawbones existed in ancient Egypt and survives in modern Africa. It is not surprising, therefore, to find that the jawbone has been looked upon as a spiritual wand, an invincible weapon, and a shrine.

Jeanne Des Anges, Sister

Jeanne de Belcies entered the Ursuline order in 1622 and

eventually became the head of their house at Loudon. She confessed that Urbain Grandier, a priest, had made a pact with the Devil and sent demons into the bodies of eight Ursuline nuns. The demons in her own body were named Leviathan, Behemoth, Asmodeus, Isacaaron, Ballam, Gresel, and Aman.

Jesus and Exorcism

Exorcism had an important place in the life of Jesus. Mark relates (1.32, 34) that many who were sick and possessed came to him and were healed. Matthew (8.16 f.) confirms Jesus' power to drive out evil spirits and interprets it as the fulfillment of Isaiah's prophecy (53.4). Luke (4.40 f.) agrees with Mark. Specific references to Jesus' power to drive out evil demons abound in the Gospels: Luke 4.41, 6.18, 7.21, 13.32; Mark 1.14 f., 3.10 f., 16.17 f.; Matthew 4.23 f., 8.16, 10.1, 8.

Jettatura

The Italian name for the Evil Eye. The superstition is widespread in southern Italy. See Evil Eye.

Jetzirah

The *Sepher Jetzirah* (Book of the Creation) is the most occult of all the extant Cabalistic works. It explains the evolution of the universe in terms of a system of correspondences and numbers. God is said to have created the universe by 32 paths of secret wisdom, corresponding with the 22 letters of the Hebrew alphabet and the 10 fundamental numbers. These 10 primordial numbers, from which the whole Universe evolved, are followed by the 22 letters divided into 3 Mothers, 7 double consonants, and 12 simple consonants.

Jewish Demonology

The Old Testament, with its stress on monotheism, con-

313

tains only incidental references to a deep-rooted and persistent belief in the existence of demons. The *shedim*, angels of destruction (*Exodus* 12.23 and *II Samuel* 24.16), were imported from Babylon and later identified with heathen idols. The seirim, hairy demons resembling the jinni in the ancient belief of the heathen Arabs, were thought to inhabit the wilderness. Originally representing the unsubdued forces of nature, they became the devils after whom the children of Israel "have gone a whoring" (*Leviticus* 17.7).

The Baylonian Lilitu became the first she-demon of the Jews, Lilith. She was supposed to have borne Adam many children before abandoning him for the demon Samael, and to have hated the descendants of Eve. She may also be the "terror by night" mentioned in Psalms 91.5 and the terrifying spirit seen by Eliphaz (*Job* 4.15).

Cherubim and seraphim probably originated as demons. Seraphim, derived etymologically from "burn," were originally fiery, flying serpents (*Numbers* 21.6), associated with scorpions (*Deuteronomy* 8.15). Serpents and scorpions became symbols of demons in the New Testament. Throughout the Middle East people believed that these creatures could cause possession.

The Old Testament does not connect Satan with demons, but apocryphal and pseudepigraphical writings dating from as early as the second century B.C. tend to ascribe all evil to powers inimical to God. Both Satan and his demons were depicted as enemies of God and men, whom they sought to lead astray. The main work on Jewish demonology is the *Ethiopian Book of Enoch*. Other works include the *Book of Jubilees,* the *Testament of the Twelve Patriarchs, Tobit,* the *Apocalypse of Abraham,* the *Apocalypse of Moses,* the *Wisdom of Solomon,* the *Martyrium Jesajae,* the *Secrets of Enoch,* and the Syriac *Apocalypse of Baruch.*

314

The devils known as shedim in talmudic tradition were supposed to share with the angels the privilege of listening in to divine deliberations and were sometimes consulted by men. Ashmedai, the king of the shedim, was supposed to have served for a time as Solomon's tutor. A shed named Joseph was said to have attended lectures in the foremost talmudic academies. Rabbi Pappa obtained valuable information from him and also had a young shed as his private servant. Rabba, a prominent sage living in Babylon in the third century, claimed that he had seen Ormuzd, son of the demon queen Lilith, on the run. Other scholars who subscribed to the belief in demons included Nahmanides (1194-1270), Hasdai Crescas (1340-1410), and Joseph Caro.

Certain demons specialized in inflicting diseases on men: Shabriri caused blindness, Palga migraine, Ben Nefilim epilepsy, Tezazith insanity, and Cardiacus melancholia. Obot (singular ob), mentioned in Leviticus, gave counsel and could call up the spirits of the dead. Yideonim were probably familiar spirits.

The Zohar teaches that the ties between husband and wife are permanent, for the husband injects a part of his soul (a *ruah*) into his wife during their first sexual union. The ruah is transmitted in diminished portions to his offspring but enough of it remains behind in the womb to punish a second husband and his offspring in case he dies and his widow remarries.

The *Ethiopian Book of Enoch* contains a comprehensive demonology. Satan and his angels existed before creation. Their fall is described in chapters 6-8. They seduced the wives of men and created the giants mentioned in the *Book of Genesis* (6.1-4):

And it came to pass, when men began to multiply on the face of the earth, and daughters were born unto

315

them, that the sons of God saw the daughters of men that they were fair; and they took them wives of all which they chose. . . . There were giants in the earth in those days; and also after that, when the sons of God came in unto the daughters of men, and they bare children to them, the same became mighty men which were of old, men of renown.

Their leaders were Azazel and Semjasa, who was bound by Michael for 70 generations. Azazel wrought such evil among men that God commanded the archangel Raphael to chain him in the wilderness (*I Enoch* 9.10). Milton made him Satan's ally:

(Satan) commands that . . . be upreared His mighty standard. That proud honor claimed Azazel, as his right, a cherub tall.

When the giants died in the flood, they became evil spirits who attacked men (*I Enoch* 15.8-9).

A second version is offered in *I Enoch* 19-21. The fallen angels, symbolized as stars, caused men to worship demons as gods, introducing lawlessness, bloodshed, and witchcraft.

Their actions necessitated the flood as punishment (8.1-3, 9.8, 64.2). They served Satan not only as tempters but also as avengers (69.12). Gadreel, one of the fallen angels, seduced Eve (69.1). The wives of the fallen angels became sirenes or sea-nymphs (19.2).

Originally demons and fallen angels were two distinct groups, but Enoch tried, not always successfully, to link them together. Later writers and the Church Fathers treated them as one group.

Azazel and his followers were to continue their work until the final judgment (*I Enoch* 13, 55). Semjasa and his horde were cast into a well of fire (10.1).

316

The leading role of Mastema, the chief of the evil spirits resulting from the union of the fallen angels and mortals, is described in the *Book of Jubilees*. To him are ascribed the unseemly attributes of the Old Testament God. Women seduced the angels sent by God to teach righteousness, and their children became demons after death (4.15, 5.6). Mastema begged God not to chain all of the disobedient angels, and God heard his plea. A tenth of the fallen angels, entrusted to Mastema to punish wayward men, turned men away from God and caused them to think evil thoughts (10.7-11, 40.8). They also taught Noah how to use herbs in treating diseases caused by demons (7.27, 10.1-13).

According to the *Testament of the Twelve Patriarchs*, the common name of Satan is Beliar, lord of evil spirits and prince of deceit. The heathen belong to him. When a man dies, one of Beliar's angels, along with one of God's angels, waits for his soul. Beliar's angels can cause sickness. The prince of the kingdom of darkness is the opponent of the God of light.

Tobit identifies as an evil demon Ashmodai, who caused Sara to kill seven husbands before she married Tobit and gained her freedom. Raphael instructed Tobit to use the ashes from the burnt heart and liver of a fish to free his wife from Ashmodai. Through Sara's nose the demon breathed in the ashes, then fled to Egypt, where he was bound by Raphael. Thus this apocryphal book offers one of the earliest descriptions of a means of warding off evil.

The *Apocalypse of Abraham* relates the temptation of Abraham by Azazel, who as a serpent had beguiled Eve. He tempted Abraham in the form of an unclean bird and was punished by an angel.

The *Apocalypse of Moses* and the *Wisdom of Solomon* identify Satan, master of the world, with the evil impulse in man. The *Martyrium Jesajae* contains the names of demons like Matanbulus, Malkira, and the three princes of evil, Satan, Belior, and Sammael. The *Secrets of Enoch* depicts Satanail and his angels as prisoners who, though they are tortured and held captive in the air, can nevertheless seize men. The Syriac *Apocalypse of Baruch* teaches that evil spirits caused men to practice magic and witchcraft. It relates encounters with demons (27.9) and the evocation of sirens and dragons.

In the demonology of the Essenes, Mastena and Belial are the angels of darkness and leaders of the evil spirits. They try to seduce the sons of light into Godlessness, magic, and necromancy. In their struggle against demons the Essenes used the names of angels, especially Michael and Gabriel, and incantations. They were experts in the art of exorcism.

In rabbinical literature are recorded many traditions, speculations, and theories that date back to pre-Christian times. There are many theories, for example, to account for the origin of demons. In addition to being identified with fallen angels and the ghosts of dead giants, they are said to be the bodiless souls created on the sixth day by God, who then began his period of rest, before he had had time to create bodies for them. Thus they became shedim or mazzikin ("avengers"). Another theory is that God punished some of the men engaged in building the Tower of Babel by turning them into shedim and ghosts. Still another theory is that demons originated as serpents. Later writers, like Josephus, held that they were the ghosts of bad men who had not been obedient to God while they lived.

As angels, demons have wings, can move swiftly, and are superior to men in knowledge. As men, they eat, drink,

318

and die. They live in the lower regions of the air. As spirits they are incorporeal and invisible, cast no shadows, and often are associated with retribution. They can make themselves visible, appearing in the shapes of men and animals. One can make them become visible by smearing ashes from the excrement of a black cat over his eyes or around his bed.

Rabbinical literature lists countless demons. They are present by the thousands in all parts of the world. Lilith had a following of 180,000 female demons. Every man has a thousand demons on his left side and a hundred thousand on his right. Only occasionally are they closely linked with Satan. They are classed as night spirits (Lilin), morning spirits (Zafrire), afternoon spirits (Tikarim), and evening spirits (Telane).

Both religious and magical practices afford protection against evil spirits. The Shema, consisting of selections from the Pentateuch, is a powerful weapon, as are certain Psalms (29, 91) and the name of the Lord. Certain plants, rings, and amulets with demons' names on them also afford protection, particularly on the Sabbath.

Sorcery is the work of demons. Solomon used a magic ring to summon spirits like Beelzebub, whom he forced to reveal their secrets. Later, because of his sins, Solomon lost his power over demons. In the hands of Kabalists, Jewish demonology continued to flourish through the Middle Ages, rejected only by Maimonides. Naamah was identified as the wife of Sammael, sister of Tubal Kain and mother of Ashmodai. Demons like Lilith were viewed as vampires and ghosts with a place in the total cosmic plan.

Jewish Magic

Derived from Babylonian and Persian sources, ancient Jewish magic stressed divination. The witch of Endor was in reality a seer, but the King James version of the injunction against divination ("Thou shalt not suffer a witch to live") was carried out to the letter by medieval Inquisitors. Most of the religious leaders of the Jews condemned both maleficium and divination.

Jewish Stone

A stone to which magic properties were attributed. Also called Lapis Iudaicus.

Jinni

A demon representing one of the forces of nature. To Moslems jinn (the plural form of jinni) may be either good or evil supernatural beings. Solomon is supposed to have possessed a magic ring which gave him power over the jinn.

Joan of Arc

At her trial in 1431 the national heroine of France was accused of dancing with fairies, invoking demons, and making a pact with the Devil. Her accusers said that the voices she heard were not those of saints and angels but voices that came from Satan, Belial, and Behemoth. Before her trial ended, the charges of sorcery and witchcraft were withdrawn, and the sentence that condemned her as a heretic makes no mention of the earlier charges.

John XII

Pope from 954 to 964. One of the youngest of all Popes when he ascended the throne of St. Peter, he was accused of having made toasts to the Devil and of having invoked other demons.

John XXII

Pope, author of bulls and letters attacking witchcraft in the first quarter of the fourteenth century. In 1326 he urged the faithful to seek and proceed against those who sacrifice to devils or worship them. . . , make an avowed pact with the devils . . . , fashion or cause to be fashioned any waxen image or anything else to bind the devil.

John Frum Movement
Preaching a return to the ritual magic of his forefathers, a native of the island of Tanna in the South Pacific declared that he was a prophet of John Frum, heir to the role of an ancient and powerful spirit. The movement, initiated in 1940, spread throughout the South Pacific and was incorporated into the Cargo Cult.

Johnson, Margaret
Seventeenth-century English witch. She was accused of having intercourse with the Devil, who appeared in the form of a cat.

Jolivet-Castelot
A high dignitary of the French Rosicrucian Society. He helped to bring alchemy back into fashion. He is said to have used transmutation to produce gold.

Jones, George Stansfeld
Modern occultist. He took the magical name of Frater Achad. He rearranged the cabalistic Tree of Life, making it into a "cosmic snowflake" symbolizing the anatomy of God and the universe.

Ju-Ju
A generic name for African magic practices. There are secret societies with strange initiatory rites, occult cults and brotherhoods that are, according to reliable evidence, furnished by European government officials and others, able to enlist the services of powerful Ju-Ju men.

These latter are knowledgeable in ancient traditional secrets that may affect life and death. They are feared by their fellows and they have demonstrated, to the knowledge of physicians, engineers, administrators who are coldly objective, that they are capable of producing phenomena inexplicable to reason. They are reputed to protect a client by fashioning apotropaic amulets. The love potions that they prepare will win over a recalcitrant or forgetful lover. On the sinister side, they may prepare powders to induce sickness, even death. They can cause illness in a designated person who shows no external symptoms or other diagnostic evidence amenable to medical diagnosis. A Ju-Ju curse is a serious matter, and may bring agonies to the victim until it is broken by certain specific rituals. Ju-Ju is practiced by women as well as by the so-called "witch-doctor" or medicine man. There is a special costume worn by the Ju-Ju man, a special cane. Devil masks are part of the equipment.

If an evil spirit enters a man, the Ju-Ju adept is called in, and in his own mysterious way he exorcises the diabolic creature as demons were exorcised since Biblical times. In the jungle and in forest areas, among the haunts of wild beasts, all kinds of hazards are to be encountered. But a medicine brewed by a Ju-Ju man is a sovereign remedy.

Witches abound, casting evil spells on an entire village, on women and cattle alike. But the superior skill and potency of the medicine man will subdue her, by remote control, by means that are telepathic and psychic. When the witch is caught, she may suffer the extreme penalty, being strangled or burned or drowned, as was the practice in the Middle Ages.

Julianus
Ancient Roman sorcerer. He is reputed to have used occult practices to banish plague from Rome. He was also known as Theurgus, the Necromancer.

Jung, Carl Gustav

Swiss psychologist (1875-1961). His emphasis on the will to live in defining the libido, rather than on the sexual drive, set him apart from Sigmund Freud, with whom he was associated until 1912. He incorporated into his work occult ideas and concepts drawn from Eastern mysticism. He stressed the cooperation of the conscious and unconscious (both individual and collective) and the development of a symbolic language between them. His theory of the collective unconscious suggests the possibility that racial memories, legends, myths, archetypes, and traits may be transmitted genetically.

Jung was the first to suggest that dreams are not simply facades for sexual fantasies and wish fulfillment. In his view they are symbolic and satisfy a basic need for spiritual significance. They compensate for the one-sided view of reality that results from cultural conditioning. We can discover their ultimate meaning only through the symbol which he defines as an image that "describes in the best possible way the dimly discerned nature of the spirit. A symbol does not define or explain, it points beyond itself to a meaning that is adumbrated but still beyond comprehension, a meaning that cannot find expression in the ordinary words of our language." Dream language welds fragments of myth, legend and fairy tale into a personal drama. Beyond rationality, in dreams, legends, myths, and the archetypes that clutter it, Jung glimpsed the collective unconscious that he posited long before LSD and other hallucinogenic agents established its existence. His emergence as the leader of the school of analytical psychology and his respect for subjective experience helped to restore myth and magic, which engrossed his attention through the years, to a position of respectability.

323

Jung, J. H. (Jung-Stilling)

German spiritualist. His voluminous writings, published near the end of the 19th century, won many converts to spiritualism. His *Pneumatology* contains many extraordinary cases of spirit intervention. It was at the urging of Goethe that he wrote his autobiography.

Junius, Johannes

Mayor of Bamberg. After his wife had been executed as a witch, he was accused of having intercourse with a demon succubus, Fuchsin, and of having been baptized Krix before Belzebuth. He was burned in 1628.

Jupiter

The influence of this planet is symbolized by the man who has lived through the turbulence of youth and has become calm and methodical, rational and strong-willed. Jupiter takes 11 years, 10 months, and 17 days to complete its long cycle. Its color is metallic blue.

K

Ka

In Egyptian religion, one of the seven parts of man. The ka
is man's spiritual double or astral body. Man receives ka at
birth. After a person dies, the ka remains near his body
for a while, reanimating it occasionally.

Kabbalah

See Cabala.

Kachinas

In American tradition, kachinas are spirits of the dead.
They leave their underground abode to appear as representatives of deities at ceremonial dances and rituals. These
benevolent spirits control the weather, fertility, harvests,
etc., and may exhibit vindictive tendencies unless properly
honored. The young, particularly among the Hopi, Navaho,
and Zuni, once played with dolls representing the Kachinas
and in this way became acquainted with their function and
importance.

Kaiga'u

Among the Trobriand Islanders, a powerful magic designed
to bewilder and ward off the *mulukuausi,* or evil sorceresses.

Kalevala

Finnish epic containing many references to sorcery. This incantation will stop the flow of blood:

Listen, o blood, instead of flowing, instead of
  pouring forth thy warm stream.
Stop, o blood, like a wall,
Stop like a hedge.
Stop like a reef in the sea:
  like stiff sedge in the moss,
  like a boulder in the field,
  like the pine in the wood.

Another incantation in the *Kalevala* banishes sickness:

O malady, disappear into the heavens:
pain, rise up to the clouds:
inflamed vapour, fly into the air, in order that
the wind may take thee away, that the tempest may
chase thee to distant regions, where neither sun
nor moon give their light, where the warm wind
does not inflame the flesh.

Kamrusepa
Hittite goddess, skilled in witchcraft. Also know as Katah-
zipuri.

Kanea
Amulets in the form of magic squares. Cabalists link each
square with a spirit and a planet.

Karagoz, Mehmet
Eighteenth-century magician. Born in Tartary, he was the
son of a shaman. He traveled to the centers of learning of
the Turkish peoples—Bokhara, Samarkand, and the monasteries of Kashgar. Seeking always to find the answer to
magical power, he traveled to India before finally settling
in Moslem Albania. He performed amazing cures, without
the use of talismans, potions, or spells, and he was quick

326

to denounce the deceptive practices of false magicians. He had many disciples and many requests for his services. He is reputed to have lifted the top off a mountain, visited the Sultan in Istanbul supernaturally and advised him personally, and caused a visitor to see himself having the hallucination of a strange but complete lifetime within the span of a few seconds.

Karcist
The magician or operator who stands inside the magic circle in carrying out his tasks.

Kardec, Allan
Assumed name of the French spiritualist Denizard Rivail (1804-69). He believed that he was the reincarnation of the ancient Druid whose name he had assumed. His doctrines were largely accepted on the continent and especially in France. His numerous works, based largely on communications received through mediums, were internationally acclaimed—and condemned by the Bishop of Barcelona. He had studied animal magnetism before his introduction into a spiritualistic circle by Victorian Sardou in 1856. His tomb at Père-Lachaise cemetery is marked by a druidic menhir.

Karra-kalf
Modern Icelandic magic. The initiate must lick the Devil, who appears in the shape of a newborn calf.

Katahzipuri
Hittite goddess, skilled in witchcraft. Also known as Kamrusepa.

Kemp, Ursula
An Englishwoman whose skeleton is displayed in the Witches' House in Bocastle, England. She was tried and executed for withcraft in 1589.

Kepler, Johannes

German astronomer (1571-1630). Somewhat humiliated by his position as confidant of the superstitious Emperor Rudolf II, he wrote:

> Astrology is indeed a foolish child, but, good gracious, where would her mother, the wise astronomy, be if she had not this foolish child! Is not the world more foolish still, so foolish, indeed, that the old sensible mother (i.e. astronomy) must be introduced to the people . . . through her daughter's foolishness . . . But when guesses are limited to yes and no, one has always about half the chances in one's favor. . . . Right guesses are remembered, failures forgotten, and so the astrologer remains in honor. (Paul Carus.)

Kerner, Justinus

German physician and spiritualist. See Hauffe, Frederica.

Keteb

According to Cabalists, the noonday devil. A fearsome figure, he personifies danger and evil.

Kether

In Cabalistic teachings, the first emanation, the power of God as Prime Mover, First Cause, the One. It stands at the apex of the first triangle on the Tree of Life. Guarded by the four "living creatures of the first chapter of Ezekiel," according to Aleister Crowley, in magical image it is a bearded old man, personified by Zeus and Jupiter, supreme gods of Greece and Rome. Its symbols are the crown (kingship) and the point (one). On reaching this sphere, the soul achieves union with God.

Keugant

In Celtic religion, the outer circle of life. See Druids.

Key of Solomon

The most famous grimoire, or handbook of magic, ever written. It exists in many versions in various languages. Josephus referred in the first century A.D. to a book supposedly written by Solomon and containing incantations for summoning evil spirits. Legend holds that the magic manual was composed by devils and hidden under Solomon's throne. A Greek version of the manual, preserved in the British Museum, may date back to the twelfth century. Most versions, in French or Latin, date from the eighteenth century. Aleister Crowley edited, translated, and—unfortunately—bowdlerized the work.

Typical of the formulas given in the *Key of Solomon* is an invocation for finding treasure:

Adonai, Elohim, El, Eheieh, Asher Eheieh: King of Kings, Existence of all Existences, be merciful to me, and look upon me Thy servant, who calls Thee with humility, and begs by Thy most holy name Tetragrammaton to be benefited.

Order Thy Angels and planetary spirits to come and be here: O Angels and planetary spirits! O all of you, spirits, I conjure you: I, the deputed of God! let God order you to come, that I ask most fervently and most humbly. Amen.

A curse may befall an enemy if his image is left in a dish of burning fumes as these words are chanted:

O commanders and friends, I conjure and command you to obey this order without hesitation: consecrate this figure in the name of (victim) and the one is against the other. Thus they are henceforth irreconcilable.

Khaib

The ancient Egyptians believed that each person had a

shadow which might at times leave the body and lead a life of its own. This shadow they called the khaib.

Khaldun, Ibn
Arab historian who belongs in the fourteenth century. He described the practices of the Nabatean sorcerers who inhabited the Lower Euphrates:

> We saw with our own eyes one of these individuals making the image of a person he wished to bewitch. The magician pronounces some words over the image, which is a real or symbolical representation of the person to be bewitched. Then he blows and emits from his mouth a little saliva and at the same time makes those organs vibrate which are used in the utterance of this malevolent formula. Next he holds over this symbolical image a cord which he has prepared, making a knot in it to signify that he made a pact with the demon who acted as his associate. A wicked spirit then comes forth from the operator's mouth covered with saliva. Many evil spirits then descend, and the result is that the magician causes the victim to be attacked by the desired evil.

Khunrath, Henry
German alchemist (born about 1560). A. E. Waite writes:

> This German alchemist, who is claimed as a hierophant of the psychic side of the magnum opus, and who was undoubtedly aware of the larger issues of Herrietic theorems, must be classed as a follower of Paracelsus. He was a native of Saxony, born about the year 1560. . . .

> The prologue directs the aspirant to the supreme temple of everlasting wisdom to know God and Jesus Christ whom He hath sent, to know also himself, and the mysteries of the macrocosmos. The whole treatise is purely mystical and magical. The seven steps leading to the

portals of universal knowledge are described in an esoteric commentary on some portions of the Wisdom of Solomon. The lapis philosophorum is declared to be identical with the Ruach Elohim who brooded over the face of the waters during the first period of creation. The Ruach Elohim is called *vapor virtutis Dei,* and the internal form of all things. The perfect stone is attained through Christ, and, conversely, the possession of that treasure gives the knowledge of Christ.

Kilcrops

Offspring of an incubus and a woman. Jean Bodine calls them "rocots."

Kingsford, Anna

Modern occultist. See Maitland, Edward.

Kischpuh

A part of the Cabala. It deals with sorcery and magic, giving specific instructions for causing sickness and death, disguising oneself as an animal, undertaking spiritual travel, etc.

Kiss

Some sorcerers, believing that souls or spirits mingle during an embrace or a kiss, use this means to gain power over a victim.

Kiss of Shame

At the Sabbat the kiss of shame (*osculum infame* or *osculum obscoenum*) came after members had completed the ritual of allegiance to Satan. Accusations of the kiss of shame were also made against the Waldenses and the Knights Templars. Guazzo described the *osculum infame* in his *Compendium Maleficarum* (1626): "Then they pay homage to him by kissing him on the rump. Having committed these and similar abominable acts, they proceed to still other infamies."

Kludde
Flemish sprite. It can be identified by its two small blue flames and by its cry, "kludde." It changes into a tree, horse, black dog, or toad.

Knorr Von Rosenroth, Christian
Cabalist (1636-1689). In 1684 he published his *Cabala Unveiled*. It is in the form of a dialogue between the Cabalist and the Christian Philosopher.

Knots
Moslem sorcerers are called Blowers on Knots because they tie knots as they perform their incantations and imbue the rope or cord with magical powers contained in their breath. It is said that a sorcerer and his two daughters once tied 11 knots in a cord and cast a spell on Mahomet. The Prophet would have died if Allah had not come to his rescue.

Konkomba Sorcery
The Konkomba, a small tribe inhabiting the Oti Plain in the Gold Coast, believe that the osuo or sorcerer uses magical medicines to cause the death of a victim. The osuo may also cause death by sending snakes to lie in wait for the victim or by sending his shadow to devour the victim's shadow. A flaming stick may be used to drive away a sorcerer.

Koshar
A Canaanite god. His name means skilful. He was also known as Hayin, dexterous, and Hasis, intelligent. He was the counterpart of the Greek Hephaestus (Vulcan), the craftsman-god. He had a forge in Crete or on the island of Carpathos. Among the Egyptians he was equated with the potter-god Ptah. Koshar was also credited with the invention of magic incantations.

332

Kramer, Heinrich

Dominican prior (c. 1430-1505) and co-author (with Jakob Sprenger) of *Malleus Maleficarum*, the source of all subsequent treatises on witchcraft. His name was Latinized as Henricus Institor.

Krata Repoa

Book describing the process of initiation into the ancient Egyptian mysteries, published in 1782. The authors, C. F. Koppen and J. W. B. von Hymmen, divided the book into seven grades: Postophoris, or keeper of the sacred threshold; Neokaros, containing many ordeals and temptations; Death, or passage of the soul; the Battle of the Shadows, in which the candidate was restored to light; the degree of Vengeance; the state of the astronomer in the presence of God; and the final grade in which the whole plan of initiation is explained.

Krishnamurti

Heralded as a prophet even at birth, he became a protégé of the Theosophical Society founded by Mme. Blavatsky, who had prophesied his appearance on earth at the opportune moment. He was considered the next in a series of great instructors who appear in this world from time to time. Following a sensational guardianship trial at Madras, he was proclaimed the vehicle of the new Messiah. He broke with the Theosophical Society and renounced his claim of messiahship in 1929. He continued his teaching, stressing the importance of a spiritual approach to life and urging mankind to change its attitudes.

Kru

Cambodian sorcerers and exorcists.

Kundalini

A Sanskrit term meaning circular or coiling energy. Prana,

the breath or life current, is used to compel the upward surge of kundalini, residing in or near the lowest of the chakras (that is, between the anus and the penis, at the level of the spine). In the course of progressive meditation "the sleeping serpent" is carried through the highest of the six chakras, resides for a while with the deity in the upper part of the head, and returns through the chakras, bringing to each a spirtualizing influence. The prana is also linked to sexual energy. Mind and breath, rhythmically united, imbued with the great magical power residing in every individual (*shaki*), and directed toward a particular goal, is the basis of sexual magic. See Chakras; Shakti.

Kundje

A form of magic practiced in New Guinea. It brings good results to the practitioner and danger to his enemies.

Kurdaitcha

Shoes worn by the Australian aborigines for ceremonial killing by black magic. They are made of emu feathers glued together with human blood.

Kurdaitja

A sorcerer and executioner among the Arunta of Australia.

Kuthun

An amulet or other item containing a written incantation and transmitted by one sorcerer at the time of his death to another sorcerer or a neophyte. The kuthun confers full or additional powers on the recipient.

Kwei

In Chinese demonology, a spirit akin to the dibbuk. It is capable of taking possession of a human body.

Kyteler, Alice

The first person accused of witchcraft in Ireland. In 1324 she was charged with sacrificing cocks to demons, preparing

334

magic herbs to kill her husband, and having intercourse with a demon named Robert Artisson. She fled to England, but her maid, Petronilla de Meath, was burned alive.

Lady Alice's four husbands had left to her and to her son William Outlaw considerable property. Her younger children tried to break the will by proving that she had bewitched her husbands. She was formally charged with renouncing Christ and the Church in order to obtain her occult powers. She cut up live animals and offered them up at crossroads to a familiar demon named Robert or Robin Artisson, who appeared variously as a cat, a dog, or an Ethiopian, the latter accompanied by two tall comrades. One of the black men carried an iron rod, which may have served as a phallic symbol as well as the sceptre of power later borne by the Devil and transformed into the trident representing power over the sky, the earth, and the netherworld.

Under the direction of her familiar demons Lady Alice became proficient in the magic arts. She learned to concoct ointments containing loathsome ingredients, used Robert Artisson as her incubus, and took part in secret candlelit meetings. When the candles were extinguished, the thirteen members of the group (the word coven does not appear in the trial records) shouted "Fi, fi, fi, amen" and entered into a sexual orgy.

The trial of Lady Alice ended with mixed results since she had escaped to England and was never heard of again. Petronilla of Meath, one of her comrades, holds the dubious distinction of being the first person burned for heresy in Ireland. Others named by him under torture were punished by beating, branding, burning, exile, or excommunication. Others escaped punishment by hiding. William Outlaw managed to escape burning by agreeing to do penance for the crime of abetting heretics.

The account of the trial is one of the most complete on record. The evidence suggests that Alice Kyteler actually did dabble in magic but that her case is a mixture of accusations drawn from knowledge of witch trials outside Ireland and the imaginations of men motivated by self-interest. Another trial did not take place in Ireland until the 17th century.

L

Laburum

A cabalistic sign. It is embodied in the Great Magical Monogram, which is the seventh and most important pantacle of the Enchiridion.

Lafond, Lucas De

Priest tried in 1340 at Toulouse and sentenced to life imprisonment for practicing necromancy and practicing blasphemous rites.

Lama

A priest or monk of the form of Buddhism called Lamaism. Tibetans restrict the term to men famed for their wisdom and saintliness. Lamaism is noteworthy for its elaborate hierarchical organization, headed by the Grand or Dalai Lama (literally, the Ocean Lama), chosen by an oracle at the time of death of his predecessor. The present head of civil and religious affairs in Tibet, regarded by the faithful as a higher god incarnate in human form, now lives in exile in Northern India.

Lambe, John

Dr. John Lambe was an English wizard who practiced prognostication. One of his adherents was said to be the Duke of Buckingham. In 1628 Lambe was stoned to death by a London mob.

La Medica, Maria

Central figure in a witch trial conducted by Brother Antonio Petoselli, a Dominican Inquisitor, in 1480. She confessed that she had been a witch for 14 years, attended the witches' assembly three times a week, worshiped the Devil as lord of the assembly, denied God and Christ, and made a pact with Lucibel. She usually paid homage to the Devil by kneeling before him completely in the nude, to pay homage to him. She invoked the Devil, whom she called Lucibel, on many occasions. Lucibel helped her to work magic, especially in curing diseases, and taught her the best ways to kill children.

Maria took part in masses celebrated in the name of the Trinity but dedicated to her master.

Lurid details of her confession must have appealed to the spectators at her trial, if not to the Inquisitors. The witches' assembly, she reported, usually included a feast followed by a sexual orgy. Witches copulated with one another, then with the Devil. She described both natural and unnatural sex acts in her confession.

Maria confessed to having bewitched 30 children. She killed half of them and released the other half from her spell. She abused the holy sacraments, using the holy chrism as an aphrodisiac or an ointment applied to divining sticks used in locating buried treasure. Her confession and repentance caused her to be spared from the stake. She was sentenced to life imprisonment.

Lamia

In classical mythology, a loathsome being with a vampire's appetite. Also called Empusa, the creature is named for the queen of Libya. Hera was jealous of Lamia, who had been loved by Zeus, and slew the queen's children. Spitefully and maliciously, Lamia robbed other mothers of their children, then tore them apart or sucked their blood. Witches, noted for their blood-sucking, were called *lamiae*. The lamiae were capable of taking on the appearance of beautiful young women. Keats popularized the story of a bride whom Apollonius of Tyana identified at the wedding banquet as a lamia.

The Greeks considered the lamiae bisexual. Philostratus wrote in his *Life of Apollonius of Tyana* (third century A.D.):

> They were wont to lust not for love but for flesh: and they particularly seek human flesh and by arousing sexual desire they seek to devour whom they wish.

In the Middle Ages lamia was the name given a witch who looked like a woman but had a horse's hoofs.

Lancashire Witches

Believing that Pendle Forest, not far from Manchester, England, was the haunt of witches and demons, Roger Nowel, a country magistrate, first seized two helpless old women, Elizabeth Demdike and Ann Chattox, then several other suspects, and promptly induced them to confess that they had been communicating with the Devil. While they were awaiting trial in Lancaster Castle, the authorities suspected that a score of witches had assembled at the home of Elizabeth Device to plot the rescue of the prisoners.

In securing the conviction of the accused the court relied mainly on the evidence presented by Elizabeth Device and her three children.

Elizabeth withheld her confession until "a young maid, Jannet Device, her own daughter, about the age of nine years, a witness unexpected," rose up and revealed "all their practices, meetings, consultations, murders, charms, and villainies." After her two children had testified against

339

her, Elizabeth made "a very liberal and voluntary confession" which she later retracted, only to have it become the chief evidence against her.

Jannet testified that a spirit in the shape of a brown dog helped her mother kill people. James corroborated her story and helped Jannet to identify most of the witches who were accused of attending the meeting at Elizabeth's home. Ten of the accused, including Elizabeth and James Device, were hanged; six were acquitted, and four were freed. In 1634, seventeen other persons, including Jannet Device, were convicted on the testimony of a young boy, but they were eventually reprieved by Charles I.

The mass trial of twenty accused witches is described in *The Wonderful Discovery of Witches in the County of Lancaster* (1613). The unusually long chapbook became a textbook on the conduct of trials for witchcraft.

Lancre, Pierre De
Author of *Tableau* (1612), based on his experiences in investigating witchcraft among the Basques.

Lapis Lazuli
A stone believed to be inhabited by deities and invested with magical properties. The Egyptians used it for fashioning scarabs.

Lapis Philosophorum
This Latin expression means The Philosopher's Stone. It refers to the alchemical concept of a universal solvent which ultimately produces pure gold.

Larva
In Roman religion, a malevolent spirit. In medieval occultism, a supernatural monster.

Lascaris
Eighteenth-century alchemist. He is supposed to have given

away a transmuting powder that enabled others to manufacture large quantities of gold.

Laurel

A tree whose leaves offer protection against evil spirits. They symbolize power, honor, and divinity. The Romans used a laurel wreath to crown royalty.

Laveau, Marie

Voodooienne or Hoodoo queen (c. 1796-1881). She usurped the power wielded earlier, in and around New Orleans, by Sanité Dédé and Marie Saloppé. She may have learned her craft from Doctor John, the most famous of the Voodoo practitioners of his time, and is said to have put the practice of Voodoo on a paying basis for the first time. She renounced any form of devil worship, insisting that her followers were Christians. Both she and her husband, a man named Paris who died before she took control of all organized rituals in the area, were free persons of color. The "Widow Paris" prospered by selling charms, removing curses, and telling fortunes. Her reputation for wisdom and magical powers drew prominent whites as well as blacks to her house.

In the yard behind her house dances were held on Friday nights. She called the figures and told the dancers exactly what to do. Her giant snake Zombi crawled over the legs of the nude dancers. Inside the cottage, thronged with people from every class, she sold amulets, love powders, and other gris-gris.

Her mantle fell to a daughter born to her and Christophe Glapion. The daughter also assumed the name of Marie Laveau and became the greatest of all Hoodoo queens in America. Like her mother, she started her career as a hairdresser, but engaged in profitable side-lines—among them, that of procuress. By the late 1880s she had lapsed into obscurity, bringing to an end the golden age of Voodoo in Louisiana.

La Voisin, Catherine

Seventeenth-century French sorceress. With the unscrupulous Abbé Guiborg, she is supposed to have inveigled Madame de Montespan into performing, nude, at a Black Mass attended by members of the French court.

Law of Correspondences

See Signatures, Laws of Magic.

Laws of Magic

The art and science of magic is based on three basic principles: (1) one may communicate with other realms, worlds, or planes of existence through the medium of the Astral Light; (2) the power of the magician is unlimited; (3) external characteristics (signatures) are signs through which everything internal and invisible can be revealed. Aleister Crowley defined magic as the science and art of causing change in accordance with the will of the magician. He claimed that he had caused angels, intelligences, and demons to appear out of the Astral Light. It is also alleged that he turned his pupil, Victor Neuburg, into a camel. The magician merges his consciousness with God, becomes identical with Him, and loses his human identification. The identification of magician and God, according to Crowley, binds magic with mysticism.

Lead

The Romans viewed lead as the magical metal par excellence. It was the metal associated with Saturn (Cronos), god of hatred, vengeance, and harvests.

Leadbetter, C. W.

Modern occultist. He wrote extensively on occult subjects, particularly clairvoyance and the perfumes of Egypt. His exposition of "thought forms" is the classic theosophical work on the physical manifestations of thought processes.

Leannan Sith

In Gaelic these words mean fairy sweetheart. Mortals are advised to shun them. The fairy lover is companionable until things go wrong; when offended he may take the life of his enemy.

Leek, Sybil

An English witch, by her own admission, who traces her ancestry back to 1134. She calls her witchcraft the Old Religion. She writes a column on astrology for a magazine, acts as a medium, and lectures and travels throughout the United States.

A woman described by the *New York Times* as "perhaps the world's best-known witch," she claims that more than 400 witch covens are active in the United States today. She is the author of *The Sybil Leek Book of Fortune Telling*, an introduction to palmistry, fortune-telling, *I Ching*, and tea-leaf reading.

Left

In black magic, the left is associated with evil. Leftward motion is executed with the intention of attracting evil influences. "Sinister" was the Latin word for both left and evil.

Legba

In Haitian Voodoo cults he is the go-between without whose help no man could communicate with the gods. His symbol, a crutch, hangs on the wall in almost every Voodoo Houmfort (temple). He is guardian of gates and fences, protector of the home, the god of every place of meeting and parting, and as Maître Carrefour (god of the crossroads), the patron of sorcerers. As one of the collective body of divinities known as *loa,* he participates in religious ceremonies.

Legba

In Dahoman religion, the name given to the "joker" who perverts all the rules and hence allows evil to manifest itself in the form of sickness, disasters, etc. His ineptitudes, malice, and carelessness pose a constant threat to society. He may also on occasion propitiate other gods on behalf of men and carry messages to human diviners.

Leicester Boy

A seventeenth-century English boy who pretended to be bewitched and succeeded in bringing about the execution of several women. He was exposed by James I. The gullible magistrate and his Sergeant Crew, who had countenanced the ravings of the boy, named John Smith, were satirized by Ben Johnson in *The Devil Is an Ass.*

Leland, Charles

American poet, scholar and littérateur (1824-1903). He was founder and first president of the Gypsy Lore Society, whose charter members included the Scottish anthropologist Sir James George Frazer. His book titled Gypsy Sorcery and Fortune-Telling, first published in 1891, was reprinted as recently as 1971, but another small book entitled Aradia, or The Gospel of the Witches is extremely rare. There may have been attempts to repress it shortly after publication, according to T. C. Lethbridge. Based on his studies of Florentine and Etruscan witchcraft, the book contains what he described as a pagan gospel of considerable antiquity. See *Aradia.*

Lemegeton

A four-part handbook of magic, also called *Lesser Key of Solomon,* written before 1500. The origin and meaning

344

of the term are obscure. The four parts of the work are Goetia, Theurgia Goetia, the Pauline Art, and the Almadel.

Le Normand, Marie
French sorceress (1772-1843). Known as Sybil of the Faubourg Saint Germain, she was one of the most famous occultists and diviners of her day. Most authorities write her off as a harmless charlatan.

Leo
In astrology, the Lion. The fifth, northern sign of the zodiac. It is equated with fire, with the power of the sun. In occultism, it symbolizes strength and courage. Cabalistically, it signifies the heart of the grand old man of the heavens, the fire vortex of physical life, and the life center of humanity.

Leprechaun
Irish fairy. A shoemaker by trade, a leprechaun is very helpful to his host. He is about two feet tall, likes wine, and wears a cocked hat, knickers, and silver-buckled shoes.

Lethbridge, T. C.
Anthropologist, disciple of Margaret Murray, and author of *Witches,* subtitled "The Investigation of an Ancient Religion Involving the Worship of Diana—the Witch Cult —Laying as Much Stress on the Consorts of the Goddess as on the Lady Herself" (1962). He traces the cult of the Mother Goddess to its paleolithic origins, relating it to the decline of totemism.

Leti's Calendar
An Egyptian document purporting to predict the day and hour most appropriate to any given undertaking. Composed by the magician Leti, it divides the day into three parts and ascribes each part to various gods who control events.

There is a complete copy of the calendar in the British Museum.

Levi, Eliphas

(1810-1870). The real name of this French occultist was Alphonse Louis Constant. He was trained for the priesthood, but was expelled for his views. After an unfortunate marriage, he dedicated himself to occultism, and also gave instructions to disciples. He professed to have conjured the spirit of Apollonius of Tyana in 1854. Among other writings, he produced a *History of Witchcraft,* in which he stresses mystical interpretation of the occult elements in Nature.

Born in Paris about 1810, he is said to have been reincarnated as Aleister Crowley. A. E. Waite, the learned English occultist, said that Lévi's *Doctrine and Ritual* contained the secrets of an occult society into which Lévi had been initiated and from which he had been expelled.

He was the first to lend his efforts to the task of rehabilitating magic after it had been largely discredited by science. It was he who applied the concept of Astral Light to magical operations.

Lévi defines magic and describes the conditions for attainment of the knowledge and power of the sorcerer:

> Magic is the traditional science of the secrets of Nature which has been transmuted to us from the Magi. By means of this science the adept is invested with a species of relative omnipotence and can operate superhumanly— that is, after a manner which transcends the normal possibility of men. Thereby many illustrious hierophants, such as Mercurius Trismegistus, Osiris, Orpheus, Apollonius of Tyana, and others whom it might be dangerous or unwise to name. . . .

To attain the SANCTUM REGNUM, in other words, the knowledge and power of the Magi, there are four indispensable conditions—an intelligence illuminated by study, an intrepidity which nothing can check, a will which cannot be broken, and a prudence which nothing can corrupt and nothing intoxicate. TO KNOW, TO DARE, TO WILL, TO KEEP SILENCE—such are the four words of the Magus, inscribed upon the four symbolical forms of the sphinx.

Levitation

A supernatural phenomenon giving rise to the impression that an object or a human being is floating in the air without direct or indirect support. Associated with saints, mediums, fakirs, and those who practice magic, it is supposed to have been accomplished by Simon the Magician, Apollonius of Tyana, and Marie d'Agréda.

Accounts of levitation involving humans, animals, and inanimate objects have come from many different regions, religions, and magical systems. Tibetan Buddhism contains many references to the levitations of holy llamas. The Hindus claim that adepts can learn through yoga training to perform levitation. Roman Catholicism contains many reports of levitation and divine ecstasy in the case of mystically inclined saints. Malinowski, the famous anthropologist, recorded instances of levitation among the Trobriand Islanders. Some mediums are reported to have accomplished the levitation of objects during seances, using a force known as psychokinesis.

Lewis, Matthew Gregory

English author (1775-1818), commonly known as Monk Lewis. *Castle Spectre* (1798) and *Tales of Terror* (1788) won him great popularity among people interested in the occult.

347

Leyak

A bewitched spirit, according to the Balinese, who haunts lonely roads and deserted places. These spirits are responsible for the misfortunes that befall men.

Liber Lapidum

This Latin title means *The Book of Precious Stones*. It was written around 1123 by Marbod, bishop of Rennes. He describes each gem in symbolical terms. The onyx, for instance, brings nightmares. The sapphire is a protection against terror. The jasper aids childbirth, while the sardonyx is the symbol of the inner man.

Liber Samekh

A ritual devised by Crowley to summon up the divine power within himself. It is based on a Graeco-Egyptian magical text.

Libra

In astrology, the Balance. The seventh, southern sign of the zodiac. It symbolizes equilibrium in the material universe and in the psychic zone. Esoterically, and on the intellectual plane, it signifies external perception and intuition, united as reason and foresight. Cabalistically, it represents the kidneys and loins of the grand old man of the heavens.

Ligature

Impotency resulting from sorcery. It is generally accomplished by administering potions or tying knots in threads. The most common procedure is to tie knots in a strip of leather or cord. The ligature remains in force until the knot is untied. The knot should be tied as the bride and groom are exchanging their vows. Vergil mentions a string with nine knots. Pliny recommends putting wolfgrease on the sill and lintels of the bedroom door to counteract the

348

ligature. During the Middle Ages, urine and salt were used as counteragents. Famous victims of ligature include Philippe Auguste, Theodosius, and Ahmose.

Though not so common as other forms of *maleficia*, it was widely discussed in earlier times and was generally recognized as a just cause for voiding a union about to be made and annulling one already contracted. It was also known by other names *vaecordia* (Latin), *aiguillette* (Franch), and *ghirlanda delle streghe* (Italian).

Lille Novices
Thirty-two orphan girls in a foundling home started in Lille, France, by Antoinette Bourignon (1616-1680) exploited the credulity of their benefactor by declaring

> that they had daily carnal cohabitation with the devil, that they went to the sabbats or meetings, where they ate, drank, danced and committed other illicit acts.

Lilly, William
Seventeenth-century astrologer. In addition to being the most celebrated astrologer of his time, he was a scholar and teacher of Greek. He was finally cleared of the charge of arson brought against him after he had predicted the Great Fire of London.

Linga (Lingam)
A Sanskrit word used esoterically to identify the symbol of every creative god in every nation.

Li Shao Chun
The first known Chinese alchemist. He lived during the Earlier Han Dynasty (203 B.C.-25 A.D.) and claimed to have acquired the art of transmuting cinnabar from An Ch'i. He insisted that cinnabar could be transmuted into pure gold which, when swallowed, would enable one to rise to heaven as a hsien. Shao Chun is said to have dis-

349

appeared from his coffin, leaving the clothes in which he was wrapped "like the slough of a cicada."

Little Albert

In magic of a low or vulgar order many procedures are available for securing the affection of a young lady, causing a hostile neighbor's cows to withhold their milk, etc. The *Little Albert* ("Marvelous secrets of Little Albert's natural and cabalistic magic") is devoted mainly to popular traditions involving the use of magic for immediate and practical purposes. Whole pages are inspired by Agrippa von Nettesheim's *De occulta philosophia,* but much space is devoted to love philtres, knotting, treasure-seeking, "domestic secrets," talismans, magical perfumes, charlatans, and the relations between hours and planets. It was published at Lyon, France, in 1758, and became the bible of practitioners of low magic.

Lituus

A curved rod with which the Roman augurs, dressed in their purple-bordered mantles, marked out the limits of the templum or area of observation used in taking the omens from birds in flight.

Loa

Gods of the Voodoo cult. Their desires are satisfied by acts or offerings of voodoo practitioners. The head of an afflicted family may light a candle, toss water, or place food in a place of worship. If danger threatens, he may consult the *hungan* and arrange for an elaborate ceremony.

Lodestone

A precious stone endowed with magical properties. It protects its bearer against snakebite, makes audible the voices of the gods, and cures wounds, weak eyes, headaches, hearing defects, and snakebites.

Lotapes

Ancient sorcerer, attached to the court of Pharaoh.

Loudun, Nuns of

A group of nuns whose strange behavior is detailed in Aldous Huxley's The Devils of Loudun (1952). In 1963 the Ursuline convent established at Loudun in France witnessed an outbreak of diabolical possession. Soon most of the nuns were speaking in tongues and behaving in the most extraordinary and hysterical manner. Jeanne des Anges (Mme. de Belfiel), the Mother Superior of the convent, Sister Claire, and five other nuns were the first to be possessed by evil spirits. The outbreak spread to the neighboring town and created such a stir that Richelieu appointed a commission to deal with it. After attempts at exorcism had failed, Father Urbain Grandier was arrested and charged with using sorcery to give the nuns over to possession of the Devil. The confessor of the convent protested his innocence, but to no avail. A council of judges found the marks of the Devil on his body. Even after he was burned alive at the stake on August 18, 1634, the possession of the hysterical sisters did not cease. The three exorcists who had participated in his condemnation—Lactance, Tranquille, and Surin—also came to a bad end. Lactance died insane one month later, Tranquille followed his example five years later, and Surin experienced diabolical possession for twenty years. The strange behavior of the nuns made Loudun a tourist attraction until Richelieu refused to provide further financial support for the nuns. Then their possession ceased.

Louviers, Nuns of

Several nuns and priests were involved in fantastic orgies allegedly committed from 1628 to 1642 in the little convent of the Franciscan Tertiaries at Louviers, France. At least thirty-four books detailed the accusations against

351

Madeleine Bavent and three successive directors of the convent, Father David, Father Picard, and Father Boullé. Madeleine stated in her autobiography that the Devil entered her cell in the form of a huge black cat, dragged her forcibly on the bed, and ravished her. She reported also that the priests said Black Mass at midnight Sabbats.

The perverse mingling of sacrilege and sensuality is reported in Madeleine Bavent's confession. She entered the convent in 1625, when she was 18. Father Pierre David, the chaplain of the convent, insisted that God should be worshiped naked. Madeleine was forced to take communion bare-breasted, with Father David caressing her indecently. The chaplain also taught the nuns to fondle each other and to use an artificial penis. His teachings were carried even further by Father Matthurin Picard and his assistant, Father Thomas Boullé. Picard and Boullé may have conducted Satanic rites involving cannibalism, sex orgies, and the Black Mass. These Satanic practices continued until Picard died in 1642. Many instances of hysterical paroxysms and convulsions were investigated. In 1647 Boullé was burned alive, and with him the exhumed corpse of Picard.

Love Charms
The Druids attributed magic virtues to garlic, and the reverence for this bulbous root spread to leeks and onions. A Gypsy love charm relies on the onion:

"Take an onion . . . and plant it in a clean pot never used before; and while you plant it repeat the name of the one whom you love, and every day, morning and evening, say over it;—

" 'As this root grows
And as this blossom blows,
May her heart be
Turned unto me!' "

352

Another Gypsy love charm is prepared by putting a frog into an earthen vessel full of small holes and placing it on an ant hill. After the ants have eaten away the frog's skin and flesh, the skeleton is ground into a powder, mixed with the blood of a bat, dried, shaped into a small bun, and slipped into the food of the intended lover. The charm is most effective on St. John's Day.

Low Magic
Vulgar, superstitious magic involving processes that do not require the knowledge and dedication expected of those engaging in the operations of ritual magic. Medieval grimoires and handbooks of magic offer many recipes and simple procedures for concocting love philtres, casting spells, finding lost treasure, etc.

Loyer, Pierre Le
French demonographer (b. 1550). He wrote a book which throws considerable light on the occult science of his time: *Discourses and Histories of Specters, Visions and Apparitions of Spirits, Angels, Demons and Souls Exhibiting Themselves to Men.*

LSD
Lysergic acid diethylamide, the most famous of the hallucinogenic or mind-expanding drugs. As early as 1943 Albert Hofmann, a Swiss chemist, was investigating the properties of LSD.

In the afternoon of 16 April, 1943, when I was working on this problem, I was seized by a peculiar sensation of vertigo and restlessness. Objects . . . appeared to undergo optical changes. . . . In a dreamlike state I left for home, where an irresistible urge to lie down overcame me. I drew the curtains and immediately fell into a peculiar imagination. With my eyes closed, fantastic pictures of extraordinary plasticity and intensive color seemed to

353

surge toward me. After two hours this state gradually wore off.

By 1966 former Harvard professor Timothy Leary was proclaiming the "sacred energies" of hallucinogenic drugs before congressmen, and some occultists were claiming to have had astounding mystical and religious revelations under its influence. Other users of the drug said that they had astral flights under its influence. The Tibetan *Book of the Dead,* read prior to ingestion of LSD, was said to make its effects more intense and meaningful.

The banning of LSD in most countries, except in limited experimental settings, such as the preparation of terminal cancer patients for the acceptance of death by enabling them to experience death and rebirth in a trance state, did not eliminate its use. Anyone familiar with chemistry may easily synthesize the drug.

Ergot, produced on rye bread by a fungus, has properties similar to those of LSD. Epidemics of ergotism, reported from time to time in Europe prior to the discovery of LSD, indicate that apparently opposite sensations, such as feelings of elation and despair, can be experienced at the same time. Abnormal impressions of one's own body are not uncommon, recalling the case of Alice in Wonderland. Alice ate a cake and grew so tall that she thought of writing a letter to Alice's Right Foot, Esq.

Experiences involving the use of psychedelic substances like LSD (Mexico's "magic mushrooms," for instance) in magical and religious rituals are widespread.

Lucifer
Name applied to the Devil, often linked to a fallen star or angel. The "Light-bringer" presides over the east, according to the old magicians. The first to be invoked in

354

the litanies of the Sabbat, he is according to some demonologists the grand justiciary of Hades.

Luciferiani of Brandenburg
The bishop of Magdeburg burned 14 men and women of Angermünde in Brandenburg in 1336. They were accused of worshiping Lucifer. Later, in 1384, a clergyman at Prenzlau accused his congregation of believing that Lucifer was the brother of God or God himself, denying that Christ was in the host, removing from their children the salt used at the time of baptism for protection against evil spirits, and behaving promiscuously at nightly meetings held in cellars. The Luciferiani believed that the Devil took them by night over long distances. Their heretical views and practices, particularly the wild ride, helped to forge the medieval amalgamation of witchcraft and heresy.

Luciferians
Medieval sects of occultists who mutilated Eucharistic wafers before an idol of Lucifer. The practice of witchcraft may have been initiated by a Luciferian sect in Milan. It was against this sect that Konrad of Marburg, the first German inquisitor, moved zealously in the first part of the thirteenth century. He extorted confessions from them "proving" that they were out-and-out Satanists who worshipped the Devil as creator and ruler of the world.

Lucifuge
Prime Minister of infernal spirits. He commands three subordinate spirits: Baél, Agares, and Marbas. Also known as Lucifuge Rofocale, he has power assigned to him by Lucifer over all the treasures of the world.

Lucifuges
A class of demons identified by medieval theologians, following the suggestions of John Wier. They shun the light

of day. Only by night can they fashion bodies for themselves.

Lug (Lugh)

The greatest of the Celtic heroes, he was the patron of Lyon (Lugdunum), Laon, Loudun, and Montlucon in France; Lugarus, Lugano, and Locarno in Switzerland; Luga and Luganskaya in Russia; Lugde in Prussia; Leiden in Holland; Luggude in Sweden; Lugoj in Rumania; Lugo in Spain and Italy; Lugos in Austria.

In Irish romance he was the sun god whose final conquest of the Formorians symbolizes the victory of light and intellect over darkness, represented by Balor. By his title of Ildanach (Mighty Craftsman) he is comparable to the Greek Apollo, Egyptian Ptah, and Cymric Gwydion, the great magician and giver of arts and civilization. With Bel and Dana he formed the triple-headed Celtic god who could not be named.

Lug was also the name by which Lucifer (Beelzebub, Bel, Beli, Balor) was known in many regions inhabited by the ancient Celts. Related to the Latin word *lux*, light, it was also associated with the sun. Lug was one of the lovers of the Great Mother and may have become the archangel Michael under the influence of Christianity and Pope Gregory's admonition to the clergy to turn deep-rooted pagan beliefs into Christian guise. The Plantagenets used on the reverse of their silver coins a design which could be interpreted either as a cross or a pagan sun disc.

Lugnas

One of the four major Sabbats, celebrated on August 1. Throughout the Celtic world the festival of Lug was celebrated with assemblies and harvest games.

356

Lully, Raymond (Ramon Lull)

Philosopher, logician, and alchemist (1235-1315). Born in Majorca, he wrote in Catalan and became one of the most prolific authors of his time. His books were translated into Latin. Either Raymond Lully of Majorca or another ecclesiastic of the same name was said to have been one of the most celebrated Hermetic artists of his age. It is reasonable to suppose that two authors have been confused or that the alchemical writings attributed to the philosopher are spurious. One of these, the *Clavicula* of Raymond Lully contains the arch secrets of alchemical adeptship.

The Catalan mystic also wrote a treatise on the Cabala. He may have had ties with a secret Muslim sect, The Brothers of Purity. He was said to have practiced alchemy and to have succeeded in changing base metal to gold.

Lutin

A prankish spirit of Normandy. He had many names and could assume many shapes.

Lycanthropy

Transformation of a human being into an animal, particularly a wolf.

Lynx

A Chaldean symbol of universal being, reproduced as a living sphere or winged globe. The word means "power of transmission." Eliphas Levi describes the lynx as "corresponding to the Hebrew Yod or to that unique letter from which all other letters were formed."

M

Maa Kheru

In Egyptian religion, an expression meaning "the right word." When spoken, it permitted the spirit of the dead to enter the halls of the underworld and to assume the powers of the gods.

Maat (Mat, Mut)

In Egyptian mythology, the egg produced by the union of Chaos and the Wind. Mat was the Egyptian word for both mother and matter. The same word also designated the goddess of truth and justice. The original egg later became the 0 or zero, the number of the first Tarot card. In early French decks, this card was called *Le Mat,* the fool.

Macardit

The Great Black One of the Dinka, who live in the southern Sudan. Misfortunes which are not interpreted as deserved punishment are ascribed to him.

Macrocosm

The great world or universe of which the microcosm, or man, is the epitome. One of two major cabalistic symbols into which all other symbols may be reduced, it is a six-pointed star formed with two triangles. Called the sacred seal of Solomon, it represents the infinite and the absolute.

359

The theory that a single great pattern links every element of the macrocosm with the microcosm (man) is one of the basic assumptions of magic. According to Paracelsus, every magical or cabalistic figure used to compel spirits may be reduced to two—the macrocosm or the microcosm.

Macroprosopus
The Greek word means Creator of the Great World. It is one of the four magical elements in the Cabala.

Macumba
Magic rituals and dances of Brazil. Macumba involves animism and animal sacrifices.

Madan
Elemental sprite of Hindu origin. He facilitates the malefic operations of sorcerers.

Madeleine De Demandolx, Sister
A French nun, one of the famed Aix-en-Provence nuns accused of renouncing God in favor of the Devil. She spent ten years in prison for her crimes.

Madre Natura
Secret society of Italy. Founded by members of the ancient Italian priesthood, it was a powerful order whose members worshiped and idealized nature.

Maga
A generic name for witch. The term usually denotes a pleasure-seeking witch.

Maggid
See Caro, Joseph Ben Ephraim.

Magi
The Wise Men who came from the East to Jerusalem to bring their offerings to Jesus were learned in astrology.

360

They used the stars to read the secrets of the future. The star that guided them was itself a part of the cosmological pattern and was interpreted in terms of the ancient dictum, "as above, so below." The magi saw a route traced in the heavens and accordingly charted their course on the earth below, carrying sacred and symbolic gifts. An Egyptian magical papyrus had predicted that a shining star would "descend and place itself in the middle of the chamber" and that those who had invoked the angel would see him when the star had descended and immediately "know the counsels of the gods."

Magia Posthuma
Treatise on vampirism published in 1706. It was written by Ferdinand de Schertz.

Magic
Ancient cultures made no distinction between magic and other forms of understanding and dominating the universe —science, religion, philosophy, poetry, art. High magic, especially, is an independent world view based on the belief that man is a microcosm reflecting the macrocosm, with the result that all of the world's elements—sticks and stones, plants, planets, metals, stars—are intimately fused with the lusts and longings, desires and fears, health and physical appearance of man.

The modern distinction between white magic and black magic has no basis in earlier occultism, which reached out to grasp, systematize, and ultimately control the universe. The medieval Christian view was that all magic, since it involved evil spirits and defiance of God in its attempt to control the powers of the universe, is evil. More useful than the distinction between good or white magic and evil or black magic is that which separates high magic from low magic. The former has its roots in the astrological and numerological lore of the Babylonians, the philosophical speculations of Pythagoras and early Greek thinkers, and the Persian traditions later incorporated into the Judaeo-Christian teachings (the Magi were *magoi:* seers, wise men, magicians). It was also important in gnosticism and Neoplatonism. The collection of magical writings composed in the second or third century and known as the *Corpus Hermeticum* was shaped by Gnostic influences. Later it became the keystone of the Jewish Cabala as well as of medieval Christian magic and, later, modern magic. The great Renaissance philosopher Pico della Mirandola wrote that "No science provides greater proof of Christ's divinity than magic and the Cabbala."

Low magic, practical and intended to achieve immediate goals, is more closely associated with evil-doing *(maleficium).* It involves such humble practices as urinating into a ditch to cause rain or sticking pins into a wax doll to injure an enemy. It is closely associated with witchcraft.

Cornelius Agrippa defined magic as "the true science, the most elevated and mysterious philosophy, in a word, the perfection and culmination of all the natural sciences. It is a philosophical science of intense, secret power . . . and is based on the study of the planets, elements, and stones. For all the elements of the world contain the soul of the universe." Collin de Plancy defined it as "the art of producing in nature, with the help of demons, things beyond the power of men." Albert the Great stated that "magic is very dangerous when used to discover the essence of natural things."

See Occult Philosophy; Ritual Magic.

Magic and Occultism
Magic, according to Papus (G. Encausse), differs from occult science in general in that it is a practical science whereas

the latter is mainly theoretical. Papus cautions, however, that trying to practice magic without understanding occultism is like trying to drive a locomotive without having had special training.

Magic and Witchcraft

Magic is of secondary importance in witchcraft, according to Justine Glass (*Witchcraft,* 1965). Glass divides witchcraft into two parts, operative witchcraft and ceremonial witchcraft. The former includes charms, words used in incantations, and unguents used for different purposes. Operative witchcraft includes everything having to do with magic. It is part of a tradition dating from the beginning of man's consciousness of himself as a being capable of using his will to effect changes in his world. Once religion and magic were virtually identical and one person could serve as both priest and magician. The rise of Christianity relegated magic to an inferior status. In the 19th century, however, a resurgence of interest in magic led to the revival or formation of groups or movements such as the Rosicrucians, Vril, the Golden Dawn, and the Theosophical Society. Rudolf Steiner attracted considerable attention by popularizing the notion that human mind contains the cosmos.

Magic Cake

Black millet mixed with the flesh of unbaptized children, served at the Sabbat, was supposed to enable witches to remain silent under torture.

Magic Candle

The sorcerer uses a lighted candle in discovering buried treasure. The discovery of the secret of the Magic Candle is attributed to Jerome Cardan. The *Little Albert* provides directions for concocting it:

You must have a big candle made of human tallow, and

it must be set in a piece of hazel-wood. . . . If this candle, when lighted in an underground place, sparkles brightly and makes considerable noise, treasure must be in that place, and the nearer you come to the treasure, the more the candle will sparkle. When you are quite near, the candle will go out, and you must have others in reserve. When there are good reasons for believing that treasure is guarded by the spirits of dead men, it is better for you to have wax candles which have been blessed instead of common candles, and to conjure the spirits in the name of God to declare whether you can help them to a place of untroubled rest. You must not fail to comply with their request.

Magic Carpet

A carpet made of new wool during the full moon produces oracular utterances if this incantation is used in making it:

Agla, Agla, Agla, Agla! O Almighty God, Thou art the Life of the Universe, and rulest over the four parts of that immense area, through the power of Thy Holy Name Tetragrammaton: Yod, He, Vau, He! Bless this carpet in Thy Name, as Thou blessed the cloak of Elijah in the hands of Elijah; so that, with Thy wings, I may be able to be protected against all: He shall hide Thee under His wings and under His feathers thou shalt trust, and His truth shall be thy protection.

Magic Chain

The magician must create around himself a powerful field of fluidic attraction in the visible and the invisible world, beginning with the latter. This field of attraction is the magnetic chain that will block all attacks by jealous or spiteful individuals. The adept first chooses a guide, a deceased master of magic, ancient or modern, whose doctrine and works he cherishes. The master's name, dynamized by

364

the disciple's admiration and eagerness, is the nucleus of the magic chain. In beginning every ceremony or prayer, the adept addresses himself to his beloved master, the symbol of the adept's will in the invisible realm. Then he invokes the psychical influences of the astral world. Then he invokes his own planetary spirit (the one that dominates his temperament), calling out his name three times. Next comes a prayer, then a statement of the adept's request. In case of danger, he has only to whisper the name of the master three times and he will immediately sense the chain's protective psychical influence. Once this chain is brought into being in the invisible world, it must be established as quickly as possible in the visible world. Consequently, an intellectual association with a serious and discrete friend is very useful, and is the prime reason for the formation of most occult groups. The magic circle is simply the material representation of the chain that protects the magician in the invisible world.

Éliphas Lévi made the following statements concerning the Magic Chain:

> To make the Magic Chain is to establish a magnetic current which becomes stronger in proportion to the extent of the chain. . . .

> All enthusiasm propagated in a society by a scheme of intercourse and fixed practices in common produces a magnetic current, and is maintained or increased by the current. The action of the current is to transport and often to exalt beyond measure persons who are impressionable and weak, nervous organizations, temperaments inclined to hysteria or hallucination. Such people soon become powerful vehicles of magical force and project efficiently the Astral Light in the direction of the current itself. . . .

I will go further and affirm that magical circles and magnetic currents establish themselves, and have an influence, according to fatal laws, upon those on whom they can act. Each one of us is drawn within a sphere of relations which constitutes his world and to the influence of which he is made subject. . . .

It has occurred to me frequently after experiments in the Magic Chain, performed with persons devoid of good intention or sympathy, that I have been awakened with a start in the night by truly alarming impressions and senations. On one such occasion I felt vividly the pressure of an unknown hand attempting to strangle me. I rose up, lighted my lamp, and set calmly to work, seeking to profit by my wakefulness and to drive away the phantoms of sleep. The books about me were moved with considerable noise, papers were disturbed and rustled one against another, timber creaked, as if on the point of splitting, and heavy blows resounded on the ceiling. With curiosity but also with tranquillity I observed all these phenomena, which would not have been less wonderful had they been only the product of my imagination, so real did they seem.

Magic Circle

Every magical operation is executed within the confines of a circle which symbolizes the will of the operator and protects him against external influences. The circle should be drawn with the point of a magic sword. The outer circle should be nine feet in diameter. Inside it, at intervals equal to the width of his palm, he should inscribe two other circles. The middle circle should contain astrological data, the outer circle the names of the angels of the air who rule the day chosen for the operation, and the inner circle four names of God, separated by crosses. At each of the cardinal points outside the circle he should put a penta-

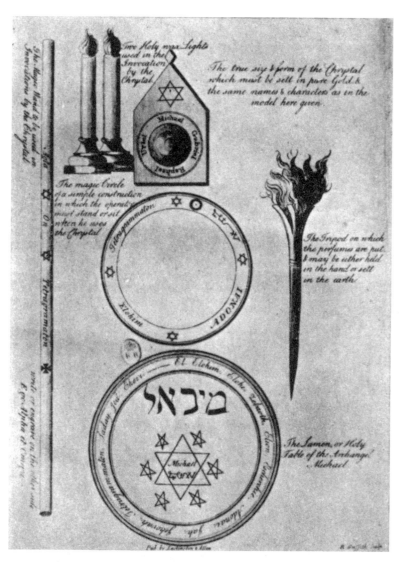

THE MAGIC CIRCLE AND THE ACCESSORIES FOR EVOCATION
Francis Barrett, *The Magus* (London, 1801).

The Two Witches
Hans Baldung Green; Stadelsches Institute, Frankfurt.

gram; inside, in the eastern half the Greek letter Alpha, and in the western half Omega.

The *Great Grimoire* outlines each step to be followed in making a magic circle:

You will begin by making a circle with the goatskin, as previously indicated, nailing down the skin with four nails. Then you will take your blood stone and trace a triangle inside the circle, beginning with the direction of the east; and you will also trace with the blood stone the great A, the small E, the small A and the small J, along with the holy name of Jesus, between two crosses, to prevent the spirits from attacking you in the rear.

After which, the karcist will gather his assistants into the circle, each in his own place, as indicated, and he will enter it himself without fear, whatever sounds he may hear; placing the two candlesticks with the two verbena wreaths on the right and the left of the inner triangle.

This done, you will begin to light your two candles, and you will have a brand new vase before you, that is, before the karcist, filled with charcoal made of willow, burnt the same day, that the karcist will light, throwing a drop of brandy on it, and a pinch of the incense and the camphor that you have, keeping the rest to maintain a constant fire, as the duration of the operation requires.

After all that has been previously mentioned has been performed, you will pronounce the following words:

"I offer you, O mighty Adonai, this purest incense, as I offer this charcoal made from the lightest wood. I offer it, O great and potent Adonai, Eloim, Ariel, and Jehovam, with all my soul and all my heart. Deign, O mighty Adonai, to accept it favorably."

Then you will also make sure not to have on your person

any impure metal: only gold and silver to throw at the spirit, wrapping it in a piece of paper that you will throw at it, so that it may do you no injury when it presents itself before the circle.

While the spirit picks up the coin, you will begin the following prayer, fortifying yourself with courage and strength and wisdom. Also see to it that only the karcist speaks. The others must maintain silence, even when the demon questions or threatens them:

"O mighty living Lord! In one and the same person, father, son, and holy spirit, I worship you with the greatest reverence, and submit to your holy and worthy protection in the deepest confidence. I believe, with the utmost faith, that you are my creator, my benefactor, my support and my master, and I declare to you that I have no other desire but to belong to you in all eternity."

The circle, drawn around the karcist with a new sword, symbolizes the separation of the wizard from the infernal powers. Honi Ha Me'agel, a first-century Hebrew magician, was known as the circle drawer because he often stood within the magic circle and produced rain. Reginald Scot's *Discoverie of Witchcraft* (1584) offered this advice:

As for the places of Magical Circles, they are to be chosen melancholy, doleful, dark and lonely; either in Woods or Deserts, or in a place where three ways meet, or amongst ruins of Castles, Abbeys, Monasteries, etc., or upon the Seashore when the Moon shines clear, or else in some Parlor hung with black . . . , with doors and windows closely shut, and waxen candles lighted.

The *Key of Solomon* provides instructions for the magician who is about to enter the magic circle. He must chant these words:

368

May all devils flee, and particularly those who are inimical to this operation! When we enter herein we call with humility that God the Almighty entering this Circle will cast down divine pleasure and prosperity and joy and charity and greeting.

May the Angels of Peace help and defend this Circle, may discord disappear from it!

Help and magnify us, O Lord. Thy Most Holy Name bless our meeting and our speech. O Lord our God, bless our entry into this Circle, for Thou art blessed for Ever and Ever!

Another formula for consecrating the magic circle is offered by Frances Barrett in *The Magus* (1801):

In the name of the holy, blessed, and glorious Trinity, proceed we to our work in these mysteries to accomplish that which we desire; we therefore, in the names aforesaid, consecrate this piece of ground for our defence, so that no spirit whatsoever shall be able to break these boundaries, neither be able to cause injury nor detriment to any of us here assembled; but they may be compelled to stand before the circle, and answer truly our demands, so far as it pleaseth Him who liveth for ever and ever and who says, I am Alpha and Omega, the Beginning and the End, which is, and which was, and which is to come, the Almighty; I am the First and the Last, who am living and was dead; and behold I live for ever and ever; and I have the keys of death and hell. Bless, O Lord! this creature of earth wherein we stand; confirm, O God! thy strength in us, so that neither the adversary nor any evil thing may cause us to fail.

Magic Darts
Lead darts were used by the Laplanders, who were once

credited with being master magicians, against their absent enemies. These magic darts were supposed to inflict grievous pains and maladies on their victims.

Magic, Definition
Papus defined magic as the study and practice of the manipulation of the secret forces of nature, the application of the dynamic human will to the rapid evolution of the living forces of nature.

Magic Formula
See Sator.

Magic Formulas and Exorcisms
The idea of magic fascinated even learned men and was responsible for the inclusion of a plethora of magic formulas and exorcisms in popular grimoires.

> There are innumerable magic formulas and exorcisms, most of them invoking God or the Trinity, or Jesus Christ, in Hebrew or Latin. . . . Among the magic symbols which are met with in old documents, the triangle, the cross, the pentagram, and the signs of the planets are preferred; but other figures, such as squares, hexagrams, circles, and fantastic combinations of irregular lines are also quite frequent. Conjurations were made according to various prescriptions; a circle was drawn at midnight where two roads cross; it was lit with wax candles made after specific recipes. The conjurer had to prepare himself by fasts and prayers, sometimes by partaking of the holy communion at church, and when at last he failed to find the treasure or to accomplish his purpose, whatever it may have been, he had reason to believe that he made some trifling mistake in his preparations. (Joseph Caro.)

Magic Girdles
Ferns gathered at midnight on St. John's Eve and arranged

to form the magic character HVTY. Magic girdles are supposed to cure diseases.

Magic, Laws of
See Laws of Magic.

Magic Lozenge
See Sky-trap.

Magic Manuals
Legend holds that the devils composed several handbooks on magic and hid them under Solomon's throne. After his death, they urged his courtiers to dig under his throne to learn how he had secured control over men, spirits, and the wind. According to the Koran:

> And they followed the device which the devils devised against the kingdom of Solomon; and Solomon was not an unbeliever; but the devils believed not, they taught men sorcery.

Magic Mirror
See Solomon's Mirror.

Magic Mushrooms
Fleshy fungi used in magical and religious ceremonies, particularly in Mexico and the southwestern region of the United States. The mushrooms (probably Psilocybe mexicana) have been used for centuries to induce visions and hallucinogenic states. See Castaneda, Carlos.

Magic, Origin of
Magic originated with man's earliest attempts to control occult forces. It synthesized psychological concepts appropriate to the manipulation of the primitive mind. Magical science was closely linked to the life and destiny of prehistoric man, and the first magicians thoroughly understood such psychological forces as inhibition and fascination. The

earliest forms of attack and defense among men may have resembled the fascination of the cat or serpent and the inhibition (complete withdrawal, death feint, "freezing") of the opossum. Men tried to charm the creatures they were trying to catch and magic, with its appeal to instinct and feeling, was their most powerful weapon.

Magic, Ritual
See Ritual Magic.

Magic Robes
In the performance of magic rites, special garments and other equipment were used by occultists as an aid in the effectiveness of the ceremonies. Among such requirements were a tunic of white linen, or a purple robe; garlands fashioned of various branches of violet, or vervain; incense and perfumes; cedar, citron, amber; poplar or oak wreaths. Black robes too were in order in certain diabolic rites: also necklaces, bracelets, beads, rings.

Magic Triangle
See Abracadabra.

Magical Diagrams
Geometrical designs representing the mysteries of creation and the divinity. They are supposed to be of special virtue in summoning spirits. The chief magical diagrams are the Triangle, the Double Triangle forming the Sign of Solomon, the Tetragram or four-pointed star formed by the interlacement of two pillars, and the Pentagram or five-pointed star.

Magical Instruments
According to Éliphas Lévi, the most important magical instruments are the wand, sword, lamp, chalice, altar, and tripod.

In the operations of Transcendental and Divine Magic, the lamp, wand and chalice are used; in the works of

Black Magic, the wand is replaced by the sword and the lamp by the candle of Cardan. . . .

The consecration of the wand must last seven days, beginning at the new moon, and should be made by an initiate possessing the great arcana, and having himself a consecrated wand. This is the transmission of the magical secret, which has never ceased since the shrouded origin of the transcendent science. The wand and the other instruments, but the wand above all, must be concealed with care, and under no pretext should the Magus permit them to be seen or touched by the profane; otherwise they will lose all their virtue. The mode of transmitting the wand is one of the arcana of science, the revelation of which is never permitted. . . .

The sword is less occult and is made in the following manner: It must be of pure steel, with a cruciform copper hilt having three pommels. . . .

The consecration of the sword must take place on a Sunday, during the hours of the Sun, under the invocation of Michaël. The blade of the sword must be placed in a fire of laurel and cypress; it must be dried and polished with ashes of the sacred fire, moistened with the blood of a mole or serpent. . . .

The magical lamp must be composed of the four metals —gold, silver, brass and iron; the pedestal should be of iron, the mirror of brass, the reservoir of silver, the triangle at the apex of gold. It should be provided with two branches composed of a triple tube of three intertwisted metals, in such a manner that each arm has a triple conduit for the oil; there must be nine wicks in all, three at the top and three in each branch. The Seal of Hermes must be engraved on the pedestal, over which must be

373

a two-headed androgyne of Khunrath. A serpent devouring its own tail must encircle the lower part.

Magical Laboratory

All of the furnishings of the magician's laboratory should be new and each item should be consecrated separately, according to Éliphas Lévi, taking into account planetary correspondences. Each item should be sprinkled with magical water, fumigated with consecrated perfumes, rubbed with consecrated ointment, and blessed with a prayer. The walls of the room should be covered with white cloth. The laboratory proper *(laboratorium)* consists of a long table covered with a thick mirror or white cloth and placed along the western side of the room. The eastern side is for the oratorium, consisting of an altar, a storage closet for magical equipment, and a closet for the symbols associated with the world's chief religions. All of these items must be bought and consecrated under the auspices of the sun. A curtain should separate the laboratorium and the oratorium. One light should be suspended from the ceiling of the eastern half of the room, another from that of the western half.

The altar should be covered with a fine white linen and should constitute a pentacle of the universe in its three planes, human, natural, and divine. In the middle of the altar there should be a pentagram, either that of Éliphas Lévi (synthetic) or that of Agrippa von Nettesheim (microcosmic):

The pentagram should be inscribed on virgin parchment or on the skin of a new-born calf. Around it should be placed seven small cubes, corresponding to the metal associated with each of the seven planets. Mercury's cube should be enclosed in the seven-pointed Egyptian star.

The water used in the magical room should be prepared ritually, under the influence of the moon but during the day. Placing his hands on the crystal vase containing the

374

water, the magician breathes upon it three times, pronouncing the name of the Tetragram and stating the purpose of the consecration. Incense should be burned as the Prayer of the Undines is uttered. Perfumes corresponding to each planet are consecrated as the Prayer of the Sylphs is pronounced.

Magical Operations

Details concerning magical operations are found in many medieval handbooks. Selections from books on ceremonial magic are found in L. Thorndike's *A History of Magic and Experimental Science* (8 vols., 1923-58), E. M. Butler's *Ritual Magic* (1959), and A. E. Waite's *The Book of Ceremonial Magic* (1961, reprint of a revised version of his *Book of Black Magic and of Pacts*, 1898).

Magicians

Demons collaborate with magicians, according to Tertullian, Origen, and Bossuet. Magicians were excommunicated by the Councils of Agde (506), Orléans (511), Narbonne (589), Reims (625), Tours (813), Paris (829), Angers (1294), Cologne (1357), and Rouen (1445).

Magick in Theory and Practice

One of the best books ever written on the subject of magic. It was published in 1929 by Aleister Crowley, the self-styled "Great Beast."

Magister Templi

One of the ten grades in Aleister Crowley's cabalistic system. It corresponds to sephira 3, Saturn. The Magister Templi tends his garden of disciples and achieves a perfect understanding of the universe.

Magus

One of the ten grades, corresponding to sephiroth, in Aleister Crowley's cabalistic system. The magus, in sephira 2, the sphere of stars, "attains to wisdom, declares his law and is a Master of all Magick in its greatest and highest sense."

Éliphas Lévi maintained that the Magus and the Microprosopus were one:

> The Magus is truly that which the Hebrew Kabalists term MICROPROSOPUS—otherwise, the creator of the little world. The first of all magical sciences being the knowledge of one's self, so is one's own creation first of all works of science; it comprehends the others and is the beginning of the Great Work. The expression, however, requires explanation. Supreme Reason being the sole invariable and consequently imperishable principle—and death, as we call it, being change—it follows that the intelligence which cleaves closely to this principle and in a manner identifies itself therewith, does hereby make itself unchangeable and as a result immortal. To cleave invariably to reason it will be understood that it is necessary to attain independence of all those forces which by their fatal and inevitable operation produce the alternatives of life and death. To know how to suffer, to forbear and to die—such are the first secrets which place us beyond reach of affliction, the desires of the flesh and the fear of annihilation. The man who seeks and finds a glorious death has faith in immortality and universal humanity believes in it with him and for him, raising altars and statues to his memory in token of eternal life.

> Man becomes king of the brutes only by subduing or taming them: otherwise he will be their victim or slave. Brutes are the type of our passions; they are the instinctive forces of Nature. The world is a field of battle, where liberty struggles with inertia by the opposition of active force. Physical laws are millstones; if you cannot be the miller you must be the grain. You are called to be king of air, water, earth and fire; but to reign over these four

living creatures of symbolism, it is necessary to conquer and enchain them. He who aspires to be a sage and to know the Great Enigma of Nature must be the heir and despoiler of the sphinx: his the human head, in order to possess speech; his the eagle's wings, in order to scale the heights; his the bull's flanks, in order to furrow the depths; his the lion's talons, to make a way on the right and the left, before and behind.

Mahatmas
See Adepts.

Maier, Michael
German alchemist (born about 1568). A. E. Waite gives this account of his life and works:

> This celebrated German alchemist, one of the central figures of the Rosicrucian controversy in Germany, and the greatest adept of his age, was born at Ruidsburg, in Holstein, towards the year 1568. . . .

> He appears as an alchemical writer a little before the publication of the Rosicrucian manifestoes. In the controversy which followed their appearance, and which convulsed mystic Germany, he took an early and enthusiastic share, defending the mysterious society in several books and pamphlets. He is supposed to have travelled in search of genuine members of the "College of Teutonic Philosophers R. C.," and, failing to meet with them, is said to have established a brotherhood of his own on the plan of the *Fama Fraternitatis.* . . .

> Many of his works are Hermetic elaborations of classical mythology, and are adorned with most curious plates. . . .

> He does not appear to have been included among the adepts, and he is now almost forgotten. His chemical

knowledge is buried in a multitude of symbols and insoluble enigmas.

Maitland, Edward
Modern occultist. He worked with Anna Kingsford during her lifetime and remained in communication with her, through a medium, after her death. With her he evolved a form of esoteric Christianity.

Ma'kheru
Egyptian sorcerer. The word derives from the Egyptian expression meaning Magic Word or Word of Truth. Based on the notion that making a statement or a promise is equivalent to having it done or fulfilling it, the Word of Truth was one of the teachings of the ancient Egyptian mysteries.

Malayan Incantations
Magic accessories—incense, rice, wax tapers—are used to cure sickness. The Malay charm is pronounced over the embers.

> If you are at one with me, rise toward me,
> O smoke:
> If you are not at one with me, rise athwart me,
> O smoke,
> Either to right or left.

A Malay charm for fever requires seven cigarettes, seven betel-leaf chews, seven bananas, parched rice, and an egg. These must be rolled up in a banana leaf and placed at a triple crossroads. Then this incantation is pronounced:

> Jembalang, Jembali, Demon of the Earth,
> Accept this portion as your payment
> And restore (name of person sick).
> But if you do not restore him

I shall curse you with the saying
"There is no god but God."

In Malayan witchcraft, each type of incense is effective
against a particular demon. Here is an invocation addressed
to the Spirit of Incense:

Zubur Hijau is your name, O incense,
Zabur Bajang the name of your Mother,
Zabur Puteh the name of your Fumes.
May you fumigate the Seven Tiers of the Earth,
May you fumigate the Seven Tiers of the Sky
And serve as a summons to all spirits,
To those that have magic power.

Maleficia

Mishaps and misfortunes suffered by persons, animals, or
property were attributed to evil spirits. Witches, classified
as *malefici*, were capable of causing mental as well as physical harm. In his *Discourse of Damned Art of Witchcraft*
(1608), William Perkins detailed their powers: raising
storms, poisoning the air, blasting corn, killing cattle, an-
noying people, procuring strange passions in the bodies of
creatures, and casting out devils. Nider (1435) compiled an
earlier list: inspiring love, inspiring hatred, causing impo-
tence, causing disease, killing, taking away reason, and in-
juring property or animals. Hex is another term for
maleficia.

Martin de Arles (1460) concluded that maleficia involved
an implicit pact with Satan. Bernard de Como (1510) decreed in his role as Inquisitor that all incurable and unex-
plainable diseases were the result of sorcery. Evidence of
harm or injury to people was sufficient basis for condemnation as a devil-worshipper.

379

Exorcistarum (1651) defines maleficia as "a vicious act directed against the body, through the power of the Devil in a tacit or public pact entered into with the witch. . . ."

Accounts of maleficia are still being reported throughout the world.

Malinowski, Bronislaw Kasper

Polish-born British anthropologist (1884-1842). He is known especially for the depth and comprehensiveness of his studies of Melanesian society. His detailed study of the function of magic in the Trobriand Islands led him to the conclusion that magic fills a gap in tribal knowledge and provides an alternative means of expression for thwarted human desires.

Malkuth

The tenth sephira, the sphere of the earth, in cabalistic teachings. It contains the force of all the sephiroth within itself. When the Tree of Life is represented as a human body, Malkuth is the union of the whole body.

Malleus Maleficarum

First published in Cologne in 1486. *Malleus Maleficarum* (The Witches' Hammer), by Jacob Sprenger and Heinrich Kramer, has subsequently reappeared in many editions in most of the countries of Europe. Its encyclopedic pages cover every phase of witchcraft. Part I identifies heresy and witchcraft; Part II analyzes evil spells; Part III specifies modes of repression (inquisitorial, episcopal, civil), interrogatories, tortures, and confessions; Part IV indicates the exorcisms to be applied. The work owes its success to the personalities of its authors, two Dominicans, and to the advice offered to witchhunters.

Its title derives from the title often given to the Inquisitors, "Hammer of heretics." Modeled on the handbooks of

Eymeric and other scholastics, it was carefully organized and fortified by papal approval. Its wide dissemination fixed the whole system of beliefs in witchcraft in the public's mind.

The *Malleus* tries to refute all arguments against the reality of witchcraft, which it defines as the most abominable form of heresy. Witchcraft involves three elements: an evil-minded witch, the Devil, and God, who must allow evil to exist along with freedom. Its four essentials are renunciation of the Christian faith, sacrificial killing of unbaptized children, giving body and soul over to evil, and copulating with incubi.

Man
According to Hitchcock, man is the secret subject of every alchemist. He adds:

> The object also is one, to wit, nature directed by art in the school of nature, and acting in conformity therewith; for the art is nothing but nature acting through man.

Man of Knowledge
Term used by Carlos Castaneda to translate Don Juan's concept of a witch. Don Juan treats drugs as an alternative or incidental route to be followed in becoming a man of knowledge. The process involves techniques for "stopping the world," or shifting to the perception of a separate reality. Splintering the ego and effacing self-consciousness, learning to "see" rather than to "look," and passing tests not unlike those set for men seeking to be initiated into the Egyptian mysteries are a part of the process.

Mana
In occultism, a power of force which affects both things and the actions of men.

381

Manannan

Brother of Bran. He is still the center of a cult on the Isle of Man. He is a powerful magician whose horse flies through the air. He moves across the sea in a ship that has neither a rudder nor sails. Some occultists believe that he was an alien visitor to the planet Earth. See Astronauts.

Mancy

Suffix derived from Greek *manteia*, meaning divination. The suffix is used in technical descriptions of various forms of divination: necromancy, based on the examination of dead bodies; oneiromancy, involving dreams; hydromancy, using water, etc.

Mandala

Magic circle, usually geometric in design. It consists of an inner circle enclosed in a square with four entrances. It combines art, magic, and psychology. Its symbology may derive from the yoga doctrine stressing complete union with the divine through meditation and concentration. It enables the devotee (sadhaka) to achieve the power of a deity whose nature it typifies.

C. G. Jung has proposed psychological interpretations of the mandala. See Signatures.

Mandragoras

Familiar demons. They appear in the figures of little beardless men.

Mandrake

A plant, mandragora officinarum, of the potato family. It is also called mandragore. It often grows in the shape of human limbs. In former times it was frequently used in love philtres, and is so mentioned in Genesis 30.14-15. It is also known as "the plant of Circe," because her witchbrews were reputedly infusions of mandrake. In the Middle Ages, the mandrake was said to grow from the sperm of men who have been hanged. The plant was supposed to have the power to predict the future, open locks, and produce gold.

Manilius, Marcus

A Roman poet who flourished in the first century A.D. He was the author of Astronomica, a didactic poem on the subject of astrology. Five books of the poem are extant. The themes treated include: the creation of the universe, the starry heavens and their disposition, the zodiacal signs, with their characteristics, aspects and subdivisions, methods of determining a horoscope, and the influence of the zodiac on human life.

Manticism

A state of prophetic frenzy. In antiquity, the pagan priests and others associated with religious cults were accustomed, while in this condition, to make prophetic pronouncements. The early Church Fathers condemned this practice.

Mantra Shastra

Brahmanical writings on the occult science of incantations.

Mantrika Sakti

The occult potency of mystic numbers, sounds, or letters in the Vedic mantras.

Marcomir

A witch is supposed to have summoned a triple-headed devil to come before Marcomir, king of the Franks.

Margaritomancy

Divination by pearls.

Maria Hebrea

A Jewess who was an alchemist. She flourished possibly in the first century A.D., in Memphis, Egypt. Her name has survived in the expression bain-marie, a term used in chemistry.

Maria La Medica
See La Medica, Maria.

Mariken Van Nieumeghen
A Dutch miracle play (c. 1500) based on the legend of a female Faust who agreed to live with the Devil for many years, obtaining his favors and presents. The play ends with the salvation of the heroine.

Mars
The planet nearest the earth is the image of the warrior. The reddish, violent planet has the warrior's courage, energy, and anger. Its influences are utilized in magic when action is called for. It is rarely used in the fabrication of pentacles, however, since its cycle is 687 days. Red is its color.

Martinet
Familiar demon who accompanies sorcerers. Sometimes he helps travelers who have gone astray.

Masleh
In rabbinical legend, Masleh is the medium through which the power of the Messiah was transmitted to the sphere of the Zodiac.

Mastema
In pre-Christian literature Mastema is frequently identified as an evil prince. In apocalyptic writings, the word designates the cosmic power of evil, identified with the evil impulse in man and with death. According to the Book of Jubilee, written before 96 B.C., he is the chief of the evil spirits resulting from the union of the fallen angels and mortals. After God intervened, he remained in control of one-tenth of the fallen angels "in order that they might

384

continue to serve Satan on Earth." He counseled God to test Abraham. In Egypt he aided the sorcerers who opposed Moses.

Master John

A fourteenth-century English necromancer. He was involved in a plot to kill Edward II by using Black Magic.

Materialization

A term used in spiritualism to denote the formation of a temporary but visible physical organization that enabled the spirit to come into touch with material objects. A spirit may appear in material form partially or wholly— as a complete body or merely as a head or hand.

Mather, Cotton

New England preacher and writer. He encouraged the Salem witchhunts. He wrote *Memorable Providences Relating to Witchcraft and Possessions* (1689) and *Wonders of the Invisible World* (1693).

Mathers, Samuel Liddel MacGregor

Visible Head of the Order of the Golden Dawn. With the help of his wife, a clairvoyant who was the sister of the philosopher Henri Bergson, he deciphered the mysterious manuscript discovered in 1884 by a London clergyman and brought to him by William Winn Westcott. The manuscript dealt with the Cabala and the Tarot. Mrs. Mathers' introduction to the 1938 edition of her husband's *Kabbalah Unveiled* indicates that the Golden Dawn explored "the intelligent forces from behind Nature, the Constitution of man and his relation to God," and the means by which man may unite with "the Divine Man latent in himself." Mathers, who took to calling himself MacGregor Mathers, Chevalier MacGregor, and Comte de Glenstrae, edited and translated magical textbooks: the *Key of Solomon* and the *Sacred Magic of Abramelin the Mage.*

Yeats frequently played chess in the Mathers household in Paris. He and Mrs. Mathers played against Mathers and a spirit. The Order of the Golden Dawn was torn by dissension after Aleister Crowley became a member. When Mathers died in 1918, his friends believed that Crowley used black magic to cause his death.

Mbwiri

In Central Africa, this is a malefic demon that enters the victim's body. The demon is exorcised by the priest-doctor of the tribe. The rite is performed over a period of some ten days or more, to the accompaniment of drinking, eating, dancing and music. This ritual coincides largely with the exorcism ceremony as practiced in Tibet and as described by the Abbé Huc in his *Travels in Tibet*.

Medea

In Classical mythology, an enchantress, daughter of Aeëtes, king of Colchis. She fell in love with Jason and helped him to slay the dragon guarding the golden fleece. Betrayed by Jason, she murdered their two children and fled from Corinth in her car drawn by dragons to Athens. There she married Argeus and gave birth to a son named Medus.

Medicine-man

Among Australian aborigines, the medicine-men initiate the tribal members into the mysteries of rituals and myths. They practice meditation, telepathy, and hypnotism. They also act as seers, treat sickness, and give protection against magic practices.

The term is frequently applied to the priests and shamans of the Indian tribes of North America.

Medium

A spiritualistic medium is supposed to be susceptible to supernatural agencies and to be able to communicate knowledge obtained from them or perform acts made possible only by their help. In theosophy, a medium is one whose unstable inner constitution functions in magnetic sympathy with components of the astral light.

The medium is generally an extremely sensitive person who can be readily "controlled" by spirits. Among the earliest mediums in America were Mrs. Fox and her daughters, whose seances consisted mainly of rappings to convey messages from the spirits to the sisters. The crowning achievement of later mediums was the materialization of hands, faces, and finally the complete forms of "controls."

Trance utterances dealing with life beyond the grave are stressed by those for whom spiritualism is a religion. Spiritualists claim that mediumistic phenomena result from the influence of the spirits of the dead on the sensitive organism of the medium.

In preliterate as well as advanced societies certain individuals act as if possessed by a supernatural force or being. They seem to convey messages from the world of the dead to the world of the living. Sometimes these mediums protest the function assigned to them; sometimes they gladly accept it. Generally they train themselves or are trained by mentors or sponsors who help them to develop their potential as mediums. Their primary role is to comfort the living by bringing them communications from the deceased. Many of the most intriguing paranormal phenomena observed after modern spiritualism came into existence in the 19th century (clairvoyance, telepathy, psychokinesis) as well as alleged proof of the existence of a spirit world and the survival of the soul involve mediumship. Mediums are also called sensitives. Some anthropologists hold that in primitive societies individuals entrusted with the role of medium (diviners, sorcerers, etc.) are the misfits or outcasts of the tribe.

Megwa

A word used in the Trobriand Islands to denote either a
spell or magic.

Mellin, Hector

French magician, inventor of a machine to protect people
against evil radiations. See Radiation Machine.

Melusian

French fay. She was wedded to a mortal count. Every Saturday she was condemned to turn into a serpent from the waist
downward. When he discovered her secret, he forced her
to wander about as a specter until doomsday.

Menat

A magic amulet worn by Egyptian gods, goddesses, kings,
priests, and officials. Inscribed with representations of a
goddess and a serpent, it was supposed to ensure fertility
and was buried with the wearer in order to renew his sex
powers in the outer world.

Mephistopheles

The story of the pact made between Faust and Mephis-
topheles recalls the ancient Chaldean incantations and the
seven evil planetary spirits mentioned in a text beginning
"They are seven! They are seven!" The name of Faust's
familiar spirit seems to be derived from Semitic words
meaning destroyer and deceiver, and joined together in the
form Mephistopheliel. See Faust; Chaldean Incantations.

Mercurius

In the writings of alchemists, Mercurius (or the planetary
spirit Mercury) is the god who discloses the secret of the
art to the initiates. He is also the soul of bodies, spirit
that has become earth, spirit that transforms the material
world. Idented with Hermes Trismegistus, he is also symbolized, like *nouns* or *pneuma,* by the serpent and called

the mediator, the original man, and the Hermaphroditic Adam.

Mercury

The fastest moving planet, Mercury completes its cycle in 88 days and can be used by the magician at least four times a year by the magician who seeks to acquire its influence. The planet represents infancy, with its overflowing of vitality and motion. Its color is that of the prism—that is, the juxtaposition of different colors.

Merlin

Enchanter belonging to the court of King Arthur. He was probably a Celtic god who in time became to be looked upon as a great sorcerer.

The reputed offspring of an incubus and the daughter of King Arthur, he was the wise counselor of four kings and played an important part in the literature of the Middle Ages.

Mescaline

The purified active principle of the mescal cactus, *Lophophora williamsii*. Long used in magic and religious rituals by the Indians of Mexico and the American Southwest, it was studied by Heffter in 1897. He described its effects on himself, saying that it produced vividly colored visual hallucinations. In 1954 Aldous Huxley praised mescaline intoxication in *The Doors of Perception*. Detailed accounts of its use in sorcery appear in two books by Carlos Castaneda, *The Teaching of Don Juan* (1968) and *A Separate Reality* (1971).

Mesmer, Franz

Austrian physician (1733-1815). He believed that medicine and religion were inseparable. Through his use of magnets, rituals, and the animal magnetism (life force) around the body, he cured hundreds of patients.

The influence of the planets he identified with magnetism. On seeing the remarkable cures of Gassner he supposed that the magnetic force must also reside in the human body, and thereupon dispensed with magnets. . . . His method was to seat his patients round a large circular vat or *baquet,* in which various substances were mixed. Each patient held one end of an iron rod, the other end of which was in the baquet. In due time the crisis ensued. Violent convulsions, cries, laughter, and various physical symptoms followed, these being in turn superseded by lethargy. In 1784 the government appointed a commission . . . (which reported) that there was no such thing as anmal magnetism, and referred the facts of the crisis to the imagination of the patient. (Lewis Spence.)

Mesmerism
The older term for hypnotism. Mesmerism is derived from Franz Mesmer (1733-1815), an Austrian physician who discovered what was called animal magnetism. The principles of his discovery are expounded in *De Planetarium Influxu:* (1) celestial, terrestrial, and animated bodies influence each other; (2) this mutual influence depends on a continuous, subtle, and universal fluid; (3) unknown mechanical laws govern this influence; (4) alternating effects are produced (flux and fluxes and refluxes); (5) the human body has magnetic properties, making it susceptible to various influences.

Metamorphosis
A change from human to animal form. Zoomorphism dates from the earliest ages of man. Nebuchadnezzar is said to have taken on animal characteristics (growth of hair and the practice of eating grass), Circe changed Ulysses' men

into swine, and Ovid reported many examples of metamorphosis. Aeluranthropy (changing into a cat), boanthropy (cow or bull), cynanthropy (dog), lepanthropy (rabbit), and lycanthropy (wolf) are types of metamorphosis. Witches and demons were supposed to be able to assume various shapes.

Isabel Gowdie repeated a number of charms used in effecting transformations:

When we go in the shape of a hare, we say thrice over:

I shall go into a hare,
With sorrow and sigh and mickle care;
And I shall go in the Devil's name
Ay while I come home again.

And . . . when we would be out of this shape, we will say:

Hare, hare, God send thee care.
I am in a hare's likeness just now,
But I shall be in a woman's likeness even now.

Methods of Seducing Souls

The Devil seduces the innocent through weariness, through their carnal desires, or through sadness and poverty. The Malleus Maleficarum provides examples of each method of seduction.

Women have complained . . . that when their cows have been injured by being deprived of their milk, or in any other way, they have consulted with suspected witches, and even been given remedies by them, on condition that they would promise something to some spirit; and when they asked what they would have to promise, the witches answered that it was only a small thing, that they should agree to execute the instructions of that master with regard to certain observances during the

391

Holy Offices of the Church, or to observe some silent reservations in their confessions to priests.

The Dominican monks who wrote the handbook and ultimate authority for the Inquisition and for both Catholic and Protestant judges, magistrates and priests engaged in the struggle against witchcraft in Europe called attention to the fact that iniquity has small and scant beginnings, that the Devil often tempts us to give way from very weariness, and that by slow degrees people are led to a total abnegation of the faith and into the arms of the Devil.

Carnal desire is more likely to be the method used by witches to seduce innocent young girls. A witch confessed before she was burned at Ratisbon that she had been seduced by some old woman.

> A different method, however, was used in the case of her companion witch, who had met the Devil in human form on the road while she herself was going to visit her lover for the purpose of fornication. And when the Incubus Devil had seen her, and had asked her whether she recognized him, and she had said that she did not, he had answered: "I am the Devil; and if you wish, I will always be ready at your pleasure, and will not fail you in any necessity." And when she had consented, she continued for 18 years, up to the end of her life, to practice diabolical filthiness with him, together with a total abnegation of the Faith as a necessary condition.

The third method of temptation is through sadness and poverty. A poor girl who has been deflowered by her lover and then scorned by him readily turns to the Devil, either for revenge or for carnal pleasure. A young man living in the Diocese of Brixen testified that he had once rejected a certain girl in favor of another. But . . . I invited her to

392

the wedding. She came . . . , raised her hand and said, "You will have few days of health after today. . . ." After a few days my wife was so bewitched that she lost the use of all her limbs, and even now, after ten years, the effects of witchcraft can be seen on her body.

Metroscopy
Divination based on the relation of the forehead to the planets. Cardano, an Italian mathematician, anticipated phrenology by assigning a planetary influence to each part of the forehead.

He was the first to notice that the wrinkles of the forehead formed a mass of configurations that differed with each person and inferred that these configurations might serve as valuable indications of personality traits.

Meung, Jean De
Poet, alchemist, and astrologer (c. 1240-1305). A. E. Waite has this to say about him:

> Jean de Meung was one of the chief figures of the Court of King Philippe le Bel. . . .

> The Romance of the Rose, "that epic of ancient France," as Éliphas Lévi calls it, has been generally considered by alchemists a poetic and allegorical presentation of the secrets of the *magnum opus*. It professes, at any rate, the principles of Hermetic Philosophy, and Jean de Meung was also the author of "Nature's Remonstrances to the Alchemist" and "The Alchemist's Answer to Nature." Hermetic commentaries have been written upon the romance-poem, and tradition has ascribed to the author the accomplishment of great transmutations.

Mialism
A necromantic offshoot of voodoo practiced in Jamaica and involving intercourse with the spirits of the dead.

Michelet, Jules

One of the most brilliant and prolific historians France has produced, Jules Michelet (1798-1874) also wrote one of the classic studies of witchcraft. His *La Sorcière* (published in English as *Satanism and Witchcraft: A Study in Medieval Superstition*) appeared in 1862 and has been called "a nightmare of the most extraordinary verisimilitude and poetical power."

Microcosm

Man, the epitome of the microcosm, symbolized by a five-pointed star. Cabalists predicate control of supernatural forces on correspondences between the macrocosm and the microcosm.

Mirabilis Liber

A collection of predictions concerning the saints and the sybils. The edition of 1522 contains a prophecy of the French Revolution. Much of the book is attributed to Saint Césaire.

Miracle of Theophile

Falsely accused of wrong-doing, Theophile turned to a Jewish magician, reputed to be in league with the Devil. Theophile sold his soul to the Devil in order to regain his possessions. Years later, through the intercession of the Virgin, he recovered his soul. The legendary Faustian prototype is supposed to have lived in the sixth century. Theophile, the Virgin, and the Devil figure prominently in the literature and art of the middle ages.

Miracles

Miraculous actions and other supernatural phenomena were, in pre-Christian and non-Christian cultures, attributed to particular personalities—holy men, priests, sorcerers—who were regarded as endowed with abnormal powers. Around certain names—Zoroaster, Lao-tzu, Buddha, Confucius, Mohammed—legends spread with regard to their birth and death, the temptations that assailed them from Satanic malefic sources.

Miraculous deeds were attributed even to followers of these figures. Such miracles, contrary to the normal laws of nature, involved healing practices, escapes from incarceration, transportation and flight. The saints in Hinduism and Buddhism performed endless miracles. They traveled through the air. They transported people across rivers, without the aid of boats. They induced rain. They controlled storms and floods. They healed chronic sickness. They removed sterility. They could pass through the earth or through a wall. They assumed any form they desired. They could achieve invisibility and invulnerability. They could produce illumination by burning a finger. They remembered past lives. They also foresaw the future. At Buddha's birth the earth quaked. At his death flowers rained from heaven around the funeral procession and fire from the heavens lit the funeral pyre. Zoroaster again and again was rescued from evil spirits who were determined to destroy him. Moses, at the court of Pharaoh, performed miracles, and Elijah the Prophet was equally a thaumaturgist. In Moslem tradition, Mohammed's ascent to heaven is the predominant miracle. The Chinese immortals too possessed supernatural powers. In Christian religion the miracles performed by Jesus form an integral part of Christian faith.

Miriam the Jewess
One of the most famous sorceresses of ancient times. She was the sister of Moses and was said to have been instructed by God himself. Many important works were attributed to her. She was also known as Maria.

Mirror, Magic
See Solomon's Mirror.

395

Mirror of Solomon
See Solomon's Mirror.

Mirror Writing
Automatic writing sometimes presented in such a form that it can be read in a mirror. Writing backwards (also called by its German name *Spiegelschrift*) is supposed to authenticate the spiritual origin of automatic writing.

Mistletoe
The Druids believed that mistletoe was a gift from heaven. They gathered it on the sixth day of the new moon marking the beginning of their month. Two white bulls were sacrificed after a white-robed priest had climbed the tree, cut the mistletoe with a curved golden blade, and given it to attendants who placed it on a white cloth. The Druids also believed that a drink made from the mistletoe cured sterility and served as a powerful antidote.

This parasitic plant is connected with many pagan rites. In Brittany it was hung in stables to protect livestock. In Scandinavian mythology, it killed the god Balder. In Sweden it was said to have the power to reveal the existence of gold. In popular belief, it was supposed to be the source of life. In Frazer's *The Golden Bough,* the myth of Balder, vulnerable only to an arrow of mistletoe, is interpreted as a symbolic account of a fertility drama of death and resurrection.

Mitote
A meeting of a peyote cult.

Modern Occultism
See Current Literature.

Modern Witchcraft, Initiation into
See Coven, Admission into.

Mohammed-Ben-Ahmed
See Abou-Ryhan.

Molay, Jacques De
Conqueror of Jerusalem and Grand Master of the Templars. He confessed under torture (and later recanted) that he had denied Christ and worshiped Baphomet, practiced sodomy, and attended diabolic feasts at which human flesh was served. He was burned on March 18, 1314, along with Guy d'Auvergne.

Molitor, Ulrich
One of the earliest writers on witchcraft, he published his *De Lamiis et Phitonicis Mulieribus* (Concerning Female Sorcerers and Soothsayers) in 1489.

Monen
A term covering the branch of cabalistic magic dealing with divination based on the computation of time and observance of the celestial bodies.

Montespan, Mme. De
Mistress of Louis XIV of France (1641-1707). In order to retain the king's dying love, she practiced occult and Satanic rites, participating in an obscene Mass, in the concoction of philtres, and, according to historical chronicles, in child sacrifice as well. Among her accomplices were a certain Abbé Guibourg, Lesage, an alchemist, and Catherine La Voisin, a notorious witch.

Moon
In magic, the moon rules over the sublunar world. Its cycle matches the sun's, with the result that it is possible for the magician to conduct any operation without having to consider the positions of any of the other planets. The moon's phases epitomize the universal law of involution and evolution in four periods. Only during its first two

phases, when the lunar influences are truly dynamic, should the magician undertake ritual operations. The color corresponding to the moon is white.

Mopses

Secret German society which celebrated the Sabbat by using the Hermetic dog instead of the cabalistic goat as an object of worship.

Mora Witches

The famous investigation of witchcraft that began at Mora, Sweden, in 1669 was inspired by reports that the Devil had gained control over hundreds of children in the vicinity and had been seen going through the country. Scores of witches were identified. The mania spread to the Swedish-speaking provinces of Finland and to Stockholm. Finally it was stopped by Urban Hjärne, a young doctor who showed that the craze depended on a morbid imagination, malice, and desire for attention.

More, Henry

English philosopher (1614-1687). Though he was an earnest champion of the fusion of reason and faith, More had a lifelong interest in the occult. He believed that he had proof that witches and devils with cloven hooves attended sabbats.

Moses

Medieval Christians linked magic with the Devil, but Jews generally traced magic back to Moses, whom they numbered among the most famous magicians of all time.

Moses De Leon

Cabalist who revealed the Zohar to the public in 1300.

Mu

A lost continent of the Pacific. Thousands of years ago, according to some occultists, it sank below the surface and disappeared, except for some outcroppings now identified as the Pacific Islands. The inhabitants of Mu (or Lemuria), related to other highly advanced cultures such as those the ancient Mayas and Incas, were scattered when water covered most of the continent.

Mule
In Gypsy mythology, the souls of the dead. The *mulé* return to life at midday following the death of their hosts. Their function is mainly to harass the living, whom they often drive to suicide.

Mulos
In Gypsy superstition, the malefic spirits of the dead. They bring sickness and trouble upon the living. Treatment, confined within the family or tribe, includes herbal concoctions and repulsive ingredients such as snake fat, pulverized insects, and the entrails of animals. The wise old women of the tribe, the repositories of Gypsy healing lore, also use spells, incantations, and charms.

Murphy, Bridey
Subject of the best seller, *The Search for Bridey Murphy* (1956), written by Morey Bernstein, multimillionaire businessman and amateur hypnotist. Mrs. Virginia Tighe, in a deep hypnotic trance, recalled memories of the childhood of Bridey Murphy, wife of an early nineteenth-century barrister in Belfast. Bernstein concluded that Bridey Murphy was a former reincarnation of Mrs. Tighe.

Murray, Gilbert
World renowned classical scholar (1866-1957). He was president of the Society for Psychical Research for 1915-1916. He experimented with thought transference, a faculty which he discovered in himself by accident. He regarded the "fringe of consciousness" as the key to telepathy.

Murray, Margaret Alice

Anthropologist, folklorist, and Egyptologist (1863-1963). She published her first work on European witchcraft in 1921 *(The Witch Cult in Western Europe)*. This book, together with her *Encyclopaedia Britannica* article on "Witchcraft," made her by far the most influential proponent of the theory that an ancient fertility religion founded on the worship of Dianus persisted through the seventeenth century. Those who reject her extravagant claims (among them, the argument that every king of England from William the Conqueror through James I was a high priest of the witch cult) credit her with stressing a point long ignored by other scholars: that pagan folk practices survived long after the rise of Christianity and constituted the substratum of witchcraft in medieval Europe. In *The Witch Cult* she writes:

Underlying the Christian religion was a cult practiced by many classes of the community, chiefly, however, by the more ignorant or those in less thickly inhabited parts of the country. It can be traced back to pre-Christian times and appears to be the ancient religion of western Europe."

Muses

The Thracians engaged in elaborate ritual to enlist the support of the nine muses in their artistic undertakings. All nine of them were daughters of Olympian Zeus and Mnemosyne, and each was in charge of a particular art: Calliope, epic poetry and eloquence; Clio, history; Erato, love poetry; Euterpe, lyric poetry and music; Polyhymnia, sacred poetry; Thalia, pastoral poetry and comedy; Melpomene, tragedy; Terpsichore, dancing and Urania, astronomy.

Mushroom Madness

An expression used to describe a pseudo-psychotic state resulting from the ingestion of certain mushrooms. Because of their hallucinogenic properties, many mushrooms often produce temporary delusions and symptoms of madness.

Myers, Frederick William Henry

English writer (1843-1901). *In Human Personality and its Survival of Bodily Death,* the noted poet, essayist, and psychic researcher set forth the potential powers of the subliminal self. He viewed the subliminal consciousness as a vast region, beneath the threshold of ordinary consciousness, embracing many phenomena associated with the supernatural.

Myomancy

Divination utilizing rodents. The entrails may be examined or the rodent may be put inside a numbered or lettered circle or square. His movements then constitute the basis for divination.

Mysteries, Egyptian

See Egyptian Mysteries.

Mysteries, Eleusinian

See Eleusinian Mysteries.

Mysteries, Greek

See Greek Mysteries.

Mystical Numerology

Pythagoras, the Greek philosopher and mathematician, conceived that the notion of friendship could be represented by a pair of numbers: 220 and 280. They were called amicable numbers. The numbers are such that each of them is equal to the sum of all the exact divisors of the other number except the number itself.

For 2000 years no other pair of numbers with such qualities had been found. From 1636 on, mathematicians have discovered examples of amicable numbers to the extent of some 400 pairs.

Mystical Spiral of Life

A movement founded by Worthington Cake, an 18th-century Irish occultist, who held that various elements (wood, stone, metals, etc.) were characterized by certain rates of spiritual vibration and could help the adept to descend the Mystical Spiral of Life, reach its vortex, and merge with the godhead. The perfect numerical representation of the spiral was supposed to be 311. Many incantations were built on that magic number. Members of the order also reported frequent cases of levitation and glossolalia.

Myth

Under the influence of Freud and Jung the study of myths has shown striking similarities between the contents and the world of the unconscious. For the primitive man (today's Aborigines are a good example) myth means a true story, all the more precious because it is sacred, exemplary, and significant. It relates the acts of supernatural beings whose deeds can be repeated by power of rites.

N

Naassenes

A Gnostic sect. Members of the sect revered the serpent (Ophis) as the symbol of secret divine wisdom. They believed that the serpent in the Garden of Eden was trying to help mankind when he persuaded Adam and Eve to disobey God. See Ophites.

Naberus

In demonology, the Marquis of Hell. He appears in the shape of a crow. He gives instruction in eloquence and the fine arts.

Nagalism

Serpent-worship. The term derives from the Sanskrit *naga*, "serpent." Nagalism was practiced in many places, including Burma, Egypt, Greece, and Mexico. See Ophites.

Nagari

The alchemists' dragon uttered these words: "I rise from death, I kill death, and death kills me. I resuscitate the bodies I have created and, alive in death, I destroy myself."

Nagual

In Mexico and in Central America, the nagual is a personal guardian spirit, thought to dwell in the body of an animal.

The term is employed in various ways by the Indians themselves and by ethnographers. The Nahuatl of Tepoztlán say that the nagual is a person who can change into an animal. In other contexts the word has been translated as guardian spirit, soul bearer, companion spirit, destiny animal, and transforming witch.

Nahemah
A name applied to the princess of all the succubi.

Nails
Like skin, blood, hair, or sperm, nails may be used in casting spells. French children are warned not to bite their nails because the Devil is ready at all times to claim them and use them against the children.

Nakedness
Witches regard the human body as a storehouse of energy whose release is hindered by clothing. For this reason they appear naked at their assemblies.

Names
To the magician a name sums up the characteristics of whatever it represents and identifies and therefore is a miniature image of and substitute for the thing itself. An early outgrowth of this notion was the use of two names, one a convenient label and the other the true or secret name of a person. Plutarch said that the secret name of the guardian deity of Rome was carefully concealed in early times. The God of Israel had an unspeakable name.

An Egyptian legend reveals how Isis tried to capture the power of the omnipotent sun god Ra by discovering his true name. The goddess collected some of his saliva (the old god dribbled and slobbered), made a venomous snake by mixing it with earth, and used the snake's bite to force him to give her his name.

404

In Islam the names of God are transcribed on amulets and pentacles, either directly or after being transposed into numbers. Mohammed is supposed to have said, "God has 99 names, or 100 less one; whoever knows them will enter paradise." The hundredth name, according to some Islamic scholars, is Allah. These names act through the magic force of the sign as well as of the sound. Among the 99 names: Aziz (Dear), Hakin (Wise), Kabir (Great), Madjid (Glorious), Rachid (Law), and Karim (Generous).

In magic and witchcraft successful invocation or exorcism may depend on exact knowledge of a name. Some people (the Hindus, for example), try to conceal the names of their children to protect them against demons. See Numerology.

Names, Divine

The science of names was developed by Jewish scholars. In their written and oral traditions, the tetragram YHWH is the most secret name of God. It was forbidden to the masses and known only within closed circles. The Talmud states that the wise teach it to their sons and disciples once a week. A 12-letter secret name is made up of the first three sephiroth: KTRHHMHTBWNH. A 24-letter name, the holiest of mysteries, was taught to the initiated. It includes the ten sephiroth:

KTRHHMHTBWNHGDWLHTPERT
GBWRHNSHYSODHODMLKWT.

Names of Power

Names or titles of ancient divinities, used in incantations to enable the magician to acquire and utilize the powers of those named. Most such names are derived from those associated with the gods of the ancient world. Modern magicians borrow heavily from Jewish magical practices and the Cabala. See Ritual Magic.

405

Names of Satan

Malleus Maleficarum, a fifteenth-century treatise by Heinrich Kramer and Jakob Sprenger, indicates that Satan may be invoked under several names, each with a special etymological significance:

> As Asmodeus, he is the Creature of Judgment. As Satan, he becomes the Adversary. As Behemoth, he is the Beast. Diabolus, the Devil, signifies two morsels: the body and the soul, both of which he kills. Demon connotes Cunning over Blood. Belial, Without a Master. Beelzebub, Lord of Flies.

Here are the names by which he is generally known in various languages:

> Arabic: Sheitan
> Biblical: Asmodeus (or Belial or Apollyon)
> Egyptian: Set
> Japanese: O Yama
> Persian: Dev
> Russian: Tchort
> Syriac: Béherit
> Welsh: Pwcca

Napoleon

The French emperor was reputed to have a familiar demon that manifested itself in the corridors of the Tuileries in Paris.

Nativity

In astrology, the Birth Moment. The instant wherein the native first inhales, thereby beginning a process of blood conditioning that up to that point had been accomplished by the receptivities of another. During the first years of life there ensues a growth of channels of receptivity to cosmic energy which results in a life-pattern of cosmic stimula-

406

tion. Nativity is also applied to a figure, or horoscope, cast or a date, moment, and place of birth, as distinguished from an electional or horary figure.

Nazar
In Iran, the spell cast by the Evil Eye.

Nebiros
Field Marshal of the infernal spirits. He has command over Ayperos, Naberus, and Glasyabolas. He has power to inflict harm on whomever he wishes, to teach the properties of things, and to predict the future.

Nebo
Name adopted by Stanislas de Guaita. The founder of the nineteenth-century Rosicrucians in France took the pseudonym from Assyrian astrology.

Nebuchadnezzar
King of Babylon from 605 to 562 B.C. Because he tried to make himself an object of worship, he was forced to eat grass and drink dew like an ox. His madness is described in the fourth chapter of the Book of Daniel.

Necromancy
Divination of the dead. Fastidious preparations are required if the necromancer is to communicate with the corpse he intends to disturb. An appropriate incantation must accompany the opening of the grave and the coffin. If the rites involve the body of a suicide, the magician commands the spirit by the flames of Banal and the rites of Hecate to reveal why it took its own life and to answer specific questions. One of the principal aims of the necromancer is to discover the future by communicating with the dead, who are no longer bound by mortal limitations and can foresee events. The modern form of necromancy is called Spiritism.

A Greek magical papyrus gives the formula for invoking spirits of the dead. The ritual was accompanied by image magic, performed on the grave of the departed:

> I place this charm down beside you, subterranean gods, Kore, Persephone, Ereschigal and Adonis, Hermes, the subterranean, Thoth and the strong Anubis, who hold the keys of those in Hades, the gods of the underworld and the demons, those untimely carried off, men, women, youths and maidens, year by year, month by month, day by day, hour by hour. I conjure you, all demons assembled here, to assist this demon. And awaken at my command, whoever you may be, whether male or female. Betake yourself to that place and that street and that house and bring her hither, and bind her.

Éliphas Lévi narrated his successful attempt to a complete evocation, following a 22-day period of preparation:

> The cabinet prepared for the evocation was situated in a turret; it contained four concave mirrors and a species of altar having a white marble top, encircled by a chain of magnetized iron. The Sign of the Pentagram, as given in the fifth chapter of this work, was graven and gilded on the white marble surface; it was inscribed also in various colours upon a new white lambskin stretched beneath the altar. In the middle of the marble table there was a small copper chafing-dish, containing charcoal of alder and laurel wood; another chafing-dish was set before me on a tripod. I was clothed in a white garment, very similar to the alb of our Catholic priests, but longer and wider, and I wore upon my head a crown of vervain leaves, intertwined with a golden chain. I held a new sword in one hand, and in the other the "Ritual." I kindled two fires with the requisite prepared substances,

and began reading evocations of the "Ritual" in a voice at first low, but rising by degrees. The smoke spread, the flame caused the objects upon which it fell to waver, then it went out, the smoke still floating white and slow about the marble altar; I seemed to feel a quaking of the earth, my ears tingled, my heart beat quickly. I heaped more twigs and perfumes on the chafing-dishes, and as the flame again burst up, I beheld distinctly, before the altar, the figure of a man of more than normal size, which dissolved and vanished away. I recommenced the evocations and placed myself within a circle which I had drawn previously between the tripod and the altar. Thereupon the mirror which was behind the altar seemed to brighten in its depth, a wan form was outlined therein, which increased and seemed to approach by degrees. Three times, and with closed eyes, I invoked Apollonius. When I again looked forth there was a man in front of me, wrapped from head to foot in a species of shroud, which seemed more grey than white. He was lean, melancholy and beardless, and did not altogether correspond to my preconceived notion of Apollonius. I experienced an abnormally cold sensation, and when I endeavoured to question the phantom I could not articulate a syllable. I therefore placed my hand upon the Sign of the Pentagram, and pointed the sword at the figure, commanding it mentally to obey and not to alarm me, in virtue of the said sign. The form thereupon became vague, and suddenly disappeared. I directed it to return, and presently felt, as it were, a breath close by me; something touched my hand which was holding the sword, and the arm became immediately benumbed as far as the elbow. I divined that the sword displeased the spirit, and therefore I placed it point downwards, close by me, within the circle. The human figure reappeared immediately, but I experienced such an intense weakness in all my limbs, and a swooning sensation came over me so quickly, that I made two steps to sit down, whereupon I fell into a profound lethargy, accompanied by dreams, of which I had only a confused recollection when I came again to myself. For several subsequent days my arm remained benumbed and painful. The apparition did not speak to me, but it seemed that the questions I had designed to ask answered themselves in my mind. To that of the lady an interior voice replied—Death!—it was concerning a man about whom she desired information. As for myself, I sought to know whether reconciliation and forgiveness were possible between two persons who occupied my thoughts, and the same inexorable echo within me answered—Dead!

I am stating facts as they occurred, but I would impose faith on no one. The consequence of this experience on myself must be called inexplicable. I was no longer the same man; something of another world has passed into me; I was no longer either sad or cheerful, but I felt a singular attraction towards death, unaccompanied, however, by any suicidal tendency. I analysed my experience carefully, and, notwithstanding a lively nervous repugnance, I repeated the same experiment on two further occasions, allowing some days to elapse between each. There was not, however, sufficient difference between the phenomena to warrant me in protracting a narrative which is perhaps already too long. But the net result of these two additional evocations was for me the revelation of two kabalistic secrets which might change, in a short space of time, the foundations and laws of society at large, if they came to be known generally.

Modern occultism treats necromancy as the art of controlling the spirits of the dead. It also brings in the notion of the astral corpse which ascends to a mysterious, ethereal plane and of the soul which finally ascends to a still higher plane, leaving the astral corpse of "body of light" in the astral plane. A man's body remains on earth, his astral corpse in an intermediate region, and his soul in still another place. The astral corpse retains a spark of life and may be brought back into the physical world unconsciously or by necromancy. From living creatures it may absorb enough life-energy to continue its shadowy existence indefinitely. Some occultists believe that spiritualists in their seances summon astral corpses rather than spirits. See Necromancy.

Nectanebus

King of Egypt in fourth century B.C. A noted magician, he was skilled in concocting philtres, in astrology, divination, and the casting of runes. He made wax figures of his forces and of enemy forces, and by observing their movements in a bowl of Nile water, he forecast his own victory. In another instance, he succeeded in circumventing disaster by a timely escape.

Needfire

In Teutonic folklore, a fire kindled to remove injury from the herd and promote prosperity. Of heathen origin, probably during a time of plague, the practice involved extinguishing hearth fires and relighting them from the new fire. The custom dates back to prehistoric times and survives in some modern settings, particularly in the lighting of fires on St. John's Day.

Neophyte

In Aleister Crowley's cabalistic system, the first of the ten ranks or grades designating the spheres through which the student must ascend if he is to wield the magical power accessible to man as the potential God. The tenth sephira is the sphere of earth.

Neshaman

In the Cabala, as taught by the Rosicrucian order, one of

411

the three highest essences of the human soul. It corresponds to the Sephira Binah.

Netsah
The seventh sephira, the sphere of Venus, in Cabalistic teachings. It stands for animal drives, instinct, impulse. It stands opposite Hod on the Tree of Life.

Neuburg, Victor
Magician (1883-1940). He was a pupil of Aleister Crowley, who allegedly turned him into a camel in the Algerian desert in 1909. They had succeeded in evoking Choronzon, the Demon of Chaos.

New Birth
A symbolic enactment of death and rebirth, conferring on a neophyte a new set of parents and powers derived from them.

New Thought
Developed by Phineas Parkhurst Quimby (1802-66), the New Thought Movement combined auto-suggestion, faith healing, and animal magnetism. Alleging that a healthy person could draw sickness from an unhealthy person, he added the power of positive thinking to his credo and in some ways anticipated Christian Science.

Newbury, Witch of
In 1642 a soldier shot a woman who was reputed to have the ability to walk on water. The "witch" was killed by his bullet.

Ngwa
A word used by the Sudanese to denote magic. The word generally means wood and is used to refer to magic only in special contexts. The material element in Zande magic, occult and known only to the practitioner, usually consists of rare roots and strange woods.

Nichusch

In cabalistic teachings, a prophetic indication. Cabalists hold that all things have a secret connection and interact with each other, with the result that practically anything—the flight of birds, cries of animals, movement of clouds, etc.—can become a prophetic indication.

Nicolai, Christoph Friedrich

German author and bookseller (1733-1811). He recounted his own supernatural experiences in a paper read before the Royal Society of Berlin. Nicolai reported that figures of deceased persons had appeared to him frequently and for long periods of time. He further reported that the apparitions vanished when his surgeon performed a blood-letting operation.

Nicromancy

Derived from the Latin *niger,* meaning black, the term nicromancy also recalls the word necromancy, derived from the Greek *nekros,* meaning corpse. Through etymological confusion "divination by examining the dead" became "black magic."

Nider, Johannes

(c. 1380-1438) Professor of theology and author of the second book ever printed on witchcraft. He wrote *Formicarius* (The Anthill) in 1435. The fifth part of the book, a discussion of the evil powers of witches, was sometimes appended to the *Malleus Maleficarum.*

Nietzsche, Friedrich

Mystically inclined German philosopher (1844-1900). He coined the phrase, "God is dead," stressed the will to power, the eternal recurrence, and the damage done by democracy. He received many of his ideas through visions.

Night-riders

The ancient Teutons thought that the souls of the dead returned to the world of the living by night or during storms to harass sleepers. The belief in such demonic spirits is the foundation of the medieval belief in terrifying night-rides or night-mares. Many stories circulated about hordes of night-flying demons and dead souls. The ninth-century Canon Episcopi states that some women were under the illusion that they rode by night "upon certain beasts with Diana, the goddess of pagans, and an innumerable multitude of women, and in the silence of night traversed great distances and obeyed her commands as their mistress." These evil incubi pressed down on the breasts of women, sucked their milk and the milk of cows, and disturbed the dreams of mortals. Part of a group of hexen ("witches") responsible for much mischief and capable of assuming many forms, they were the female counterparts of the werewolves of European legend.

Nine

A powerful magic number reflected in the nine muses, nine-day fall of Satan, nine-fold gate of hell, nine orders of angels and of devils, and the blessed state merited by the mother of nine children. In astrology the ninth house deals with communication, creativity, and ideas.

This number, according to Éliphas Lévi, is that of initiation into the sacerdotal art of magic:

> The number nine is that of divine reflections; it expresses the divine idea in all its abstract power, but it signifies also extravagance in belief, and hence superstition and idolatry. For this reason Hermes made it the number of initiation, because the initiate reigns over superstition and by superstition: he alone can advance through the darkness, leaning on his staff, enveloped in his mantle and lighted by his lamp.

414

Nine Divine Names

By uttering these nine divine and mystic names one may summon demons:

Eheieh
Iod
Tetragrammaton Elohim
El
Elohim Gibor
Eloah Va-Daath
El Adonai Tzabaoth
Elohim Tzabaoth
Shaddai

Nivasi

In Gypsy mythology, these are earth-spirits. Their daughters appear as quails in the fields, robbing grain by night. They are regarded as the Devil's bird.

Noah's Ark

Accounts of the nomadic period of their history indicate that the Israelites attributed to Noah's Ark talismanic and magical properties and regarded it as the terrestrial habitation of Yahweh. The Old Testament attributes its holiness to its contents, the Ten Commandments.

Nocticula

See Bensozia.

North Berwick Witches

The trials of witches in North Berwick, Scotland, began with seemingly miraculous cures effected by Gilly Duncan, a young servant who confessed her ties with the Devil and named her accomplices. The trials took place between 1590 and 1592 and may have inspired King James to write his *Demonology* (1597). In 1590 David Ceaton tortured his young servant Gilly Duncan, forcing her to confess that she was possessed by the Devil and to name her accomplices. Among those named were Dr. John Fian, who was charged with practicing levitation and using cadavers to make charms, and Agnes Sampson, who accused scores of men and women of attending the Sabbat and of conspiring to raise a storm and sink the ship bearing James VI from Oslo to Leith. The king survived, thanks to the power of Margaret, a cat that had been thrown into the sea, but he had Fian, Sampson, and others put to death "for witchcraft and sorcery." The North Berwick trials were the most famous ever held in Scotland.

Norton, Thomas
An English alchemist who flourished in the fifteenth century. Author of a treatise on hermetics and alchemy.

Nostradamus
French physician, astrologer, and seer whose real name was Michel de Notre-Dame (1503-1566). His book of predictions, titled *The Centuries,* has been remarkably accurate.

Nottingham Boy
See Somers, William.

Novich, Gregori
A notorious Russian monk and cultist, known to millions by the name of Rasputin (1871-1916). Possessing what seems to have been a hereditary gift of mesmerism, he initiated a new cult in which dancing and debauchery were mingled with mystical seances. He gained power over the royal family of imperial Russia after he was alleged to have performed a miracle in restoring Alexis, the young ex-czarevitch, to health. After he was murdered, his body was buried in a silver casket.

Nuctemeron
A monument of transcendent Assyrian magic, according to

its French translator Éliphas Lévi, the *Nuctemeron* was written by Apollonius of Tyana. It signifies the night illuminated by day. Levi suggests that the work may be translated as *The Light of Occultism*. Here is the English text:

The First Hour
In unity, the demons chant the praises of God: they lose their malice and fury.

The Second Hour
By the duad, the Zodiacal fish chant the praises of God; the fiery serpents entwine about the caduceus and the thunder becomes harmonious.

The Third Hour
The serpents of the Hermetic caduceus entwine three times; Cerberus opens his triple jaw, and fire chants the praises of God with the three tongues of the lightning.

The Fourth Hour
At the fourth hour the soul revisits the tombs; the magical lamps are lighted at the four corners of the circle: it is the time of enchantments and illusions.

The Fifth Hour
The voice of the great waters celebrates the God of the heavenly spheres.

The Sixth Hour
The spirit abides immovable; it beholds the infernal monsters swarm down upon it, and does not fear.

The Seventh Hour
A fire, which imparts life to all animated beings, is directed by the will of pure men. The initiate stretches forth his hand, and pains are assuaged.

The Eighth Hour
The stars utter speech to one another; the soul of the suns

417

corresponds with the exhalation of the flowers; chains of harmony create unison between all natural things.

The Ninth Hour
The number which must not be divulged.

The Tenth Hour
The key of the astronomical cycle and of the circular movement of human life.

The Eleventh Hour
The wings of the genii move with a mysterious and deep murmur; and they fly from sphere to sphere, and bear the messages of God from world to world.

The Twelfth Hour
The works of the light eternal are fulfilled by fire.

Numa Pompilius
Second king of Rome. He was supposed to have practiced magic and to have had as his advisor Egeria, a fountain nymph whose worship was associated with that of Diana at Nemi.

Numbers
The law of correspondence finds its first expression in numbers. Philolaus, a disciple of Pythagoras, wrote: "Numbers are the sovereign, autogenous force that maintains the permanence of the cosmic forces. . . . One can see the nature and power of numbers manifesting their strength not only in demonic and divine things but also in all the activities and thoughts of men."

According to Paul Carton (*La Science occulte et les Sciences occultes,* 1935), numbers are the symbols of the whole hierarchy of creation. "Number one is the symbol of the original, creative, governing, and unifying force." Number two is the equilibrium of opposing forces; three, the generation

418

of three forces in one, or creation itself. Four is the first individual arrangement of elements, forms, and temperaments; five, the human head originating plans and directing the four members of the body as they execute these plans; six, wisdom, or the realization on earth of the divine triune; seven, the hierarchy of the elements that account for individual forms and their evolution. Eight is the reflection of four, the order and power of the four angles and four sides of the square. Nine is the harmony of three worlds—life, mind, and matter. Ten is the unity of the cube (six sides and four angles) and the source of a new act of creation.

Numerology

A survival of the ancient magical theory of names. Names are infinite in their diversity but all may be reduced to a finite set of numbers, usually from 1 to 9, occasionally with the addition of 11 and 22. Leonard Bosman, in *The Meaning and Philosophy of Numbers* (1932), stated:

> The power which the student may draw into himself when trying to realise the inner meaning of these great names and posers is sometimes so great as to cause a physical breakdown.

The simplest way to find the number corresponding to a name is to turn each letter into a number. Two systems are used. The Hebrew system, which also relies on knowledge of the Greek alphabet, does not use the figure 9 and writes the letters under the other numbers:

1	2	3	4	5	6	7	8
A	B	C	D	E	U	O	F
I	K	G	M	H	V	Z	P
Q	R	L	T	N	W		
J		S			X		
Y							

The modern system places the letters of the alphabet under the numbers 1-9.

1	2	3	4	5	6	7	8	9
A	B	C	D	E	X	G	H	I
J	K	L	M	N	F	P	Q	R
S	T	U	V	W	O	Y	Z	

Using either system, the digital root is obtained by adding the number equivalents for each letter of a person's full name and reducing the sum to one digit: J (1) + O (6) + H (8) + N (5) + S (1) + M (4) + I (9) + T (2) + H (8) = 44 = 8. Thus 8 is the digital root of 44 and the number corresponding to John Smith's name. It reveals his personality, character, life style, and future. The name also contains vowels and consonants whose sums, respectively, are the heart number and the personality number. The birth number is found by adding the digits of one's date of birth: July 27, 1924 becomes 7 27 1 9 2 4 50 5. If it fails to harmonize with the number of his name, the person born on that date may expect to be torn by inner conflict.

Traits or qualities are associated with the numbers of names. One denotes resoluteness and drive. Two is associated with femininity, three with imagination, four with industry, and five with resourcefulness. Six is the number of happiness and harmony, seven of mysticism and scholarship, eight of power and worldly involvement, and nine of lofty mental and spiritual achievement.

Nyoro Diviners
The Nyro in rural Bunyoro, Uganda, consult diviners whenever they are in trouble. The most common technique of divination is by cowry shells. Other mechanical techniques used by diviners include casting strips of leather on an animal skin, squeezing the juicy leaves of the muhoko,

rubbing a moistened stick, and examining the pattern created by tossing twigs into water. The technique of divination through possession by a spirit is perpetuated by a cult of spirit mediumship based on the Chwezi spirits and/or later additions of non-Chwezi spirits such as Irungu, the spirit of the bush.

O

Oak

Regarded as sacred by both the ancient Hebrews and Druids, the oak is also used as a toothache cure. The Semitic tribes carved idols from oak, and primitive Christians often used oak in fashioning images of Christ and the saints. The Druids worshiped the spirit of the oak, treated the mistletoe growing on it as a sacred symbol, and performed magic rites under its branches.

Oak Apple

An applelike gall produced on the leaf of an oak by a gallfly. When placed in a container of water underneath an infant's crib, it may float, indicating that the child is the object of fascination or possible possession.

Obeah

A cult originated by the Ashanti, who predominated among the African natives brought to the West Indies. The chief center of the cult is Jamaica. Claude McKay, the twentieth-century Jamaican poet, wrote: "Obeah is black people's evil God. Of the thousands of native families, illiterate and literate . . . there were few indeed that did not worship and pay tribute to Obi, the god of Evil. . . ." Its practioners, called obeah men or women, rely on sorcery, magic rituals, poisonous herbs, and fear, in casting spells, locating missing items, and causing sickness and accidents.

Among the items used by the obeah man are blood, feathers, teeth, grave dirt, rum, egg-shells, cards, mirrors, camphor, sulphur, myrrh, incense, asafoetida, shells, wooden images, and strangely shaped sticks. The obeah man is engaged to make love philtres, exorcise evil spirits, inflict harm on a disliked person, prevent theft, etc. An obeah man who uses incantation at home may appear in court to influence witnesses, jury, and judge.

Obereit, John Hermann
Mystic and alchemist (1725-1798). Born at Arbon, Switzerland, he worked for a long time to perfect the process of transmutation. According to A. E. Waite:

He inherited from his father a taste for transcendental chemistry, and the opinion that metals could be developed to their full perfection, but that the chief instrument was the grace of God, working in the soul of the alchemist. . .

He celebrated, he informs us, a mystical marriage with a seraphic and illuminated sheperdess named Theantis, the ceremony taking place in a castle on the extreme summit of a cloud-encompassed mountain.

Occult Philosophy
Éliphas Lévi gives a good synthesis of occult philosophy in his *Doctrine of Transcendental Magic:*

Behind the veil of all the hieratic and mystical allegories of ancient doctrines, behind the darkness and strange ordeals of all initiations, under the seal of all sacred writings, in the ruins of Nineveh or Thebes, on the crumbling stones of old temples and on the blackened visage of the Assyrian or Egyptian sphinx, in the monstrous or

424

marvellous paintings which interpret to the faithful of India the inspired pages of the Vedas, in the cryptic emblems of our old books on alchemy, in the ceremonies practised at reception by all secret societies, there are found indications of a doctrine which is everywhere the same and everywhere carefully concealed. Occult philosophy seems to have been the nurse or god-mother of all intellectual forces, the key of all divine obscurities and the absolute queen of society in those ages when it was reserved exclusively for the education of priests and of kings. It reigned in Persia with the Magi, who perished in the end, as perish all masters of the world, because they abused their power; it endowed India with the most wonderful traditions and with an incredible wealth of poesy, grace and terror in its emblems; it civilized Greece to the music of the lyre of Orpheus; it concealed the principles of all sciences, all progress of the human mind, in the daring calculations of Pythagoras. . . . Such was Magic from Zoroaster to Manes, from Orpheus to Apollonius of Tyana, when positive Christianity, victorious at length over the brilliant dreams and titanic aspirations of the Alexandrian school, dared to launch its anathemas publicly against this philosophy, and thus forced it to become more occult and mysterious than ever. . . .

Science, notwithstanding, is at the basis of Magic, as at the root of Christianity there is love, and in the Gospel symbols we find the Word Incarnate adored in His cradle by Three Magi, led thither by a star—the triad and the sign of the microcosm—and receiving their gifts of gold, frankincense and myrrh, a second mysterious triplicity, under which emblem the highest secrets of the Kabalah are allegorically contained. Christianity owes therefore no hatred to Magic, but human ignorance has ever stood in fear of the unknown. The science was driven into hid-

425

ing to escape the impassioned assaults of blind desire; it clothed itself with new hieroglyphics, falsified its intentions, denied its hopes. Then it was that the jargon of alchemy was created, an impenetrable illusion for the vulgar in their greed of gold, a living language only for the disciple of Hermes. . . .

Furthermore, there exists in Nature a force which is immeasurably more powerful than steam, and a single man, who is able to adapt and direct it, might change thereby the face of the whole world. This force was known to the ancients; it consists in a Universal Agent having equilibrium for its supreme law, while its direction is concerned immediately with the Great Arcanum of Transcendental Magic. By the direction of this agent it is possible to modify the very order of the seasons; to produce at night the phenomena of day; to correspond instantaneously between one extremity of the earth and the other; to see, like Apollonius, what is taking place on the other side of the world; to heal or injure at a distance; to give speech a universal success and reverberation. This agent, which barely manifests under the certain methods of Mesmer's followers, is precisely that which the adepts of the Middle Ages denominated the First Matter of the Great Work. The Gnostics represented it as the fiéry body of the Holy Spirit; it was the object of adoration in the Secret Rites of the Sabbath and the Temple, under the hieroglyphic figure of Baphomet or the Androgyne of Mendes. . . . On penetrating into the sanctuary of the Kabalah one is seized with admiration in the presence of a doctrine so logical, so simple and at the same time so absolute. The essential union of ideas and signs; the consecration of the most fundamental realities by primitive characters; the trinity of words, letters and numbers; a philosophy simple as the alphabet, profound and infinite as the Word; theorems more complete and luminous than those of Pythagoras; a theology which may be summed up on the fingers; an infinite which can be held in the hollow of an infant's hand; ten figures and twenty-two letters, a triangle, a square and a circle; such are the elements of the Kabalah. Such also are the component principles of the written Word, reflection of that spoken Word which created the world! All truly dogmatic religions have issued from the Kabalah and return therein. Whatsoever is grand or scientific in the religious dreams of the illuminated, of Jacob Böhme, Swedenborg, Saint-Martin and the rest, is borrowed from the Kabalah. . . .

We have sketched rapidly the history of occult philosophy; we have indicated its sources. . . . Magical power comprehends two things, a science and a force: without the force the science is nothing, or rather it is a danger. To give knowledge to power alone, such is the supreme law of initiations. Hence did the Great Revealer say: 'The kingdom of heaven suffereth violence, and the violent only shall carry it away.' The door of truth is closed, like the sanctuary of a virgin: he must be a man who would enter. All miracles are promised to faith, and what is faith except the audacity of will which does not hesitate in the darkness but advances towards the light in spite of all ordeals, and surmounting all obstacles? It is unnecessary to repeat here the history of ancient initiations: the more dangerous and terrible they were, the greater was their efficacy. Hence, in those days, the world had men to govern and instruct it. The Sacerdotal Art and the Royal Art consisted above all in ordeals of courage, discretion and will. . . .

After passing our life in the search for the Absolute in religion, science and justice; after revolving in the circle of Faust, we have reached the primal doctrine and the first book of humanity. At this point we pause, having discovered the secret of human omnipotence and indefinite progress, the key of all symbolisms, the first and final doctrine: we have come to understand what was meant by that expression so often made use of in the Gospel—the Kingdom of God.

Occult Philosophy
Title of Agrippa von Nettesheim's defense of magic as a composite of religious doctrine, occultism, and scientific knowledge.

Occult Universities
Works on the occult sciences allude to the existence of learning centers in various countries. Salamanca was supposed to have had several occult universities. Many lecturers taught alchemy during the Middle Ages. Much earlier occult centers were reported to have flourished in Egypt and Babylonia. Mme. Blavatsky insisted that a great school of occultists existed in Tibet.

Occultism in America
Early in 1973 New York's Museum of American Folk Art put on display a collection of sorcerers' tools and magical artifacts dating back to the time when the first settlers manifested their fascination with the occult. Included in the collection were a book of voodoo recipes dating from 1796 and a statuette now used by a coven of witches in Brooklyn.

Occultism Today
See Current Literature.

Och
In works on magic, Och is listed as one of the seven Olympian Spirits who rule the world. He is the master of the sun.

Ochnotinos
A demon named in an ancient Hebraic incantation, used to

428

banish fever. The fever subsided as the demon's name was uttered in diminishing size:

Ochnotinos

Chnotinos

Notinos

Tinos

Inos

Nos

Os.

Od
See Aura.

Odic Force
See Aura.

Odyle
See Aura.

Odyllic Force
Subtle energy issuing from every substance in the universe but perceptible only to mediums and occultists, who may use it to perform magic acts.

Ogres
Huge humanlike creatures renowned for their strength and ugliness. Many mythological heroes tested their courage and skill against these malevolent beings.

Oiik
Among the Nanchi in the Congo, evil spirits or demons that cause sickness, earthquake, and death.

Oinomancy
A method of divination by observing of wine spilt into various forms.

Old Religion
Term designating a cult believed by some students of witch-

cratt, mainly those inspired by the writings of Margaret Murray and her followers, to incorporate the essential tenets of a prehistoric religion. These students hold that the idea of a Supreme Being antedates the Old Testament and was fairly widespread. Traces of the Old Religion appear in the Vedas of India, in ancient Persian manuscripts, and in the earliest esoteric writings of the Egyptians. Thousands of years before Paul wrote that "In Him we live, and move, and have our being," the ancient adepts or Magi had taught the essential truths of all the great religions of the world. They taught that the physical world and the mental world existed in the continuum of one great mind, the eternal reconciler of all opposites, the source of all things at all levels, the ultimate and absolute repository of wisdom and knowledge. Man with his limited intelligence could never comprehend the incomprehensible. But knowledge of God was accessible to man through his perception of truth and spiritual values; God revealed himself as perfection, love, light, and beyond that, Mystery. The ancient belief was summed up in thc formula carved on ruined temples: "I am all that is, all that was, all that will be, and no one shall lift my veil."

Witches have always believed in monotheism, in the immortality of the soul, and in the possibility of being reborn among those with whom they share bonds of love and affection. They believe that witchcraft is hereditary. It is transmitted from generation to generation within a family. Moreover, the guardians of the ancient faith are reincarnated witches. Justine Glass (*Witchcraft,* 1965) even finds points of similarity between the Old Religion and the traditions of the Cabala.

In England the Old Religion persisted in spite of the efforts of inquisitors and persecutors until the 18th century. Vestiges of pagan practices are said to survive today in France and England.

Olympian Spirits

According to the occult writers, seven Olympian Spirits rule the world. They are also called the Seven Stewards of Heaven.

Om (Aum)

A mystic syllable used in Hinduism, occultism, primitive masonry, and syncretic cults practiced in modern youth communes which have recently sprung up all across the United States. The Hindu syllable originally denoted assent but is now the most solemn of all words heard in India. A mantra representing the triple constitution of the universe, it is used as an invocation, a benediction, an affirmation, and a promise. It is generally placed at the beginning of sacred scriptures and prefixed to prayers. The three component parts of the syllable are the Absolute (Agni or Fire), the Relative (Varuna or Water), and the relation between them (Maruts or Air). The mystic syllable is called the Udgitta and is sacred with both Buddhists and Brahmins. It is chanted each evening before dinner by members of youth communes after they have joined hands and stood for two or three minutes in silent meditation.

Om Mandi Padme Hum

A mystical interjection addressed to the Bodhisattva Padmapani. The magical words are frequently engraved on walls to protect Tibetan buildings and villages.

One

The number of God. The characteristics assigned to it by numerologists are power, purposefulness, activity, innovation, and leadership.

Oneiromancy
Divination based on dreams but excluding the interpretation of numbers.

Onimancy
Divination utilizing the fingernails. The size and configuration of the moon and spots appearing on a nail enable the diviner to make his prediction.

Some diviners restrict onimancy to predictions based on the examination of the nails of the right hand of an unpolluted youth after oil of walnuts mingled with tallow has been applied to them.

Onion
Regarded as a symbol of the universe by the ancient Egyptians, the onion was supposed to have miraculous properties. It could absorb poison and, when applied to the victim's stomach, serve as an antidote to most philtres and potions.

Onomancy
A form of divination by observing the letters that form a person's name.

Ooscopy
Divination based on an egg. Ooscopy is used to determine the sex of an unborn child. The pregnant woman simply keeps an egg between her breasts until it hatches, then uses the sex of the chicken to determine the sex of her child.

Opening of the Mouth
A ceremony which originated among the early inhabitants of the valley of the Nile. Ancient formulas were recited during the performance of ceremonial rites to reconstitute the body of a person who had died and restore to it its *ba* and *ka*, its living soul and the ghostly double of this soul,

given to the person at birth. Originally, the ceremony was performed on a statue and consisted in using holy water and other substances to purify the statue, presenting the foreleg of a slain ox to the statue, touching its eyes, nose and ears with various magical instruments, and pronouncing a formula which ended, "the mouth of every god is opened." Finally, the statue was invested with royal insignia and a sacred meal was served on the altar. The king had the sacred duty to perform the reanimation rites for his deceased father.

Ophiel
The spirit of Mercury, whose day is Wednesday. Ophiel is one of the Seven Olympian Spirits who rule the world.

Ophites
Gnostics who revered the serpent (Ophis) as the symbol of secret divine wisdom. Members of the sect believed that the serpent was trying to help Adam and Eve when he persuaded them to eat of the tree of knowledge.

Opposites, Doctrine of
The existence of pairs of opposites in nature underlies the development of a magical theory based on the search for the mysterious One that reconciles all diversity in unity. The alternation of day and night, life and death, hot and cold seasons, calm and storm led to the belief that opposites were manifestations of something of which they themselves were a part. The search for the pathway to the One through the reconciliation of opposites recalls the Hegelian dialectic with its thesis, antithesis, and transcendent synthesis. It requires the magician to experience and master all things and to bring into proper balance all the forces at his command—love and hate, instinct and reason, good and evil. Many magical rituals and ceremonies focus on summoning up and unleashing the strong instinctive forces

433

secreted in the innermost depths of human nature. Not man the animal or man the thinker but the *whole* man has to be raised to the power of infinity.

Sex has its part in the doctrine of opposites. An ancient Jewish legend reconciled the belief that man was made in the image of God, who can be described as neither male nor female, by depicting Adam as bisexual. In one version Adam's right side was masculine, his left feminine, until God separated the two halves. In the other version Adam and Eve were joined back to back until God split them. Progress through the union of opposites is illustrated in the mating of male and female, which results in the creation of a new being. The magician must go one step beyond the ordinary if he is to regain the status held by Adam before the first division occurred. The magician must become bisexual. He accomplishes this goal by cultivating the female side of his nature without impairing his masculinity. The reverse is true of the sorceress. Both male and female magicians may carry the process to the point of deliberate homosexuality. An alternate method is copulation, which joins man and woman into one bisexual creature with two backs and constitutes a mystical appoach to the One. As Eliphas Levi phrased it, "Generation is in fact a work of the human androgyne; in their division man and woman remain sterile."

Sex orgies, common in the pagan world in which magic is rooted, were described in detail by many of those accused of witchcraft during past centuries. Rarely, however, can sorcery be written off as a mere justification for sex orgies. The notion that sex is something dirty and unworthy of the divine has no place in magic. Myths formulated in ancient times attribute all life in the universe to the procreative powers of the gods. Aeschylus describes Nature as

434

the offspring of earth and sky. The sky "passionately longs to penetrate" the earth, and accomplishes this through the rain that impregnates the earth and causes it to bring forth "for mortals pasturage for flocks and Demeter's livelihood." Each year the king of the ancient Sumerians practiced sacred copulation with a priestess representing Inanna. The symbolic union with the goddess of procreation, here as in many other societies, was to ensure the fertility of the land and an abundance of crops.

Magical theory holds that mere sensual indulgence has no place in the magician's life. A sorcerer who fails to control the sex-drive fails to achieve the perfect balance of opposites necessary for his operations. Inhibitions, guilt feelings, and repressions must be overcome or banished if the magician is to experience and control the universe. Thus magical ceremonies focusing on the release of man's driving forces are essential elements of witchcraft but they transcend mere delight in sensual pleasures. Symbolic union with God is achieved by sexual intercourse not only by pagan adepts but also by religious mystics.

Oracle Head
In the alchemical tradition, the oracle head seems to point to an original human sacrifice. Such sacrifices may have been made for the purpose of summoning up familiar spirits. A severed head, prepared according to prescribed rites, was supposed to reveal to people their inmost thoughts and to answer questions addressed to it. Gerbert of Reims, who later became Pope Sylvester II, was believed to have a golden head with oracular powers. The alchemical head may be connected with the teraphim, considered by Rabbinic tradition to have been a decapitated skull or a dummy head.

The oracle head was also known in ancient Greece and may

go back to the severed head of Osiris, which was linked with the notion of resurrection. Aelian swore that the head of Archonides was preserved in a jar of honey by his friend Cleomenes of Sparta, who consulted it as an oracle. Similar powers were attributed to the head of Orpheus.

Oracles
For centuries the Greek oracles served as prime sources of divination and prophecy.

> The most famous Oracles were those at Delphi, Dodona, Epidaurus, and Trophonius, but others of renown were scattered over the country. Perhaps one of the earliest was that of *Aesculapius,* son of Apollo, and called the Healer, the Dream-sender because his healing was given through the medium of dreams that came upon the applicant while sleeping in the temple courts, the famous temple-sleep. This temple, situated at Epidaurus, was surrounded by sacred groves. . . . Famous beyond all was that of Apollo, the *Delphian oracle* on the Southern slopes of Parnassus . . . , built above a volcanic chasm amid a wildness of nature which suggested the presence of the unseen powers. Here the priestess, the Pythia, so named after the serpent Pytho whom Apollo slew, was seated on a tripod placed above the gaseous vapours rising from the chasm. . . . The *Oracle of the Pelasgic Zeus at Dodona,* the oldest of all, answered by signs rather than inspired speech. . . . The *Oracle of Trophonius* was also of great renown. Here there were numerous caverns filled with misty vapours and troubled by the noise of hidden waters far beneath. In this mysterious gloom the supplicants slept sometimes for nights and days, coming forth in a somnambulic state from which they were aroused and questioned by the attendant priests. (Lewis Spence.)

Delphi, to the south of Parnassus, was a magnificent temple

436

dedicated to Apollo, the god of eloquence. An inscription engraved on the pediment of the temple read: "Let no man enter this temple if his hands are unclean." Everyone who visited the temple had to bring a gift. Soon the place was filled with treasures and gifts from Greeks and foreigners. Apollo's statue stood at one end of the temple. Behind the cave was the entrance to a cave. Plutarch wrote that the entrance to the cave was discovered when goats feeding nearby suddenly had convulsions. The shepherd and others who explored the cave seemed to be in a trance. In their state of confusion they murmured incomprehensible words. The priests decided that such behavior was not simply the result of noxious gases issuing from the cave but an attempt of Apollo to communicate his wisdom to mankind in their language. Once each month a virgin, Pythia, went down into the cave. Her mind overpowered by the gases, she was supposed to utter the wisdom that Apollo had chosen to communicate to mankind through her.

Pythia, her head crowned by laurel leaves, sat on a tripod. Sometimes she had to struggle with the pythons that had had been dedicated to Apollo, their conqueror. At first the virgins were chosen for their beauty from the most important families of Delphi. After one of them fled with a handsome young man, the minimum age was raised to 50.

Apollonius of Tyana left a detailed account of his visit to the oracle at Delphi. Purification in holy water was followed by the sacrifice of a bull and a goat to the god. Apollonius entered the temple holding an olive branch decorated with a ribbon of white wool (matching that encircling Pythia's head). He went behind the statue of Apollo and into the cave, but attendants would not allow them to approach Pythia, who, after much delay, finally sat down on her tripod. Her chest expanded, her face flushed and paled. She began to tremble nervously but uttered nothing intel-

437

ligible. Her convulsions became more violent, she foamed at the mouth, and her hair stood on end. She tore the band from her forehead (the priests forced her to remain on the tripod), howled loudly, and uttered a few words which the priests quickly set down. He had asked whether his name would be remembered through the ages. The answer was that it would be, but only because of slander. Like other egotistical inquirers, he tore up the paper on which the answer was written.

Ordeals

Various tests were employed by tribunals established to try those accused of witchcraft. These included the ordeal by corpse, cold water, boiling water, fire, and the cross. In the ordeal by water the right hand of the accused was tied to the left foot, the left hand to the right foot, and the victim was thrown into a vat of cold water to determine whether he would sink. When hot water was used, the hand of the accused was plunged into the container in search of a ring, then bound for three days. If no injuries were discovered, the accused was presumed to be innocent. In the ordeal by fire, the accused had to carry a red-hot bar several steps. In the ordeal by the cross, the accused had to stand before a cross with outstretched arms.

Order of the Golden Dawn

Occult society whose members included W. R. Yeats, Algernon Blackwood, Austin Osman Spare, Arthur Machen, the Astronomer Royal of Scotland, and Allan Bennett, an eccentric who renounced his Catholic faith when he discovered the mechanism of childbirth, and Austin Osman Spare. Founded in England, the society at its peak had lodges in London, Edinburgh, Bradford, and Weston-super-Mare. Its most precious possession was a mysterious manuscript discovered on a London bookstall in 1884. It was deciphered by Samuel Liddell Mathers, who replaced William Wynn

Westcott, an authority on Cabala, as Visible Head of the Order of the Golden Dawn. The occult group modeled its doctrine of "assumption of God-forms" on the Egyptian system of magic, in which there is an attempt to merge with the consciousness of a god in animal form.

Orias
Count of Hell. He is an expert in astrology and in metamorphoses. He carries a serpent in each hand.

Orkoiyot
Powerful African sorcerers who divine by casting lots, examining the entrails of a goat, or utilizing information gained from visions and dreams. Their mana is so powerful that no one can touch them with impunity. They exact payment for their services in curing spells and sicknesses.

Orphean Egg
Doctrine ascribed to Orpheus and predicated on the assumption that the whole universe has the form of an egg, and everything in it strives to attain the same form. The doctrine is related to the magical theory of correspondences between the microcosm and the macrocosm. To Orpheus are attributed these words:

> God, the uncreated and incomprehensible Being, created all things; the ether proceeded from him; from this the unshapely chaos and the dark night arose, which at first covered all things. The unshapen mass was formed into the shape of an egg, from which all things have proceeded.

Orphic Magic
Egyptian influences entered Greece mainly through Orpheus and Pythagoras, who had been initiated into the Egyptian mysteries. The irresistible power of Orpheus' music compelled the rocks, trees, and animals to follow him and storms to rise or abate at his command. His music enabled him

to overcome the powers of darkness, descended to Hades, find his beloved Eurydice, and bring her back to the rim of the living world. Even after his head was cast on the shores of Lesbos, jealous women having dismembered his body, it retained the power to utter oracles. He instructed the Greeks in medicine and magic, and for long afterwards the power of healing was ascribed to magical formulae, incantations, and charms inscribed on Orphic tablets.

Osthanes
According to Pliny, Osthanes was a great magician who brought from Asia the system of magic practiced by the Greeks.

Ouija Board
A flat surface or board containing letters, numbers, and one-word answers such as yes, no, and maybe. One or more hands are placed on a marker, called a planchette, and spiritual forces guide the marker as it spells out the answers to questions and makes predictions. The name probably derives from the words for "yes" in French and German, *oui* and *ja*.

Ovid
Roman poet. (43 B.C.-17 A.D.) In *Metamorphoses* he attributes this invocation to Medea, the most famous magician of Greek mythology: O night, faithful preserver of mysteries. . . . With your help I stir up the calm seas by my spell; I break the jaws of serpents with my incantations. I bid ghosts to come forth from their tombs.

Ozark Witchcraft
According to Vance Randolph *(Ozark Superstitions),* the hill people of the Ozarks practice a form of witchcraft in which a key element of the initiation ceremony involves sexual intercourse between a neophyte and a male member

of the cult, who acts as the Devil's representative. For three nights in succession, the initiate and the cult member, meet at midnight, in the dark of the moon, in the family burying-ground of the woman seeking admission. There she formally renounces her faith, learns the secret of the cult, and recites the Lord's Prayers backwards. Cultists report that "the witch's initiation is a much more moving spiritual crisis than that which the Christians call conversion."

P

Pact with the Devil

The *Key of Solomon* offers explicit instructions for formalizing a pact with demons.

When you want to make your pact with one of the principal demons that I have just named, you will begin, on the evening before the pact, by cutting, with a new knife that has never been used, a wild nut-tree twig that has never borne fruit and that is like the thundering rod already described, at the exact moment that the sun appears on the horizon.

This being done, you will fortify yourself with a blood stone and consecrated candles, and you will then choose a spot for the operation where nobody can disturb you. You may even make the pact in a secluded chamber in a hut of some old ruined castle, because the demon has the power of transporting whatever treasure he pleases to that spot.

After which, you will trace a triangle with your blood stone, and that only the first time that you make the pact. Then you will set the two candles on the side, placing the sacred name of Jesus behind, to prevent the spirits from inflicting any harm on you.

Then, you will stand in the middle of the triangle, with

the mystic wand in your hand, with the great invocation to the demon, the clavicule, the request that you want to make, with the pact and the dismissal of the demon, as indicated in the model of the cabalistic triangle of pacts.

Having performed scrupulously all that is indicated, you will begin to recite the following invocation with confidence and assurance:

Emperor Lucifer, Master of all the rebellious spirits, I beg you to be favorable in the invocation that I make to your great Minister Lucifuge Rofocale, as I wish to make a pact with him. I beg you also, Prince Beelezebub, to protect me in my enterprise.

O Count Astorath! Be propitious, and bring it to pass that, this very night, the great Lucifuge appear to me in human form and without any evil odor, and that he grant me, by means of the pact that I shall offer him, all the wealth that I need.

O great Lucifuge! I beg you to leave your abode, in whatever region of the earth it may be, to come and speak to me. Otherwise I shall constrain you by the power of the great living God, his dear Son, and the Holy Spirit.

Obey promptly, or you will be tortured eternally by the force of the potent words of the Great Key of Solomon that he himself used to bind the rebellious spirits to accept his pact.

So, come forth instanter! Or I shall torture you endlessly by the force of these powerful words of the Key: Aglon, Tetragram, vaycheon stimulamaton y expares retragrammaton oryoram irion esytion existion eryona onera brasim moym messias soter Emanuel Sabbot Adonai, te adoro et invoco.

The notion of a pact which seized the minds of the scholas-

444

tics and the Inquisitors implied a direct and deliberate tie with the Devil or demons. Though the notion precedes Christianity and is mentioned by Lucan, among other pagan writers, it did not become widespread until the early middle ages. The story of St. Basil (c. 380) is the earliest Christian legend involving such a pact. The legend of St. Theophilus, who died about 540, was translated into Latin in the eighth century. Gerbert and Faust later appeared as central figures in pact legends.

According to the *Great Key* attributed to Solomon, to command the forces of nature one must first learn the names, qualities, and jurisdiction of the six demons empowered to make pacts. Each of the six is served by three lesser demons: Lucifuge by Baël, Agares, and Marbas; Satanachia by Pruslas, Aamon, and Barbatos; Agaliarept by Buer, Guseyn, and Botis; Fleuretty by Bathym, Pursan and Aligar; Sarganas Sarganatas by Loray, Valefar, and Forau; and Nebitos by Ayphos, Naberus, and Glasyalabolas. See Conjuration; Gaufridi, Louis.

Pacts with Demons

The method of making a pact with demons varies according to the practices associated with different witches. According to the *Malleus Maleficarum,* the method of the most powerful class of witches, those capable of performing every sort of witchcraft and spell, is similar to that used by the other classes.

Now the method of profession is twofold. One is a solemn ceremony, like a solemn vow. The other is private, and can be made to the devil at any hour alone. The first method is when witches meet together in conclave on a set day, and the devil appears to them in the assumed body of a man, and urges them to keep faith with him, promising them worldly prosperity and length of life;

and they recommend a novice to his acceptance. And the devil asks whether she will abjure the faith . . . and she swears with upraised hand to keep that covenant. The devil demands the following oath of homage to himself: that she give herself to him, body and soul, for ever, and do her utmost to bring others of both sexes into his power.

On September 19, 1398, the University of Paris expressed its alarm over the practice of magic and drew a distinction between natural magic and supernatural magic, which always required the making of a pact with demons.

Pactum Expressum
A pact entered into by a witch and a demon in writing, verbally, or by signs.

Pactum Tacitum
An assumption on the part of a witch that Satan collaborates in an undertaking.

Paigoels
Hindu devils. Some of them have individual names and are tempters of men. Others enter the bodies of men and possess them.

Paladino Eusapia
Internationally famous Italian spiritualistic medium (1854-1918). She performed in the major cities of Europe. She was investigated by many noted men, among them Professor Cesare Lombroso, the Italian criminologist and psychiatrist and representatives of the British Society for Psychical Research. She was able to produce spirit emanations but finally was caught using trickery. Yet some of the phenomena she produced, which were coldly and effectively tested and investigated, were beyond any one definitive and conclusive explanation.

Palas Aron Azinomas
An ancient formula for invoking a demon.

Palou, Jean
French historian (1918-67). In his study of Witchcraft *(La Sorcellerie)*, he follows Michelet in ascribing the origins of witchcraft to economic and social forces.

Pan
A lustful, energetic god whose cult spread throughout the Hellenic world. Pan was half man and half goat. A leader of satyrs, he is said to have participated in celebrations of the witches' Sabbat.

Papa Guede
The voodoo deity evoked by cultists on the Day of the Dead. Dr. François Duvalier, who was elected ruler of Haiti in 1957 on a program of "Africanism," was called Papa Guédé by his back-country supporters.

Papus
See Encausse, Gérard.

Papyrus of Setna
A papyrus reputedly discovered by Prince Setna Kha-em-ust, son of Rameses II. The text says that the Egyptian prince was told of the existence of the papyrus by an old man, who said that the magic book contained two spells written by Thoth himself. One spell bewitched heaven and earth; the second could return the dead to life. The prince found the papyrus in a tomb but was punished for disturbing the peace of the dead. The second text presents three magical tales, all characteristically Egyptian.

Paracelsus
The name adopted by Theophrastus Bombastus von Hohenheim (1493-1541), one of the most famous physicians and

occultists of the Middle Ages. He regarded the life of man as inseparable from that of the universe and disease as the result of a separation of the three mystic elements of which man is compounded—salt, sulfur, and mercury.

Paranormal

Resembling ordinary phenomena but without an identifiable physical cause. Events beyond the range of ordinary sensory experience are said to be paranormal or paraphysical.

There are countless instances of psychic or paranormal phenomena in relation to man and to the cosmos that have challenged scientific investigation. The East in particular is rich in such phenomena. Levitation is practiced by some Tibetan lamas. Hindus can pierce the body without the appearance of any blood or injury. Afghan mystics, holy men or gurus perform strange feats. Spirits are materialized: demons that pullulate in the air. Mystic shamans abound as healers, while evil spirits prowl the jungle depths.

Parapsychology

A branch of psychology that investigates psychical and psychophysical phenomena such as telepathy, apparitions, visions, premonitions, automatic writing, states of impersonation, clairvoyance, materialization of spirits, telekinesis. Supporters of parapsychological manifestations included the philosophers Fichte, Schelling, and Hegel. Some paranormal phenomena may have religious interpretations to persons undergoing the experience. The source for an intensive study of this entire field is the London Society for Psychical Research. In the U.S.A. Dr. Rhine of Duke University has been internationally prominent in parapsychological investigations.

Parapsychology embraces the scientific study of two classes of psi communication, extrasensory perception (ESP) and

448

psychokinesis (PK). A phenomenon is regarded as parapsychical when it is beyond physical principles of explanation. Psi phenomena are strange events involving people and appearing to stand clear of explanation by known natural law. Parapsychology has developed largely under the influence of Dr. Rhine, for 38 years director of Duke University's Institute of Parapsychology. The scientific investigation of psychical phenomena had first been investigated systematically in the nineteenth century. At Cambridge University a group of English scholars helped the physicist William Barrett, the clergyman W. Stainton Moses, and the classical scholar F. W. H. Myers launch a movement which soon attracted the outstanding British intellectuals. William James played a similar role in the United States. William McDougall helped J. B. Rhine to establish a parapsychology laboratory at Duke University. See Psychical Research.

Pare, Ambroise
The sixteenth-century "Father of Modern Surgery" believed that demons could transform themselves quickly into any desired shape, into "serpents, toads, screechowls, hoopoes, crows, goats, donkeys, dogs, cats, wolves, bulls. . . . They even take on human bodies, alive or dead."

Paregoric
Camphorated tincture of opium, well known in medieval Europe as an elixir.

Paris Witch Trial
The first secular trial in Europe for witchcraft took place in Paris in 1390. Jehenne de Brigue, called La Cordière, confessed that she had practiced witchcraft, and she implicated Macette de Ruilly. Both were burned alive at the Pig Market on August 19, 1391.

Past-masters
See Dreaming.

Patience Worth

Many volumes written in late medieval prose and poetry are attributed to Patience Worth by Mrs. John H. Curran, a medium who first communicated with her by means of a ouija board. Patience Worth claimed to have lived in 17th-century England and to have been killed in America by Indians. Her works include *The Sorry Tale,* an account of the life and times of Christ.

Patron of Witchcraft

Among the Greeks and Romans, Hecate was the goddess most often invoked by witches. Represented with three heads or three bodies corresponding to the three phases of the moon—new, full, and old—she ruled the night and darkness, ghosts, tombs, and dogs. As Luna, the moon, she appeared in the sky; as Diana she stalked the earth; and as Prosperine she ruled over the underworld. Hecate seems to have been forgotten in early Christian times, but memories of Diana survived and gave rise to the belief that mortals could ride with her at night. See Night-Riders.

Pazalas

Ancient Chaldean magician, to whom were attributed, later, collections of prophecies and charms.

Pcuvushi

In Gypsy lore, these are beneficent earth-spirits.

Pearls

The early Greeks and Romans wore pearls as amulets or talismans. Pearls were therefore often made into a crown.

Pectoral

Decorative breastplate worn by the Jewish high priest. It originated in Egypt as an amulet embellished by stones with well-defined magical properties. The tradition was adopted by the Israelites, who used twelve precious stones to represent the twelve tribes of Israel: emerald for Reuben, agate for Asher, etc. In Egypt the high priest wore a pectoral with representations of Ra and Ma, the gods of light and justice.

Pedomancy
Divination utilizing the human foot. It is especially popular in the Orient.

Pentacle
Originally a five-pointed star or pentagram, the pentacle became a designation for any symbol or figure used as a talismanic device.

A medieval grimoire known as the *Key of Solomon* tells how to make and consecrate pentacles:

> The pentacles are to be made on the day of Mercury, and in its hour. The Moon is to be in a sign of air earth, and waxing, and her days shall be the same as those of the Sun. Retire to a specially prepared room or other place, set aside for this purpose, with your companions. It is to be censed and perfumed with magical incense and fragrances. . . . We with humility beg and implore thee, Majestic and Holiest One, to cause the consecration of these Pentacles, through thy power; that they may be made potent against all the Spirits, through thee, Adonai, Most Holy, for ever and ever.

The *Key of Solomon* also contains an incantation to be used in consecrating pentacles:

> O Adonai, Omnipotent, El, all-powerful, Agla, holiest, On, most righteous, Aleph and Tau, the Beginning and the End! O thou that hast caused everything through thy knowledge! Thou, who elected Abraham as thy servitor, and who promised that all the nations should be blessed by his progeny; and thou who hast manifested thyself to thy slave Moses as a flame in the Burning Bush; who

451

enabled him to walk dryshod through the Red Sea! Thou, who gavest him the Law upon Sinai, thou, who gave to thy servant Solomon these Pentacles, of thy mercy unequalled, that souls and bodies might be saved!

We with humility beg and implore thee, Majestic and Holiest One, to cause the consecration of these Pentacles, through thy power: that they may be made potent against all the Spirits: through thee, Adonai, Most Holy, for ever and ever.

Éliphas Lévi called the pentacle (Pantacle) a complete and perfect synthesis expressed by a single sign and serving to focus

all intellectual force into a glance, a recollection, a touch. It is, so to speak, a starting-point for the efficient projection of will. Nigromancers and goëtic magicians traced their infernal Pantacles on the skin of the victims they immolated. The sacrificial ceremonies, the manner of skinning the kid, then of salting, drying and bleaching the skin, are given in a number of Clavicles and Grimoires. . . .

The initiatory symbolism of Pantacles adopted throughout the East is the key of all ancient and modern mythologies. Apart from knowledge of the hieroglyphic alphabet, one would be lost among the obscurities of the Vedas, the Zend-Avesta and the Bible. The tree which brings forth good and evil, the source of the four rivers, one of which waters the land of gold—that is, of light—and another flows through Ethiopia, or the kingdom of darkness; the magnetic serpent who seduces the woman, and the woman who seduces the man, thus making known the law of attraction; subsequently the Cherub or Sphinx placed at the gate of Edenic sanctuary, with the fiery sword of the guardians of the symbol; then regeneration

452

by labour and propagation by sorrow, which is the law of initiations or ordeals; the division of Cain and Abel, which is the same symbol as the strife of Anteros and Eros; the ark borne upon the waters of the deluge like the coffer of Osiris; the black raven which does not return and the white dove which does, a new setting forth of the dogma af antagonism and balance—all these magnificent kabalistic allegories of Genesis, which, taken literally and accepted as actual histories, merit even more derision and contempt than Voltaire heaped upon them, became luminous for the initiate, who still hails with enthusiasm and love the perpetuity of true doctrine and the universality of initiation, identical in all sanctuaries of the world.

The pentacle, according to Jean Marquès-Rivière *(Amulettes, Talismans et Pantacles,* 1972), artificially created according to the complex laws of correspondences, became a great stellar talisman, a microcosm capable of dominating the individual and condensing the hidden energies of the cosmos. It is a "metaphysical equation" summing up a religious thought and elaborate philosophical conceptions. It introduces a vision of the cosmos foreshadowing scientific knowledge as well as "the premises of a symbolic and philosophical geometry." Faust no longer seeks to control the magical powers of the pentacle outlined on the window of his laboratory. It has become his metaphysical revelation, "a quasi-divine entity, an angelic form, an intellectual prayer."

Pentagram
According to Éliphas Lévi the Pentagram signifies

The domination of the mind over the elements, and the demons of the air, the spirits of fire, the phantoms of water and ghosts of earth are enchained by this sign.

Equipped therewith, and suitably disposed, you may behold the infinite through the medium of that faculty which is like the soul's eye, and you will be ministered unto by legions of angels and hosts of fiends. . . .

For the wise man, to imagine is to see, for the magician, to speak is to create. It follows that, by means of the imagination, demons and spirits can be beheld really and in truth; but the imagination of the adept is diaphanous, whilst that of the crowd is opaque; the light of truth traverses the one as ordinary light passes through clear glass, and is refracted by the other, as when ordinary light impinges upon a vitreous bloc, full of scoriae an foreign matter. That which most contributes to the errors of the vulgar is the reflection of depraved imaginations one in the other. But in virtue of positive science, the seer knows that what he imagines is true, and the event invariably confirms his vision.

Paracelsus, that innovator in Magic, who surpassed all other initiates in his unaided practical success, affirms that every magical figure and every kabalistic sign of the pantacles which compel spirits, may be reduced to two, which are the synthesis of all the others; these are the Sign of the Macrocosm or the Seal of Solomon, the form of which we have given already, and that of the Microcosm, more potent even than the first—that is to say, the Pentagram, of which he provides a most minute decription in his occult philosophy. If it be asked how a sign can exercise so much power over spirits, we inquire in return why the whole Christian world bows down befort that Sign of the Cross? The sign is nothing by itself, and has no force apart from the doctrine of which it is the summary and the logos. Now, a sign which summarizes, in their expression, all the occult forces of Nature, a sign which has ever exhibited to elementary spirits and others a power greater than their own, fills them naturally with respect and fear, enforcing their obedience by the empire of science and of will over ignorance and weakness. By the Pentagram also is measured the exact proportions of the great and unique Athanor necessary to the confection of the Philosophical Stone and the accomplishment of the Great Work. The most perfect alembic in which the Quintessence can be elaborated is conformable to this figure, and the Quintessence itself is represented by the Sign of the Pentagram.

Lévi discussed at length the consecration of the Pentagram.

The Pentagram, which in Gnostic schools is called the Blazing Star, is the sign of intellectual omnipotence and autocracy. It is the Star of the Magi; it is the sign of the Word made flesh; and, according to the direction of its points, this absolute magical symbol represents order or confusion, the Divine Lamb of Ormuz and St. John, or the accursed goat of Mendes. It is initiation or profanation; it is Lucifer or Vesper, the star of morning or evening. It is Mary or Lilith, victory or death, day or night. The Pentagram with two points in the ascendant represents Satan as the goat of the Sabbath; when one point is in the ascendant, it is the sign of the Saviour. The Pentagram is the figure of the human body, having the four limbs and a single point representing the head. A human figure head downwards naturally represents a demon—that is, intellectual subversion, disorder or madness. Now if Magic be a reality, if occult science be really the true law of the three worlds, this absolute sign, this sign ancient as history and more ancient, should and does exercise an incalculable influence upon spirits set free from their material envelope.

The sign of the Pentagram is called the Sign of the

Microcosm, and it represents what the Kabalists of the book Zohar term the Microprosopus. The complete comprehension of the Pentagram is the key of the two worlds. It is absolute philosophy and natural science. The sign of the Pentagram should be composed of the seven metals, or at least traced in pure gold upon white marble. . . .

The Pentagram is consecrated with the four elements; the magical figure is breathed on five times; it is sprinkled with holy water; it is dried by the smoke of five perfumes, namely incense, myrrh, aloes, sulphur and camphor, to which a little of white resin and ambergris may be added. The five breathings are accompanied by the utterance of names attributed to the five genii, who are Gabriël, Raphaël, Anaël, Samaël and Oriphiel. Afterwards the Pentacle is placed successively at the north, south, east, west and centre of the astronomical cross, pronouncing at the same time, one after another, the consonants of the Sacred Tetragram, and then, in an undertone, the blessed letters ALEPH and the mysterious TAU, united in the kabalistic name of AZOTH. . . .

The old magicians traced the sign of the Pentagram upon their doorsteps, to prevent evil spirits from entering and good spirits from departing. This constraint followed from the direction of the points of the star. Two points on the outer side drove away the evil; two points on the inner side imprisoned them; the only on the inner side held good spirits captive. All these magical theories, based upon the one dogma of Hermes and on the analogical deductions of science, have been confirmed invariably by the visions of ecstatics and the paroxysms of cataleptics, declaring that they are possessed by spirits. The G which Freemasons place in the middle of the Blazing Star signifies GNOSIS and GENERATION, the two sacred words of the ancient Kabalah. It signifies also

GRAND ARCHITECT, for the Pentagram on every side represents an A. By placing it in such a manner that two of its points are in the ascendant and one is below, we may see the horns, ears and beard of the hierarchic Goat of Mendes, when it becomes the sign of infernal evocations.

The Allegorical Star of the Magi is no other than the mysterious Pentagram; and those three kings, sons of Zoroaster, conducted by the Blazing Star to the cradle of the microcosmic God, are themselves a full demonstration of the kabalistic and magical beginnings of Christian doctrine. One of these kings is white, another black and the third brown. The white king offers gold, symbol of life and light; the black king presents myrrh, image of death and of darkness; the brown king sacrifices incense, emblem of the conciliating doctrine of the two principles. . . .

All Mysteries of Magic, all symbols of the Gnosis, all figures of occultism, all kabalistic keys of prophecy are summed up in the Sign of the Pentagram, which Paracelsus proclaims to be the greatest and most potent of all signs. Need anyone be surprised therefore that every Magus believes in the real influence exercised by this sign over spirits of all hierarchies? Those who set at naught the Sign of the Cross tremble before the Star of the Microcosm. On the contrary, when conscious of failing will, the Magus turns his eyes towards this symbol, takes it in his right hand and feels armed with intellectual omnipotence, provided that he is truly a king, worthy to be led by the star to the cradle of divine realization; provided that he KNOWS, DARES, WILLS and KEEPS SILENT; provided that he is familiar with the usages of the Pentacle, the Cup, the Wand and the Sword; provided, finally that the intrepid gaze of his soul corresponds to those two eyes which the ascending point of our Pentagram ever presents open.

Pentagram

Official organ of the Witchcraft Research Association. According to a recent article published in the periodical, the basic teachings of the "Craft" have always been crystal clear, but prejudice, misunderstandings, and distortions have hidden these teachings. It contains the germ of the tradition of the ancient mysteries and harks back to the days when the sorcerer was a respected member of the community. He was not feared but welcomed into the home, for he had the power to heal and help. He knew the secrets of telepathy, precognition, second sight, astral travel, and the power of prayer. Modern sorcerers look upon the Craft as a means of creating a link between the material world and the spiritual world, utilizing techniques known for thousands of years.

Pentalpha

A design formed by five interlacing A's and used in divination and the conjuration of spirits.

Perkins, William

Puritan preacher (1555-1602). His *Discourse on the Damned Art of Witchcraft* (1608) supplanted the *Demonology* of James VI.

Perkins, William

See Witches, Requirements for Condemnation.

Persian Demonology

According to Zoroaster, whose teachings fill the *Avesta*, one of the world's oldest books, an evil spirit identified first as Angra Mainyu and later as Ahriman has existed throughout eternity. He has the prime function of leading men astray. He created the archfiend Aeshma, five other demons *(Daeva)* of equal rank, and a host of lesser fiends *(daeva* and *druy),* such as the dragon Pairikas. Demons fill the air, dwell in unclean places and animals (snakes, rats, frogs, cats, and mice), and can possess men. Though they prefer to work in the dark, they can make themselves visible. They can also be identified by their foul stench.

The Persian demons are personifications and primary causes of certain sins: lust, anger, pride, avarice, deceit. Cleanliness protects men against these demons. Useful also are fire and certain animals: dogs, cocks, and asses. Demons are put to flight by the name of Ahura Mazda, leader of the powers of light, and by texts from the holy books, recited four times. Each year the sorcerer-priest drives away countless demons by putting on a fire the horn of an animal slain on a certain day and holding above the fire written incantations which are later affixed to a red door under which sand has been strewn.

Pert Em Hru
The Egyptian Book of the Dead, a guide to the Nether Regions for the souls of the dead and a kind of manual of instructions.

Peter of Albano
A thirteenth-century Italian philosopher and astrologer who wrote on magic. He was reputed to have had associations with Satanic forces.

Peterson, Joan
Called the "Witch of Wapping," she was accused of possessing familiar demons (a black dog and a squirrel) and of casting spells. She was hanged in London on April 12, 1652.

Petra
A ruined site in the mountain of Hor, between the Dead Sea and the Red Sea, near the border of Jordan. The site

lies in a rock basin on the eastern side of the region called the Valley of Moses or the Wadi 'Araba. According to the books attributed to Moses, the first inhabitants of Petra were the Horites (Cave Dwellers). High in the mountain can be seen a temple, a theater, and palaces, cut into the sides of the cliff. The tombs, more ancient than these structures, offer evidence of an early Nabatean settlement, leading scholars to conclude that Petra was their famous capital and the center of their caravan trade.

The fact that the majestically executed facades of the structures that adorn the cliff are only that—not entrances to real palaces or buildings but simply designs behind which lies an empty corridor—has led to much speculation. For some of those who see the ancient pyramids, Stonehenge, and Mayan temples as evidence of the existence of a Superior Race, Great Initiators, a Secret Tradition, or prehistoric astronauts, behind the facade was the sanctuary where candidates were initiated into the craft of high magic. See Astronauts; Hyperboreans.

Petro

One of the three great rites or divisions of Voodoo, the Pètro division includes a group of evil gods or angels. Ibos, who identifies himself as the red god, is associated with blood, with fire, and with the red cult of Voodoo, the cult of the blood sacrifice. Other deities in this division of Voodoo includes Pétro, the Zandor, Ti Jean Pié Fin, and Marinette Bois-Chèche.

Peyote

A small cactus *(Lophophora williamsii)* used as a mild intoxicant and to induce visions. The hallucinogenic properties of the plant were known to the ancient Aztecs. Today Indians of the Southwest and Mexico, though they have accepted Catholicism, refuse to abandon their peyote ritual.

They look upon the peyote button (the word peyote derives from Nahuatl *peyotl,* meaning caterpillar, and referring to the downy center of the button) as being the flesh of God. Still other Indians of the Southwest use the psychedelic buttons to promote communion with spirits and to induce visions.

Phallicism
A form of nature worship in which the generative principle in nature is symbolized by the male organ or phallus. The custom is characteristic not only of primitive religions but also of sophisticated cultures. Anciently prevalent among the Semites, it was later adopted by the Greeks. Often occurring as a form of sympathetic magic, it may assume an orgiastic character in ceremonies, as in the *Sakti puja* of the Indians.

Philocaption
Inordinate love of one person for another, according to the authors of the Malleus Maleficarum. Devils through temptations and sorcerers through spells, the best known and most general form of witchcraft, can cause philocaption. Like others who are bewitched, victims of philocaption may have recourse to five remedies: a pilgrimage to a holy shrine; true confession and contrition; the sign of the Cross and prayer; lawful exorcism using solemn words; and prudent treatment of the offending witch.

Philosophus
In the cabalistic system of Aleister Crowley, the Philosophus must ascend through sephira 7, corresponding to Venus, before he can reach the highest rank or grade and wield the magical power belonging to man as the potential God. Here he completes his moral training and is tested in "Devotion to the Order."

461

Philotanus

A lesser demon who helps Beliel to turn humans to pederasty and sodomy.

Phoenix

Derived from an Egyptian word meaning lapwing or heron, the phoenix was in Egyptian religion an embodiment of the sun god (Ra). His periodical resurrection was interpreted as a guarantee of the resurrection of the dead and gave birth to many legends. Fabled to live 500 years or longer, the bird was consumed by fire only to rise again from its own ashes and begin a new life cycle, its youthful freshness restored. In subsequent religions it became a symbol of immortality, reincarnation, and magic.

Phrenology

The study of the relation of the conformation of the skull to mental faculties and traits of character. Robert Thidd foreshadowed phrenology in attempting to symbolize the "mystery of the human head" and the manner in which "the celestial word enters into the cranium." Systems of phrenology were described by the Swiss mystic Johann Kaspar Lavater (in collaboration with Goethe) and by the German physician F. J. Gall. According to Lavater's system, the face is divided into three worlds: the forehead is the divine world; the triangle formed by the nose and eyes, together with the forehead and mouth, is the psychical world; the jaw and chin are the physical world.

Gall, a Viennese medical philosopher, believed that the proportions of the head yielded a complete portrait of its possessor. His notions were introduced into America in 1832 and popularized by Johan Gaspar Spurzheim, his disciple. Quack practitioners caused it to fall into disrepute toward the end of the 19th century.

Phylactery

Anything worn as an amulet or a charm. In Judaism, it is a small square leather box containing strips of parchment. On these strips are written scriptural passages (Exodus 13.1-10 and 11-16; Deuteronomy 6.4-9 and 11.13-22). Jews wear one such box on the head and another on the left arm during prayers except on holy days, as reminders that they must keep the law.

Phyllorhodomancy

Divination from rose leaves, following the same principles as tea-leaf reading.

Phrygian Cap

A red, peaked cap, symbolizing the tip of the phallus and recalling the practice of circumcision. It is the sacred cap of the Rosicrucians and the ancestor of the mitre used in different religious faiths.

Physiognomy

Divination by facial features is based on the notion of a connection between the human body and the universe. The art of discovering temperament and character from outward appearance enjoyed great popularity in the nineteenth century. As early as 1619, Robert Fludd had explored the interconnection between the microcosm of Man and the macrocosm of the universe.

Picatrix

A handbook of magic translated from Arabic in 1256. It became the black Bible of sorcerers. According to one modern initiate, M. Gehem, it is the most complete book that exists on black magic but available translations are inaccurate or incomplete, for those who try to explain it are struck by a curse.

Its magic is based on groupings of planets and fixed stars.

These astral combinations engender infinitely powerful forces. According to M. Gehem the authentic manuscript of the *Picatrix* contains terrible secrets: how to use the Ray of Silence to destroy a city, make flying machines, and influence or kill people from a distance. Some occultists believe that Moslem sages alone have preserved the scientific secrets of the Atlanteans. Here are some of the secrets recorded in the *Picatrix*:

> To destroy objects (houses, a town, etc.), make an image under the ascendant of the town if you know it or at the hour of the ascendant of the interrogation. Put this ascendant and its Lord in one of the houses of the moon that will be dominant and join to it the Lord of the house of the ascendant Lord with the tenth dwelling and its Lord, the whole in the hour of the interrogation. Then bury this image if you can in the middle of the town or under the ascendant of this interrogation.

> To destroy an enemy, make two images, one at the hour of the sun Lelion ascendant and the moon falling from the angle of the ascendant the other in the hour of Mars under the ram ascendant Mars and the moon falling and making this image resemble a man who beats another man then bury it at the hour of Mars when the first face of the ram rises. Having done that, you can exercise control over your enemies and have mastery over all their activities.

The formulas contained in the *Picatrix* are hard to decipher. They are supposed to be intelligible only to the initiate.

Pickingale, George
British sorcerer (d. 1909). The last "Master of Witches" at Canewdon in Essex, England, he died at the age of 93. See Canewdon.

Pico Della Mirandola

Italian sage (1463-94). He is supposed to have advanced the study of magic, which he called "the noblest part of the natural sciences." His *Strige* was the first important work on witchcraft to be published in Italy.

Tradition holds that he had mastered jurisprudence and mathematics before he was out of his teens, and that he had also waded far into the seas of theology and philosophy. He traveled from Italy into France, where he made a close study of the work of Raymond Lully. His erudition aroused suspicion, with the result that his activities were brought to the attention of the Inquisition and he was accused of heresy. He published a defense of the ideas and theories promulgated in his lectures. Pope Alexander VI granted him absolution in 1493.

Pico della Mirandola spent his last days in Florence, where he continued his cabalistic studies and delved occasionally into alchemy.

He published the fruits of his biblical studies in *Heptaplus*, a cabalistc account of the Book of Genesis. In this mystical work he derived Plato's doctrines from Moses. His major work on cabalistic, theological, and philosophical subjects *(Conclusiones Philosophicae, calabisticae et theologicae)* was issued in 1495.

Pike, Albert

Leading figure in the Scottish Rite of Freemasonry and author of a Masonic classic, *Morals and Dogma of the Ancient and Accepted Scottish Rite of Freemasonry* (1872). Sensational reports attributed to Dr. Bataille made Pike the founder of a diabolic order of Freemasonry and possessor of a bracelet used to summon Lucifer.

Pike, Bishop James A.

In recent years Bishop Pike was the subject of violent controversy for his unorthodox views on the Church, its functions, and its effectiveness. Bishop Pike, until recently Bishop of the Protestant Episcopal Diocese of California, left his Church, accused of heresy. His "open communion" policy was attacked, as were his sermons on doctrine and race.

With his wife, a former missionary, he founded in 1966 the New Focus Foundation, directed toward a fresh appraisal of Christian doctrine and its purpose.

Of immediate and particular interest is Bishop Pike's view of life after death. In collaboration with his wife, he published *The Other Side,* an account of his communication with his dead son, only a few months before he perished on the Sinai desert.

Bishop Pike wrote for the popular press and appeared frequently on television, expounding his new religious orientation.

Pillars of the Temple

An intriguing account of the pillars standing before Solomon's Temple is recorded in Éliphas Lévi's Doctrine of Transcendental Magic:

> Boaz and Jakin are the names of the two symbolical Pillars before the principal entrance of Solomon's Kabalistic Temple. In the Kabalah these Pillars explain all mysteries of antagonism, whether natural, political or religious. They elucidate also the procreative struggle between man and woman, for, according to the law of Nature, the woman must resist the man, and he must entice or overcome her. The active principle seeks the passive principle, the *plenum* desires the void, the serpent's jaw attracts the serpent's tail, and in turning about upon himself, he, at the same time, flies and pursues him-

self. Woman is the creation of man, and universal creation is the bride of the First Principle.

When the Supreme Being became a Creator, He erected a JOD or a phallus, and to provide a place in the fulness of the uncreated light, it was necessary to hollow out a cteïs or trench of shadow equivalent to the dimension determined by his creative desire, and attributed by him to the ideal JOD of the radiating light. Such is the mysterious language of the Kabalists in the Talmud, and on account of vulgar ignorance and malignity, it is impossible for us to explain or simplify it further. What then is creation? It is the house of the creative Word. What is the cteis? It is the house of the phallus. What is the nature of the active principle? To diffuse. What is that of the passive? To gather in and to fructify. What is man? He who initiates, who toils, who furrows, who sows. What is woman? She who forms, unites, irrigates and harvests. Man wages war, woman brings peace about; man destroys to create, woman builds up to preserve; man is revolution, woman is conciliation; man is the father of Cain, woman is the mother of Abel. What also is wisdom? It is the agreement and union of two princples, the mildness of Abel directing the activity of Cain, man guided by the sweet inspirations of woman, debauchery conquered by lawful marriage, revolutionary energy softened and subdued by the gentleness of order and peace, pride subjugated—by love, science acknowledging the inspirations of faith. . . .

Furthermore, the universe is balanced by two forces which maintain it in equilibrium, being the force which attracts and that which repels. They exist alike in physics, in philosophy and in religion; in physics they produce equilibrium, in philosophy criticism, in religion progressive revelation. The ancients represented this mystery by

467

the conflict between Eros and Anteros, the struggle between Jacob and the angel, and by the equilibrium of the golden mountain, which gods on the one side and demons on the other encircle with the symbolic serpent of India. It is typified also by the caduceus of Hermanubis, by the two cherubim of the ark, by the twofold sphinx of the chariot of Osiris and by the two seraphim—respectively black and white. Its scientific reality is demonstrated by the phenomena of polarity, as also by the universal law of sympathies and antipathies.

The undiscerning disciples of Zoroaster divided the duad without referring it to unity, thus separating the Pillars of the Temple and endeavouring to halve God. . . .

So there are two forces in the moral region, one which attacks and one which restrains and expiates. They are represented in the mythos of Genesis by the typical personalities of Cain and Abel. Abel oppresses Cain by reason of his moral superiority; Cain to get free immortalizes his brother by slaying him and becomes the victim of his own crime. Cain could not suffer the life of Abel, and the blood of Abel suffers not the sleep of Cain. In the Gospel the type of Cain is replaced by that of the Prodigal Son, whom his father forgives freely because he returns after having endured much.

Piper, Mrs. Leonora E.

An American spiritualist medium. She possessed marked powers, particularly in the matter of communication with the dead. Among those who investigated her capacities were the noted psychologist William James and Sir Oliver Lodge. She first became entranced in the company of a professional clairvoyant, in 1884. Later the famous trance medium was controlled by numerous spirits, including Bach and Longfellow.

468

Her discourses and writings present compelling evidence supporting the actuality of spirit communication.

In 1885 she came under the observation of the Society for Psychical Research, and her principal control became Dr. Phinuit. Henceforth her trance utterances and writings were carfully analyzed by members of the S. P. R. In some instances she seems to have given information not conceivably known to any of the participants in the seance. She also took part in cross-correspondences sittings. She achieved fame in England as well as in her native America.

Pisces

In astrology, Fishes. The twelfth southern sign of the zodiac. It represents dissolution of matter followed by resurgence. Esoterically, this sign represents the flood and is the last emanation of the watery trigon. Cabalistically, it signifies the feet of the archetypal man and the mechanical forces of humanity.

Planchette

Usually heart-shaped, the planchette is a small slice of wood used in divination and named for M. C. Planchette, a 19th century spiritualist. When the fingers of the diviner or diviners are rested lightly on the board, it moves without conscious volition on the part of the operator, tracing out the answers to questions.

Planetary Angels

Cabalists assign to each planet a higher and a lower angel. Saturn's spirits are Zaphkiel and Cassiel, Jupiter's Zadkiel and Tachiel, Mars' Camael and Samael, the sun's Raphael and Michael, Venus' Haniel and Anael, and Mercury's Michael and Raphael. The moon has only one planetary angel, Gabriel. They may be used as names of power in incantations.

Planetary Influences

The seven planets recognized by ancient astrologers are supposed to influence the development of the mind and character of an unborn child. Saturn confers judgment. Jupiter generosity, Mars hatred and violence, the sun knowledge and memory, Venus concupiscence, Mercury joy and pleasure, and the moon virtue. Saturn's influence on the body of the child is dominant at the time of conception. Jupiter replaces Saturn during the second month, Mars the third, the sun the fourth, Venus the fifth, Mercury the sixth, and the moon the seventh. Saturn again exerts its influence during the eighth month, and Jupiter again replaces Saturn during the ninth month. The child at birth comes a complete being under the influence of these same planets, called by the ancients the Gods of Nature.

The child born under the influence of Saturn is dark-skinned, he has a thick head of hair and a heavy beard. He is mean, untrustworthy, quick-tempered, and melancholy. He prefers a coarse life and has all the bad physical and moral qualities that go with it.

Jupiter's child is handsome and bright-eyed. His two upper front teeth are big and wide apart. He is good, dependable, and modest. He likes fine clothes, has good taste, and will live a long time. He is compassionate, benevolent, virtuous, and sincere.

A child born under the influence of Mars has a reddish complexion, as if sunburned, short hair, small eyes, and an ugly body. He is fickle, deceitful, shameless, and subject to emotional outbursts. He sows discord and dissension.

The sun's child is plump, handsome, and perhaps hypocritical. Some say that he is learned, pious, and rich. The child of Venus is also handsome and wise. He loves music, pleasure, dancing. He is candid and out-going. Mercury

470

produces a well-proportioned child with a handsome beard. He is intelligent, studious, eloquent, sociable, and of modest means. He gives good advice, keeps his word, and chooses good companions. By contrast, the moon's child is flighty, untrustworthy, incompetent.

Planetary Spirits
Cabalists assign a spirit to each of the seven planets recognized by their system. Saturn's spirit is Aratron, Jupiter's Betoi, Mars' Phaleg, the sun's Och, Venus' Haegit, Mercury's Ophiel, and the moon's Phul. Like the planetary angels, they are names of power.

Planetary Talismans
The talisman of Saturn protects the bearer against the danger of death by apoplexy, cancer, poisoning, or violence. It protects women against the perils of childbirth. It should be made during the hours governed by the spirit of Saturn. (The same rule applies to the fabrication of talismans under other planetary influences.) On one side of the talisman should be engraved the Saturn Square, on the other the hieroglyphic figure of the planet:

SATURN

FACE   REVERSE

471

This talisman should be made of pure lead, smoothly polished on both sides. It should be executed on Saturday, when the moon is in the first 10 degrees of Taurus or Capricorn. The mystical names linked with the numbers of Saturn (corresponding to the number of digits in one line of the magic square of Saturn, the total number of digits in the square, the sum of the numbers making up one line of the square, and the sum of all the numbers in the square) are as follows:

> 3——AB
> 9——HOD
> 15——IAH
> 15——HOD
> 45——AGIEL (Intelligence)
> 45——Zazel (Daimon)

Saturn's angels are Zaphkiel (higher angel) and Cassiel (lower angel). The planetary spirit is Aratron. (In the cabalistic tradition, each planet was assigned specific characteristics, or signatures, as well as numbers, angels, and spirits of daimons.)

The talisman of Jupiter brings the wearer the sympathy and good will of others. It protects him against worries, death by violence, and accidents. This talisman should be executed upon a round piece of tin, polished on both sides. The sum of Jupiter's square, which must be carved on the face of the metal, is 34 in one direction and 136 when all of the numbers are counted each time they appear in the square.

The other side of the talisman contains the hieroglyphic figure of the planet, which is a man dressed in priestly garments and holding a book which he seems to be reading.

JUPITER

FACE   REVERSE

4	14	15	1
9	7	6	12
5	11	10	8
16	2	3	13

Above his head is a bright star and the word Jupiter. The mystical numbers and names of Jupiter are:

4——ABBA
16——TAIE
16——EHIE
34——ELAB
136——JOPHIEL (Intelligence)
136——HISMAEL (Daimon)

Jupiter's day, Thursday, is ruled by the angel Sachiel.

The talisman of Mars offers protection against the attacks of any dangerous enemy. Its influence wards off the danger of death in battle or in a quarrel, from fever, or from an epidemic. It is made from pure iron, smoothly polished on both sides. It must be fashioned on a Tuesday when the moon is moving through the first ten degrees of Capricorn or Sagittarius. The face of the talisman should show Mars' square, consisting of 25 numbers whose sum in any direction is 65 and whose combined total is 325. The reverse side should contain the hieroglyphic figure of the planet, an armed soldier holding a shield in one hand and a sword in the other.

473

FACE

11	24	7	20	3
4	12	25	8	16
17	5	12	21	9
10	18	1	14	22
23	6	19	2	15

The mystical names corresponding to the numbers of Mars

5——HE
25——ZEI
65——ADONAI
325—GRAPHIEL (Intelligence)
325—BARBAZEL (Daimon)

The talisman of the sun draws the favor and good will of powerful men to the wearer. It protects him against heart disease, fainting, epidemics, and fire. It is made from pure gold. The face of the talisman contains a six-column square. The sum of each column is 111 and of all columns, 666. The reverse contains the hieroglyphic figure of the planet, a king seated on his royal throne a lion lying at his feet:

SUN

FACE

REVERSE

6	32	3	34	35	1
7	11	27	28	8	30
19	14	16	15	23	24
18	20	22	21	17	13
25	29	10	9	26	12
36	25	33	4	2	31

474

The mystical names of the numbers of the sun are:

6——VAU
6——HE
36——ELOH
111—NACHIEL (Intelligence)
666—SORATH (Daimon)

The angel for Sunday is Michael.

Those who wear Venus' talisman are assured of preserving harmonious, affectionate relationships between themselves and their mates. It protects the wearer against envy and hatred, and it is a good defense against poisoning, whether accidental or planned. Put in an enemy's drink, it will turn his hatred into affection and loyalty. The talisman is made from a piece of pure copper. The magic square of Venus contains 49 numbers, arranged in 7 columns. Each column totals 175 and all columns total 220. The reverse of the medal contains the hieroglyphic figure of the planet, a woman with Cupid and his flaming arrow beside her.

VENUS

FACE

REVERSE

22	47	16	41	10	35	4
5	23	48	17	42	11	29
30	6	24	49	18	36	12
13	31	7	25	43	19	37
38	14	32	1	26	44	20
21	39	8	33	2	27	45
46	15	40	9	34	3	28

VENUS

The mystic names corresponding to the numbers of Venus are:

7——AHEA
49——HAGIEL (Intelligence)
1252——BNE SERAPHIM (Intelligences)
175——KEDEMEL (Daimon)

Friday, the day of Venus, has three angels: Anael, Rachiel, and Sachiel. Anael is also the planetary spirit.

Mercury

The influence of Mercury protects the wearer of its talisman against epilepsy and madness, murder and poisoning. Hidden in the basement of a store, it draws customers and profits. It is fashioned on Wednesday, when the moon is passing through the first 10 degrees of Gemini or Scorpio. It is made of an alloy of silver, tin, and mercury. The magic square of Mercury consists of 64 numbers arranged in 8 columns. The sum of each column is 260 and of all columns, 2,080. The reverse side of the medal contains the hieroglyphic figure of the planet, an angel holding a caduceus.

MERCURY

FACE

8	18	59	5	4	62	63	1
49	15	14	52	53	11	10	56
41	23	22	44	45	19	18	48
32	34	35	29	28	38	39	25
40	26	27	37	36	30	31	33
17	47	4	20	21	43	42	24
9	55	54	12	13	51	50	16
64	2	3	61	60	6	7	57

REVERSE

The mystic names and corresponding numbers of Mercury are:

476

```
  8——ASBOGA
 64——DIN
 64——DONI
260——TIRIEL (Intelligence)
280——TAPHTHARTHARATH (Daimon)
```

Wednesday's angels are Raphael, Miel, and Seraphiel. Mercury's planetary angels are Michael and Raphael. The planetary spirit is Ophiel.

The moon's influence protects travelers and people residing in a foreign land. A talisman executed under the moon's influence protects the wearer against death by shipwreck, epilepsy, dropsy, apoplexy, and madness. It is made from pure silver. On one side is the moon's magic square, containing nine columns. The sum of each column is 369. The sum of all columns is 3,321. The reverse of the talisman contains the hieroglyphic image of the planet, a woman standing on the moon's crescent and holding another crescent in her hand.

Pliny the Elder
Roman encyclopedist (23-79 A.D.).

The author of the voluminous *Natural History* found an element of truth in magic:

> We may rest assured that magic is a thing detestable in itself. Frivolous and false, it still contains some element of truth in it.

Poimandres
One of the books included in the *Corpus Hermeticum*. It describes how the Universal Intellect revealed itself to Hermes-Thoth:

> He looked me squarely in the face until I trembled before his gaze. Then as he again raised his head, I saw

477

how in my own mind *(nous)* the light embracing countless possibilities became an infinite Whole, while the fire,
contained by an almighty power that surrounded it, had
become motionless. That is what I managed to grasp
rationally. . . . While I was completely absorbed in my
vision, he spoke again: "In the mind you have now seen
the prototype, the origin, the eternal beginning. . . ."

Poltergeist

A spirit assumed to create disturbances and otherwise un-
explained noises. The word means "noisy ghost." A seventeenth-century manual gives a formula for exorcising a
poltergeist:

> I adjure you, ancient serpent, by the Judge of the living
> and the dead, by the Creator of the universe, who has
> power to send you to Gehenna, that you depart forthwith
> from this house. He orders you to do so, cursed devil,
> who ordered the winds and the sea and the tempests. He
> orders you who ordered you to go back. Hearken, there-
> fore, Satan, and be afraid, and withdraw, subdued and
> prostrate.

These noisy, troublesome spirits are generally activated by
the presence of adolescent girls. They are invisible but
capable of performing physical acts that disturb a household
and threaten the security of its occupants. Some modern
psychic researchers believe that poltergeists are not spirits
but telekinetic manifestations of adolescents whose hostility
toward others is the driving force behind the movement of
physical objects in their environment.

Poltersberg

According to Martin Luther, on a high mountain in Germany, called Poltersberg, there is a pool. "If one throws a
stone into it, instantly a storm arises. . . . This lake is full
of demons. Satan holds them captive there."

Polyglot Invocation

A powerful spell uttered in Greek, Hebrew, and Syriac is binding on the spirit invoked. It is found in a Graeco-Egyptian magical manuscript.

I call upon thee that didst create the earth and bones, and all flesh and all spirit, that didst establish the sea and that shakest the heavens, that didst divide the light from darkness, the great regulative mind, that disposeth everything, eye of the world, spirit of spirits, god of gods, the lord of the spirits, the immovable Aeon, Iaoouei, hear my voice.

I call upon thee, the ruler of the gods, high-thundering Zeus, Zeus, King. Adonaid, lord, Iaoouee. I am he that invokes thee in the Syrian tongue, the great god, Zaalaer, Iphphou, do thou not disregard the Hebrew appellation, Ablanchanalb, Abrasiloa.

For I am Silthakhookh, Lailam, Blasaloth, Iao, Ieo, Nebouth, Sabiothar, Both, Arbathiao, Iaoth, Sabaoth, Patoure, Zagoure, Baroukh Adonai, Eloai, Iabraam, Barbarauo, Nau, Siph.

Popes Accused of Being Sorcerers

From the tenth century onward a number of popes were accused of being sorcerers. Gerbert reputedly sold his soul to the Devil to win the papacy, under the name of Silvester II. Benedict IX, who became Pope at the age of 12 and was accused of being a member of Silvester's school, was followed by a number of ecclesiastical sorcerers: Laurence, Archbishow of Melfi, John XX, Gregory VI, and Gregory VII. The latter, who was sentenced as a magician and necromancer at the Synod of Brixen, was said to be able to cause lightning merely by shaking his sleeve.

Porphyry

A Neoplatonic philosopher (c. 232-305 A.D.). He was a

pupil of the great Neoplatonist Plotinus. Like the early Greek philosophers, Porphyry had a profound belief in demons and in their malefic practices which required secret rites and formulas, invocations and conjurations to dispel them. Among Porphyry's works is a mystical treatise On the Return of the Soul.

Post, Sarah

The last witchcraft trial in the United States was held at Ipswich, Massachusetts, in 1693. Sarah Post of Andover was freed after standing trial on the charge of signing a pact with the Devil.

Power, Cone of

See Cone of Power.

Practicus

The third grade or rank in Aleister Crowley's cabalistic system. The student completes his intellectual training in sephira 8, corresponding to mercury, and studies the Cabala.

Prana

In Hindu and Buddhist teachings, prana is the breath or life-current. It is used mainly to compel the upward surge of the mystic fire called kundalini, which can also be expressed sexually. Breath and mind, rhythmically directed toward a particular goal, is the basis of sexual magic. See Kundalini.

Prayer

In magic, the aim of prayer is the momentary fusion of the indvidual consciousness and the supreme consciousness. Prayer is first and foremost a magical ceremony and the necessary starting point of any undertaking. But in ritual magic prayer is not a mechanical, habitual movement of the lips, it is an act involving both the will and the mind.

Before he prays the magician must have fasted for at least

three hours. He should meditate for five minutes, after breathing slowly and deeply three times. He should then turn successively toward the four cardinal points, beginning with the east. He should invoke each of the spirits or angels of these cardinal points. After completing the cycle, he should meditate for three minutes, then turn to the east and pray, his arms extended, his palms upward. See Angels of the Four Cardinal Points.

Precognition
Foreknowledge, awareness of events before they occur. The word also designates the ability to predict future occurrences.

Prediction
The passion for probing into the future is so intense nowadays that all sorts of techniques, both old and more recent, have been revived and promoted. A large number of such procedures concern the daily routine, domestic affairs, personal situations. One of the most popular methods in common vogue is the use of numerology. Interpretation of numbers and their impact on persons and events have become a major issue. Gambling, especially in races, appeals to practitioners in numerological calculations.

A trip taken for business or pleasure is conditioned by consultation of certain numbers and combinations of such numbers. Numbers too affect the good or unfavorable days for moving to a new location, a new apartment. Lucky days are determined similarly by numerical observation. These practices are referred back to antiquity, to ancient procedures among the Egyptian priesthood, among Chinese wizards, and among the priests of the pagan mystery cults of Phrygia and Mesopotamia.

Prelati, Francois
Florentine "expert in the prohibited art of geomancy," he

481

helped Gilles de Rais (1404-40) to invoke evil spirits.

Premonition

Forewarning or anticipation of an event. independent of conscious reason. Occultists believe that many people have the capacity to receive intuitional messages but fail to allow this capacity to develop adequately. Those who fail to act upon the messages they receive destroy faith in the process and lose the ability to receive other messages.

Preparations for Magical Operations

The Magus who wished to devote himself seriously to magical works, according to Éliphas Lévi, must first fortify his mind against the danger of hallucination and fright. He must also purify himself without and within for forty days. The number is sacred, and its very figure is magical. In Arabic numerals it consists of the circle, which is a type of the infinite, and of the 4, which sums the triad by unity. In Roman numerals, arranged after the following manner, it represents the sign of the fundamental doctrine of Hermes and the character of the Seal of Solomon.

```
        X                           X
      X   X                       X   X
                                    X
        X
```

The purification of the Magus consists in the renunciation of coarse enjoyments, in a temperate and vegetarian diet, in abstinence from intoxicating drink, and in regulating the hours of sleep. . . .

All clothes, furniture and vessels made use of must be also washed carefully, whether by ourselves or others. All dirt is evidence of negligence, and negligence is deadly in Magic. The atmosphere must be purified at rising and retiring with a perfume composed of the juice of laurels, salt, camphor, white resin and sulphur, repeating at the same time the four Sacred Words, while turning successively towards the four cardinal points. . . .

The Magus must be isolated at the beginning and difficult to approach, so that he may concentrate his power and select his points of contact; but in proportion as he is austere and inaccessible at first, so will he be popular and sought after when he shall have magnetized his chain and chosen his place in a current of ideas and of light. . . .

So far as may be possible, we must avoid the sight of hideous objects and uncomely persons, must decline eating with those whom we do not esteem, and must live in the most uniform and studied manner. We should hold ourselves in the highest respect and consider that we are dethroned sovereigns who consent to existence in order to reconquer our crowns. We must be mild and considerate to all, but in social relations must never permit ourselves to be absorbed, and must withdraw from circles in which we cannot acquire some initiative. Finally, we may and should fulfil the duties and practice the rites of the cultus to which we belong. Now, of all forms of worship the most magical is that which most realizes the miraculous, which bases the most inconceivable mysteries upon the highest reasons, which has lights equivalent to its shadows, which popularizes miracles, and incarnates God in all mankind by faith. This religion has existed always in the world, and under many names has been ever the one and ruling religion.

Price, Harry

Ghost-hunter. He made a name for himself by exposing fraudulent British mediums and founding the National Laboratory for Psychical Research. His investigations of Borley Rectory, which he called "the most haunted house in England," stirred violent controversy among psychical researchers. Legends of a 14th-century nun, murdered following an illicit love affair, visions of headless men, and poltergeist phenomena were associated with the house. Price wrote two books on the subject, *The Most Haunted House in England* (1940) and *The End of Borley Rectory* (1945).

Prickers

The notion that the Devil's mark was insensitive to pain gave rise to a class of witch-finders known as prickers. Matthew Hopkins, the self-styled English Witch-Finder General, used pricking along with other "methods of discovery." In his *Laws and Customs of Scotland* (1678), Sir George Mackenzie wrote:

> This mark is discovered among us by a pricker, whose trade it is and who learns it as other trades; but this is a horrid cheat, for they allege that if the place bleed not, or if the person be not sensible, he or she is infallibly a witch.

Prickers owed their success largely to deception and terror. Some of them used bodkins with retractable blades; others soon discovered that victims of horror frequently experience temporary anaesthesia.

Persons suspected of being witches were examined for signs that they had been branded by Satan's mark. If no such mark was visible, they were stuck with long pins. It was assumed that they would feel no pain when the pin was stuck into the invisible devil's mark.

Psalterium Mirable
See Secret of Secrets.

Psellus, Michael Constantius
Greek philosopher (c. 1020-79). He wrote on alchemy and

demonology. He described Hecate's Circle (Hecate was the patroness of witchcraft) in these words:

Hecate's Circle is a golden sphere, enclosing a sapphire in the centre, turned by a thong of bull's hide, and having characters through the whole of it. They made conjurations by turning this: and they are wont to call such things wheels, whether they have a spherical or triangular or any other shape whatsoever. Shaking these, they uttered unintelligible or beastlike sounds, laughing, and striking the bronze. It accordingly teaches the operations of the rite, or the motion of such a circle, as possessing secret power and it is called "Hecate's" as being dedicated to Hecate: and Hecate is a divinity among the Chaldeans.

PSI
Term used to designate the human capacity for extrasensory perception and psychokinesis, whether latent or fully developed.

Psilocybin
The active ingredient of Mexico's "magic mushrooms."

Psychagogues
This expression, of Greek origin, means conjurer of the spirits of the dead.

Psychedelic
Producing hallucinations, consciousness expanding, giving rise to mystical and religious experiences. Psychedelic agents are used in occult rites because they heighten awareness and produce impressions susceptible of mystical or occult interpretations.

Psychic
A person subject to spiritual possession or influences. The word is synonymous with medium or sensitive.

Psychic

This is a recently founded bi-monthly magazine, published in California. It is devoted to every aspect of psychic phenomena and related topics. It is designed to present material of substance to the general public and bring about open discussion among proponents and detractors. The first issue included an interview with Jeane Dixon, who has been called the "seeress of Washington"; an article on ESP in Eastern Europe and Russia; and a piece on the Lost Continent of Atlantis.

Psychical Research

Since William James and Oliver Lodge took the first steps toward establishing a solid basis for the investigation of psychical happenings, researchers have accumulated a vast amount of data. Experiments have been conducted under controlled conditions in apparitions, clairvoyance, psychokinesis, telepathy, and other related fields, and the results of these experiments have been published in scholarly journals: *Journal of the American Society for Psychical Research, Journal of Parapsychology,* and the *Proceedings* and *Journal* of the Society for Psychical Research in London. Gardner Murphy, past president of the American Psychological Association, has selected and analyzed much of this material in his book *Challenge of Psychical Research* (1961).

Psychokinesis (Pk)

A physical event involving people and not subject to explanation by known natural law. An individual with psi ability seems to be able to use his will to cause objects to move. The notion is related to levitation.

Psychomancy

This is the practice of divination by conjuring the spirits of the dead. In ancient Greece psychomancy was a common practice.

486

Psychometry

The faculty of reading a person's character by holding in one's hand an object belonging to that person. J. R. Buchanan is supposed to have discovered this faculty which many mediums possess.

A medium may have the ability to detect radiations emitted by an object and use them to judge a person's character. Peter Hurkos is widely known for his ability to help officials solve crimes, locate missing persons, etc., by using psychometry.

Psylli

A class of persons thought in ancient times to have had the power to charm snakes.

Ptolemy (Claudius Ptolemaeus)

Alexandrian astronomer (c. 100-170), mathematician, and author of the thirteen-volume work familiarly known as the *Almagest*.

Pyramid Tests

Beginning in the Fifth Dynasty (c. 2400 B.C.) the Egyptians covered the walls of the interior chambers of pyramids with hymns and magic spells to be used by the deceased king as he ascended to heaven. Magic spells were also used by each new ruler to achieve identification with Osiris.

Pyramid Texts

The earliest religious Egyptian writings so far known, from about 2,500 B.C. Concerned with the mortuary ritual practiced to ensure the resurrection of the dead pharaoh, they contain the ideas and beliefs of the ancient Egyptians. The ritual of embalming, intended to purify the corpse and to revivify it, was patterned on the rites believed to have been performed by other deities to raise Osiris to life again. The dead pharaoh was identified in ritual with Osiris.

The Pyramid Texts intersperse embalming rituals, funeral rites, incantations, hymns, prayers, and myths. Material bearing even a remote relation to magic or religion seems to have been included.

Pyramids

Apart from the intricate mathematical and architectural calculations involved in the building of the Egyptian pyramids, these structures have been mystically and symbolically interpreted in terms of man, his spiritual ascent, and, in general, the evolutionary process of mankind. See Astronauts; Initiators.

Pyromancy

Divination utilizing fire and the smoke that arises from it.

Pythagoras

Mystically oriented Greek philosopher (c. 582-507 B.C.). A mathematician and a dreamer, he seems to have been acquainted with Indian mysticism and Egyptian magical thinking. As a teacher, he divided his pupils into two classes: the neophytes, who possessed only the most obvious and general truths; and the initiates, who devoted all their material possessions to the community in which they came to live and gain access to both scientific and mystical teachings.

The master communicated with his chosen pupils from behind a curtain over a novitiate of either three or five years, during which time they had to preserve strict silence, practice vegetarianism, and lead a simple life. He was seen only at night, when he appeared wearing "a long garment of the purest white, with a flowing beard and a garland upon his head." He encouraged his followers to believe that he was the divine Hyperborean Apollo, and that he had chosen to dwell on earth in human form to encourage men to approach him and give him their confidence. He claimed to have been reincarnated in successive ages, and to have visited the dwelling place of departed souls.

Pythagoras was initiated into the secret doctrines of Egypt. His novitiate was long and taxing, and included the rite of circumcision. He was said also to exhibit many of the strange powers attributed to Indian miracle-workers. He left no writings but his views are known through Empedocles and were adopted by Plato. He taught the theory of reincarnation, recalling that he had appeared in various human forms in successive ages; the secrets of miraculous medicine, rejuvenation, and necromancy; and the method of producing rain, storm, or sunshine. His supernatural exploits included the taming of a wild bear by whispering in its ear, calling down an eagle from its flight, and appearing simultaneously at two distant places, one in Italy and the other in Sicily. He returned to Italy after an absence of a year and claimed that he had been journeying through the infernal regions.

One of his disgruntled pupils inflamed the populace and caused them to set fire to the Pythagorean college. Later Pythagoras took refuge in the Temple of the Muses, where he died of his privations following a forty-day siege.

Pythia
See Oracles.

Q

Quail

In Gypsy mythology, the Devil's bird. The daughters of the Nivasi, earth-spirits, appear by night as quails to steal corn from the fields.

Queen of Elfame (Elfin)

In some of the Scottish witchcraft trials, the Queen of Elfame or Elfin was mentioned as the presiding deity of the witches' sabbat. She was said to copulate with male witches.

Queen of Night

In the twelfth century John Salisbury wrote that a few ignorant men and women believed that the Queen of Night, or Herodias, summoned them to nightly meetings. Children were eaten, vomited up whole, and returned to their cradles by the presiding goddess.

Queen of the Sabbat

Although most Sabbats were said to be presided over by a male, in the early 17th-century Basque witches had a Queen of the Sabbat who was the Devil's principal bride.

Quimby, Phineas Parkhurst

American physician (1802-66), founder of the New Thought movement, based on animal magnetism, auto-suggestion, and the power of positive thinking. He may have been the first person to use the expression mental healing.

Quindecemviri
Guardians of the Sibylline Books. The fifteen men appointed by the Roman dictator Sulla were the only ones permitted to read the manuscripts in which were embodied the secrets of human destiny.

Quirardell, Corneille
Franciscan astrologer. He was born at Boulogne towards the end of the 16th century. He wrote several treatises on astrology.

Quirinus (Quirus)
A juggling stone. It is found in the nest of the hoopoo. It evokes a confession from a sleeper on whose chest it is placed.

R

Rabdos
A demon, said to have been a wise man at one time. Known as the strangler, he personifies the *rhabdos* or wand, one of the supreme emblems of magical power. The wand or rod is also a phallic symbol.

Rada
In the Voodoo cult, the rada is the royal rite of the sun. It bears the name of the snake which personifies Dangbe, the supreme deity.

Haitian Voodoo cults acknowledge three great rites or divisions, the Rada, Congo, and Pétro. Only the Rada division includes good or benevolent deities. Among them are Legba, Agouè, Taroyo, Aïda Ouèdo, Damballah Ouèdo Maîtresse Philomise, Papa Piè, Erzulie Dantor, Erzulie Fréda Dahomin, Ati Danyon Monkè, Ogou Badagris, Ogou BalindjO, and Ogou Feraille.

Radiation Trap
The French weekly newspaper Quatre et Trois reported recently (July 30, 1947) that Hector Mellin, a magician and inventor, had perfected a machine "to capture and return evil radiations."

Rahats
See Adepts.

Rahu

A Hindu devil whose name means The Tormenter. People worship him to ward off the attacks of evil spirits.

Rais, Gilles De Laval De

French nobleman and soldier (1404-40). He fought beside Joan of Arc and was named Marshal of France at the age of twenty-three. He delved into alchemy, invoked evil spirits, and signed a pact with the demon Baron. He sacrificed children to obtain favors from Satan and was arrested by the Inquisition. He was hanged and burned at Nantes on October 6, 1440. See Gilles de Rais.

Raju Sathyanarayana

An Indian mystic and miracle worker, known to his followers as Baba. Born in 1917, he claims to be the reincarnation of Krishna. He is reputed to have performed many miraculous cures, to have produced sandalwood statuettes of Krishna from the sand by magic, to have turned water into gasoline, and to have cured himself of heart attacks which he had taken on himself in order to spare the life of another person. His goal is to restore justice to the world by teaching men how to follow the "moral path."

Rakshasa

A hideous Indian demon. He appears in folktales as a black creature with yellow hair, wearing a wreath of entrails.

Ramakrishna

The best-known Hindu saint of modern times (1836-86). Visionary as a child, he was attracted by the lives of great religious figures. He founded monasteries in India, dedicated to the principle that all religions are one. Visions of Rama, Krishna, Siva, Kali, Allah, and Jesus became part of his life. His famous disciple Swami Vivekananda said that he was "the embodiment of all the past religious thought of India."

Rappings

Knocking or rappings frequently accompany poltergeistic disturbances and are closely associated with the beginnings of spiritualism. The famous Rochester Rappings began in 1848. See Hydesville.

Rapport

The name used by spiritualists to denote a community of sensations that links the medium and someone actually present at a seance or represented by some personal object.

Rasputin

See Novich, Gregori.

Rauwolfia Serpentina

A tropical plant chewed by East Indian holy men engaged in meditation. Mahatma Gandhi chewed the sacred plant regularly. The powerful tranquilizer called reserpine is extracted from it.

Recordi, Peter

Carmelite monk condemned by the Inquisition at Carcassonne in 1329. He was accused of having made images of wax, spittle, and toads' blood and of summoning the Devil and sacrificing to him a butterfly. Recordi was accused of hiding his images, which he had consecrated to the Devil, in the homes of women with whom he hoped to have sexual intercourse.

Red Book

The sabbat opened with a ritual of allegiance to Satan, who then opened his red book and called the roster of those present.

Red Dragon

Handbook on magic. It is based on the *Grand Grimoire*.

Red Man

The demon of the tempests. He is supposed to vent his

anger in the form of storms when a rash voyager disturbs his peace.

Redfearne, Alison
One of the Lancashire witches, hanged in 1612. She was only 11 years of age.

Reich, Wilhelm
Psychiatrist. A pupil of Freud, he developed a theory of the importance of an unobstructed orgasm. His theory involves a substance which he called orgone and for which he constructed a special box. In this box he saturated his patients with the potent, energizing, cosmic substance which he called orgone.

Reincarnation
According to Gerald B. Gardner, whose writings include *Witchcraft Today* (1955), modern witches believe in reincarnation and direct their prayers to the Lord of the Underworld. Their great goddess descended to the underworld, became the bride of the Lord of the Dead, and could presumably influence his decision concerning the time and place a person was to be reborn.

Rejuvenation
See Elixir of Life.

Relatio
A confession of guilt based on affirmative answers to a list of prepared questions. The questions were generally put to those accused of witchcraft while they were undergoing torture.

Religion and Magic
Sir James Frazer drew a rigid distinction between religion and magic, saying that the former supplicates the powers of the Universe while the latter tries to compel them. Re-

jecting this notion, most modern historians of religion stress the fact that all religions contain magical elements. Moreover, both magic and religion attribute an I-Thou relationship to man and his Universe.

Reuchlin, Johann
German scholar (1455-1522), author of *The Kabalistic Art* and *The Mirific Word.* His writings profoundly influenced Agrippa von Nettesheim.

Rhabdomancy
Divination utilizing a rod. An arrow is shot toward an object to which are attached several answers. The correct answer is the one pierced by the arrow.

Rhasis
Alchemist (c. 850-932). The celebrated Arabian physician and alchemist, whose true name was Mohammed-Ibn-Secharjah Aboubekr Arrasi, was born in Iraq. His oriental panegyrists call him the Imam of the scholars and western admirers describe him as the Galen of the Arabians. Avicenna profited by reading some of the 226 treatises ascribed to him. His writings, like those of Geber, enlarge on the planetary correspondences, or on the influence exerted by the stars in the formation of metallic substances underneath the earth.

Rhine, J. B.
Parapsychologist. In 1965, after 38 years of service at Duke University's Parapsychology Laboratory, he retired and became director of the Institute of Parapsychology of Durham, North Carolina. With Professor William McDougall, he founded the *Journal of Parapsychology* in 1937. His books include *Extrasensory Perception* (1934) and *New World of the Mind* (1953).

Rhombos
In Greek religion, a small piece of wood which was whirled

on a string to produce a loud droning sound. Used in primitive Greek ritual, it has as its counterpart the modern bull roarer.

Richard II
Plantagenet king of England (1367-1400). It has been suggested that he was the accepted head of a witch cult since he was able to put down a rebellion that had cost the life of a chancellor and head of the church. Watt Tyler's Rebellion, also known as The Peasants' Revolt (1381), was directed primarily against the church. Simon of Sudbury, who was both chancellor and archbishop of Canterbury, was seized and beheaded, and London was threatened by the rebels. Richard, son of the Black Prince and a descendant of the founder of the Order of the Garter, notwithstanding his tender age, was able to persuade the rebel army to return home. Margaret Murray has inferred, since the peasants had already shown their contempt for the church and the law, that Richard represented something more than these powers and was the accepted head of a rival religion. She believes that the whole Plantagenet family were devotees of a witch cult.

Rides with Diana
As early as 1370 the Inquisition at Milan indicted a woman for claiming that she went out at night as a member of the society of Diana to eat, drink, and steal from the wealthy. Near Isère, in France, it was reported in 1395 that revelers celebrated every three years a festival at which they elected a king and then went out to do mischief. Tyrolese women claimed to have ridden out together at midnight on animals in the company of Diana, Herodias, or Percht (Bertha). In 1423 a woman living near Basel was sentenced to death after she had confessed to having practiced maleficum and ridden out at night on wolves.

498

Rider of the White Horse

A female ghost astride a white horse. She has been observed by many Europeans, and her presence portends war.

Ripley, George

Alchemical philosopher (d. 1490). A. E. Waite writes:

This illustrious alchemical philosopher, whose works paved the royal road to the initiation, in after times, of his still more illustrious pupil, the sublime and mysterious Philalethes, entered, at an early age, among the regular canons of Bridlington, in the diocese of York. The tranquillity of monastic life afforded him a favourable opportunity for the study of the great masters in transcendental chemistry, but he found himself notwithstanding incompetent for their full comprehension, and in considerable consequent disappointment he determined to travel, persuading himself that he should discover in the conversation of philosophers what he could not glean from books.

In Italy, Germany, and France he became acquainted with various men of learning, and was present at a transmutation which was performed in Rome. He proceeded afterwards to the island of Rhodes, where a document is supposed to exist testifying that he gave £100,000 to the Knights of St. John of Jerusalem. He was dignified by the Pope, which fact, on his return to Bridlington, excited the jealousy of his brethren, and in consequence of their hostility he entered the Carmelite order at Butolph, in Lincolnshire, and, by an indulgence from Innocent VIII, had permission to live in solitude, exempt from cloistral observances, and in his now uninterrupted leisure he wrote twenty-four books, some scientific, and others on devout subjects. The "Twelve Gates of Alchemy" he composed in 1471, and he declares that any of his experiments recorded from 1450 to 1470 should be entirely discredited, as he wrote them from theory, and found afterwards by practice that they were untrue. Hence it may be concluded that he employed twenty years in mastering the secrets of the science. He died at Butolph in 1490.

Rishis
See Adepts.

Ritual Ablution
An initiatory rite using water to purify the corpse from the contamination of death and to revivify it. It was practiced not only in Egypt but also in the mystery religions of the Graeco-Roman world.

Ritual Magic
The object of ritual magic is to control powerful supernatural forces. To do so, the magician has recourse to impressive ceremonial. He tries to summon up from the spirit world some kind of supernatural power—a spirit, a cosmic force, a demon, a god. The name that the magician uses to identify it is not important.

Ritual magic is grounded on analogy, the analogy between man and his universe. The magician uses ceremony as a visible demonstration of his identity with a superhuman power. He assumes that just as human beings are moved, persuaded, or inspired by ceremonial (witness the flag salute in thousands of classrooms each day), so are the driving forces of his universe. He moves purposefully to the right to attract the support of the forces of good, to the left to activate the forces of evil. In the magical tradition of the West, the left is the side of evil, the right the side of good. He uses mimicry, gestures, garments, incantations, and other aids in creating a state of mental and emotional intoxication that carries him beyond his normal self and confers upon him superhuman powers. He stimulates his imagination to the utmost degree until he reaches a mental state in which he feels that he is the god or cosmic force whose power he covets.

European ritual magic is rooted in human nature and has left its traces in the earliest archaeological sites. A melange of cultures, religions, and philosophies of the eastern Mediterranean area had already absorbed a welter of ideas from Egypt and the Middle East before Christianity gained ascendancy: from the ancient mystery religions in which a ritually inspired identity with a god was the adept's goal; from Gnostics whose ordered hierarchy of supernatural forces were subject to magical control; from a body of Jewish mystical doctrines known today as the Cabala.

Alchemy taught that man could become immortal and omnipotent by concentrating on certain secret symbols and processes. Number mysticism derived from both Greek and cabalistic sources. Belief in astrology was widespread, and magicians tried to harness the influences of the stars for their own purposes. Grimoires which abounded after the 18th century, based mainly on the medieval *Key of Solomon,* indicate the general patterns of traditional rituals.

In the ritual of conjuration the magician first prepares himself and his equipment. He may fast, bathe, practice chastity, or resort to any other means of initiating the process of raising his mind to that high state of concentration necessary for the conjuration.

Equipped with a knife, sword, wand, and brazier, he draws a magic circle, steps inside it, and in a series of incantations causes a spirit to appear. After forcing the spirit to answer his questions or to perform his commands, he dismisses it.

A spirit is summoned by incantation, which is the magical

501

use of language. A mixture of prayer and command, couched in solemn and striking language, the incantation is founded on the belief that saying a thing is so makes it so. The magician chants names and attributes of a god as a means of bringing the god under his control. The name of a god is supposed to contain the god's power, and to pronounce the name is to bring that power into operation. Names of power were drawn from many sources but mainly from the Greek and Egyptian. The grimoires prescribe the use of the names of Jesus and other Biblical figures even in diabolical operations. Meaning and sound are both important in the incantation, which is chanted rhythmically and with gradually increasing force. The incantations are repeated again and again as the ritual proceeds and the magician works himself up into a state of frenzied intoxication. In this state his inner energies reach their highest pitch as he forces the spirit to appear and submit to him. The fumes from the brazier, the motions he makes with his wand and sword, sometimes the wounding or killing of a living creature, sometimes the achievement of orgasm—all are important elements of the ritual, but the most important single ingredient contributing to the attainment of the climactic stage is the hypnotic chanting of words of power.

Some modern magicians follow the precedent set by the grimoires. Others choose Graeco-Egyptian models. Mac-Gregor Mathers, for instance, invoked the goddess Isis in his "Egyptian Masses." His pupil Aleister Crowley turned instead to Gnostic sources for his models.

Rituale Romanum
A liturgical book "The Roman Ritual" contains all the rites normally administered by a priest, including the rite of exorcism. See Exorcism, the Rite of.

Robert, Armande
See Carcassonne Trials.

Robert the Devil

Son of a Norman duke and duchess, he used his great physical strength to minister to his evil passions. His mother explained his evil tendencies by saying that he had been born in answer to prayers addressed to the Devil. A hermit ordered him to remain silent, take his food from the mouths of dogs, feign madness, and provoke abuse from common people. He became the court fool to the emperor and delivered the city from the Saracens three times, each time on the advice of a heavenly messenger. He appears in an old French romance as Robert le Diable.

Rodier, Paul

See Carcassonne Trials.

Roland, Pierrille

See Carcassonne Trials.

Roman Astrology

The ancient purpose of astrology was to reduce the notions of the heavenly bodies to mathematical precision. It was concerned with the influence of these bodies on human life.

The temples of Mesopotamia were the earliest to record this view. When the Orient came into contact with Greece, and later on Rome came in contact with Hellenic culture, the emphasis on astrology grew until it reached its height in Roman Imperial times. The astrologers who practiced their skill in casting horoscopes were called Chaldaei and mathematici. A major field of knowledge that was deeply affected by astrology was the practice of medicine.

Roman Demonology

In Roman folklore a *larva* or the goddess Ceres was supposed to possess a man, who then was regarded as *larvatus* or *cerritus*. To the Romans, however, possession meant mental illness. Epilepsy was treated as a singular disease and

503

called *morbus comitialis* because people who had come together had to disband when one of them suffered an epi-
leptic attack. Epileptics were spat upon because people
believed that spit had a protective quality.

Roman Incantations

The Romans had magic formulas for almost every occasion.
A magic tablet supplies a curse against the horses of one's
opponents:

> I summon you demon and hand over to you these horses
> to keep them and bind them so that they cannot move.

An ancient formula for banishing pain is supplied by an
anonymous Roman:

> On a paper hung round the neck:
> "An ant has no blood nor bile:
> flee, uvula, lest a crab eat you."

Cato, in *De Agri Cultura,* offers an incantation for dislocated bone:

> Huat hanat huat
> Ista pista sista
> Domiabo damnaustra.

Rose

A flower symbolizing beauty, purity, and power. To the
Greeks and Romans it was an emblem of silence (*sub rosa,* in
secret, recalls the ancient practice of hanging a rose at
entertainments to signify that nothing said there should
ever be divulged), to alchemists the source of ingredients
for love philtres, and to Moslems a reminder of the tear
that dropped from the Prophet's eye and brought it into
existence. Some mystics contemplate the rose in search of
illumination.

The secret of the rose is so closely guarded that only a

504

few initiates are supposed to understand its deepest meaning. It is the symbol par excellence of closely guarded secrets, for it is one of the rare flowers that remains closed around its heart until it opens its corolla in anticipation of death. Most secret societies (Freemasons, Templars, Rosicrucians) have the rose as one of their most esoteric emblems. Jean de Meung's *Romance of the Rose* explores some of the meanings attached to the rose by medieval occultists.

Rosicrucians

A fraternal organization whose purpose is the investigation and study of cosmic and natural laws. Centuries old, it aims to awaken the faculties and talents of man for greater personal attainment.

It is not a religious or sectarian body, nor has it political ambitions. It does not promulgate concepts that are contrary to accepted public morals and customs. The headquarters are in California, with branches in New York and Pennsylvania. The symbol of the organization is a Rosy Cross. The organization is also concerned with the symbolism of the swastika and the pyramids.

The name of the order derives from that of the founder, Christian Rosenkreutz, who is said to have died in 1484, at the age of 106, after being initiated into the order in the Holy Land, and to have transmitted knowledge to eight initiates. The Danish astrologer Max Heindel claimed to have been visited in Berlin by invisible spirits who instructed him to reestablish the old secret society. He completed construction of a Rosicrucian Temple south of Los Angeles in 1920.

The order has spread throughout the Western world and indulged in alchemy, astrology, and other occult practices. Members of the order believe that the faithful may learn the secrets of life through ritual, study, and spiritual development. See Bernard, Raymond.

Ruby
A gem that protects the wearer against famine, pestilence, and witchcraft.

Ruilly, Macete De
See Brigue, Jehanne de.

Rumi, Jalaluddin
Founder of the 13th-century Sufi Order of Maulawi Dervishes in Persia. He wrote six books honoring the Dervishes, whose complicated dances have cosmic significance.

Runes (Futhark)
The word rune means mystery in its earliest usage in English and related languages. From the outset, runes were associated with magic, divination, and other rites. The runic alphabet later became the storehouse of pagan Germanic rites. The twenty-four runes of the common Germanic *futhark* (alphabet) were used to evoke or ward off the power contained in their names. In Germanic mythology, Woden hung upon the world-ash Yggdrasil for nine nights, tormented by hunger and pain, until finally he glimpsed the runes which he then seized and passed on to men. Runes are credited with the power of resurrecting the dead and are associated with health, fertility, love, etc. Belief in rune-magic survived until the seventeenth century.

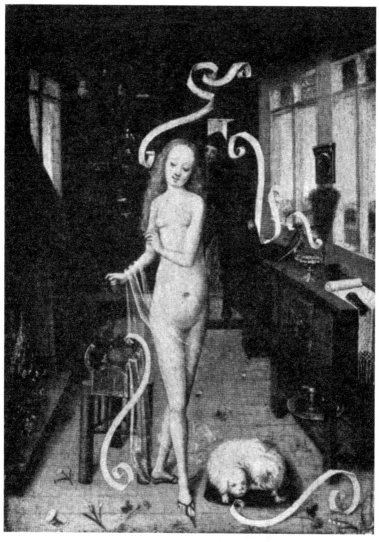

WITCH PREPARING A PHILTRE
Notice the familiar, the Satanic spirit that attends her in animal form, crouching at
her feet.
(By an Unknown Master of the Flemish School, middle 15th century)
Leipsig Museum.

THE SABBATH, OR THE REUNION OF THE SORCERERS
An old sorcerer offers a child to Satan, who is
pictured as a he-goat
From a painting by Goya in the Prado

S

Saba

The wife of Finn and mother of Oisin. In Ossianic legend, she appeared in the form of a fawn and was captured by Finn in the chase. The enchanter who had forced her to assume the shape of a fawn later lured her from Dun Allen by appearing to her in the likeness of her husband, who had gone to fight the Northmen.

Sabbat

A periodic gathering of witches and warlocks wonderworkers and necromancers in dark forests, secluded caves, abandoned ruins, or even in sanctified places such as the Blokula Church in Sweden. Throughout the continent of Europe and in the British Isles, the adepts gathered to celebrate their lascivous devotion to the infernal demons, indulging in frenzied orgies, back-to-back dancing in the dark, demonic conjurations, and obscene sacrifices.

The Latin and French spelling of the word sabbath, may have been used to designate witches' assemblies because of its association with the Jews, who were constantly persecuted by medieval Christians. Some scholars say that the term is derived from the French expression *s'ébattre*, "to frolic."

Special meetings were held on certain evenings each year, but the dates are somewhat uncertain. In some regions the great feasts were held on February 2 (Candlemas), the Eve

507

of May 1 (Walpurgis Night), August 1 (Lammas), and October 1 (Hallowe'en). These days recall the old Celtic divisions of the year, May 1 (Beltane) and November 1 (Samhain), and the two subdivisions, beginning on February 1 and August 1.

The first sabbat on the modern witches' calendar is marked by the winter solstice, called Yule ("wheel"). It is one of four minor sabbats. The others are marked by the spring equinox, the summer solstice, and the autumnal equinox. The four major sabbats correspond to All Saints' Day, Candlemas, May Eve, and August 1.

Justine Glass (*Witchcraft*, 1965) maintains that witches' assemblies are traditionally gay affairs; witches talk and laugh together, celebrate their rites, and enjoy cakes and wine. Esbats differ from the sabbat in that they are less solemn occasions and never take up business. It can be no more than a social gathering, serving to keep the members in touch with each other. It is held during a full moon.

Sabbathi
In Jewish rabbinical legend, the angel assigned to the sphere of Saturn in the celestial hierarchies.

Sabellicus, Georgius
A late 15th-century magician. Though generally looked upon as a charlatan, he styled himself "The most accomplished Georgius Sabellicus, a second Faustus, the spring and center of necromantic art, an astrologer, a magician, consummate in chiromancy, and in agromancy, pyromancy and hydromancy to none that ever lived."

Sacred Mushroom
A hallucinogenic plant, probably *Psilocybe mexicana*, used for pleasure, curing, witchcraft, and the attainment of states

of ecstasy. American Indians have widely employed the sacred mushroom and other hallucogenic plants since before the arrival of the conquistadors. Don Juan, the key figure in Carlos Castaneda's *The Teachings of Don Juan: a Yaqui Way of Knowledge*, related the use of the sacred mushroom to the acquisition of power, which he called an "ally."

Sacred Words

The *Malleus Maleficarum* advocates the use of sacred words to protect a person against harm from witches. The surest protection for places, men, or animals are the words IESUS NAZARENUS REX IUDAEFORUM, written in four places in the form of a cross. To these may also be added the name of the Virgin, the names of the evangelists, or the words of St. John: "The Word was made Flesh."

Safed

A city in Palestine. In the sixteenth century Safed became the center of Cabalism, the Hebraic mystical system.

Saga

According to Michelet, the Saga or Wise Woman was the sole healer of the people of Europe for a thousand years. If her cure failed, she was called a witch. Generally, she was called Bella Donna (Beautiful Lady). She gathered plants to heal and save, yet was often looked upon as the Devil's bride, "the mistress of the Incarnate Evil One." Paracelsus declared when he burned the whole pharmacopoeia of his time, in 1527, at Bayle, that the sorceresses had taught him all he knew.

Sagittarius

In astrology, the Archer. The ninth, southern sign of the zodiac. It represents the corporeal and the spiritual elements constituting man. Esoterically, it represents the organizing power of the mind as well as retribution. Cabalistically, it signifies the thighs of the grand old man of the heavens and represents stability and authority.

St. Albans

A member of a witch coven of St. Albans, naked except for a string of beads, justified her participation in the celebraton of one of the great annual festivals of the British witches, All-Hallows Eve, by saying, "We are not anti-Christian. We just have other means of spiritual satisfaction." She was referring to a celebration that occurred in 1963, involving incantations, nudity, and frenzied dances.

St. Augustine

The Numidian bishop of Hippo (354-430) argued that magic could be performed only with demonic help. He held that demons, after being cast out of heaven, wandered through the air and sought the ruin of men. Whereas they could change their form since they were spiritual beings, men did not have such power. Shape-shifting must therefore be considered an illusion.

Saint-Germain

Eighteenth-century French occultist. The Count of Saint-Germain was attached to the court of Louis XV. He claimed to be two thousand years old, to speak and write many Oriental and Western languages, and to have achieved invisibility. He wrote an occult book entitled *La Très Sainte Trinosophie* (The Most Holy Triple Philosophy). Of disputed origin, he claimed to have known Christ and the apostles. He also claimed extraordinary powers of alchemy, including the ability to transmute metals and make diamonds from pure carbon. He lived in France, England, and Russia before moving to Schleswig, where he engaged in magical practices with the landgrave Karl of Hesse. He died about 1784.

510

St. James

Patron of alchemists and of all cosmological arts and scientists. His pilgrim's staff, criss-crossed by two ribbons and crowned with a round knob, is similar to Hermes' staff. His shrine at Compestela, in Spain, contains a statue showing him with the staff in his hand.

St. John's Dancers

See St. Vitus' Dancers.

St. Medard, Convulsionaries of

See Convulsionaries of St. Médard.

St. Vitus' Dancers

Though the dance craze had appeared in the 13th century, it did not reach pandemic proportions until the following century. The Tarantella dancers began to attract attention about 1350 in Apulia. By 1400 the mania had engulfed northern Italy. The dance craze reached its peak in northwestern Europe about 1430, but outbreaks continued until the 16th century. Typically, half-naked dancers performed their frighteningly grotesque gyrations in groups in some town or village until they fell from exhaustion.

The frenzied dancers called out the names of demons as they moved in a circle, stepping over those who had already fallen. They may have been victims of hysteria, imploring the demons to cease tormenting them, but some authorities charged them with trying to invoke demonic help.

Also called St. John's Dancers in the north, they were for the most part poor, illiterate, unmarried women.

The authorities cured one group of frenzied dancers by bringing them to a chapel of St. Vitus (a fourth-century martyr) at Strasbourg during an outbreak of the mania in 1418.

Salagrama

A stone invested with magical properties. Hindus wear it as an amulet or place it in the hand of a dying man to give him comfort and hope.

Salamanca

Spanish city long associated with sorcery. According to the Rumanian Gypsies, there was near the city a college where the secrets of nature, the language of animals, and the magic arts were taught by the devil in person. Located deep in the mountains, the college accommodated ten students at a time. When they had completed their course, one of them was detained by the professor, assisting him in managing storms and thunderbolts. A deep lake served as the cauldron in which the thunderbolts were fashioned and as the sleeping dragon's lair.

Salamanders

In the medieval theory of elementals, particularly as formulated by Paracelsus, salamanders were associated with fire and were assumd to be composed of the most subtle parts of the sphere of fire (in contrast to sylphs, formed of air particles, and nymphs, formed of water particles). Some demonographers make Romulus the offspring of a salamander and an incubus.

Salem Witches

Much has been written concerning the most famous witchcraft trials in North America. Among the best works are Charles Wentworth Upham's *Salem Witchcraft* (1867), Marion Lena Starkey's *The Devil in Massachusetts* (1949), and Arthur Miller's play *The Crucible* (1953), in which a link is established between the Salem witch hunters and McCarthyism. The affair began when two young girls, influenced perhaps by Indian tales, became hysterical. Collective hysteria spread until it had assumed frightening proportions. More than three hundred persons were arrested. In 1692, thirty-one persons, including six men, were convicted. Three died in prison, nineteen were hanged, and one (Sarah Dustin), though exonerated, died in prison because she was unable to provide for her upkeep.

Saliva
Widely regarded as a life fluid or substance containing the spirit of the person producing it (hence the expression "the spit and image," reconstructed in folk etymology as "spitting image"), the saliva or spit of a person is applied to an effigy, which then may be acted upon to wound or heal the person.

Salt
In magic, salt is used to ward off demons. All devils are supposed to detest salt. As a preservative, it is contrary to their nature.

Sacred to the gods, salt wards off evil by suggesting that a god may appear wherever it is present. Since evil spirits traditionally cluster near a person's left side, one may frighten them away by throwing a pinch of salt over the left shoulder.

Samhain
Associated with one of the four major sabbats celebrated by witches, Samhain (November 1) was the beginning of the Celtic winter half year. It was also the time for observing a feast of the dead, with many harvest rites. On this occasion mortals were believed to be in close touch with the

dead. All Saints' Day now falls on November 1, the day after Halloween.

Samothracian Mysteries

Greek mysteries centered around four shadowy deities, Axieros the mother, her son and daughter, Axiocersos and Axiocersa, and Casindos, their offspring and the originator of the universe.

The festival probably symbolized the creation of the world, also the harvest and its growth. Connected with this was the worship of Cybele, goddess of the earth, of the cities and fields. Her priests, the Corybantes, dwelt in a cave where they had their ceremonies, including a wild and orgiastic weapon-dance. (Lewis Spence.)

Sanguis

Feast of blood, celebrated in honor of the Phrygian goddess of fertility. See Cybele.

Sapphire

A precious stone that protects the health of the wearer.

Sardonyx

A semi-precious stone worn as an amulet or ingested in powdered form. It protects its user against witchcraft and nullifies evil spells.

Sardou, Victorian

French dramatist (1831-1908). A student of occultism and spiritualism, he achieved great facility as a medium for spirit drawings.

Sargatanas

Brigadier of the infernal spirits. He controls Loray, Valafar, and Foraü. He has the power to confer invisibility, to transport people everywhere, to open any lock, and to teach every trick. He commands many demonic brigades.

Sator Formula

The most famous of all magic squares. It has been found inscribed on ancient walls, drinking vessels, etc. It is recommended for finding witches, extinguishing fires, fulfilling wishes, and many other purposes.

The Sator formula (Sator arepo tenet opera rotas) was used throughout the Roman world as early as 200 A. D. At Doura, on the Euphrates, it was painted on a wall in red ink:

R O T A S
O P E R A
T E N E T
A R E P O
S A T O R

It traveled across the western world. The Copts named each of the five nails of the Cross after one of the five verses of the Sator. It was used during the middle ages as a charm, in magical circles, and in esoteric groups. Its literal translation, the object of much misguided speculation, is practically meaningless. Specialists have translated it variously as "The planter is at the plow, the plowing engages the wheels," and "Arepo the sower (planter) carefully guides the wheels."

An esoteric meaning underlies the magical use of the formula. Félix Grosser de Chemnitz discovered its occult meaning. When the 25 letters of the formula are arranged in the form of a cross marked off by the letters A and O (Greek Alpha and Omega), they form the Latin words Pater Noster, the opening words of the prayer known to all Christians and a reminder of the omnipresence of the one who is the "Alpha and Omega" of all things.

515

```
                    A

                    P
                    A
                    T
                    E
                    R
A   P A T E R N O S T E R   O
                    O
                    S
                    T
                    E
                    R

                    O
```

The Christian cross is formed by the word *tenet* in the Sator square:

```
R O T A S
O P E R A
T E N E T
A R E P O
S A T O R
```

It is possible that the Sator formula remained as mute testimony of a persecuted faith long after the fish, mysterious initials, cryptograms, doves, and other symbols had ceased to be closely guarded secrets.

Saturn

Like the waning moon, Saturn is the favorite of practitioners of black magic. It symbolizes age, sadness, and long experience. It takes 29 years and 187 days to complete its cycle. Those born under its influence may expect a long but difficult life. Its color is that of lead: metallic black.

Saturn Square

A magic square used to attract Saturn's influence. It is the oldest magic square known and appears in I Ching. It consists of three rows of three figures because Saturn is the third sephira, or agency through which God manifested himself in the production of the universe:

$$4 \quad 9 \quad 2$$
$$3 \quad 5 \quad 7$$
$$8 \quad 1 \quad 6$$

Saunders, Alex

The leading witch of Great Britain. His biography, *King of the Witches,* was written by June Johns.

Savigliano, Antonio Da

Dominican Inquisitor who conducted a series of witch trials in 1387-88 and brought to light a number of practices associated with Catharism, Waldensianism, and witchcraft. Under torture the first heretics tried at Pinarolo and Turin in Lombardy implicated many people and described a sect of such moral excellence that only its members could be saved. The sect taught a mixture of Catharist and Waldensian doctrines: the Devil rules created all material things and rules this world. A pregnant woman is filled with the Devil and her child can achieve salvation only by joining the sect. Masters distributed consecrated bread (*consolamentum*) to the heretics before their death to prevent their spirit from transmigrating into a lower form of life. One who chose to live on after receiving the bread became a confessor and was called a magister or perfectus.

The heretics were also accused of practicing sorcery. Once or twice a month they held a synagogue, where they renounced their faith and gave their allegiance to Satan. They heard sermons, feasted and consumed loathsome drinks, turned out the lights, and engaged in a sexual revel.

A witch named Bilia admitted that she fed her familiar toad meat, bread, and cheese, then used its feces and human hair to concoct a powder for use in the liquids served at the synagogue.

The members of the sect swore upon a red book, possibly one containing the names of evil angels, that they would never leave the sect nor reveal its secrets. They believed that Satan would eventually overcome God.

Scalinger
A familiar demon who belonged to Jerome Cardan.

Scapular
Two square pieces of cloth linked by strings and worn over the shoulders under the clothing, signifying membership in an order. The scapular was used to pre-Christian times as protection against malevolent forces. Today it is worn by some Catholics to signify religous devotion.

Scarabaeus
The dung beetle, symbolic in Egyptian religion of the male generative principle and of resurrection.

Schemhamproras
Seventy-two divine names discussed in the Cabala.

Schropfer, Johann Georg
German necromancer who initiated many followers into occultism.

Schwagel, Anna Maria
The last person officially executed for witchcraft in Germany. She was put to death on April 11, 1775, after confessing that she had copulated with the Devil.

Science and Magic
A coherent view of the world forms a solid link between science and magic. In *Giordano Bruno and the Hermetic*

Tradition (1964) France Yates argues that the greatest scientists of the Renaissance were magicians. Both Marsilio Ficino and Giordano Bruno accepted the world view of magic since science had not yet formulated its own world view.

Scientology
An eclectic system of thought with occult overtones. A refinement of Dianetics, Scientology stresses the removal of the engrams (emotional and pain-laden blocks) that inhibit the flowering of an individual's potential self through a process called auditing. L. Ron Hubbard, before he founded Scientology, was a science fiction writer.

Scorpio
In astrology, the Scorpion. The eighth, southern sign of the zodiac. It represents the human span of life. Esoterically, the Scorpion signifies death and deceit, the allegorical serpent that tempted Eve. Cabalistically, it represents the pro-creative system of humanity.

Scot, Michael
Scottish magician (c. 1175-1232). Astrologer at the court of the Emperor Frederick II, Scot wrote numerous books on the occult, ranging from necromancy to alchemy, dream-interpretation, divination. He was himself credited with magic potency. Many legends were current about his skills in sorcery. He is mentioned by Dante.

Scott, Sir Walter
Scottish novelist and poet (1771-1832). Shortly before his death he made an important contribution to the study of the supernatural, writing *Demonology and Witchcraft*. Typical of such writing is his discussion of Beltane, following an examination of Celtic rites:

Remains of these superstitions might be traced till past

the middle of the last century, though fast becoming obsolete, or passing into mere popular customs of the country, which the peasantry observe without thinking of their origin. About 1769, when Mr. Pennant made his tour, the ceremony of the Baaltein, Beltane, or First of May, though varying in different districts of the Highlands, was yet in strict observance, and the cake, which was then baked with scrupulous attention to certain rites and forms, was divided into fragments, which were formally dedicated to birds or beasts of prey that they, or rather the being whose agents they were, might spare the flocks and herds.

Scrapfaggot Green (Witch of)
In 1944 an American bulldozer pushed aside a stone that had imprisoned the Witch of Scrapfaggot Green, in Essex County, England, and released a malicious poltergeist. According to press reports, many strange events occurred— bells rang, haystacks were scattered, and huge stones were carried considerable distances.

Seal of Solomon
See Solomon's Seal.

Seance
A meeting of spiritualists held for the purpose of communicating with the dead. At least one member of the group must have mediumistic powers. The seance-room is generally darkened and the actual seance may be preceded by music. Sitters take their places around the table and join hands, forming a chain. Each person puts his thumbs together and allows his little fingers to touch the person on either side of him. The sitters are at the mercy of spirits, who announce their presence by rappings, tilting the table, etc., until the chain is broken.

Second Sight
The power of discerning the invisible or of foreseeing future

events. The term has been largely replaced by the more modern one, precognition.

Secret Book of John
See Apocryphon Iohannis.

Secret Name of God
Speculation concerning the secret name of God soon spread to the sacred texts and oral traditions drawn by the Jews from many sources. These secret traditions, carefully preserved in closed circles, were the basis of the Cabala. Gradually the Cabala embraced Egyptian, Babylonian, Syrian, Gnostic, Greek, and Arabic traditions. In the Middle Ages a mass of documents and texts were added, and these were the foundation of magical science as it existed then and as it still exists in the western world.

Secret Names
In many societies people believe that to discover the name of a person or supernatural being is to gain power over him. Hence the use of hidden or secret names. The hidden name of the Egyptian god Re was known only to Isis. Marduk, the Babylonian god, had fifty secret names.

Secret of Secrets
One tradition holds that the Secret of Secrets is a ritual to be employed to establish contact with the angels to whom God entrusted the government of the world. Solomon is supposed to have transmitted his wisdom and knowledge in a two-part document of which translations still exist. The second part of the document, the *Psalterium Mirabile,* is a collection of the psalms of David with a key to their mystical and magical interpretation. The key explains how they are to be used to secure wealth, power, honor, love, security, and protection against all dangers.

Psalm 137, according to the key, can be used to kindle love

in the heart of a man or woman. The rite has to be performed at dawn on Friday, following the new moon; oil from a white lily has to be poured into a crystal goblet; the psalm is recited and the planetary spirit of Venus (Hamiel, Haniel, or Anael) is invoked, as is the name of the beloved; the name of the planetary spirit is engraved on a piece of cypress, which then is dipped into the oil and rubbed over the eyebrows; finally, the piece of cypress is tied to the right arm. Whenever the person who has carried out the cermony touches another person, love will spring up in the latter's heart.

Solomon is alleged to have used the rites contained in the *Secret of Secrets* to achieve absolute power, only to be destroyed by his gigantic feats, his wealth, and the universal adulation to which he was subjected. His egotism caused him to lose the qualities that accounted for his greatness. Hoards of lovely damsels adorned his court and brought with them alien religions. Jehovah had to share the Mount of Olives with rival gods—Astarte, Venus, Moloch. Solomon's preference may have gone to the cow-headed goddess of Egypt, Hathor, to whom he offered flowers, and animals symbolizing the elements of the earth, air, and water. Moloch required human sacrifices, and infants were thrown into a bronze statue in the image of God as drums and cymbals drowned their cries.

Secret of Secrets (The)
Handbook of magic. *The Secret of Secrets,* also called *True Black Magic,* is a French version of the *Key of Solomon.* It was published in 1750.

Secret Tradition
Lewis Spence gives a lengthy account of the secret tradition. A few excerpts follow.

It has long been an article of faith with students of occultism that the secret tenets of the various sciences embraced within it have been preserved to modern times by a series of adepts, who have handed them down from generation to generation in their entirety. There is no reason to doubt this belief, but that the adepts in question existed in one unbroken line, and that they all professed similar principles is somewhat improbable. But one thing is fairly certain, and that is, that proficiency in any one of the occult sciences requires tuition from a master of that branch. . . . We have satisfactory evidence that the ancient mysteries were receptacles of a great deal of occult wisdom, symbolism, magical or semi-magical rite, and mystical practice in general; and we are pretty well assured that when these fell into desuetude among the more intellectual classes of the various countries in which they obtained, they were taken up and practised in secret by the lesser ranks of society, even the lowest ranks, who are in all ages the most conservative, and who clung faithfully to the ancient systems, refusing to partake in the rites of the religions which had ousted them. The same can be posited of magical practice. The principles of magic are universal, and there can be no reason to doubt that these were handed on throughout the long centuries by hereditary castes of priests, shamans, medicine-men, magicians, sorcerers, and witches. But the same evidence does not exist with regard to the higher magic. . . . We speak . . . of that spiritual magic which, taken in its best sense, shades into mysticism. . . . The undisturbed nature of Egyptian and Babylonian civilisation leads to the belief that these countries brought forth a long series of adepts in the higher magic. We know that Alexandria fell heir to the works of these men, but it is unlikely that their teachings were publicly disseminated in her public schools. Individuals of high magical standing would however be in possession of the occult knowledge of ancient

523

Egypt, and that they imparted this to the Greeks of Alexandria is certain. Later Hellenic and Byzantine magical theory is distinctly Egyptian in character, and we know that its esoteric forms were disseminated in Europe at a comparatively early date. . . . Regarding alchemy, the evidence from analogy is much more sure, and the same may be said as regards astrology. These are sciences in which it is peculiarly necessary to obtain the assistance of an adept if any excellence is to be gained in their practice. . . . In the history of no science is the sequence of its professors so clear as is the case in alchemy, and the same might almost be said as regards astrology, whose protagonists, if they have not been so famous, have at least been equally conscientious. . . . But the individual tradition (in the occult sciences) was kept up by an illustrious line of adepts, who were much more instrumental in keeping alive the flame of mysticism than even such societies as those we have mentioned. Mesmer, Swedenborg, St. Martin, Pasqually, Willermoz, all laboured to that end. . . . The line may be carried back through Lavater, Eckartshausen, and so on to the seventeenth century. These men were mystics besides being practitioners of theurgic magic, and they combined in themselves the knowledge of practically all the occult sciences. . . . The occultists of to-day . . . recognise that their forerunners of the seventeenth and eighteenth centuries drew their inspiration from older origins, and they feel that these may have had cognisance of records and traditions we are not aware of. The recovery of these is perhaps for the moment the great question of modern magic. But apart from this, modern magic of the highest type strains towards mysticism, and partakes more than ever of its character. It disdains and ignores ceremonial, and exalts psychic experience.

524

Seducing a Girl

A 15th-century book, written in a mixture of Yiddish and Hebrew, contains the prescription (written backwards) for seducing a girl.

You must make a waxen image of a female, emphasizing her sex organs. Write across the breast and back: "(name), daughter of (father's name) and daughter of (mother's name)." Then say, "Let it be thy will, O Lord, that (name's as above) burn with a strong passion for me." Bury the image carefully, taking care not to break its limbs. Leave it for 24 hours. Dig it up again and wash it in water three times, once in the name of the Archangel Michael, once in the name of Gabriel, and once in the name of Raphael. Dip it in urine, then dry it. To arouse the girl's passion, pierce the heart of the figure with a brand-new needle.

Senda

An Eskimo goddess who rules over the sea mammals and punishes men for their wrongdoings. The sorcerer must endure many hardships to reach her, stroke her hair, express contrition for his misdeeds, recount the sufferings of his people, and listen to her account of the taboos that have been broken by his people. He then returns to his people and leads them in a mass confession. Senda returns lost souls, heals sickness, and allows animals again to roam across the land.

Sender

In telepathy, the person who initiates a form of communication. Some people seem to be more adept than others in sending messages. Mediums are sometimes referred to as receivers. It seems that urgency, as in the case of impending disaster, facilitates telepathic communication even among people who are not ordinarily considered to be gifted with telepathic powers.

Sepher Yetzirah
Cabalistic text attributed to Adam. Known in English as the Book of Creation, it describes for the first time the magic potency of combinations of Hebrew letters.

The ancient cabalistic treatise discusses the creation of the universe through the symbolism of the ten numbers (sephiroth) and the twenty-two letters of the Hebrew alphabet. Together, the ten numbers and the twenty-two letters are called the thirty-two paths of wisdom. See Sephiroth.

Sephiroth
Ten successive emanations from God, each of them containing less of the divine substance. The cabalists teach that God is the total of all things, the sum of all ideas, and that man is God in miniature. The soul can climb the hierarchy of the sephiroth and man can become God on earth. Occult groups which teach the theory of the soul's descent and ascent through the ten spheres may have ten corresponding grades. In Crowley's system, the student begins as a Neophyte (Sephira 10, or the earth), moves on to become a Zelator (9, the moon), Practicus (8, Mercury), Philosophus (7, Venus), Adeptus Minor (6, the sun), Adeptus Major (5, Mars), Adeptus Exemptus (4, Jupiter), Magister Templi (3, Saturn), Magus (2, sphere of the stars), and Ipsissimus (1, sphere of God). *Sepher Yetzirah* teaches that the "Ten ineffable Sephiroth have ten vast regions bound to them," following the Pythagorean concept of the importance of the numbers from 1 to 10, the basis of all things. A complicated system of correspondences was worked out by Crowley. Traditionally, the ten Sephiroth are arranged to form the Tree of Life, illustrating the underlying pattern of the universe and its essential unity. Number 1, Kether

(Supreme Crown), is the first emanation, the Force of God as Prime Mover or First cause. Then come 2, Hokmah (Wisdom); 3, Binah (Understanding); 4, Hesed (Love); 5, Geburah (Power); 6, Tiphereth (Beauty); 7, Netsah (Endurance); 8, Hod (Majesty); 9, Yesod (Foundation); and 10, Malkuth (Kingdom). When the Tree is shown as a human body, Malkuth is the union of the whole body. It contains the forces of all the Sephiroth. The kingdom of the earth, which is its sphere, is also the kingdom of God. See also Ten Evil Sephiroth.

One basis for designing pentacles is provided by the secret correspondences believed to exist between the ten sephiroth, the divine names, the classes of angels, cosmological elements, and part of the human body.

CORRESPONDENCES

Sephiroth	Meaning	Divine Names
1. Kether	Crown Principle of Principles	"I am" Ehyeh
2. Chochmah	Wisdom Male aspect of Unity	Yah
3. Binah	Passive intelligence, Mother	YHWH Tetragram
4. Gedullah (Hesed)	Grace, Mercy, arm of Life	El
5. Geburah (Pahad)	Justice, hand of death	Eloah

527

6. Tiphereth	Beauty heart	Elohim
7. Nesakh	Triumph	Yhwh Shebaoth
8. Hod	Glory	Elohe Shebaoth
9. Yesod	Generation	El-Khayy
10. Malkuth	Royalty harmony	Adonai

Classes of Angels	Cosmology	Part of the Body
Hayyoth	Heaven of Fire	Head
Ophannim	Prime Mover	Brain
Arelim	Zodiac	Heart
Hashmalim	Saturn	Right Arm
Seraphim	Left Arm	Jupiter
Shinamim	Mars (Sun)	Heart
Tarshishim	Sun (Mars)	Right leg
Son of God	Venus	Left leg
Ishim	Mercury	Genital Organs
Cherubim	Moon	Feet

Éliphas Lévi gives the following explanations of the Ten Sephiroth:

1. KETHER.—The Crown, the equilibrating power.
2. CHOKMAH.—Wisdom equilibrated in its unchangeable order by the initiative of intelligence.
3. BINAH.—Active Intelligence, equilibrated by Wisdom.
4. CHESED.—Mercy, which is Wisdom in its secondary conception, ever benevolent because it is strong.
5. GEBURAH.—Severity, necessitated by Wisdom itself, and by goodwill. To permit evil is to hinder good.
6. TIPHERETH.—Beauty, the luminous conception of equilibrium in forms, intermediary between the Crown and the Kingdom, mediating principle between Creator and creation—a sublime conception of poetry and its sovereign priesthood.
7. NESAKH.—Victory, that is, eternal triumph of intelligence and justice.
8. HOD.—Eternity of the conquests achieved by mind over matter, active over passive, life over death.
9. YESOD.—The Foundation, that is, the basis of all belief and all truth—otherwise, the ABSOLUTE in philosophy.
10. MALKUTH.—The Kingdom, meaning the universe, entire creation, the work and mirror of God, the proof of supreme reason, the formal consequence which compels us to have recourse to virtual premises, the enigma which has God for its answer—that is to say, Supreme and Absolute Reason.

Setna, Papyrus of
See Papyrus of Setna.

Seton Alexander
One of the few alchemists credited by his contemporaries with the transmutation of metals. Early in the seventeenth

century, Seton Alexander, who took for his first name the designation of a fishing village near Edinburgh, traveled widely in Europe and convinced many observers of his rare ability to change lead into gold.

Seven

The number seven is esoterically associated with various phenomena, personalities, concepts. The seven deadly sins are traditional. Medically, seven is linked with the healing rhythm. The Bible contains many references to seven: Balaam's seven altars, seven years served by Jacob, seven kine. The seventh day of the seventh month was, among the Israelites, a time when a seven-day feast began. Physiologically, there are seven internal organs, seven tissue systems, seven compartments of the heart. In mythology and folklore, spells last for seven years. Ancient India had seven gods. Among the Israelites, oaths were confirmed by seven witnesses. The mystery cult of Mithra involved seven gates, seven altars. There are seven penitential psalms, seven sacraments.

The mystical and sacred number is also associated with the seven holy days in the Jewish year, God's resting on the seventh day, the seven-year reign of pagan priests in the Old Religion, and the seven deadly sins.

Lugulannemundu, the great Sumerian king, erected a temple with 7 gates and 7 doors to the goddess Nintu in the city of Adab more than 4,000 years ago. Joshua and his men circled the walls of Jericho for 7 days before destroying it by shouting as they circled it the seventh time on the seventh day. The Book of Revelation is replete with number symbolism in which 7 figures prominently. The mysterious importance of the number 7, unique in that it is indivisible and cannot be multiplied by another number to produce a number between one and ten, may relate to the seven-day cycle of the moon. Ptolemy credited the moon with govern-

530

ing the cycle of life and death on the earth. Occultists hold that the number 7 governs the cycles and rhythms of life. Its characteristics are wisdom and mystery.

Éliphas Lévi maintained that the number seven represented supreme magical power:

> The septenary is the sacred number in all theogonies and in all symbols, because it is composed of the triad and the tetrad. The number seven represents magical power in all its fulness; it is the mind reinforced by all elementary potencies; it is the soul served by Nature; it is the SANCTUM REGNUM mentioned in the Keys of Solomon and represented in the Tarot by a crowned warrior, who bears a triangle on his cuirass and is posed upon a cube, to which two sphinxes are harnessed, straining in opposite directions, while their heads are turned the same way. This warrior is armed with a fiery sword and holds in his left hand a sceptre surmounted by a triangle and a sphere. The cube is the Philosophical Stone; the sphinxes are the two forces of the Great Agent, corresponding to JAKIN and BOAZ, the two Pillars of the Temple; the cuirass is the knowledge of Divine Things, which renders the wise man invulnerable to human assaults; the sceptre is the Magic Wand; the fiery sword is the symbol of victory over the deadly sins, seven in number, like the virtues, the conceptions of both being typified by the ancients under the figures of the seven planets then known. Thus, faith—that aspiration toward the infinite, that noble self-reliance sustained by confidence in all virtues—the faith which in weak natures may degenerate into pride, was represented by the Sun; hope, the enemy of avarice, by the Moon; charity, in opposition to luxury, by Venus, the bright star of morning and evening; strength, superior to wrath, by Mars; prudence, hostile to idleness, by Mercury; temperance, opposed to gluttony, by

531

Saturn, who was given a stone instead of his children to devour; finally, justice, in opposition to envy, by Jupiter, the conqueror of the Titans. Such are the symbols borrowed by astronomy from the Hellenic cultus. In the Kabalah of the Hebrews, the Sun represents the angel of light; the Moon, the angel of aspirations and dreams; Mars, the destroying angel; Venus, the angel of loves; Mercury, the angel of progress; Jupiter, the angel of power; Saturn, the angel of the wilderness. They were named also Michael, Gabriel, Samael, Anael, Raphael, Zachariel, and Orifiel. . . .

The virtue of the septenary is absolute in Magic, for this number is decisive in all things: hence all religions have consecrated it in their rites. The seventh year was a jubilee among the Jews; the seventh day is set apart for rest and prayer; there are seven sacraments, etc. The seven colours of the prism and the seven musical notes correspond also to the seven planets of the ancients, that is, to the seven chords of the human lyre. The spiritual heaven has never changed, and astrology has been more invariable than astronomy. The seven planets are, in fact, the hieroglyphic symbols of the keyboard of our affections. To compose talismans of the Sun, Moon or Saturn, is to attach the will magnetically to signs corresponding to the chief powers of the soul; to consecrate something to Mercury or Venus is to magnetize that object according to a direct intention, whether pleasure, science or profit be the end in view. The analogous metals, animals, plants and perfumes are auxiliaries to this end. The seven magical animals are: (a) Among birds, corresponding to the divine world, the swan, the owl, the vulture, the dove, the stork, the eagle and the pewit; (b) among fish, corresponding to the spiritual or scientific world, the seal, the cat-fish, the pike, the mullet, the chub, the dolphin,

532

the sepia or cuttle-fish; (c) among quadrupeds, corresponding to the natural world, the lion, the cat, the wolf, the he-goat, the monkey, the stag and the mole. The blood, fat, liver and gall of these animals serve in enchantments; their brain combines with the perfumes of the planets, and it is recognized by ancient practice that they possess magnetic virtues corresponding to the seven planetary influences.

Seven Deadly Sins

Peter Binsfield lists the demons credited with the power to provoke people to commit the seven deadly sins:

> Lucifer: Pride
> Mammon: Avarice
> Asmodeus: Lechery
> Satan: Anger
> Beelzebub: Gluttony
> Leviathan: Envy
> Belphegor: Sloth

Seven Stewards of Heaven

Works on magic list seven stewards of heaven by whom God rules the world: Bethor, Phaleg, Och, Hagith, Ophiel, Yadiel, Phul. Magicians use special ceremonies to invoke each of these seven celestial spirits. They are also called the Olympian Spirits since they rule over the Olympian Spheres, embracing 196 regions.

Sex and Sorcery

The fusion and interpenetration of sex and sorcery, documented time and again in the witch trials of Europe, was complete by the early 16th century. Generally the sabbat reached its climax when lights were extinguished and the cult members satisfied their lusts. The sex orgy was described, not infrequently with embellishments, in confession after confession. Sometimes perversions, such as homosexual practices and sex positions other than those accepted as normal, are detailed in the official records. Demons or the Devil himself, after assuming the form of incubi or succubi, attended to the sexual needs of those who attended the Sabbat.

Toward the end of the 15th century ritual copulation with the Devil became a standard part of the orgy. In trials at Artois in France the female members of the cult took pleasure in giving themselves over to demons in the form of various animals. Both men and women had ritual intercourse with Satan, who changed from male to female form in carrying out his function. Various crimes against nature, including sodomy and homosexuality, are listed in trial records.

A more chilling account of sexual orgies appears in the records of trials held at Arras, France. According to these records, the Devil's whole body, including his penis, is cold, and he collects his corrupt yellow sperm from humans. Fear, not pleasure, causes men and women to submit to him.

In the Dionysiac cult, the rites of Tantric Buddhism, and other practices known throughout the world, sexual release is linked with ecstatic religious experiences.

Sextus V
One of several popes linked to sorcery. He was accused of making a compact with the Devil in order to be raised to the chair of St. Peter.

Sexual Magic
See Kundalini, Shakti.

Sexual Union
Sexual union with the Devil is an essential element of witchcraft. According to Vance Randolph's *Ozark Supersti-*

tions, a Devil's representative, a man who is already a member of the cult, has intercourse with a woman initiate for three nights in succession. The rite occurs at midnight, in the dark of the moon, at the family burying-ground of the would-be witch. Women who have been initiated into a cult report that the initiaton "is a much more moving spiritual crisis than that which the Christians call conversion."

Shaddai
One of the Nine Mystic Names used to summon demons.

Shaddai
One of the ten divine names assigned in the rabbinical legend of the angelic hierarchies. It rules the sphere of the moon, causes increase and decrease, and has control over the jinn and protecting spirits.

Shakti
The great magical power residing in every individual, according to the esoteric teachings of Hinduism and Buddhism. Magic powers belong to the adept who can stay the shakti at any of the six chakras or lotuses situated at intervals along the spinal column. The *Yoga Vasishtha,* an ancient Hindu work, contains a classic description of the awakening of the shakti, visualized as a sleeping serpent coiled at the base of the spine:

> Filled with prana, the kundalini darts upward. She then becomes stiff and erect, like a stick or an excited serpent. If the various physical orifices then are closed, the body fills with prana and experiences fundamental changes in its material and physical components.

Shaving
Those suspected of having relations with Satan were shaven. The reasons deduced were mainly these: the suspect might conceal charms in the hair; the hair might conceal devil's

marks; and a demon might be hiding in the suspect's hair, advising her what to say and do.

Sheila-na-gig

Term of doubtful origin, representing the female principle of fertility. Figures symbolizing the Great Mother, they represent a woman squatting in a position that draws attention to her sex organs. Some authorities interpret their presence in the churches of England (a good example are those found in the church of Whittelsford, Cambs) as proof of the co-existence of two rival religions for several centuries, the Old Religion of paganism and the new faith of Christianity.

Shield of Solomon

A hexagram or six-pointed star formed by two equilateral triangles.

Shri Yantra

The lineal representation of the Great Mother conveyed by the Astral Light to the ancient seers of India. They saw her as a pattern of interlaced triangles.

Sibillia

Italian sorceress. Her trial opened at the secular court of Milan on April 30, 1384. She was alleged to have gone out with Oriente every Thursday night as a member of a society. Oriente instructed her followers in divination. They ate every kind of animal except the ass; afterwards Oriente resurrected the slaughtered animals. Condemned to wear two red crosses as a penance, Sibillia was tried again in 1390 as a recidivist. At the second trial the Inquisitors succeeded in identifying Oriente with Diana and Herodias.

Sibylline Books

Manuscripts embodying the secrets of human destiny. The sibylline books were attributed to the sibyls or prophetesses

536

of the ancient world. Tacitus says that they were stored in the Capitol in Rome, then moved to the temple of Apollo Palatinus. What happened later is not clear. The Cumean books existed until 339 A.D., when Stilikon destroyed them. Eight books in Greek and Latin are said to remain from the later sibylline books. They contain predictions couched in mysterious and symbolic terms.

Sickness
Sickness and death frequently are attributed to malevolent spirits or witches. Sorcery is posited as the explanation of such misfortunes as sickness. A significant part of witch-lore is made up of factors that might explain the actions of witches in raising storms, destroying crops or cattle, and causing sickness and death among men. Witches are said, for instance, to be greedy for meat; consequently they will sickness and death on their neighbors in order to share the funeral feast.

Sidereal Body
The spirit or soul, commonly described as radiant and immortal. It is released at death.

Sigil
An image possessing the powers of the stars or supernatural powers. See Signatures.

Signatures
Basic to the practice of magic is the doctrine of signatures or law of correspondences. Magicians believe that external characteristics stand for inner qualities, that outward signs can lead them to discover everything internal and invisible. In an incantation containing a god's name, the Astral Light causes a lineal figure typifying the nature of the god named to appear. Magic seals, sigils, yantras, and mandalas owe their origin to Doctrine of Signatures. Indian mystics saw the lineal figure or signature of the Great Mother as a

pattern of triangles called the Shri Yantra. A god's signature is the lineal representation of him transmitted by the Astral Light. The seer's role is to reveal these symbols to the worshiper who, by concentrating on the tangible representation of the symbol communes with the deity. At the height of his ghostly operations, the magician sees the image of the god he is invoking; harmonizing himself with this god's nature, he loses consciousness of his human identification and identifies himself with god. See Laws of Magic.

The doctrine of signatures is developed in the Zohar:

> As the firmament is marked with stars and other signs meaningful to the wise, the skin that serves as man's outer covering is marked with wrinkles and lines meaningful to the wise; and these skin marks are especially meaningful on the face. . . . Both the lines on the hand and those on the fingers conceal great mysteries.

The law of signatures goes beyond the microcosm and embraces correspondences linking nature in its entirety. Everything that exists, animal, mineral, or vegetable, bears the signature of the microcosm and the macrocosm. An occult law of correspondences governs the creation and the operation of the universe. This law operates on the basis of analogy, whether of form or of effect. Human hair is linked to moss and hair-like plants. The head bears a likeness to nuts. Spagyric medicine used such correspondences in treating diseases, linking the quince and lemon to the heart, mushrooms to the liver, the orchis to the testicles, cassia to the intestines. See Astrological Correspondences.

Signora
In the early sixteenth-century Italian witches were said to be presided over by *la Signora* (the Lady), who wore a golden robe at the Sabbat.

Silcharde

One of the demons who may be summoned by a necromancer. Bread will induce him to appear between three and four o'clock on Thursday morning.

Silence

In European witch trials the ability of the accused to remain silent under torture was interpreted as a sign of guilt.

Silver Belle

A spirit allegedly materialized and photographed at a seance held in the United States.

Silvester II

Pope accused of being a sorcerer (d. 1003). Gerbert, known as Pope Silvester II, is said to have been drawn to the great magical school of Cordova, in Moorish Spain. There he learned Arabic and is said to have first imported Arabic numerals to Europe and to have initiated the use of the clock. He was only one of a number of Popes who, from the tenth century onward, were regarded as sorcerers. He was supposed to have evoked a demon in his bid to obtain the papacy.

He was one of the most learned men of his day, a proficient in mathematics, astronomy, and mechanics. It was he who introduced clocks, and some writers credit him with the invention of arithmetic as we now have it. It is not at all improbable that his scientific pursuits seemed to savor of magic. . . . The brazen head which William of Malmesbury speaks of as belonging to (him), and which answered questions in an oracular manner probably had its origin in a similar misinterpretation of scientific apparatus. . . . By the aid of sorcery he is said to have discovered buried treasure and to have visited a marvelous underground palace, whose riches and splendour vanished at a touch. His very tomb was believed to possess the powers of sorcery, and to shed tears when one of the succeeding popes was about to die. (Lewis Spence.)

Simon Magus

Simon the Magician is mentioned in Acts 8:5-24 and is frequently referred to by early Chrisian writers. A sorcerer who had been converted to Christianity, he was reputed to have had a companion, Helena, who had become enslaved to matter. Having fallen under the power of evil angels, she had occupied, successively, a number of mortal bodies, including that of Helen of Troy. Simon is said to have promulgated an Oriental doctrine in which he was the first Aeon or Emanation, the first manifestation of the primal deity, the Word, the Paraclete, the Almighty.

Sinistrari, Ludovico Maria

Italian demonologist (1622-1701). Professor of theology at Pavia University and author of *De Daemonialitate* (On Demoniality), discovered in 1875. He concentrated on the problems that arise from relations between devils and humans.

Siva

In many Indian homes Siva is worshiped as the male principle—the lingam or phallus. Mahadevi is worshiped as the female principle—the yoni.

Six

A sacred number. The creation was accomplished in six days. Six is the multiple of the first even number and the first odd number. It therefore symbolizes the reconciliation of the two opposing forces of nature.

Sixteen

Because of the number of ways in which it can be expressed (2 2 2 2, 4 4, etc.), sixteen signifies power, strength, unity, and perfection. In incantations 16 steps, figures, parts, etc.

540

constitute a perfect offering which the gods cannot ignore.

Sixth Sense
A latent, undeveloped, extrasensory faculty, also known as the psi faculty or the human capacity for ESP.

Skin Remedy
A Gypsy incantation is supposed to cure diseases of the skin:

Duy yákhá hin mánge	I have two eyes
Duy punrá hin mánge	I have two feet
Dukh ándrál yákhá	Pain from my eyes
Já ándre punrá!	Go into my feet!
Já ándrál pçuv	Go from my feet
Já ándre pçuv!	Go into the earth!
Já ándrál pcuv	Go from the earth
Andro meriben!	Into death!

Skryer
A medium, particularly one who has access to the Cosmic Records. Madame Blavatsky and Rudolph Steiner are among those who have recorded their findings.

Sky-trap
A geographical region bounded by Florida, the Bermudas, Puerto Rico, and Jamaica is called the Sky-trap in America and the Magic Lozenge (or Triangle of Death) in Europe. In this zone ships and their crews are said to disappear without leaving a trace. Aircraft have suffered the same fate. On December 5, 1945, five Avengers, American bombers, departed from their base at Fort Lauderdale, Florida, on a routine flight. About two hours later, as they were returning to the airport, the control tower received a message indicating that the pilots could not see the earth and did not know where they were. Their conversations with each other revealed that they were in a state of confusion or derangement. The planes disappeared. Search planes failed

541

to find any trace of the missing bombers. Beginning in 1948, mysterious disappearances multiplied: in January a passenger plane with 40 passengers, and in December a DC-4; in 1949, a transport plane; in 1959, two supply planes; and in 1963, a supply ship and trawler. No one has yet advanced a rational explanation of these seemingly supernatural occurrences.

Slate Writing

A popular spiritualistic performance in which writing mysteriously appears on a slate. The medium and the sitter occupy opposite ends of a table in a typical seance. Both hold an ordinary slate and pencil pressed against the underside of the table and wait for a message from the spirit-world to be inscribed on it. Spiritualists themselves admit that genuine mediums, owing to the uncertainty of their powers, may at times be forced to resort to fraud.

Smaragdine Table

The Tabula Smaragdina, a work on alchemy published in the sixteenth century and attributed to Hermes Trismegistus, is said to condense the whole of magic on a single page. Certain Masons and Cabalists allege that it was found by Abraham's wife on the body of Hermes. See Emerald Table.

Smith, Christopher Neil

One of perhaps a dozen exorcists now practicing in England. He is the vicar of St. Saviour's in Hampstead, London. He casts out spirits by laying his hands on the victim. He is kept busy the year round, according to the *London Sunday Times*.

Smith, John

Called the "Leicester Boy," in 1607, at the age of five, accused several women of bewitching him. Later, in 1616,

542

he caused nine other victims to be hanged. He was finally exposed by James VI, king of Scotland.

Societies for Psychical Research

The phenomena associated with clairvoyance, premonitions, telepathy and similar practices were known in proto-historical times. But organized research into such occurrences did not begin until the middle of the nineteenth century. In 1882 the Society for Psychical Research was established in England. It has investigated mediumship, precognition, and clairvoyance.

In 1885 an American Society for Psychical Research was founded, but it was dissolved in 1905. A similar society, the American Institute for Scientific Research, was established in 1904. In 1922 the Institute changed its name to the American Society for Psychical Research. Similar societies have been established in other countries, notably in France, where the Institute Métaphysique Internationale was founded in 1920.

Society for the Reparation of Souls

An occult sect founded by Abbé Boullan and Adèle Chevalier in 1859. It was centered around sex-magic. On at least one occasion, ritual murder was practiced.

Society of the Inner Light

Group formed by Dion Fortune, a serious student of the Cabala.

Solar System Bodies, Influence of

In astrology, in external affairs, the solar system bodies exercise influences as follows:

Sun: leaders in authority.
Moon: public life.
Mercury: business.
Venus: social activities.

Mars: weapons of war.

Jupiter: material wealth.

Saturn: poverty, decay.

Uranus: power, authority.

Neptune: popular movements.

Pluto: idealistic organizations.

Solification

Mystical union with the power of the sun. Solification was one of the goals of the Mithraic cult.

Solomon

King Solomon, traditionally known as an arch magician, used a spell to banish the infernal beings sent by the king of demons to extract human hearts:

> Lofaham,
> Solomon,
> Iyouel,
> Iyosenaoui.

Solomon's Mirror

A mirror used in divination. It is made from a shining, well-polished plate of fine steel, slightly concave. The blood of a pigeon is used to inscribe on the plate four names: Jehovah, Eloym, Metatrofn, Adonay.

Place the mirror in a clean and white cloth, and when you behold a new moon during the first hour after sunset, repeat a prayer that the angel Anaël may command and ordain his companions to act as they are instructed; that is, to assist the operator in divining from the mirror. Then cast upon burning coals a suitable perfume, at the same time uttering a prayer. Repeat this thrice, then breathe upon the mirror and evoke the angel Anaël. The sign of the cross is then made upon the mirror for forty-five days in succession—at the end of which period Anaël

544

appears in the form of a beautiful child to accomplish the operator's wishes. . . . The perfume used in evoking him is saffron. (Lewis Spence.)

Solomon's Ring

Solomon is said to have possessed a magic ring enabling him to command the angels and all the forces of nature. See Solomon's Stones.

Solomon's Seal

A six-pointed star formed by two intersecting triangles. It symbolizes the macrocosm. In alchemical tradition the natural order of the elements is represented by a cross or by concentric circles. If a cross is used, its point corresponds to the quintessence (*quinta essentia*, fifth essence). If concentric circles are used, earth is the middle point and fire the outer circle. This natural order may also be represented by the individual parts of the seal. That is, in the two intersecting equilateral triangles, the one pointing upward corresponds to fire, the one pointing downward to water. The triangle pointed upward, cut by the upturned base of the other triangle, forms the symbol for air. The same symbol, when reversed, stands for earth. Thus the complete six-sided seal symbolizes the synthesis of the four elements and the union of all opposites.

Solomon's Stones

According to a Moslem legend, eight angels gave Solomon a precious stone which invested him wth absolute power over them and over the winds when the stone was turned toward the heavens. Four other angels gave him a stone which, when placed on his head, allowed him to command every living creature on the earth or in the water. Another angel brought him a third stone which he could use to level mountains, dry up seas and streams, and make the earth fertile. Finally, a fourth stone gave him control over the spirits that inhabit the region between the earth and heaven. He placed the four stones on a ring and acquired control over the whole world.

Solomon's Throne
Devils are reputed to have hidden magic manuals under Solomon's throne. See Magic Manuals.

Solomon's Triangle
Éliphas Lévi dealt at length with Solomon's Triangle. Here are some of his views:

> The perfect word is the triad, because it supposes an intelligent principle, a speaking principle and a principle spoken. The Absolute, revealed by speech, endows this speech with a sense equivalent to itself, and in the understanding thereof creates its third self. So also the sun manifests by its light and proves or makes this manifestation efficacious by heat.

> The triad is delineated in space by the heavenly zenith, the infinite height, connected with East and West by two straight diverging lines. With this visible triangle reason compares another which is invisible, but is assumed to be equal in dimension; the abyss is its apex and its reversed base is parallel to the horizontal line stretching from East to West. These two triangles, combined in a single figure, which is the six-pointed star, form the sacred symbol of Solomon's Seal, the resplendent Star of the Macrocosm. The notion of the Infinite and the Absolute is expressed by this sign, which is the grand pantacle —that is to say, the most simple and complete abridgement of the science of all things.

> Grammar itself attributes three persons to the verb. The first is that which speaks, the second that which is spoken to, and the third the object. In creating, the Infinite

546

Prince speaks to Himself of Himself. Such is the explanation of the triad and the origin of the dogma of the Trinity. The magical dogma is also one in three and three in one. That which is above is like or equal to that which is below. Thus, two things which resemble one another and the word which signifies their resemblance make three. The triad is the universal dogma. In Magic—principle, realization, adaptation; in alchemy—azoth, incorporation, transmutation; in theology—God, incarnation, redemption; in the human soul—thought, love and action; in the family—father, mother and child. The triad is the end and supreme expression of love; we seek one another as two only to become three.

Somatomancy

A term coined by William A. Lessa to describe the whole range of divination from the human body. It includes phrenology, chiromancy, and astral physiognomy.

Somers, William

Better known as the Nottingham Boy, he brought notoriety to England's only exorcist, John Darrell. In 1597 Darrell was invited to exorcise William Somers. One incident followed another as William Somers feigned possession and accused numbers of innocent people of practicing witchcraft. Somers finally admitted that he had used trickery, that "by working the spittle in his mouth, he foamed till the froth ran down his chin."

Sons of Midnight

Members of an occult society in London. In the last decades of the seventeenth century and on into the eighteenth, they engaged in sinister, demoniac activities.

Soothsaying

This is the practice of foretelling events and the interpretation of dreams, visions, omens and portents by priests who

547

were considered under the immediate influence of the gods. In Babylonia, soothsaying was closely associated with astrology and hepatoscopy. Under the Roman Empire, too, soothsaying was widely influential and frequently affected imperial policies.

Among the ancient Arabs, it was believed that persons with familiar spirits possessed powers of prediction. Among the Hebrews the nabi was a form of soothsaying. The nabi or speaker was the herald or messenger of the deity of the spirit.

Sorcerer
An adept in the occult, bound to Satan for knowledge and skill in magic. Traditionally, he is represented as having a fixed stare. He keeps his occult power only so long as his feet touch the ground.

In 1591 J. G. Godelman defined sorcerers as those who by evil spells, dire curses, etc. harm and destroy the lives and health of men and beasts. See *De Magis*.

Sorcerers, Names of
In Europe a witch or sorcerer was identified variously as *sortiarius* or *sortilegus* (one who reads the *sortes* or lots—a diviner); *strix, striga, stria,* or *strigimaga* (at first a screech-owl, then a vampire, and finally a witch); *lamia* or *lama* (derived from the name of the legendary queen of Libya, who roamed the world seeking revenge for the slaying of her children by jealous Hera); *masca* or *talamasca* (probably derived from a verb meaning "to eat" since witches were thought to feed on children); *maleficus* (a person who works evil magic); *scobax* (derived from the Greek word for screech-owl or the Latin *scoba,* broom); *gazarius* (corrupted form of Catharus, a member of the Catharist sect, influenced by the Hebrew root *gaz,* "to cut," which recalled the ancient custom of cutting open animals and using their entrails to forecast events); *waudensis* (from the heretical

548

Sorcerer Condemned to Death by the Inquisition

SORCERIES.

A. A Witch.
B. A Spirit raised by the Witch.
C. A Friar raising his Imps
D. A Fairy Ring.
E. A Witch rideing on the Devill through the Aire.
F. An Inchanted Castle.

sect called Waldenses); *herbarius* (one who gathers herbs); *factura* (probably derived from the Latin *factus,* "maker" of spells; *pythonissa* (prophetess); *divinator* (one who divines); *mathematicus* (wizard); *necromanticus* (one who uses a corpse to forecast the future); *veneficus* (one who concocts potions); *tempestarius* (one who makes storms); *incantator* (one who enchants); *wicce, wicca* (one who casts spells or forecasts the future, the etymon of the modern form *witch;* and German *Hexe* (night-spirit, derived from Old High German *hagazussa*).

Sorcery
The use of power gained through control of supernatural forces. In a strict sense, sorcery is universal and timeless, whereas witchcraft is limited for the most part to the period between 1450 and 1750 and to the Christian nations.

In 1591 Johann Georg Godelman published an occult treatise entitled *De Magis.* He defines therein sorcerers as those who by evil spells, dire curses, and the sending of foul spirits, by potions prepared by the Devil or through illicit arts from corpses of hanged men, harm and destroy the health and lives of men and beasts.

As used in this book, sorcery embraces the world of the supernatural and methods or practices through which men have tried to gain control over or enlist the help of supernatural forces. The word probably derives ultimately from *sors,* meaning "lot, decision by lot, fate, destiny."

Sorcery and Witchcraft
The idea of pact was the chief means of linking sorcery and witchcraft. Both Aristotelians and scholastics admitted that some magic could be worked naturally, with the help of demons. In return for their services, the demons required a pact. It was Albertus Magnus who drew the distinction between implicit pact and explicit pact. A face to face covenant

with the Devil results in an explicit pact. One who performs an act requiring the services of a demon makes an implicit pact with that demon. William of Auvergne made all magic an offshoot of an implicit pact. Since Aquinas extended the argument to include even astrology, Christianity has labeled all magic demonic.

Sortilege
Divination by lots. It is widely used and is one of the most ancient practices.

Sortilege is today synonymous with magic or sorcery, but the word originally referred to the act of opening the Bible at random for the purpose of divination. The Latin *sortilegium,* from which it derives, meant reading of the lots.

Souberet
French sorcerer who summoned two demons, Avarus and Superbus. He was burned in 1437.

Soulis, William
Fourteenth-century Scottish noble, professed Satanist, and reputed performer of human sacrifices. Known as the Black Lord of Hermitage, he was also credited with having made a pact with the Devil.

Spare, Austin Osman
Artist and member of the Order of the Golden Dawn. He used symbolic pictures to call forth atavistic urges hidden deep in the mind. He claimed that he could prepare himself to carry a heavy load easily by closing his eyes and visualizing a picture conveying an image of the which symbolized the strength of tigers. He died in 1956, in Brixton, England, in poverty and obscurity.

Speaking in Tongues
See Glossolalia.

Spectral Evidence

The Devil who made a pact with a witch could not be subpoenaed to provide evidence against the accused. Evidence of association with the Devil therefore had to be supplied by the accused, by other confessed witches, or by innocent victims of the accused. Torture was used to induce the accused and confessed witches to provide evidence. Innocent victims claimed that they could see the spirit or specter of the accused torturing them. This evidence was accepted by the courts.

Spee, Friedrich Von

Professor of theology at Wurzburg (1591-1635). He was the author of *Cautio Criminalis,* an attempt to put an end to the unjust persecution of those accused of witchcraft.

Spell

A spoken word or formula to which some magical power is ascribed. The uttering of words in a set order, generally one prescribed by tradition, is the essential part of magic in many cultures. In the Trobriand Islands, for instance, the word for spell (megwa) also means magic. Great importance frequently is attached to the exact wording of a spell, but individual changes within the prescribed frame are sometimes permissible.

Spence, Lewis

English writer and popularizer of occult and metaphysical subjects. His major work, *An Encyclopaedia of Occultism,* subtitled "a compendium of information on the occult sciences, occult personalities, psychic science, magic, demonology, spiritism, mysticism, and metaphysics," was published in 1920 and reissued in 1959.

Spina, Alfonso De

Fifteenth-century Spanish theologian. He used Jewish sources to prove "according to the doctrine of the Talmud"

551

that the Jews are the children of the Devil. He was the author of the first book on witchcraft to be printed in Strasbourg. His *Fortalicium Fidei* ("Fortress of Faith"), written in 1460, identifies ten kinds of demons.

Spina, Bartolommeo
Theologian and author of *Quaestio de Strigibus* (On Witches), published in 1523. He advocated spectral evidence and expressed his belief in transvection, sexual intercourse with demons, and metamorphosis.

Spirit Photography
There have been many attempts to capture on film manifestations of ectoplasm or spiritual entities durng seances. Opportunities for fraud abound, and psychical researchers hesitate to accept as valid photographs offered as proof of the presence of spirits of the dead at seances. In some instances photographs of living people are said to reveal the unsuspected presence of spirits in the same surroundings.

A phenomenon of a most extraordinary kind has shown itself in America. Mr. Mumler, a photographer of Boston and a medium, was astonished, on taking a photograph of himself, to find also by his side the figure of a young girl, which he immediately recognised as that of a deceased relative. The circumstance made a great excitement. Numbers of persons rushed to his rooms, and many have found deceased friends photographed with themselves. The matter has been tested in all possible ways, but without detection of any imposture. An account of the particulars will be found in the 'Spiritual Magazine' of December 1862, and of January of the present year (1863). (William Howitt.)

Spiritism
The French form of spiritualism, particularly as developed from the doctrines of Allan Kardec. One of its main tenets is the doctrine of reincarnation.

Spiritualism

The belief that spirits of the dead communicate with the living by means of physical phenomena, such as by rapping, in trance states, usually with the help of a medium. Most existing knowledge supporting the view that life continues in spirit form after death comes from mediums. Usually during a seance a medium or sensitive claims to be able to receive messages from spirits seeking to communicate with the world of the living. Although spiritualism has existed in diverse forms throughout time, present-day spiritualism derives mainly from 19th-century practices.

Spiritualism had enlisted in its cause some of the best European minds long before it made its appearance in America, where it originated as an ordinary visitation of the type familiar to Germans as that of a Poltergeist and, spreading with almost lightning rapidity, assumed new and startling forms. Soon spiritualism was accepted by more than three million people of all classes, professions, and persuasions.

The spot in which the eventful origin of the American movement took place is thus described by Mr. Dale Owen, who had visited it:

'There stands, not far from the town of Neward . . . a wooden dwelling . . . a village . . . known under the name of Hydesville; being so called after Dr. Hyde, an old settler, whose son is the proprietor of the house in question. . . .'

Such was the humble abode where the great American spiritual movement commenced. A Mr. Michael Weekman, it appears, had occupied the house about the year 1847, and had been troubled by certain knockings, for which he could find no explanation. On the 11th of December of that year, Mr. John D. Fox, of Rochester, a respectable farmer, moved into this house. . . . His family

553

consisted of himself, his wife, and six children; but only the two youngest were staying with them at the time—Margaret, twelve years old, and Kate, nine years. It appears that the family of Mrs. Fox had long previously evinced medium power. She was of French descent, and her husband of German, the original name being Anglicised from Voss to Fox. Mrs. Fox's grandmother had been possessed of second-sight, and saw frequently funerals, whilst living in Long Island, before they really took place. Her sister, Mrs. Elizabeth Higgins, had similar power. . . . Thus open to spiritual impressions the Foxes entered the house at Hydesville, and from the very commencement they were disturbed by noises, but at first attributed them to rats and mice. In the month of January 1848, however, the noises assumed the character of distinct knockings at night in the bedrooms, sounding sometimes as from the cellar below, and resembling the hammerings of a shoemaker. These knocks produced a tremulous motion, since familiar enough to spiritualists. In the furniture, and even in the floor. The noises increased nightly, and occasionally they heard footsteps in the rooms. The children felt something heavy, as of a dog, lie on their feet when in bed, and Kate felt, as it were, a cold hand passed over her face. Sometimes the bedclothes were pulled off. Throughout February, and to the middle of March, the disturbances increased. Chairs and the dining-table were moved from their places. Mr. and Mrs. Fox, night after night, lit a candle and explored the whole house in vain. Raps were made on doors as they stood close to them, but on suddenly opening them no one was visible. . . .

The child (Kate) had evidently heard it suggested that it was the devil who made the noises, and if so, he was an obliging devil, for he immediately responded to the challenge. This at once attracted attention. Kate Fox made

554

the mere motion with the thumb and finger, and the raps regularly followed the pantomime, just as much as when she made the sound. She found that, whatever the thing was, it could *see* as well as hear. 'Only look, mother!' she said, bringing together her thumb and finger as before. The rap followed.

'This at once,' says Mr. Owen, 'arrested the mother's attion.' "Count ten," she said, addressing the noise. Ten strokes were distinctly given. "How old is my daughter Margaret?" Twelve strokes! "And Kate?" Nine! "And what can all this mean?" was Mrs. Fox's thought. . . . "How many children have I?" she asked aloud. Seven strokes. "Ah!" she thought, "it can blunder sometimes." And then aloud, "Try again!" Still the number of raps was seven. Of a sudden, a thought crossed Mrs. Fox's mind. "Are they all alive?" she asked. No answer. "How many are living?" Six strokes. "How many are dead?" A single stroke; she had lost one child.

'She then asked if it was a man? No answer. Was it a spirit? It rapped. She next asked if the neighbours might hear it, and a Mrs. Redfield was called in, who only laughed at the idea of a ghost; but was soon made serious by its correcting her, too, about the number of her children, insisting on her having one more than she herself counted. She, too, had lost one; and when she recollected this, she burst into tears. The spirits always reckon all the children, whether so-called dead or alive, as still living. They admit no such thing as death.' (William Howitt.)

Spiritualism is devoted to the study of psychic phenomena. The belief is that such phenomena can be explained in terms of incarnate or discarnate spirits who are interested in the living. The inception of spiritualism in modern times is assigned to the year 1848, when the Fox sisters gave fantastic exhibitions of their power to evoke spirits of the dead. In 1893 the cult was organized as the N.S.A., with headquarters in Washington.

The spiritualist seminary at Morris Pratt Institute in Whitewater, Wisconsin, is the first of its kind. A famous spiritualist camp is Lily Dale, in New York State. Harry Houdini, the magician and contortionist, devoted considerable time to an investigation of the claims of spiritualism. He conducted a rousing, publicized campaign. He repeatedly exposed fraudulent practices of mediums and publicly denounced them. His conclusions led him to reject totally and categorically all such claims of communication with the spirits.

On the other hand, Sir Oliver Lodge, the English physicist who died in 1940, pursued psychical research that induced him to a belief in communication between the living and the dead. In *Raymond, or Life and Death,* he published an account of his experiments in which he described his communication with his dead son Raymond.

Sir Arthur Conan Doyle, too, who died in 1930, was in his later years deeply interested in spiritualism. He lectured and wrote passionately and sincerely on the subject. More recently Bishop Pike has published an account of his communication with his dead son.

Spiritualistic Circles
Groups of persons who meet periodically for the purpose of holding seances for spirit communication. At least one member of a circle must be a medium. Spiritualistic circles generally consist of 12 persons.

Star of Bethlehem
This star is commonly conjectured to have been the conjunction of Saturn, Jupiter, and Mars, which occurred about 2 B.C. It is assumed that the astrologers, the "wise men of

the East," were trying to locate a child born at the point in terrestrial latitude and longitude from which this triple conjunction would occur in the same celestial geographical location. As this was one of the grand mutations, it was presumed that a child born at the exact place and hour that would posit this important satellitium at the cusp of the Tenth House would be marked by Destiny to become the initiator of a new epoch in the history of the world.

Sulphur
A yellow powder which, when mixed with molasses, water, or wine, protects the consumer against evil forces.

Sprenger, Jakob
Fifteenth-century Dominican. With Heinrich Kramer he wrote *Malleus Maleficarum* (The Witches' Hammer), a guide for discovering and punishing witches.

Spunkie
A Scottish goblin, popularly believed to be the agent of Satan. He preys on travelers who have lost their way.

Squassation
Torture designed to make those accused of witchcraft name their accomplices. Philip Limborch's *History of the Inquisition* (1692) gives a detailed description:

> The prisoner hath his hands bound behind his back, and weights tied to his feet, and then he is drawn up high on high, till his head reaches the very pulley. He is kept hanging in this manner for some time . . . , and on a sudden he is let down with a jerk, by slacking the rope, but kept from coming quite to the ground, by which terrible shake his arms and legs are all disjointed, whereby he is put to the most exquisite pain.

Stake
With the exception of England and New England, witches

were burned at the stake: alive in Italy and Spain, often after strangulation in France, Scotland, and Germany. Jean Bodin recommended the use of green wood to prolong the suffering of recalcitrant witches.

Staus Poltergeist

In 1860-62, on the shores of Lake Lucerne, in the village of Staus, an outbreak of poltergeist haunting occurred in the home of M. Joller, a lawyer and member of the Swiss national council. Finally the poltergeist began to persecute M. Joller, chasing him from room to room. Things were thrown about by invisble hands, and strange noises were heard. People flocked by the hundreds to witness the phenomena. The turmoil ceased only when the Joller family, which had been subjected to much ridicule, departed from their ancestral home.

Stevenote De Audebert

French witch. At her trial in 1616 she produced a pact she had made with Satan.

Stigmati Diaboli

Devil's marks. Cotton Mather believed that witches were branded by the Devil:

> I add, why should not witch marks be searched for? The properties, the qualities of those marks are described by divers weighty writers.

The Devil's mark or seal (*sigillum diaboli*) was frequently confused with the witch's mark, and these terms came to be used interchangeably by many people. See Devil's Marks, Witch's Marks.

Stoicheomancy

Divination by opening the works of Homer or Vergil and reading the first verse seen.

Stolen Children

In the Middle Ages fairies were thought to steal children and substitute for them little monsters to which they had given birth. These children were given over to the Devil or sacrificed at the sabbat.

Stolisomancy

Divination by observing a person's attire. Augustus believed that because his valet had buckled his right sandal to his left foot, a military revolt was indicated.

Stonehenge

Eric Neuman, a disciple of C. G. Jung, in his book *The Great Mother: an Exploration of the Archetype,* sees the trilithon (two huge stones standing upright and having a third stone as their lintel) as a symbol of the Great Mother or womb giving birth each year to the dead sun-god.

Erich von Daniken sees Stonehenge as evidence of the presence on this earth of astronauts who remained among the terrestrial inhabitants long enough to instruct them in the arts and sciences.

Storm-raising

A power attributed to witches. As early as the eighth century, the Archbishop of Canterbury admitted that sorcerers had the power to cause storms. In 1489 Ulrich Molitor reported that witches were commonly thought to have the power to provoke lightning and hail.

Strangulation

Method of killing witches before burning them, provided they did not retract their confessions. Strangulation was accomplished by garroting or hanging.

Strappado

A form of torture commonly used to make witches name their accomplices. It was less severe than squassation. In both forms of torture the victim was bound and hoisted in the air. In squassation he was suddenly dropped to within a few inches of the floor. The German word for strappado is *Zug*. In Italian the expression *tratti di corde* is also used.

Strix
Medieval designation of a sorceress. The word is associated etymologically with "screech-owl." Its plural form is striges. The strix was believed to suck the blood of children.

Succubus
An evil spirit thought to assume the shape of a female for the purpose of having intercourse with a man. See Incubus.

Summis Desiderantes
A papal bull, promulgated by Innocent VIII on December 5, 1484, containing the theory of magic and demonology. It ordered Kramer and Sprenger, two inquisitors of the Order of the Preaching Friars, to proceed with firmness in the suppression of heresy.

Summoning Spirits
Agrippa von Nettesheim, in *Occult Philosophy (De occulta philosophia)*, gives instructions for summoning spirits.

If you would call any evil Spirit to the Circle it first behooveth us to consider and to know his nature, to which of the planets he agreeth, and what offices are distributed to him from the planet.

This being known, let there be sought out a place fit and proper for his invocation, according to the nature of the planet, and the quality of the offices of the same Spirit, as near as the same may be done.

For example, if his power be over the sea, rivers or floods, then let a place be chosen on the shore, and so of the rest.

In like manner, let there be chosen a convenient time,

both for the quality of the air—which should be serene, quiet and fitting for the Spirits to assume bodies—and for the quality and nature of the planet, and so, too, of the Spirit: to wit, on his day, noting time wherein he ruleth, whether it be fortunate or unfortunate, day or night, as the stars and the Spirits do require.

These things being considered, let there be a circle framed at the place elected, as well for the defence of the invocant as for the confirmation of the Spirit.

In the Circle itself there are to be written the general Divine names, and those things which do yield defence unto us; the Divine names which do rule the said planet, with the offices of the Spirit himself; and the names, finally of the Spirits which bear rule and are able to bind and constrain the Spirit which we intend to call.

Sun

The influence of the sun varies with its position in the Zodiac. Bright Apollo represents youth with its generosity, noble ambition, pride, boldness, and inexperience in practical things; it also represents art with its divine intuition and its horror of vulgarity. The color corresponding to the sun is gold (yellow).

Superstitions

Modern occultists hold that there is a grain of truth at the heart of most superstitions. As Eliphas Levi explained it, "Superstitions are instinctive, and all that is instinctive is founded on the very nature of things; skeptics of all times paid too little heed to this fact."

Swastika

A symbol in the form of a cross with the ends of the arms bent at right angles. Also called a fylfot, it is found in remains from the Bronze Age, in many modified forms, throughout Europe and Asia. Derived from a Sanskrit word meaning welfare, it was used as a religious symbol by both Jains and Buddhists. Brahman priests call it the pramantha, or lighting stick, recalling the primitive method of producing fire by turning a stick in a small hollow formed at the intersection of two pieces of wood. The swastika was also used in China and Japan, and by Indian tribes in North, Central, and South America. It was used in the sun worship of the Kickapoos and Pottawatomies. As a talisman it brings good luck to its bearer. It is also called a gammadion.

SWASTIKAS

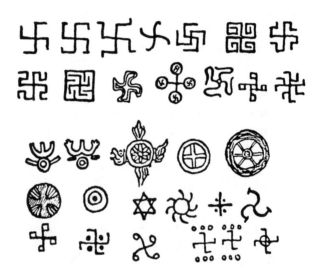

Different forms of the Swastika

Surin, Father Jean-Joseph
Seventeenth-century exorcist. The learned Jesuit was called to exorcise the famous Ursulines of Loudun. He succeeded in his mission but was possessed by demons who dominated his life for twenty years.

562

Swedenborg, Emanuel

One of the greatest mystics of all time (1688-1772). He probably influenced Theosophy more than any other mystic or seer. As an astronomer, mathematician, physiologist, naturalist, and philosopher, he commanded the esteem of his contemporaries.

It was in 1734 that he published his *Prodomus Philosophiae Ratiocinantrio de Infinite* which treats of the relation of the finite to the infinite and of the soul to the body. . . .

About the age of fifty-five a profound change overtook the character of *Swedenborg*. Up to this time he had been a scientist, legislator, and man of affairs; but now his enquiries into the region of spiritual things were to divorce him entirely from practical matters. His introduction into the spiritual world, his illumination, was commenced by dreams and extraordinary visions. He heard wonderful conversations and felt impelled to found a new church. He says that the eyes of his spirit were so opened that he could see heavens and hells, and converse with angels and spirits. . . . He claimed that God revealed Himself to him and told him that He had chosen him to unveil the spiritual sense of the whole scriptures to man. . . .

His *Divine Love and Wisdom* is the volume which most succinctly presents his entire religious systems. God he regards as the Divine Man. Spiritually He consists of infinite love, and corporeally of infinite wisdom. From the divine love all things draw nourishment. The sun, as we know it, is merely a microcosm of a spiritual sun which emanates from the Creator. This spiritual sun is the source of love and knowledge, and the natural sun is the source of nature; but whereas the first is alive, the second is inanimate. There is no connection between the two worlds of nature and spirit unless in similarity of construction. Love, wisdom, use; or end, cause and effect, are the three infinite and uncreated degrees of being in God and man respectively. The causes of all things exist in the spiritual sphere and their effects in the natural sphere, and the end of all creation is that man may become the image of his Creator, and of the cosmos as a whole. This is to be effected by a love of the degrees above enumerated. Man possesses two vessels or receptacles for the containment of God—the will for divine love, and the Understanding for divine Wisdom. Before the Fall, the flow of these virtues into the human spirit was perfect, but through the intervention of the forces of evil, and the sins of man himself, it was much interrupted. Seeking to restore the connection between Himself and man, God came into the world as Man; for if He had ventured on earth in His unveiled splendour, he would have destroyed the hells through which he must proceed to redeem man, and this He did not wish to do, merely to conquer them. The unity of God is an essential Swedenborgian theology, and he thoroughly believes that God did not return to His own place without leaving behind Him a visible representative of Himself in the word of scripture, which is an eternal incarnation, in a threefold sense—natural, spiritual and celestial. Of this *Swedenborg* is the apostle; nothing was hidden from him; he was aware of the appearance and conditions of other worlds, good and evil, heaven and hell, and of the planets. "The life of religion," he says, "is to accomplish good." "The kingdom of heaven is a kingdom of uses." One of the central ideas of his system is known as the Doctrine of Correspondences. Everything visible has belonging to it an appropriate spiritual reality. Regarding this Vaughan says: "The history of man is an acted parable; the universe, a temple covered with hieroglyphics. Behmen, from the light which flashes on certain exalted moments, imagines that he receives the key to these hidden significances—that he can interpret the Signatura Rerum. . . . According to Swedenborg, all the mythology and the symbolisms of ancient times were so many refracted or fragmentary correspondences—relics of that better day when every outward object suggested to man's mind its appropriate divine truth. Such desultory and uncertain links between the seen and the unseen are so many imperfect attempts toward the harmony of the two worlds which he believed himself commissioned to reveal. The happy thoughts of the artist, the imaginative analogies of the poet, are exchanged with Swedenborg for an elaborate system. All the terms and objects in the natural and spiritual worlds are catalogued in pairs. . . ."

In his work Heaven and Hell, Swedenborg speaks of influence and reciprocities—Correspondences. . . . By correspondence man communicates with heaven, and he can thus communicate with the angels if he possess the science of correspondence by means of thought. In order that communication may exist between heaven and man, the word is composed of nothing but correspondences, for everything in the world is correspondent, the whole and the parts; therefore he can learn secrets, of which he perceives nothing in the literal sense; for in the word, ther is, besides the literal meaning, a spiritual meaning —one of the world, the other of heaven. (Lewis Spence.)

Swimming
Trial by water *(iudicium aquae)*, an ancient means of de-

termining innocence or guilt, was incorporated in witch-craft trials. The witch's thumb was tied to her toe. If she floated and failed to sink, she was deemed guilty.

Sword
Separation by the sword is a recurrent theme in alchemical literature. The sword is used to divide the philosophical egg, to separate the elements, and to restore the primitive state of chaos in order to produce a perfect body. It is pre-figured in the flaming sword of the angel guarding paradise.

Symbolism
"It is in and through symbols," says Carlyle, "that man, consciously or unconsciously lives, works, and has his being." His words apply pertinently to magic in all its forms. Under the influence of Freud, Jung, and their successors, the study of symbols and myths has revealed striking similarities between their content and the unconscious.

Alexander Marshack, a researcher at Harvard's Museum of Archaeology and Ethnology, identified a bone recently un-earthed in France as a key find. He surmised that the bone dated from the period of the Acheulian hunters (as long as 150,000 years ago). The bone, part of an ox rib found at Pech de l'Aze, France, had symbols engraved on it and provided "the first clue" to the origins of later symbolism. Marschack said that the symbols were probably intended for use "in a ritual or ceremonial act."

Sympathetic Magic
The ancient view of the underlying unity of all things, summed up in the expression "as below, so above," is at the heart of sympathetic magic. Sympathetic magic is based on the principle that like affects like, that a desired result may be acheved by mimicry, imitation, incantation, etc.

System of Correspondences
Necromancers use a system of correspondences to control

566

the occult forces of the universe. Planets, metals and colors are linked in this manner: Sun, gold, yellow; Moon, silver, white; Mercury, quicksilver, grey or neutral; Venus, copper, green; Mars, iron, red; Jupiter, tin, blue; Saturn, lead, black.

T

Table Lifting

A familiar form of levitation. Frequently at seances tables or other objects appear to rise from the floor, tilt, and move about.

Attributed to the agency of spirits by practitioners, the phenomenon has been explained rationally by Faraday and others as the result of unconscious motor action.

Tages

Etruscan seers reputed to have the power to read the future from the entrails of animals.

Taigheirm

A magical sacrifice of black cats to the devils of the underworld, formerly practiced in Scotland. In the seventeenth century two exorcists, Allan and Lachlain Mclean, were supposed to have held a Taigheirm in Mull and to have received the gift of second sight.

Talisman

The talisman is a magical rite in symbolic form. It exerts its power over things directly, by virtue of its intrinsic qualities. Whereas other rites have acquired a religious significance through the workings of external forces (gods, spirits, etc.), it has remained at the primitive stage. Signs used for transcribing language, always invested with magical properties, first took the form of morphograms. That is, they were visual representations of sounds associated with concrete objects. Sometimes these representations were based on the configuration of objects, sometimes on one or more phases of their actions: a human figure represented a man; four sheep, a herd; two weapons, strength. The primitive signs constituted a universal graphic language. Furthermore, they preserved the magical properties of the spoken word, even after a sacred rite had ended.

Talismans, Hindu
See Hindu Talismans.

Talismans, Planetary
See Planetary Talismans.

Tana
Probably the Etruscan form of Diana. See Aradia.

Tandritanitani
An African curse so powerful as to make the victim accept the advent of death, retire to his hut, and waste away. The victim's only hope is to find a sorcerer capable of concocting an effective countercharm.

Tanit, Sign of
Symbol used for more than a thousand years to express the hopes and beliefs of the Punic civilization. Its primitive form was that of a trapezium closed by a horizontal line at the top extending beyond its adjacent sides like the extended arms of a human body and surmounted in the middle by a head-like circle. It appears as a good-luck symbol in many buildings and on stelae.

Tarantella Dancers
See St. Vitus' Dancers.

Tarot

The oldest surviving card game. The curious pack of cards that make up the Tarot are still used in a game called tarocchini in Italy and tarot in France. The pack is used in fortune-telling and is believed by many occultists to have originated in Egypt, as a storehouse of ancient lore. An alternate hypothesis attributes its invention to a committee of learned Cabalists who met in Fez in the year 1200. The modern Tarot pack contains four suits of fourteen cards each and twenty-two trumps. The suits are Swords (Spades), Cups (Hearts), Coins or Pentacles (Diamonds), and Wands or Staffs (Clubs). The cards in each suit are the King, Queen, Knight, Page (Knave or Jack), Ten, Nine, Eight, Seven, Six, Five, Four, Three, Two, and Ace. The trumps are usually placed in this order, beginning with zero and continuing through twenty-one: Fool, Juggler, Female Pope, Empress, Emperor, Pope, Lovers, Chariot, Strength, Hermit, Wheel of Fortune, Justice, Hanged Man, Death, Temperance, Devil, Falling Tower, Stars, Moon, Sun, Day of Judgment, World. The cards are rich in symbolism and lend themselves to a variety of interpretations, particularly when studied as elements in a system of correspondences based on the *Sepher Yetzirah.*

When used in divination, the cards are shuffled, divided into 10 packs, and distributed according to the pattern formed by the cabalistic Tree of Life, forming the Tree of Cards. A modern work on the Tarot is Basil Ivan Rakoczi's *The Painted Caravan* (1954).

Tasseography

This term denotes the reading of leaves, their shape and position, in a teacup, with a view to predicting the subject's future and coming events.

Taurus

In astrology, the Bull. The second, northern sign of the zodiac. Taurus is equated with the procreative function. In occultism its genius is symbolized as Aphrodite. Cabalistically, the sign represents the ears, neck, and throat of the grand old man of the skies. Thus Taurus is the silent, patient principle of humanity.

Tchovekhano

Among the Turkish Gypsies, a term denoting a ghost or spirit.

Tears

In European witch trials the inability of the accused to shed tears even when subjected to torture was taken as a most certain sign of guilt, according to the most famous of all books about witchcraft, the Malleus Maleficarum.

> It has been found that even if the witch is urged and exhorted by solemn conjurations to shed tears, she will be unable to weep. She may, however, assume a tearful aspect and smear her cheeks and eyes with spittle to make it appear that she is weeping.

Teats

Ivory figurines exhibiting multiple breasts and dating from paleolithic times have been found throughout the ancient world and are thought to offer proof of the prevalence of a Great Mother cult which survived in some regions as the witch cult. Witch-hunters considered the presence of extra teats on the bodies of women to be proof of their guilt. These extra teats were simply abnormal growths or tumors, but they were enough to condemn many victims to the stake. Witches were thought to feed their animal familiars from these extra teats.

Telekinesis

The ability to use the power of the mind to cause objects to move.

Telepathy

The ability of one mind to communicate directly with another, without the aid of visual signs or articulated speech another, without involvement of the channels of sense. Referred to also as a psi ability, it may permit a person to receive and transmit ideas, images, sounds, and words. Thought transference accurately describes the phenomenon, but the expression "mental telepathy" is redundant.

Templars

The Knights Templars or Knights of the Temple, a military and religious order first established at Jerusalem about 1118 to protect the Holy Sepulcher, became involved in one of the longest and most complex witch trials in history. Originally quartered in a palace next to the building known as Solomon's Temple, the members of the order were bound by vows of chastity and poverty. After the Saracens conquered Palestine, however, the Templars spread over Europe and acquired considerable wealth and power, largely through donations, as well as a number of political enemies. Accusations of heresy began in 1305 and resulted in the final suppression of the order by the Council of Vienne in 1312.

Many different trials were held and the allegations made against them were multiple. The initial order for their prosecution charged that they did not consider sodomy a sin, that initiates had to kiss the buttocks, navel, and mouth of the prior and caress him obscenely, and that to be admitted to the order postulants had to deny God and renounce Christ as a false prophet. The formal renunciation of Christianity included spitting upon the cross three times,

573

trampling it underfoot, and urinating upon it. They were accused of kissing and adoring an idol shaped like a golden calf or in the form of a bearded human head, of wearing around their necks an amulet previously placed around the idol's neck, and of invoking demons. Their priests were accused of failing to consecrate the host at mass. Baphomet, their great idol, was kept at Montpelier. Lesser representations of the idol were kept in every chapter house.

The Devil and his demons appeared to the Templars variously as succubi or as a huge black cat. They had intercourse with the succubi and bestowed on the cat the *osculum infame*. From the ashes of dead Templars or their own illegitimate offspring they concocted potions to work magic.

That the charges against them were exaggerated seems certain. While some Templars may have been guilty of practicing some form of sodomy, heresy, paganism, or sorcery, the persecution of the order and confiscation of its wealth issued mainly from political ambitions.

Ten Emanations
In Cabalistic mysticism, God manifests himself in ten emanations or Sephiroth. His divine attributes are: Wisdom, Reason, Knowledge, Greatness, Strength, Beauty, Eternity, Majesty, Principle, Sovereignty.

Teonanacatl
The sacred mushroom of the Indians of the Southwest and Mexico. Generally used in religious rituals presided over by curanderos, they produce visions and states of exhilaration or ecstasy. The usual dosage is 15, and the active hallucinogenic agent has been identified as psilocybin.

Tephramancy
Divination from the ashes left by the victims of a sacrifice.

574

Teraphim

Oracular objects. Jacob's teraphim were taken from him by his daughter Rachel. The allusion to this episode in the Bible is the earliest recorded indication of their existence.

Terragon

Henry III was charged with having a familiar spirit named Terragon. D'Aubigné, the great Protestant poet, accused the French king of conducting black masses at the Louvre.

Tetractys

Ten as the sum of 1, 2, 3, and 4. In Pythagoreanism, it is the basis of the numerical pattern underlying the universe, represented as dots forming a triangle:

```
        .

     .     .

  .     .     .

.     .     .     .
```

The Pythagoreans held the Tetractys in great awe, considering the first four numbers to be the source of all numerical combinations, or "eternal Nature's fountain-spring."

Tetragram

In his extensive account of the Tetragram, Éliphas Lévi made these observations:

> Affirmation, negation, discussion, solution: such are the four philosophical operations of the human mind. Discussion conciliates negation with affirmation by rendering them necessary to each other. In the same way, the philosophical triad, emanating from the antagonism of the duad, is completed by the tetrad, the four-square basis of all truth. . . .

> The Kabalistic Tetragram, JODHEVA, expresses God in humanity and humanity in God. The four astronomical

cardinal points are, relatively to us, the yea and the nay of light—East and West—and the yea and the nay of warmth—South and North. As we have said already, according to the sole dogma of the Kabalah, that which is in visible Nature reveals that which is in the domain of invisible Nature, or secondary causes are in strict proportion and analogous to the manifestations of the First Cause. So is this First Cause revealed invariably by the Cross—that unity made up of two, divided one by the other in order to produce four; that key to the mysteries of India and Egypt, The Tau of the patriarchs, the divine sign of Osiris, the Stauros of the Gnostics, the keystone of the temple, the symbol of Occult Masonry; the Cross, central point of the junction of the right angles of two infinite triangles; the Cross, which in the French language seems to be the first root and fundamental substantive of the verb to believe and the verb to grow, thus combining the conceptions of science, religion and progress.

The Great Magical Agent manifests by four kinds of phenomena, and has been subjected to the experiments of profane science under four names—caloric, light, electricity, magnetism. It has received also the names of TETRAGRAM, INRI, AZOTH, ETHER, OD, Magnetic Fluid, Soul of the Earth, Lucifer, etc. The Great Magical Agent is the fourth emanation of the life-principle, of which the sun is the third form.

Thaumaturgist

In Greek this term denotes a wonderworker. It has been applied to various reputed magicians and also the various saints noted for miraculous phenomena. Among these saints were St. Gregory Thaumaturga and St. Philomena, who is called the Thaumaturga of the nineteenth century.

576

Theomancy

The part of the Cabala dealing with the study of divine mysteries. Those who have mastered theomancy control demons and angels, and they have the ability to see into the future and perform miracles.

Thessaly

After the Persians invaded their land, the Thessalonians became famous for their sorceresses. Their practices embraced a wide field, from calling down the moon to concocting love or death potions.

Theurgy

A mystic cult established by Iamblichus, a mystic and Neoplatonist philosopher who flourished in the fourth century A.D. The theurgists were the priests associated with the temples of Egypt and Greece and the Middle East. They practiced ceremonial magic and evoked the images of the gods.

Thread

A red thread or cord was considered in medieval times to be the mark of a witch. The belief springs from the Jewish ritual mentioned in Leviticus and in Isaiah 1:18. Aaron is told to select a goat for Azazel, to put all the sins of Israel on the head of the goat, and to send the goat into the wilderness. The Jews performed the ritual until 70 A.D. They tied to the head of the scapegoat a scarlet thread, recalling the words of the prophet, "though your sins be as scarlet, they shall be white as snow."

Three

A sacred number with magical associations.

In numerology, 3 is the number of creation, the natural symbol for the male genitals (1 is the erect penis), and the first number capable of reconciling opposites and creating more numbers.

Three Symbolical Animals

The bull, the dog, and the goat are, according to Éliphas Lévi, the three symbolical animals of Hermetic magic. They are the summation of Egyptian and Indian traditions.

The bull represents the Earth or Salt of the Philosophers; the dog is Hermanubis, the Mercury of the sages—otherwise, fluid, air and water; the goat represents fire and is at the same time the symbol of generation. Two goats, one pure and one impure, were consecrated in Judea; the first was sacrificed in expiation for sins; the other, loaded with those sins by imprecation, was set at liberty in the desert—a strange ordinance, but one of deep symbolism, signifying reconciliation by sacrifice and expiation by liberty! Now, all the fathers of the Church, who have concerned themselves with Jewish symbolism, have recognized in the immolated goat the figure of Him Who assumed, as they say, the very form of sin. Hence the Gnostics were not outside symbolical traditions when they assigned this same mystical figure to Christ the Liberator. All the Kabalah and all Magic, as a fact, are divided between the cultus of the immolated and that of the emissary goat. We must recognize therefore a Magic of the Sanctuary and that of the wilderness, the White and the Black Church, the priesthood of public assemblies and the Sanhedrin of the Sabbath. The goat which is represented in our frontispiece bears upon its forehead the Sign of the Pentagram with one point in the ascendant, which is sufficient to distinguish it as a symbol of the light.

Thumbscrews

A common and effective method of extracting confessions from those accused of witchcraft. A small vise was used to crush the tip of the finger to a pulp. A simpler method involved the application of pressure on the thumb or toe by

578

means of a piece of string. Also known as pilliwinks, the screws, thumbikins, and (in French) *grésillons*.

Thunderbolt

In many cultures the thunderbolt and the axe are invested with protective powers. In Germany it is called the Donneraxt or Donnerstein. The Greeks called it Astropelakia, the Latins Gemma cerauniae, the Spaniards Piedras de rayo, the Chinese Rai-fu-seki (the battle-axe of the guardian of Heaven), and the Hindus Swayamphu (the self-originated).

The so-called thunderbolt is confused with the prehistoric sone axe both bearing the same name in many lands. As this axe is often also a hammer it is evident that it may have been sacred to Thor. . . . The prehistoric axe was probably regarded as gifted with fetish power, even in the earliest age. (Charles Leland.)

Tibetan Book of the Dead

The Bardo Thodol is a guide for the dead man who must spend forty-nine days awaiting his rebirth. The first part of text (Chikhai Bardo) describes the psychic aspect of the moment of death. The second part (Chönyid Bardo) describes the dream state that follows death. The third part (Sidpa Bardo) reveals the secrets of the birth instinct and prenatal events. Instructions are intended to fix the dying man's attention on the nature of his visions. The book is said by some interpreters to cloak the mystical teachings of the ancient gurus. Seen as a guide to the death and rebirth of the ego, it stresses the attainment of freedom by remembrance of certain teachings. The Tibetan title of the book means "Liberation by hearing on the after-death plane."

Tibetan Talismans

Mysticism and primitive sorcery blend in the fabrication. and use of talismans in Tibet. Certain objects or symbols appear frequently: the lotus flower, the three jewels (representing Buddha, his teaching, and his church), the seven precious stones (the wheel of Buddhic law, the sacred gem, the stone of a faithful woman, the gem of a good minister, the white elephant, the horse, the stone of a victorious warrior), the eight glorious emblems (golden fish, sacred umbrella, sea-shell of victory, benefic design, banner of victory, sacred vase, lotus, and wheel), the Chinese trigrams, and the swastika. The formula OM MANI PADME HUM protects many towns and buildings.

Tibetan Witchcraft
The indigenous animistic Bon cult of Tibet is based on ancestor-worship, superstition, and witchcraft.

Tiphereth
The balancing force between Hesed and Geburah the vital energy of the life-force, and the sixth sephira, representing the sphere of the sun, in cabalistic teachings.

Tiresias
Ancient Greek necromancer, afflicted by the gods with blindness but endowed with the gift of prophesy.

Tlingit Indians
As recently as 1957 several members of the Tlingit tribe of Indians living at Angoon, on Admiralty Island off the coast of Alaska, were accused of practicing witchcraft. A child's death was the occasion for a sequence of magic rites. Cats and dogs were burned in sacrificial ceremonies, while two young Indian girls were beaten with "devil clubs."

Toad
The toad has long been associated with sorcery. In 1610 a man who had been initiated into the Spanish Association of Witches testified that on admission to the association he had been given a real toad and had had a mark resembling a toad stamped on his eyelid. The toad had the

power to make its master invisible, transport him to distant places, and change him into the form of an animal.

I have been informed by gypsies that toads do really form unaccountable predilections for persons and places. The following is accurately related as it was told me in Romany fourteen years ago, in Epping Forest, by a girl. "You know, sir, that people who live out of doors all the time, as we do, see and know a great deal about such creatures. One day we went to a farmhouse, and found the wife almost dying because she thought she was bewitched by a woman who came every day in the form of a great toad to her door and looked in. And, sure enough, while she was talking the toad came, and the woman was taken in such a way with fright that I thought she'd have died. But I had a laugh to myself; for I knew that toads have such ways, and can not only be tamed, but will almost tame themselves. So we gypsies talked together in Romany, and then said we could remove the spell if she would get us a pair of shears and a cup of salt. Then we caught the toad, and tied the shears to make a cross —you see!—and with it threw the toad into the fire, and poured salt on it. So the witchcraft was ended, and the lady gave us a good meal and ten shillings."

. . . The toad is an emblem of productiveness, and ranks among creatures which are types of erotic passion. I have in my possession a necklace of rudely made silver toads, of Arab workmanship, intended to be worn by women who wish to become mothers. Therefore the creature, in the Old World as well as in the New, appears as a being earnestly seeking the companionship of men. (Charles Leland.)

Witches were especially fond of toads, pampering them as if they were children and dressing them in scarlet silk and

581

green velvet capes for the celebration of the Sabbat. They wore bells around their necks and were baptized at the Sabbat. Thy were supposed to have in their heads stones which changed color in the presence of poison and could be used as an antidote against it. Pierre Delancre says that a witch ordinarily was attended by several demons. These demons sat on her left shoulder. Having assumed the shape of a two-horned toad, they were visible only to those familiar with witchcraft.

Toledo
According to Michelet, Toledo was the Holy City of sorcerers and sorceresses. Their association with highly civilized Jews and Moors enabled them to form at Toledo a sort of university of their own.

Toltecs
Ancient rulers of all civilized parts of Mexico. They claimed descent from Quetzalcoatl, the Precious Twin, who was both the planet Venus as the Morning Star and the Feathered Serpent, and whose descendants alone among the Mexican nobility could rule the country. See Atlantis.

Tongues, Speaking in
See Glossolalia.

Tornait
In Greenland, the Eskimos' belief is that various spirits, known as tornait or tartat or tungat, become helpers of the shaman or medicine man. In Alaska the tornait are Beings that are not the souls of visible beings but have strange forms of their own. They are usually evil and harmful. They are known as the Half-People, the Wanderers, the mountain Giants. These tornait, in groups or communities, are in turn controlled by superior, more potent agents.

Torralva, Eugenio
Sixteenth-century magician. According to his own confes-

sions, he had the ability to travel over long distances in the twinkling of an eye and to foretell the future. A physician to the Emir of Castille, Dr. Torralva, had studied in Rome, where a Dominican monk had placed at his service a familiar spirit. Zakiel, as the spirit in the form of a fair young man was called, appeared at Torralva's request, provided him with money, transported him to distant places on a stick. Sentenced to prison on a charge of heresy, Torralva obtained release through his powerful friends.

Torture

A witch generally could not be executed unless she confessed her guilt under torture. The first stage of torture, called preparatory torture (question préparatoire), was designed to force a confession. It consisted mainly of threats, including the viewing of the torture chamber. Final torture (question définitive) consisted of the ordinary torture followed by the extraordinary torture (question extraordinaire). The strappado generally was employed for the ordinary torture, and squassation for the extraoridnary torture. The purpose of the final torture was to force the accused to name accomplices.

Other methods of torture included piercing of the tongue of the accused, forcible feeding on herrings cooked in salt, thrusting knotted clouts down the throat of the victim and pulling them up again with a string, denial of water, immersion in hot salt water containing lime; the wooden horse, many kinds of racks, the wheel, the heated iron chair, leg vises, and thumbscrews; and pouring hot water or moulten lead into the boots of the accused.

Totem Animals

The totem concept was widespread in paleolithic times, according to T. C. Lethbridge, and were replaced by beliefs in gods and goddesses in human form. Sometimes the change was only partial, with the result that Pan retained his horns and the legs of a goat, while Diana in the form of the three-headed Hecate represents the fusion of three totems. Metamorphoses of gods into animals recall the totemistic beliefs of earlier times as do the frequent appearances of the devil or priest of a coven in animal guise, representing the totem animal coupling with the Great Mother to ensure the fertility of the tribe.

Touch
The authors of the Malleus Maleficarum advised the judge at a witch trial not to allow himself to be touched physically by the accused, "especially in any contact by their bare arms and hands." With the help of the Devil a witch could bewitch the judge by touching him, looking at him, or uttering words in his presence, particularly when torture was being used.

Toulouse Trials
Like the proceedings conducted earlier at Carcassonne, those initiated at Toulouse in June 1335 resulted in the burning of persons accused of sorcery. Among the 8 persons burned at the stake were Anne-Marie de Georgel and Catherine Delort. Both middle-aged witches were tortured before they were burned. Both confessed that they had served Satan for 20 years and had surrendered themselves to him in this life and the next. The trial of 63 persons at Carcassonne is important to historians of witchcraft because it was one of the first instances of the use of torture to force confessions from the accused.

A few years later, in 1352, the Inquisition condemned 7 persons for trying to persuade a goat to take them to the sabbat and sentenced 8 others to life imprisonment for selling their souls to the Devil and practicing magic, and sent to the stake 8 others for using incantations or the evil eye to kill children. The following year the trial of 68 persons on the charges of magic and heresy elicited the first fully authenticated reference to ritual dancing at the sabbat. Some of the cult members were accused of dancing in a magic circle and parodying Church ceremonies.

Both women admitted that they had gone to the sabbat many times on Friday or Saturday night, that many other men and women went there with them, and that the sabbats were held sometimes in one place and sometimes in another.

See Carcassonne Trials; Delort, Catherine; Georgel, Anne Marie.

Trance
A sleeplike state characterized by increased or heightened susceptibility to the supernatural world and a corresponding decrease in sensory and motor contact with the physical world. In this altered state of consciousness a mystic sometimes merges with the godhead, enters the astral world, or communicates with supernatural beings. The medium or sensitive may enter into a trance for the purpose of allowing a spirit to take possession of him and use him in communicating with a living person.

Transcendental Magic
See Occult Philosophy.

Transmutation
In a spiritual sense, the alchemical transmutation of lead into gold is man's redemption, his regaining the original nobility of human nature. See Flamel, Nicholas; Helmont, J. B. van; Helvetius, Jan. F.

Transvection

The flight by night with the aid of a broomstick, a cleft stick, a distaff, or even a shovel, was a salient feature of witchcraft. Transvection was first illustrated in Ulrich Molitor's *De Lamiis* (1489). Here three witches are shown riding through the air on a long forked stick. One has the head of an ass, another that of a bird, and the third that of a calf.

The *Malleus Maleficarum* explains the method of transvection:

> Now the following is their method of being transported. They take the unguent which, as we have said, they make at the devil's instruction from the limbs of children, particularly of those whom they have killed before baptism, and anoint with it a chair or a broomstick; whereupon they are immediately carried up into the air, either by day or by night, and either visibly or, if they wish, invisibly. . . . And although the devil for the most part performs this by means of the unguent, to the end that children should be deprived of the grace of baptism and of salvation, yet he often seems to effect the same transvection without its use. For at times he transports the witches on animals, which are not true animals but devils in that form; and sometimes even without any exterior help they are visibly carried solely by the operation of the devil's power.

Travertine

A marble which protects the wearer against witchcraft.

Tree of Life

In cabalistic teachings, the Tree of Life represents the underlying pattern of the universe and its fundamental unity. It is a model of God, the universe, and man. It consists of three triangles containing two opposing forces together with a third force which balances and reconciles them, plus one remaining sephira at the bottom.

Tremblers of the Cevennes

Protestant convulsionaries. During the 16th century they spread from the Cevennes in France over almost the whole of Germany. They had visions, communicated with spirits, and performed many miraculous cures.

Tresilian, Robert

English magician. In 1388 he was accused of using diabolical names and a demon's head in his magic practices.

Treves

Site of several witchcraft trials. Five witches were burned by Father St. Maximim in 1572. Johann von Schonenburg persecuted Protestants and witches there between 1581 and 1589. Flade, the civil judge, was too lax and was put to death as a witch. Father C. Loos protested Flade's execution and was exiled. Peter Binsfeld was in full control during the climactic years of the witch hunters (1587-1594), when fifteen hundred persons were brought to trial.

Trevisan, Bernard

Alchemist (b. 1406). A. E. Waite has this to say about him:

Bernard Compte de la Marche Trévisan is accredited by the popular legends of France with the powers of a sorcerer in possession of a devil's bird or familiar spirit; nevertheless, he is called "the good," and enjoyed a particular reputation for benevolence.

Descendant of a distinguished Paduan family, Bernard Trévisan began to study the time-honoured science of alchemy about the time that Basil in Germany, and the two Isaacs in Holland were prosecuting their labours with supposed success. His father was a physician of Padua, where he himself was born in the year 1406. The account of his alchemical errors must rank among the most curious anecdotes in the annals of occult chemistry. . . .

For fifteen years he continued his preliminary experiences, and at the end of that time he had purchased a perfect knowledge of all the highways and byways of alchemical rogueries, and was intimately acquainted with an enormous variety of substances, mineral, metallic, and otherwise, which did not apparently enter into the composition of the stone philosophical. He calculates the cost of these experiences to have been roughly six thousand crowns. . . .

At Rhodes he became acquainted with *un grand clerc et réligieux*, who was addicted to philosophy, and commonly reported to be enjoying the philosophical stone. He managed to borrow eight thousand florins, and laboured with this monk in the dissolution of gold, silver, and corrosive sublimate; he accomplished so much in the space of three years that he expended the funds he had raised, and was again at the end of his resources. Thus, effectually prevented from continuing the practice, he returned to the study of the philosophers, and after eight years, at the age of seventy-three, he professes to have discovered their secret. By comparing the adepts and examining in what things they agree, and in what they differ, he judged that the truth must lie in those maxims wherein they were practically unanimous. He informs us that it was two years before he put his discovery to the test; it was crowned with success, and notwithstanding the infirmities of old age, he lived for some time in the enjoyment of his tardy reward.

The chief work of Trévisan is *La Philosophie Naturelle des Métaux*. He insists on the necessity of strong and discreet meditation in all students of Hermetic philosophy.

Their operations must wait on nature, and not nature on their arbitrary processes.

Triads
See Barddas.

Trolls
In Teutonic mythology, supernatural beings, variously conceived as dwarfs or giants and fabled to inhabit caves and hills. They are generally malevolent creatures.

Turquoise
A light blue semi-precious stone believed by the Arabs to be a good luck charm.

Twardowsky
The Polish Faust. He had written the fateful pact with his own blood on an ox-hide. One day when he was astounding others with his feats, he was reminded by the Devil that the appointed hour had come. He first sought protection by approaching a sleeping infant, then surrendered when reminded that a gentleman cannot break his word.

Twelve
In mystic numerology this number has special significance. It appears in mythology, folklore, and in esoteric concepts. The cosmos was divided into twelve signs called the Zodiac. In pagan cults, there were frequently groups of twelve: gods, followers, leaders. In Greek mythology, Hercules performed twelve labors. In the Bible, Jacob is recorded as having twelve sons. Mithra had twelve associates. King Arthur had his twelve knights. The year has twelve months. There are, too, the twelve days of Christmas. Mystically, for a number of reasons, twelve has been called "the perfect number."

Twenty-eight
A mystical number representing one aspect of the perfec-

589

tion of God. Because of its correspondence with the lunar cycle, the number is invested with special powers.

Twenty-one

A number with powerful magical properties. A multiple of two perfect numbers, three and seven, 21 originally symbolized majesty and power. Twenty-one salutes were offered as a final tribute at the funeral of kings, laying the basis for the modern practice of welcoming or bidding a last farewell to heads of state.

Two

The first of the even numbers, associated with woman and wickedness. Its characteristics are those traditionally ascribed to femininity—sweetness, docility, modesty—together with a strain of malice and deceit. It is the Devil's number. In the Pythagorean-inspired theory of opposites, it is passive and weak in contrast to the characteristics (active and powerful) assigned to one, the number of God.

Typtology

Communication with spirits by means of rappings.

U

Umbilical Cord

In European folklore, the umbilical cord if not carefully preserved by immersion in water or fire may cause the person from whom it has been severed to die by drowning or fire.

Universities for Sorcerers

The occult arts were taught at centers of higher learning in Egypt, Babylonia, Greece, Arabia, and Mexico. Centers for the teaching of the occult art, magic, and alchemy also existed in medieval Europe.

Universities, Occult

See Occult Universities.

Uraeus

In Egyptian religion, the sacred asp, symbol of immortality. Some occultists link representations of the uraeus, still visible on the walls and facades of temples, to visitations of astronauts who came from outer space to serve as the initiators of mankind. At the temple of Denderah, for example, winged discs flanked by serpents are said to recall visitations by astronauts from other planets. See Astronauts.

Urban VIII

In 1628 Pope Urban VIII tried to use magic to ward off

an eclipse. Fearing that the eclipse would signal his own death, the Pope employed Tommaso Campanella, a magician and an ex-Dominican friar. Relying on the great magical doctrine of "as below, so above," they used two lamps to represent the sun and the moon and five torches for the planets. They sealed off a room and filled it with jewels, plants, and colors associated with the sun and the benevolent planets, Jupiter and Mars. They drank liquor distilled under the influence of these planets and played appropriate music. Their attempt to create a propitious universe to replace the hostile one outside was successful, for the Pope lived on until 1644.

Urim and Thummin
Divination reputedly based on the casting of lots. It was practiced by the ancient Hebrews and is mentioned in the Book of Samuel.

Uroboros
The tail-eating serpent, used by Greek alchemists to symbolize the unity of the sacrificer and sacrificed.

Utchat
Amulet worn by Egyptians as a protection against evil forces. It is commonly called the Eye of Horus.

V

Vaecordia

The Latin name for ligature. Guazzo's *Compendium Malefi-carum* (1608) classifies this form of *maleficia* under seven headings:

1. When one partner is made hateful to the other.
2. When there is a physical separation of the partners.
3. When the emission of semen is prevented.
4. When the semen is infertile.
5. When a man's penis remains flabby.
6. When natural drugs prevent conception.
7. When the female genitals contract or the male organ retracts.

Valafar

Duke of Hell. On good terms with robbers, he has the head of a thief and the body of a lion. He is one of three demons in the service of Sargatanas, brigadier general.

Valentine, Basil

Occult philosopher (fl. 15th century A.D.). His life and works are described by A. E. Waite:

> One of the most illustrious of the adept philosophers is unquestionably Basilius Valentinus, born at Maycnce, and made prior of St. Peter's at Erfurt in 1414. . . .

Basil Valentine denounces the physicians of his time with the fury of Paracelsus. The most ancient systems of chemical philosophy are preserved in his experiments. He exalts antimony as an excellent medicine for those who are acquainted with alchemical secrets. . . .

Every letter and syllable of the "Triumphal Chariot of Antimony" is declared to have its special significance.

"Even to the pointes and prickes" it bristles with divine meaning and mysteries. The metrical treatise on the first matter of the philosophers declares that this stone is composed of white and red, that it is a stone, and yet scarcely a stone; one nature operates therein. Those who desire to attain it, Basil elsewhere informs us, must labour in much prayer, confess their sins, and do good. Many are called, but few chosen to this supreme knowledge. The study of the works of the philosophers and practical experiment are both recommended. There is much in the writings of Basil, in his suggestive if impenetrable allegories, in his curious Kabbalistical symbols, and in his earnest spirituality, to suggest a psychic interpretation of his aims and his principles. This is particularly noticeable in the "Triumphal Chariot of Antimony," and yet it is clear from this remarkable work, which is the masterpiece of its author, that Basil Valentine was one of the most illustrious physical chemists of his age.

Valley of Moses
See Petra.

Vallin, Pierre
Central figure in a witch trial that began at La Tour du Pin in Dauphine on March 15, 1428. He confessed that for 63 years he had served Beelzebub. He paid homage to his master by kissing his thumb, denied God, and defiled the cross. He had sacrificed his daughter Françoise to Beelzebub

when she was only six months old. He had invoked the Devil to raise storms, fly to the sabbat, and perform other maleficia. At the witches' assembly (synagogue) he had had sexual intercourse with Beelzebub, who appeared there as a young girl, and had joined with others in consuming the flesh of innocent children.

Questioned later by secular authorities, who noted that he had been convicted of practicing magic, he named four accomplices. Philippe Baile, a representative of the higher secular authority, was bothered by the fact that these accomplices were all dead. He insisted that the Devil was urging Pierre to conceal the names of living accomplices. Under torture Pierre named the woman who had first led him astray, togther with people from all social classes. He also said that the eight men and twelve women whom he named had ridden to witches' meeting on sticks.

Valonia
The dried acorn cups of certain oaks. It contains tannin, used in tanning sole leather, and was believed to be a magical cure. Ink made from the acorn of the valonia oak was used for writing spells.

Vampires
A dead person who returns from the grave in spirit form to destroy and suck the blood of mortals. Living sorcerers are supposed to assume the same shape for similar purposes.

Vaudois
French term for members of the heretical Waldensians. After the heretics gained a reputation for sexual depravity, early in the 15th century, the term frequently was used to denote a sex fiend. The Waldensians, who had at first taken vows of poverty and asceticism, became identified with witchcraft. *Vauderie* was used interchangeably with Sabbat.

595

Vaughan, Thomas

Seventeenth-century occultist and brother of the poet Henry Vaughan. Writing under the name of Eugenius Philalethes, he published two small volumes containing five tracts. One of them was titled Magia Adamica; Or the Antiquity of Magic and the descent thereof from Adam downward proved (1650). An Anglican priest, he wrote: "That I should profess magic . . . is impiety with many but religion with me. It is a conscience that I have learned from authors greater than myself and scriptures greater than both. Magic is nothing but the wisdom of the Creator revealed and planted in the creature." He asserts that the high art of magic has always been in this world. "The magicians had a maxim among themselves 'that no word is efficacious in magic unless it be first animated with the Word of God.' " The common man misunderstood and debased what wise men in all generations had known. Persecuted, the wise men hid their knowledge. The foolish resorted to charms and "studied to bind the Devil." The great persecutors denounced and destroyed the wise and the foolish alike. He names as inspired spirits Cornelius Agrippa, Libanius Gallus, Johannes Trithemius, Georgius Venutus, and Johannes Reuchlin.

Veleda

Prophetess of the ancient Germans. Rarely seen, she lived on a high tower and entrusted her oracular counsel to messengers.

Venus

The morning star, Venus symbolized feminine youth, seduction, love in all its modalities. Its influence can be utilized only rarely since it has a cycle of 224 days. The color corresponding to Venus is green.

Vervain

Sacred herb used to sprinkle the altars of Jupiter to drive away evil spirits. The druids used it in connection with many superstitions. They gathered it at daybreak. Later demonologists believed that a crown of vervain helped to evoke demons.

Verver

Occult signs made with cornmeal by a voodoo priest. The verver are made on the ground in sacred places where tables are set up, heaped with food for the *loa*.

Vessel

Though many alchemists used obscure and symbolic language to make the true meaning of their writings appear inaccessible to vulgar minds, the secrets of the Great Art were fairly widely known, except for the secret of the vessel. Jacob Boehme caused many alchemists to fear that this great secret soon would be revealed to all. The secret was that Man was the vessel, the true laboratory, according to Hitchcock. Without knowledge of this vessel, no one can achieve the magistery. Man's life is the great distillery, the thing distilling, and the thing distilled. Self-knowledge is the foundation of the alchemical tradition. See Hitchcock.

Vetis (Veltis)

An evil spirit imprisoned in a copper cauldron by Solomon and unwittingly freed by the Babylonians. Working directly under Satan, Vetis specializes in corrupting the souls of those who seek to worship God.

Viguier, Paule

See Carcassonne Trials.

Vila

A Gypsy term for a witch. Certain men, the seventh or twelfth child in a family, are thought to be able to gain the love of a vila.

Villanova, Arnold De

Alchemist (born about 1245). A. E. Waite gives a brief account of his life and work:

> His skill in Hermetic philosophy has been generally recognised. His contemporary, the celebrated Jurisconsult, John Andre, says of him: —"In this time appeared Arnold de Villeneuve, a great theologian, a skilful physician, and wise alchymist, who made gold, which he submitted to all proofs." Arnold has also the character of writing with more light and clearness than the other philosophers. His alchemical works were published in 1509, in one folio volume. His *Libellus de Somniorum Interpretatione et Somnia Danielis* is excessively rare in its original quarto edition. Several alchemical and magical works are gratuitously ascribed to him. . . .
>
> The *Thesaurus Thesaurorum* and the *Rosarium Philosophorum,* the *Speculum Alchemiae* and the *Perfectum Magisterium,* are the most notable of all his alchemical treatises.

Vintras, Pierre

Nineteenth-century French occultist. He announced that he was a reincarnation of Elijah and founded a mysterious sect, the Work of Mercy, which boasted a collection of miraculous communion wafers. Eliphas Levi examined the bloody hosts and concluded that they bore the markings of the Devil. After Vintras died in 1875, the sect was led by a defrocked priest, the Abbé Boullan.

Virgo

In astrology, the Virgin. The sixth, northern sign of the

zodiac. It represents the dual hermaphroditic form. In esoteric writings it symbolizes chastity and, on the intellectual plane, the realization of hopes. Cabalistic, it symbolizes the solar plexus of the grand old man of the heavens. Thus it represents the assimilating and distributing functions of the human organism.

Virgula Furcata

A Latin term meaning a forked rod. This is the divine rod used by dowsers. It is so called by Agricola, the metallurgist who flourished in the sixteenth century. The divining rod, however, need not be forked.

Virility

Gypsies mixed cow's blood, beans, and burned hair taken from the parents of a boy in order to produce a concoction to insure his virility. To insure the femininity of a girl, they substituted pumpkin or sunflower seeds for the beans.

Visconti, Girolamo

Fifteenth-century Italian professor and Dominican provincial of Lombardy. He wrote his *Little Book of Witches* about 1460, preparing the ground for acceptance of the *Malleus Maleficarum*.

Visions

According to Éliphas Lévi, visions operate in this manner:

All forms correspond to ideas, and there is no idea which has not its proper and peculiar form. The primordial light, which is the vehicle of all ideas, is the mother of all forms, and transmits them from emanation to emanation, merely diminished or modified according to the density of the media. Secondary forms are reflections which return to the font of the emanated light. The forms of objects, being a modification of light, remain in the light where the reflection consigns them. Hence the Astral

599

Light, or terrestrial fluid, which we call the Great Magnetic Agent, is saturated with all kinds of images or reflections. Now, our soul can evoke these, and subject them to its DIAPHANE, as the Kabalists term it. Such images are always present before us, and are effaced only by the more powerful impressions of reality during waking hours, or by preoccupation of the mind, which makes our imagination inattentive to the fluidic panorama of the Astral Light. When we sleep, this spectacle presents itself spontaneously before us, and in this way dreams are produced—dreams vague and incoherent if some governing do not remain active during the sleep, giving, even unconsciously to our intelligence, a direction to the dream, which then transforms into visions.

Vital, Hayyim

Mystic and cabalist (1543-1620). Born in Safed, he transmitted to posterity the written and oral traditions entrusted to him by Isaac Ashkenazi. Many of the mystic writings dictated to him were interred with him at his request since they were considered by the Ari (Ashkenazi) to be too sacred for a sinful generation's eyes. Later, two cabalists obtained permission from Vital in a dream to exhume these writings. After the Ari died, Vital became the acknowledged master of the Cabala. In one of his works, the *Sefer Hagilgulim* (Book of Reincarnations), he explained how the souls of the dead, from Adam and Eve until the present, were reborn in the bodies of prominent persons.

Voodoo

A cult originating in African religious practices and popularly identified with witchcraft in the West Indies and parts of the United States. Voodoo ceremonies, derived from Dahomey, center around the idea of propitiating the *loa*. Offerings to the loa, gods whose desires must be satisfied by the cultists, may take the form of a lighted candle, food, or

600

water. They may be made by an individual or, if more elaborate ceremonies are required by the *hungan* (voodoo priest). Despite persistent efforts to eradicate it, voodoo has survived for three centuries in its New World setting.

Possible origins of the word Voodoo vary from the French expression *veau d'or,* golden calf, to *Vodu,* or its corrupted forms *Vodun* and *Vaudou,* used in the West African countries of Dahomey and Togo to designate a number of gods and spirits.

The occult practices from which Voodoo has evolved may survive in Africa today in the form of Juju. Rooted in the distant past, Juju may have sprung from ophiolatry or snake worship. The name is applied today to both magical practices and the one who has mastered htem. The use of Juju in casting spells is prevalent in different regions of Africa. Practitioners rely on possession by a supernatural power, knowledge of herbalism, and psychic powers. See Haitian Voodoo.

Voodoo Dances
Drums and dancing are important in Voodoo ritual. The dance called *Voodoo zépaule* is danced with the shoulders (French *les épaules*). The Banda is a lively dance of the dead, also known as the dance of the *Guédés,* and involves mainly the execution of deft hip movements. Here the dancers imitate the movements of the dead leaving their tombs. Performed traditionally during the first two days and nights of November, it has almost passed out of existence. In performing the *Yanvallou* the dancers bend their bodies and knees reverently. Still another dance, the *Mahi,* involves mainly the feet and demands great muscular effort.

W

Wab
In Egyptian religion, priests or "divine fathers" who offered sacrifices to the gods.

Wadi 'Araba
See Petra.

Waite, A. E.
Modern scholar of occultism. In addition to *The Pictorial Key to the Tarot* (1910), he wrote *Lives of the Alchemystical Philosophers* (1888), *Book of Black Magic and Pacts* (1898), *The Real History of the Rosicrucians* (1887), *The Doctrine and Literature of the Kabalah* (1902), and *The Hidden Church of the Holy Grail, its Legends and Symbolism* (1909), and *The Secret Tradition in Alchemy* (1926).

Wakanda
In American Indian tradition, the name of the impersonal power or force behind reality. This universal principle of such tribes as the Sioux is similar to the mana, orenda, or manito of other cultures.

Walder, Sophie
Dr. Bataille claimed that Sophie Walder had been commissioned to spread Satanic Freemasonry in Switzerland. He revealed the details of her conversion to Christianity and her account of the secrets of Freemasonry. See Bataille, Doctor.

Walpurgisnacht

This expression refers to the first night in May. At this time witches and demoniac creatures were wont to assemble to celebrate their gruesome orgies and Satanic rituals.

Wand

The *True Grimoire* contains an incantation to be used in making the magician's wand:

> I beg thee, O Great Adonai, Eloim, Ariel, Jehovam, exert thy beneficence towards me, and give to this rod as I cut it the power and the virtue of the rods of Jacob, of Moses, and of Joshua the powerful!

> I beg Thee, O Great Adonai, Eloim, Ariel, Jehovam, to place in this wand the entire strength of Samson, the anger of Amanuel, and the blasting power of the mighty Zariatnatmik, he who will revenge against sin on the Day of Judgement. Amen.

Wangas (Ouangas)

Haitian magic; it is associated with spells and incantations, good-luck charms, and the use of leaves and herbs. A murder wanga found near Gonaives in 1921 contained feathers and stones; the bones of a snake, lizard, squirrel, bat, frog, and hen; images of wax and clay; and other miscellaneous items. Here is the formula for a protective wanga: small pieces of gold, silver, lead, iron, bronze, thrunde-stone, river sandstone, dogwood gum; fire ashes, fire smoke, an eye without an eye, and a tail without a tail; a cross from a cemetery, a leaf of Congo peas, a new thimble, a set *of* needles, and hairs taken from the center of the head. Leave the wanga on your window during seven Fridays.

Warboys Witches

Three persons were convicted of witchcraft at the conclusion of the most widely discussed trial in England before 1600.

Eigentliche Abbildung der ehemaligen
Probe und Reinigung der Hexen
auf dem kalten Waßer.

The Water Test
If the person under the water test failed to drown it was taken as evidence
of guilt. If the person drowned, then of course he or she was innocent.
(E. D. Hauber, Bibliotheca sive Acta et Scripta Magica, Vol. 1, Pt. 3;
Lemgo, 1738.)

SORCERER SELLING MARINERS THE WINDS TIED UP IN
THREE KNOTS OF A ROPE

Olaus Magnus, *Historia de gentibus septentrionalibus*.

The convictions were based on charges made by the five daughters of a prominent resident of Warboys, Robert Throckmorton. The case is reported in *The Most Strange and Admirable Discovery of the Three Witches of Warboys,* a pamphlet published in London in 1593.

Watchers
Celestial beings whose task it was to watch the throne of God. These were the angels who "saw the daughters of men that they were fair," had their eyes and senses deflected, and descended to the earth, ten-score strong. From the mystery of their plunging into a separate mode of existence sprang the giants who "devoured mankind"; from their sexual union with women sprang the giants who taught men the arts and occult science, the secrets of making weapons, of divination and magic.

Watchers of the Heavens
In astrology, this expression was applied by the Persians, about 3000 B.C., to the four Royal Stars, then to the angels of the zodiac: the Watcher of the East, then at the vernal equinox—Aldebaran; the Watcher of the North, which then marked the summer solstice—Regulus; the Watcher of the West, then at the autumnal equinox—Antares; the Watcher of the South, which then marked the winter solstice—Fomalhaut.

Waxen Images
Small figures made of wax or clay, used by necromancers to inflict harm on the body of an enemy. Belief in *maleficia* by means of waxen images is both primitive and universal.

Weir, Thomas
Famous Scottish wizard, executed in 1670. His sister, Jane, was charged with him, for incest, sorcery, and consulting "witches, necromancers, and devils."

Welsh Seers

Giraldus Cambrensis (1146-c. 1220), the Welsh historian and geographer, in his Description of Wales, has the following account of soothsayers:

Among these Welsh people there are—and you will not find them elsewhere—certain men called Awenithion, that is, inspired. When consulted on some doubtful issue, they immediately go into a frenzy as though beside themselves and finally become prophetic. They do not however utter the desired answer forthwith: but through much devious circumlocution, through a spate of talk, trivial and meaningless rather than coherent, yet expressed altogether in ornate language, lastly in some verbal byway, the seeker who observes the reply carefully will find a clear answer. And so finally they are roused by others from this ecstatic state as though from a deep sleep, and are forcibly brought back to consciousness almost by violence. Now you will find two remarkable characteristics about them. After their reply, unless violently aroused and awakened, they do not usually become inspired after such a frenzy. Once awakened, they will recall nothing about what was uttered by them in their trance. Thus if they happen to be consulted on this point or any other and have no reply, they will explain in quite other, different terms: perhaps they speak through inspired and possessed spirits, though in ignorance. These gifts generally come to them in sleep through visions. For some believe that, as it were, sweet milk or honey is poured into them: while others think that a card with writing on it is placed on their mouths.

Wenham, Jane

(d. 1730) The last trial of a woman for witchcraft in England occurred in 1712. Jane Wenham, known as "the wise woman of Walkerne," was convicted by a jury of "conversing familiarly with the devil in the form of a cat." The judge obtained a reprieve, and the accused was pardoned.

Werewolf, Variant Names for

In the Middle Ages, the werewolf was called guerulfus. In Old English the term werewolf itself meant man-wolf. In French, the equivalent is loupgarou. In Danish, vaerulf. In Swedish, varulf. In Greek, lukokantzari. Slavonic languages know the phenomena as volkulaku, vokodlak, wilkodlak.

Westcar Papyrus

Egyptian text dating from the 18th century B.C. and devoted to tales of magic.

White Witches

Leaders of covens of suburban housewives consider witchcraft a pre-Christian faith. Some of them claim to be versed in ancient Celtic lore and to use their powers for good ends only. Like Louise Huebner of Los Angeles, they are contemptuous of satanic rites "based on sexual perversions."

Wier, John

Physician (1515-88). A tutor to the sons of François I, he wrote *De Praestigiis* (On Magic), published in 1563 and later revised and abridged as *De Lamiis* (On Witches). He made a distinction between harmless witches who worked no evil and wicked magicians who actually conspired with Satan. Also Johann or Johan Vierus or Weyer.

Wights

Spirits visible only to those gifted with second sight. If they should leave the mounds, trees, and waterfalls where they dwell, evil or bad luck might follow.

Williamson, Cecil

A practicing sorcerer living in Bocastle, England. He is the proprietor of the Witches' House, said to be Europe's most extensive museum of black magic. He describes their initial appearance as a little globular moisture, like a frog blowing bubbles. The globule keeps growing up to the size of a football. . . . As it expands, it takes on a glasslike, luminously blue appearance, and you see a human head forming inside.

Eventually . . . , the head is full sized, and sometimes you even get speech from it. Often, the light becomes too dazzling for the eyes; then, suddenly, the globe is gone.

Willow
If a person sits under the willow or "devil's tree" and loudly curses God, the devil will invest him with nefarious supernatural powers.

Willow-knots
To win the love of a girl, according to Gypsy lore, a youth should find some willow twigs that have grown together into a knot. After cutting them and putting them into his mouth, he should repeat these words:

> I eat thy luck.
> I drink thy luck.
> Give me that luck of thine,
> Then thou shalt be mine.

Wishart, Janet
An Aberdeen witch, burned alive after she had been indicted for casting a spell on Alexander Thompson and performing other Satanic acts.

Witch
In England a witch is defined as "a person who hath conference with the Devil to consult with him or to do some act."

Now applied to a female magician, the term stems from the Old English word wicca, designating a male magician. A witch may appear to be young and beautiful but is actually old, repulsive, branded with the Devil's Mark and clothed in the Devil's Girdle. She eats human flesh, drinks human blood, fashions mannikins to represent humans, disrupts the forces of nature, is responsible for changelings, wreaks vengeance on those who scorn her, copulates with those she desires, summons the infernal hosts, and has recourse to a vast array of formulas, implements, and agents in conducting her goetic operations. Since witchcraft reached its apogee during the Middle Ages, many designations for witches are in Latin, the common literary vehicle: incantatrix, lamia, maga, malefica, saga, sortilega, strix, venefica.

Witch-burning
Throughout the Middle Ages and later, witch-burning was prevalent in Europe and America. Official records show that the practice was widespread until the eighteenth century.

Seven thousand witches were burned at Trèves, five hundred within three months at Geneva (1513), eight hundred at Wurzburg, fifteen hundred at Bamberg. During the reign of terror that encompassed all of Europe between 1300 and 1600, according to Michelet, everywhere the administration of justice was the same. Men were blinded and turned into cruel savages "by the poison of their first principle, the doctrine of Original Sin. Thus "the judge is always sure of doing justice. . . . In every case the decision is a foregone conclusion."

Witchcraft Act
The Witchcraft Act of 1735 stipulated that witchcraft did not exist and that anyone claiming to possess supernatural powers would be prosecuted. It was not until 1951, however, that the British struck the last reference to witchcraft from their laws.

609

Witchcraft and Paganism

According to Jeffrey Burton Russell (*Witchcraft in the Middle Ages,* 1972), an unselfconscious and fluctuating continuity of phenomena prevalent in ancient pagan beliefs and practices survived through the Middle Ages even in the absence of dogmas and institutions. Since its elements—a magical word view, folk traditions relating to the hunt and agriculture, the practice of sorcery, and a tendency to oppose public opinion and authority "by consorting with supernatural powers described by the Church as evil"—were only vaguely defined, witches were strongly influenced by local conditions and did for the most part what people expected them to do.

Witchcraft and Sorcery

In many languages the equivalent of the word witch means "sorcerer." Many of the elements of European witchcraft are also found in the sorcery of other societies. Among the fifty motifs common to both traditions are these: disturbances of the air; traveling on brooms, cats, beehives, or other vehicles; animals roaming by night to carry out missions for their masters; metamorphosis; the use of magic ointments to cause changes to occur; night meetings; choice of holy days for meetings; regarding bees as evil spirits; associating blackness with evil; believing that witches leave their bodies to roam about; cannibalism; associating witches with certain animals—cats, dogs, frogs, toads, mice, lizards, owls, horses, and cocks; nudity and the circular dance; crossroads, the evil eye, and ligature; pacts with demons; sexual orgies including copulation with demons; the use of salt to ward off evil and sticks as magic wands; and the tendency to link witchcraft primarily with females.

About one-third of the components of witchcraft in medieval Europe originated in sorcery: flight, shapeshifting,

610

cannibalism, nocturnal activities, and the use of ointments, familiars, and demons.

Witchcraft as a Historical Phenomenon
In his scholarly and definitive treatment of the subject, Jeffrey Burton Russell identifies eight degrees of skepticism regarding European witchcraft: (1) No one really believed in the fraud perpetrated by the Inquisitors and their collaborators. (2) Though no one believed that he was a witch, many people were deluded into believing that witches existed. (3) Some deluded people believed that they were witches. (4) Some of what self-proclaimed witches believed and practiced was derived "from old pagan cults, folklore, sorcery, and heresy." (5) The beliefs and practices described in medieval trial records are not falsified. Witches worshiped the Devil and did substantially what they were accused of doing, "though these beliefs and practices were constantly evolving." (6) Since ancient times a formal witch cult of the type described by Margaret Murray and some modern occultists has existed virtually unchanged. (7) Flight, shape-shifting, and other weird phenomena associated with witchcraft are real. (8) These and other supernatural phenomena prove that the Devil and his minions are present among us. Burton concludes that the first seven positions are historically feasible but that the reality of witchcraft is best stated in positions three, four, and five. These conclusions, stated in his *Witchcraft in the Middle Ages* (1972), are based on his examination of a vast amount of primary and secondary source material.

Witchcraft Burnings
In a recent book titled *Witchcraft* (1965) Justine Glass states that 9 million men and women were executed during the centuries of persecutions to which the witches were subjected.

Witchcraft, Initiation Into
See Coven, Admission into.

Witchcraft, Methods of Recruitment
See Methods of Seducing Souls.

Witchcraft Research Association
In *Witchcraft* (1965) Justine Glass, a member of the England Witchcraft Research Association, stated that the founding of this organization in 1964 was an important event, one that signaled the emergence of a new attitude toward the "Craft" itself and gave witches from all over England an opportunity to communicate freely and openly with each other, following centuries of persecutions that had kept them apart.

Witchcraft Theorists
Among those who wrote on the subject of witchcraft prior to the publication of *Malleus Maleficarum* were the following: Johannes Nider, Jean Vineti, Johann Hartlieb, Nicholas Jacquier, Alphonsus de Spina, Girolamo Visconti, Petrus Mamor, Ambrogio de Vignati, Jordanes de Bergamo, and Jean Vincent.

Johannes Nider was the author of the second book ever printed about witchcraft. Written about 1435 and published about 1475, the book does not mention the sabbat. The Dominican professor and prior called his book *Formicarius.*

Jean Vineti, an inquisitor at Carcassonne, was the first to identify witchcraft as a heresy, in *Tractatus cotra Demonum Invocatores,* which he wrote about 1450.

The idea of the sabbat was developed in *Errores Gazariorum,* by an anonymous Savoyard Inquisitor, around 1450. Hartlieb wrote the first German book on witchcraft, *Buch aller verbotenen Kunst, Unglaubens und Zauberei,* about 1456.

Jacquier's *Flagellum Haerticorum Fascinariorum*, the first major definition of witchcraft as a new heresy, was written in 1458 and published in 1581. The first book ever printed about witchcraft was Alphonsus de Spina's *Fortalicium Fidei*, published in Strasbourg in 1467. The Franciscan (a converted Jew) wrote the book in 1458. The first witchcraft book written in French was *La Vauderye de Lyonois*, composed in 1460 by an anonymous inquisitor at Lyons.

Visconti, an inquisitor of Lombardy, maintained in 1460, in *Lamiarum sivi Striarum Opusculum*, that to defend witches is heresy.

Petrus Mamor, canon and regent of the University of Poitiers, described the sabbat in *Flagellum Maleficorum*, written about 1462 and published in 1490. Ambrogio de Vignati, a jurist and professor at Padua, Bologna, and Turin, urged caution with accusations by accomplices in his lectures, published in 1581 as *Tractatus de Haereticis*. Jordanes de Bergamo, master of theology at Cortona, treated witchcraft as a heresy in *Quaestio de Strigis*, composed about 1470. Jean Vincent, a French prior, rejected witchcraft and accepted magic in *Liber Adversus Magicas Artes*, written about 1475.

Pope Innocent VIII issued his bull "Summis desiderantes affectibus" in 1484. He appointed Jakob Sprenger and Heinrich Kramer as inquisitors to intensify withcraft trials. The two inquisitors published about 1486 the *Malleus Maleficarum*, which reprinted the bull and developed the theory of witchcraft as a heresy into a rigid code that became the handbook of inquisitioners and judges for the next three centuries. After them came Ulrich Molitor, Symphorien Champier, Sylvester Prierias, Samuel de Cassini, Geiler von Kayserberg, Trighemius, Bernard de Como, Ulrich Tengler, Andreas Alciatus, Pietro Pompanazzi, Gianfrancesco Pon-

613

zinibio, Pico della Mirandola, Bartolomeo Spina, Paulus Grillandus, Pedro Cirvelo, and Francisco de Vitoria.

Molitor held, in *Tractatus de Pythonicis Mulieribus* (1489), that even if witchcraft is an illusion, it should be punished as if real. Pietro Pompanazzi, a professor at Padua, wrote *De Naturalium* (1520) and *Effectuum Causis* (1556), escaping punishment by claiming that as a philosopher he might be skeptical and still, as a Catholic, truly believe the teachings of the Church. Ponzinibio, in *Tractatus de Lamiis* (c. 1520), opposed the witchcraft delusion and the conduct of trials by the Inquisition. Pico della Mirandola published the first Italian book about witchcraft (*Strega,* 1524). Bartolomeo Spina, Master of the Sacred Palace, opposed the views of Ponzinibio in *Quaestio de Strigibus* (1525). Pedro Cirvelo, inquisitor at Saragossa, published the first Spanish book about witchcraft (*Reprobación,* 1539).

Witches and Sorcerers
Though the two terms are generally synonymous, during the centuries of persecution known (after Hansen) as witch-madness a distinction was made: witches had made a compact with the Devil and promised to serve; sorcerers had learned their craft from the Devil but remained free agents.

Witches, Names of
In Europe witches were often called *Vaudenses* (Waldensians), *Gazarii* (Catharists), or *haeretici* (heretics). Older names were *lamiae, mascae,* and *striae* or *strigae.*

Witches of Dauphine
A series of witch trials were held in the old French province of Dauphiné, 1421-40. Most of those brought before the Inquisition were poor peasants or shepherds, and most were accused of invoking demons who appeared variously as a black crow, dog, cat, rooster, or dog, or as a pale young man, a ruddy man, a knight in black armor, or a giant with

614

eyes as large as those of a steer. He could also appear, however, as a Negro or one of the little people known in folklore as leprechauns, gnomes, or kobolds. The demons were called by many names: Lucifel, Barrabarri, Borrel, Corpdiable, Ginifert, Griffart, Guillaume, Guillemet, Guli, Jean, Juson, Pierre, Revel, and Tartas.

Witches of Pendle Forest
See Lancashire Witches.

Witches, Requirements for Condemnation
In his *Discourse of the Damned Art of Witchcraft,* published in 1608, six years after his death, the Protestant minister William Perkins set forth the requirements for the condemnation of a witch. His views were particularly influential during the mid-seventeenth century wave of witchcraft persecution in England. According to his book, a witch could be condemned if found guilty under one of three headings: uncertain or less sufficient proof, presumptions of guilt, and just and sufficient proofs. Guilt could be presumed under seven headings:

1. Notorious defamation is a common report of the greater sort of people with whom the party suspected dwelleth, that he or she is a witch. This yieldeth a strong suspicion.

2. If a fellow-witch or magician give testimony of any person to be a witch, either voluntary, or at his or her examination, or at his or her death.

3. If after cursing there followeth death, or at least some mischief; for witches are wont to practice their mischievous acts by cursing and banning.

4. If after enmity, quarrelling, or threatening, a present mischief doth follow.

5. If the party suspected be the son or daughter, the

manservant or maidservant, the familiar friend, near
neighbour, or old companion of a known and convicted witch.

6. If the party suspected be found to have the devil's
mark.

7. If the party examined be inconstant or contrary to
himself in his deliberate answers.

Witches, Types of

According to the *Malleus Maleficarum* there are three types
of witches: those who injure but cannot cure, those who
cure but cannot injure, and those who can perform both of
these functions. Among those who injure, one class is capable
of performing every sort of witchcraft. They eat and devour
children of their own species, raise hailstorms and tempests,
cause sterility in men and animals, sacrifice unbaptized
children to devils,

> They make horses go mad under their riders; they can
> transport themselves from place to place through the air,
> either in body or in imagination . . . ; they can cause
> themselves and others to keep silence under torture . . . ;
> they can show to others occult things and certain future
> events . . . ; they can see absent things as if they were
> present; they can turn the minds of men to inordinate
> love or hatred; they can at times strike whom they will
> with lightning, and even kill some men and animals; they
> can make of no effect the generative desires, and even
> the power of copulation, cause abortion, kill infants in
> the mother's womb by a mere exterior touch; they can
> at times bewitch men and animals with a mere look,
> without touching them, and cause death; they dedicate
> their own children to devils.

These demons were charged with worshiping the Devil,

616

making a pact with him, and bestowing on him the osculum infame. They were said to have sacrificed to him black cats and firstborn children, to have cooked the flesh of their own children in order to provide ingredients for their magic powders, and to have demonstrated their loyalty to the Devil by trampling upon the cross, abstaining from mass, and refusing to kiss the cross, adore the host, or cross themselves.

The Dauphiné witches constituted a sect. They assembled regularly at sabbats, usually on Thursdays. The Devil bore them across great distances to their meeting places. They also rode to the assemblies on black horses, red mares, or sticks smeared with special ointments. At their Sabbats, they danced, took part in sexual orgies, frequently coupled with demons or the Devil himself, who appeared as a black cat or in human shape, with bright, terrifying eyes, wearing black clothing and a crown. He visited imprisoned witches, helping them in their struggles against the Inquisitors or in their attempts to escape torture by committing suicide.

Witch of Endor
King Saul, attacked by a Philistine army, sought advice from the Witch of Endor (I Samuel 28). She summoned the spirit of Samuel, his predecessor:

> And Saul perceived that it was Samuel, and he stooped with his face to the ground, and bowed himself.

The episode was widely discussed by seventeenth-century believers in witchcraft.

Witch's Cradle
A leather device suspended from a crossbar or ceiling by a chain or piece of rope. It was used by witches in medieval Europe to travel into subjective realities. A metal frame based on the same principle enables Robert Masters and

Jean Houston to induce altered states of consciousness in their experiments at the Foundation for Mind Research, near Nyack, New York. The subject is blindfolded, strapped into the cradle, and spun around until his consciousness is altered. The cradle breaks down the cultural trance or normal consciousness, liberates the mind, and creates its own trance state, according to the researchers.

Word

Éliphas Lévi stressed the word in his *Doctrine of Transcendental Magic:*

> I have said that revelation is the word. As a fact, the word, or speech, is the veil of being and the characteristic sign of life. Every form is the veil of a word, because the idea which is the mother of the word is the sole reason for the existence of forms. Every figure is a character, every character derives from and returns into a word. For this reason the ancient sages, of whom Trismegistus is the organ, formulated their sole dogma in these terms: "That which is above is like unto that which is below, and that which is below unto that which is above."

Word Magic

In both high magic and low magic the essential power of the word is a common element. Word magic is worldwide, as is the belief that one gains power over a person or thing by having power over the corresponding name. In the Judaeo-Christian tradition the Tetragrammaton, preferably with the letters reversed, is used in the most terrible magical spells. YHWH, the four letters representing the Name of God, figured in some of the most powerful magical spells.

The ancient Egyptian mysteries taught that a word retained its power unless used lightly or inappropriately. Pronounced solemnly and purposefully, the word led to the fulfillment

618

of a wish, command, or promise. The magical word was called Ma'kheru. One who said, "I promise to do such and such," unless he fulfilled his promise, weakened the power of his word and lessened the likelihood of his success. Saying a thing was equivalent to making it so.

Wraith
An apparition or "double" closely resembling its prototype and generally supposed to be an omen of death.

X

Xaphan

Demon of the second rank. At the time of the expulsion of the angels who sided with Lucifer, he suggested setting fire to Heaven. Now he fans the coals in the furnaces of Hell.

Xezbeth

Demon of lies, fairy tales, and imaginary prodigies.

Xibalba

The Quiché equivalent of the Greek Hades.

Xilka

The first word in an ancient formula used to invoke malefic demons. The complete formula is *Xilka, Xilka, Besa, Besa.*

Xiuhcoatl

The fire serpent of the Aztecs of Mexico. The companion of Xiuhtecuhtli, the god of fire, he is the object of the Plumed Serpent cult.

Xylomancy

Divination by casting sticks or twigs on the ground and interpreting their positions. Milfoil stalks were used by the Chinese in divination, giving rise to the elaborate system presented in I Ching.

Y

Yachu and Pila
Divinities of the Apa Tanis. Himalayan tribesmen sacrifice fowls to them to obtain the release or escape of a prisoner of war.

Yakori Bengeskro
A Gypsy expression meaning "Devil's Eye" and referring specifically to the berries of the elder tree. Many occult operations among the Gypsies are associated with the elder tree.

Yaksha
In Indian folklore, a class of demons who eat human beings.

Yaku
In the shamanistic religion of the primitive Vedas living on the island of Ceylon, the yaku are considered to be dangerous spirits, capable of possessing a dancer and causing him to fall to the ground.

Yam
The Canaanite god of the sea, rivers, lakes, and springs. He is also called Ruler of the Stream and Leviathan. He is represented as a dragon.

Yama (Yima)
In Persian mythology, the ruler of the land of the dead.

Yaqui Sorcery

See Castaneda, Carlos.

Yantra

A mystic diagram, usually drawn on a tablet of copper or some other metal. When used in connection with the appropriate mantra, its power is irresistible. See Signatures.

Yawn

A yawn is considered to be dangerous since it gives demons a chance to enter the body. Whoever yawns may ward off danger by making the sign of the cross on the mouth with his thumb whenever he feels the urge to yawn.

Y Ching

See I Ching.

Yeats, William Butler

Irish poet (1865-1935). His magical name as a member of the Order of the Golden Dawn was Daemon est Deus Inversus (The Devil is God Reversed). He was a frequent guest in the Parisian home of Samuel Mathers.

Yekum

According to the Book of Enoch (68.4) the demon Yekum seduced the sons of the holy angels and persuaded them to come down to the earth and copulate with mortals.

Yesod

In cabalistic teachings, the balancing force between Netsah and Hod. It is the ninth sephira, the sphere of the moon. It is associated with the aphrodisiac mandrake, and it represents the genitals when the sephiroth are matched with parts of the body. It is the dark depths of the personality in which the true self is hidden.

Yezidis

A sect of Devil-worshipers living in Armenia and the Cau-

624

casus and speaking the Kurdish language. They call the Devil Melek Taus and represent him as a peacock. Their sacred texts were collected and translated into French by F. Nau (*Recueil de textes et de documents sur les Yézidis,* 1918).

Yggdrasill
In Norse mythology, the giant ash tree. It spread its branches over the whole world and beyond the heavens, and it extended its roots into Niflheim, presided over by Hel, the queen of the dead.

Yidams
In Tibetan occultism, mysterious agents with diabolical associations.

Yin
In Chinese magical practices, yin is the dark, negative, female principle. It is associated with evil.

Yoga
Derived from the Sanskrit word meaning union, the word yoga now signifies pathway to God and embraces a series of rites and doctrines which lead the practitioner to God. Bhakti yoga is the path of love and devotion; hatha yoga outlines a system of physical exercises for the development of abnormal physical and psychical powers; ingni yoga concentrates on union with an abstract divine principle rather than with an anthropomorphic god; karmic yoga, the path advocated by Lord Krishna in the Bhagavad Gita, stresses work; and raja yoga, the royal path, focuses on meditation and elimination of sensory perceptions.

In Hinduism, yoga includes various physical disciplines designed to enable the ascetic to gain control over specific forces, to possess occult powers, and to achieve union with Brahma. Eight stages of yoga are generally enumerated: (1)

yama, or restraint; (2) niyama, or religious observances of various kinds; (3) asana, or particular postures; (4) pranayama, or methods of controlling breathing; (5) pratyahara, or withdrawal of consciousness from external objects; (6) dharana, or mental concentration; (7) dhyana, or abstract contemplation; and (8) samadhi, or union with Brahma.

Yoga-levitation
In yoga, levitation applies to walking over water, over thorns, or remaining suspended in the air. To achieve levitation, asserts Patanjali, who flourished around the second century B.C., mastery is required over one of the vital airs named udana, which resides at the throat center.

Yomael
One of the rebellious angels who swore allegiance to Samiaza. He is mentioned in the Book of Enoch.

Young, Alice
The first witch executed in America. She was hanged on May 6, 1647.

Z

Zabulon
A demon accused of possessing one of the nuns of Loudun. See Loudun, Nuns of.

Zachaire, Denis
Sixteenth-century French alchemist. He is remembered chiefly for a short work on the philosophy of metals (*Opuscule de la Philosophie de Métaux*, 1567), later translated into Latin.

Zadkiel
In the Jewish rabbinical legend of the celestial hierarchies, he is the ruler of Jupiter.

Zaebos
Grand count of Hell. Of gentle disposition, he manifests himself in the shape of a handsome soldier mounted on a crocodile.

Zagam
Grand king and president of Hell. He shows himself in the form of a bull with the wings of a griffin. He can change water into wine, blood into oil, copper into gold. He has 30 legions at his command.

Zahoris
Spanish wizards capable of seeing through objects and dis-

covering hidden items, often by virtue of a pact signed with the Devil.

Zakiel

An Arabian genie who appears in the form of a handsome young man. Dr. Eugenio Torralva was served by a familiar spirit named Zakiel, according to a confession made after the doctor had been seized by the Inquisition.

Zambri

In medieval Christian legend, the opponent of Pope Sylvester I (314-355). Zambri killed a fierce bull by whispering in its ear the name of the Jewish god (the Devil). The Pope restored the bull to life with the name of Jesus, proving the superiority of Christianity over Judaism.

Zaratus of Media

Ancient Chaldean sorcerer. The Chaldeans were famed practitioners of the occult arts.

Zavehe

One of the leaders of the angels who turned against God and swore allegiance to Samiaza. See Book of Enoch.

Zazel

One of the leaders of the rebellious angels, mentioned in the Book of Enoch. He turned against God and swore eternal allegiance to Samiaza.

Zebulon

In medieval legend, a magician associated with the Vergil cycle. He appears as Abulon, the one who provides the love potion, in Beaumont and Fletcher's *The Custom of the Country* (1619 or 1622).

Zedechias

An eighth-century Cabalist who is supposed to have caused regiments of sylphs to appear publicly and to invite men to

628

join them in their kingdom. The sylphs put at the disposal of their guests airships and the aurora borealis.

Zehut
One of the names by which the Egyptian god Thoth was first known.

Zelator
The second grade or rank in the hierarchy leading in occult teachings to the sphere of God. Certain practices established for the Zelator, who occupies sephira 10, the sphere of the moon, resemble yoga.

Zephar
Grand duke of Hell. According to John Wier, he induces men to practice pederasty.

Ziito
A famous sorcerer who performed incredible feats at the court of King Wenceslaus in Prague toward the end of the 14th century. One of his most famous exploits was summarized by Lewis Spence:

> On the occasion of the marriage of Wenceslaus with Sophia, daughter of the elector Palatine of Bavaria, the elector, knowing his son-in-law's liking for juggling and magical exhibitions, brought in his train a number of morris-dancers, jugglers, and such entertainers. When they came forward to give their exhibition Ziito remained unobtrusively among the spectators. He was not entirely unnoticed, however, for his remarkable appearance drew the attention of those about him. His oddest feature was his mouth, which actually stretched from ear to ear. After watching the magicians for some time in silence, Ziito appeared to become exasperated at the halting way in which the tricks were carried through, and going up to the principal magician he taunted him with incompe-

tency. The rival professor hotly defended his performance, and a discussion ensued which was ended at last by Ziito swallowing his opponent, just as he stood, leaving only his shoes, which he said were dirty and unfit for consumption. After this extraordinary feat, he retired for a little while to a closet, from which he shortly emerged, leading the rival magician by the hand. He then gave a performance of his own which put the former exhibition entirely in the shade. He changed himself into many divers shapes, taking the form of first one person and then another, none of whom bore any resemblance either to himself or to each other. In a car drawn by barn-door fowls he kept pace with the King's carriage. When the guests were assembled at dinner, he played a multitude of elfish tricks on them, to their amusement.

The bishop of Olmutz, Dulsavius, chronicled the exploits of Ziito in his *History of Bohemia*. Some of Ziito's magical feats later were attributed to Faust.

Zines
In the Bahamas, the name given to spiritualists who are able to enter a trance state and communicate with a spirit.

Zodiac
In astrology, a branch of the occult arts, the examination of the sky, the stars, the planets, the zodiacal signs, their relations to each other and their movements were studied with mathematical precision in order to find what influences were exerted by the celestial bodies on the conduct and fate of man: when these influences were most potent or weakest.

The signs of the zodiac mark the twelve compartments of heaven. The six northern stars are:

630

Aries	Cancer
Taurus	Leo
Gemini	Virgo

To each of these names is assigned a mystic symbol. The six southern signs are:

Libra	Capricorn
Scorpio	Aquarius
Sagittarius	Pisces

The zodiac was divided into two sections of Sun and Moon. Each half consists of six signs. The signs of the Moon of Night are: Aquarius, Pisces, Aries, Taurus, Gemini, Cancer. The signs of the Sun or Day are: Leo, Virgo, Libra, Scorpio, Sagittarius, Capricorn.

By means of scrupulous calculations the astrologer could determine the degree of influence exerted by the planets in relation to the zodiac. The issues to be determined astrologically concerned life; wealth; inheritance; land; wife, city, children, parents; health, sickness; marriage; death, religion, travel; honors, character; friends; enemies, captivity.

Zodiacal Metals
In astrology, zodiacal metals are those of the planetary Rulers, as follows:

Aries-Scorpio: Iron
Taurus-Libra: Copper
Gemini-Virgo: Mercury
Cancer: Silver
Leo: Gold
Sagittarius-Pisces: Tin
Capricorn-Aquarius: Lead

Zodiac and Character
The signs of the zodiac are assumed to exert strong influ-

ences on personal traits, abilities, and potentialities. In a general sense, for instance, Aries is associated with mental ability. Taurus implies physical force. An adaptable nature is under the patronage of the Gemini. Cancer, on the other hand, stresses conservative tradition. Leo is exhuberant and dominating. Virgo is critical. Libra is equated with justice. Daring men with initiative look toward Scorpio as their protector. Sagittarius denotes a dynamic personality. Humane traits belong to Aquarius, while a humble modesty hides behind Pisces.

Zohar

In Hebrew, the meaning of this term is The Book of Splendor. It is the most important work of the Cabala, the Judaic mystical philosophical system.

The Zohar was first published in 1558, at Cremona, and numerous editions have appeared since then in many countries.

The authorship was ascribed to Tannaite scholars belonging in the first century A.D. Along with the Zohar is the Book Bahir, which is also Cabalistic. Together they form the chief corpus of Cabalistic literature. The Book Bahir stresses letter-mysticism, the interpretation of sounds. Among other subjects discussed are the mystical significance of the human organism, creation, light and its emanations, reincarnation. The Book Bahir is written in Hebrew: the Zohar, in an Aramaic dialect.

The Zohar presents a mystical interpretation of creation, man, the concept of evil, demons, the transmigration of the soul, and the Messiah.

Zombi

A corpse which is presumed to move and act as if it were alive. In vodan (voodoo) cults, a human whose soul has been possessed by another person through evil magic and whose body is at the disposal of the magician. In West African voodoo cults, the zombi was the deity of the python. In the West Indies, the zombi is the snake god in the voodoo rite, a supernatural power capable of entering and animating a corpse. Many inhabitants of the West Indies believe that the dead can be returned to life and made to work as zombies, or mindless, mechanical beings.

Zombism
A cult of the West Indies, imported from West Africa. The rites, performed by the practitioners of voodoo, are centered around the cult of the zombi, the supernatural power that can reanimate the dead.

Zosmimos of Panopolis
A third-century alchemist and non-Christian Gnostic. He was probably an adherent of the Poimandres sect and a follower of Hermes. In his treatises, he relates a number of visions combining pagan and Christian elements. He is the author of an encyclopedia of alchemy.

Zotzilha Chimalman
The Maya god of light and darkness. He lives in a cave and struggles against Kinich Ahau. His struggle symbolized the eternal conflict between day and night.

Zracne Vile
In Gypsy mythology, these are evil spirits of the air.

Zschokke
German mystic and seer. He moved to Switzerland at an early age and was active in 19th-century Swiss politics. He called his own peculiar gift his "inward sight." He described his gift in his *Autobiography.*

It happened to me sometimes, on my first meeting with strangers, as I listened silently to their discourse, that their former life, with many trifling circumstances therewith connected . . . has passed quite involuntarily . . . before me. During this time I usually feel so entirely absorbed in the contemplation of the stranger life, that at last I no longer clearly see the face of the unknown. . . . I became more attentive to the subject and . . . would relate the subject of my vision. It was invariably ratified.

Zulus

The Associated Press reported on March 30, 1964, that witch doctors continue to play an important role in the lives of the Zulus of South Africa. Though the *Abathakathi* or enchanters are a dying breed, the *Isangoma* or witch doctors are expanding their clientele and numbering whites among their patients. They are consulted on many occasions: childbirth, sickness, rainmaking, foretelling the future, banishing evil spirits. The Isangoma bases his diagnosis of an illness on the pattern performed by bones which are cast on the ground by the patient. The profession is determined by the spirits of the Isangoma's ancestors. If, on their advice, a man embraces the profession, he must live as a hermit for two years and undergo many ordeals.

During his apprenticeship he is initiated into the secrets of witchcraft. To become a bona fide witch doctor he must kill with his own hands a huge python, eat its raw flesh, and participate in ceremonies marked by ritual dances and extending over a forty-eight hour period. One of the oldest witch doctors of Johannesburg, Nkayipi Dumisani, insists that bones never deceive the one skilled in reading them. Others blame the patient who casts the bones in case a diagnosis is wrong.

Zurich Exorcists

In February, 1969, six persons were convicted of causing the death of Bernadette Hasler, a Swiss girl of seventeen whom